DEATH ON SMALL WINGS

Neville . C. Atkinson

Col Muammar Gadaffi

Death on Small Wings

Tales of a Presidential Pilot

by

Neville C. Atkinson

Librario

Published by

Librario Publishing Ltd.

ISBN: 1-904440-78-9

Copies can be ordered via the Internet
www.librario.com

or from:

Brough House, Milton Brodie, Kinloss
Moray IV36 2UA
Tel/Fax No 00 44 (0)1343 850 617

Printed and bound by
DigiSource UK Ltd, Livingston

To Lesley, my wife, without whose love,
assistance and memory
this book could never have been written

Contents

Foreword by John Simpson CBE

I met Neville Atkinson nearly thirty years ago, when I went to Libya to interview Colonel Ghadaffi for the BBC; then, as now he was a controversial and elusive figure, who was regarded in Britain with deep hostility. The Colonel sent his private plane to fly us from Tripoli to the area of desert near Sirte where he was living. I was frankly amazed to find that the pilot, the man he trusted to fly him around the world, was British, had flown for the Fleet Air Arm, and still used his Royal Navy rank. We didn't have much time to talk, but as I said goodbye to him I remember thinking that one day he could write a fascinating book about his experiences.

This is it – and it is even more fascinating than I could have known. Neville Atkinson has flown a remarkable number of interesting people around the skies of Africa and the Middle East, and has come into contact with everyone from presidents to leading terrorists. It takes a special kind of man to ask Carlos the Jackal to sign a copy of Forsyth's 'Day of the Jackal', but Neville did it. 'The name is sheer "bullshit"', Carlos wrote above his signature, meaning Forsyth's title. There's a photograph of it on p. 335.

Neville's stories are fascinating, and the book is unput-downable. I admire him for writing it, and for doing his difficult and dangerous job so professionally. There must have been occasional clashes of loyalty, but Neville seems always to have dealt with them in the most honourable fashion. Most of all, though, I admire him for staying his own man. He wasn't a courtier, even though he was constantly in the company of the men who regarded themselves as kings and emperors. When they asked him what he thought, he told them in no uncertain manner.

This is the book of an adventurer, certainly, but is is also the book of a man who has remained true to himself and loyal to his principles. And above all it is a book full of enjoyment and excitement.

London, July 2006

List of Illustrations   page

One of our Falcons on the ground at Medina. I was sent to jail for taking this picture in a religious place (the 2nd holiest in the Islamic world). The religious police relented when our passenger Kweldi Hamidi returned to the aircraft and I was released.

Special Flight's new Gulfstream II being built at the Gulfstream factory in Savannah, Georgia, USA.

CHAPTER ONE

Let There Be Light

The first missile snaked up towards our Falcon 20, closely followed by a second. I was mesmerized. Surely someone must have made a ghastly mistake. Did they not realize the aircraft was full of passengers? Of course they did! Egypt was at war and this was no accident. Whoever ordered this atrocity on an unarmed civil aircraft must know the name of everyone on board. My death would be completely incidental to the main aim of terminating the target passenger. As captain of this aircraft I had to take immediate action if life was to continue beyond the next few seconds.

Then, suprisingly, I became aware that time appeared to be running super-slowly, despite the massive explosive device speeding unerringly towards our obliteration at many times the speed of sound. Ridiculously, I ran through a list of excuses for the military officer holding us in his sights. He thinks we are an Israeli fighter – after all we look like a fighter at first glance. He's brushed against the big red 'fire' button and the missiles were launched accidently. Perhaps he's gone insane.

All of course absolute nonsense There could be no confusion about any of the details regarding LN999, our radio call sign, as we were being guided to this rendevous with death by Egyptian military radar controllers and these missiles were clearly fired from Cairo Airport, our published destination.

Three miles below lay a scene of incredible beauty, as old as time itself and steeped in biblical history. Stretching 16,000 feet directly underneath, out to the vastness of the Sahara Desert, lay the plain of Giza, on the edge of Cairo's sprawling metropolis. The Sphinx and the three Great Pyramids of pharaohs Khufu (Cheops), Khafre and Menkaure stood out vividly in the morning sun, where Jesus had stood entranced at this, the seventh wonder of the ancient world, 3,000 years old when he gazed upon these huge man-made structures.[1] At first, it seemed almost sacrilegious to contemplate violent death in these beautiful surroundings – especially when it was one's own violent death being contemplated.

Yet this place was no stranger to wanton slaughter. Khufu's funeral extravaganza had these plains of Giza running in human blood. Pharaoh was accompanied into the afterlife by hundreds of his fellow Egyptians, bodyguards, household

---

[1] The only Egyptian reference to Jesus in the New Testament is the Flight into Egypt following his birth. Hallowed Islamic tradition, on the other hand, has the Prophet Jesus visiting a number of sites of antiquity. (See also p.229.)

staff and even members of his own family. Not a kindly death either, just a quick slit of each throat with a razor-sharp blade wielded by the presiding priestess of the goddess Hathor, and a terminal cascade of their warm lifeblood spurted into the desert sand as they joined their pharaoh on his journey to eternity.

Life as a night-fighter pilot in the Fleet Air Arm of the Royal Navy had often been laced with excitement and even danger, but had never extended to a bunch of Egyptians heaving quantities of expensive Russian missiles in my direction at hypersonic speeds, with or without copious quantities of highly destructive Semtex explosive at the front end. At first glance these missiles looked like outsize telegraph poles, and their black bodies sporting long white lateral zigzag lines did nothing to pacify the twenty-four terrified eyes peering out at them from their intended target.

How did I ever come to be in such an extreme predicament as this?

The Court Line Aviation interview panel at Luton, who offered me the job as 'Chief Pilot designate' of Libya's Special Flight, made no mention of any form of extreme danger in their job description. On the contrary, they were at great pains to emphasize the positive aspects that would surely be experienced by me and my family as we enjoyed life in the sun-drenched splendour of Tripoli, Libya's capital city, and the many exotic destinations that we would visit. I was offered what I judged was a low average salary for a job described as a prestigious position, but following family discussions of aspects like tax-free status and other perks, Court Line's offer was accepted. After all, I was leaving the Royal Navy after twenty-three years service and being an unemployed pilot, even with a top civil pilot's licence, was a most unattractive proposition.

Life never stands still and before taking up the new appointment the Libyan Special Flight had become the Libyan Presidential Flight following a bloodless coup d'état. Well, *c'est la vie*. We did not know King Idris, now ex-King, personally – though he had once demanded my court martial through a signal to the British Admiralty for my allegedly causing the Queen to spill her tea, but that's another story – so Colonel Gadaffi was now the Head of State and my new boss.

Court Line organized a Fan-Jet Falcon 20 ground school conversion course in Bordeaux at the Dassault factory, to teach me the intricacies of the new aircraft and its systems, but the necessary actual flying would wait until arrival in Libya. Compared to the complexity of the naval fighters that hitherto had been my regular workhorses, the Falcon 20 was an interesting piece of kit, although technically not too demanding. Its French equipment had the usual specific numbers to learn: hydraulic systems, pumps and pressures; electricity generators, AC and DC amps and volts; and how to exchange each for the others when any failed.

The author preparing to fly a Sea Vixen FAW2

The Author during a flying display

The actual mechanics of flying these smooth-looking Machines just had to be simpler than landing 40 tonnes of Sea Vixen, underslung with live weaponry onto the pitching, rolling deck of HMS *Centaur*, then the smallest aircraft carrier in the world, at night, in the fury of an Atlantic gale, so I was confident, even relaxed about the technicalities needed to safely operate the Falcon. For the first time I would fly an aircraft with American engines, General Electric CF700s, but they soon would become familiar and proved as reliable as the Rolls-Royce ones that I knew. They had a unique character and needed dedicated effort to learn their idiosyncrasies, but they eventually rewarded my efforts by saving my life more than once.

As we grappled with unbelievably complex emergencies, unknown in the practical world of actual flying, I realized that we had absorbed everything about the equipment and how to treat it in ways that the original designers could never have imagined. Hydraulic pumps normally operating at 3,000 psi could be persuaded to provide 100 psi for the wheel brakes, if needed, or even 115 volts 400 cycles AC for the flight instruments in the event of electrical failures. The alternative routes and conversions of one form of power to another and back again were absorbed, apparently concealed in the obligatory French coffee.

This intimate level of familiarity was necessary to deal with unfortunate failures that invariably manifested themselves on filthy stormy nights above the jungles of darkest Africa, with the fuel gauges proclaiming 1,000 lbs available (*i.e.* not very much), the runway lights failing intermittently because of Ramadan celebrations, nobody replying on the radio and all the alternative airfields within range being suddenly closed. The captain's seat then becomes a very lonely place and total knowledge of the failed or failing system is crucial.

Our arrival in Libya was complicated by President Gadaffi using the London scheduled Boeing 727 to attend a meeting in Calcutta. We drove up and down the M1 like a yo-yo for a week, trying to hitch a flight to take up my new appointment, wondering all the while whether accepting the job had been a sensible decision.

Eventually a French-built Caravelle complete with French crew arrived at Heathrow with *Libyan Arab Airlines* freshly painted on its side and with all the china and cutlery sporting crests of the Kingdom of Libya Airlines. It conveyed my wife, Lesley, my eight-year-old daughter, Trudi, and me to Tripoli in first-class comfort, with food and hospitality of superb quality – our son, Nigel, was stuck (much to his annoyance) in St Peter's School, York. An hour and a half later, as the aircraft coasted out over the harbour above Nice, the captain, Pierre, walked back from the cockpit to welcome us all to the new job and to assure us that we would be happy living in Tripoli. Although this was obviously a gesture of friendship

Ramadan Sharif, Personnel Director of Esso Oil Company, on his citrus farm with Trudi, Lesley and Nigel.

that I would have shown myself in similar circumstances, we were all incredibly reassured by his positive attitude and his good wishes. He took Trudi up to the cockpit to see what went on at the sharp end and obviously impressed our young daughter considerably. She returned to her seat ten minutes later with an intriguing old-fashioned grin on her face that was never fully explained, but it was quite significant that she never forgot his name.

As we walked into Tripoli's airport building I realized that it had been my bedroom ten years earlier, when an aircraft crash whilst attempting to land aboard HMS *Eagle* had necessitated flying a fuel-starved 802 Squadron Sea Hawk south into the desert, searching for an airfield and a bed for the night.

Pierre caught up with us all as the first suitcases disgorged down the baggage chute and shepherded us inside the customs hall to meet the immigration and customs officials. Our credentials were established with them from the outset and the fact that he introduced us to them proved to be far more important than all our complex documentation. We soon realized that the Libyan people put great store on personal introductions by people they already knew and liked. Our many suitcases were speedily blessed with the obligatory customs stamps without question, whereas we noticed that some of the other passengers were being thoroughly searched. Maybe, we thought, this new life would have some privileges that we had not considered.

Terry Danby, the Special Flight Chief Pilot, met us whilst the last box of our belongings was located. His was the first really familiar face that we met that evening and as chairman of the Court Line interview panel at Luton Airport, he had already done his best to paint an accurate picture of life and work in this new environment. He drove us the 25 miles into Tripoli city and to our apartment overlooking the Mediterranean, trying to explain all the new sights, sounds and intriguing smells of what was to become our home for the next ten years.

The huge crimson ball of the sun was slowly descending into the vastness of the Sahara Desert to the south-west. It seemed to us to be making a flamboyant stage exit with truly theatrical extravagance as we sped along the dual carriageway into town to the sound of Terry's running commentary. We three gazed towards the blinding orange glow as it sank slowly into the vast area of yellow sand dunes that seemed to stretch like an unruly discoloured sea towards infinity. I'm afraid we heard only a very small part of the pearls of wisdom being directed at us. The details of Libya's history, economics and our new boss's idiosyncracies and expectations could be absorbed at a later date. Now was a night of pure magic, stimulating the excitement of anticipation and all three of us delighted in it to the full.

As we drew up to the square building containing the apartments of five members of our team we all suffered from bad cases of 'information overload'. Jani Serkowski and Stephen Sparrow, two of Special Flight's captains, came out to help unload the pile of suitcases and boxes, which, with the three of us and the chauffeur, had filled the battleship grey Peugeot 404 estate.

Terry had his priorities absolutely right by taking us into our own flat where bottles of VSOP Courvoisier Brandy, ginger ale, lemon and ice were waiting on the dining-room table for us to make a couple of relaxing horse's necks. As we sauntered around our new home exploring the rooms, drinks in hand, Terry opened our oven and removed a steaming pot of shorba, a spicy Libyan lamb stew that he had prepared earlier. To complete the hospitality, he set the table with a couple of bottles of vintage Bollinger champagne in the centre and our first meal proceeded to the comforting sound of popping corks. Knowing that Libya was a well-publicized 'dry' country should have prompted us to enquire further, but that would have been churlish, so we all decided to relax, go with the flow and let the small details take care of themselves. Life was improving beyond our wildest expectations.

Around 9 o'clock, as the conversation subsided, our host leaped to his feet to leave saying that he appreciated we would be quite tired. As he disappeared from sight he said that he would give us a knock about 6.30 for a spot of water-skiing and, without waiting for a response, he left. We all looked at each other, more for confirmation than anything else, as we said queryingly, 'Water-skiing?' Perhaps he was talking to somebody outside on the stairway, we decided as we tucked Trudi into her bed and then settled into our own giant seven-foot-wide bed with a gently rotating silent fan suspended above. The sounds and smells outside the open windows were completely strange to us, but at 32°C, we were warm, with full bellies, feeling no pain and the cicadas chirped a lullaby as we dispensed with the lone cotton sheet and totally surrendered into the arms of Morpheus.

Whatever dream I was enjoying when Terry hammered on the door must have been naval orientated because I leapt out of bed convinced that I was needed on the bridge to take over as Officer of the Watch – but which watch and indeed which ship eluded me. Then slowly the memory of the water-skiing threat of the night before penetrated a befuddled consciousness. A glance out of the window revealed a very attractive, athletic young lady sporting a pretty bikini, and two barefooted men in swimming trunks, one of whom was Terry, manoeuvring a large rubber boat complete with 40 horsepower Johnson outboard engine and its trailer onto the tow bar of a diminutive blue Volkswagen Beetle.

The Atkinson trio somehow struggled to the scene of action to a welter of introductions shouted by Terry, the VW driver, through his open window as the car slowly gathered pace in the general direction of the mirror-smooth sea half a mile downhill. The young lady was Ollie, a nurse working at the oil company clinic and the live-in girlfriend of the other man, Dick Hayward, one of Special Flight's four 'flying engineers' who acted as cabin stewards in flight and maintenance engineers whilst on the ground. Trudi was thrown into the boat whilst the four of us leapt onto the buoyancy tubes and steadied ourselves with the boat's lifelines. A minute later, our unlikely party rolled onto the hard-packed, clean, sandy beach where the boat effortlessly arrived in the water as if it knew its own way.

Taking stock of the situation demanded a precautionary paddle or two to check the temperature of the crystal clear, oily smooth water, which was protected from the open Mediterranean by a coral reef some 300 metres out from the beach. We had the whole lagoon to ourselves and before we left the sand Dick pointed out our flats topped with a prominent flagpole. He explained that if there was an unexpected call to scramble one of our Falcons and any of the skiers were on duty a green flag would be hoisted up the flagpole by those remaining, who would shortly arrive at the beach with a car to whisk the crew member or members to the airport. It was a foolproof system that never failed when needed.

As the boat gathered pace westwards along the lagoon with its six life-jacketed occupants, the pitch of the engine decreased momentarily. Ollie threw a pair of waterskis overboard and jumped into the water close by. The ski rope snaked out over the stern and the boat circled round to pass the hand bar close to the skier. A shout of 'ready' was the signal for full power and up popped Ollie, like a cork out of a bottle. She kicked off one ski and was soon established on a single ski, cutting through the frothy wake, sometimes appearing to be overtaking the speeding boat. The three of us were very impressed, but the others seemed to regard the performance as pretty normal.

The sea outside the reef seemed almost as calm as the water inside the lagoon so with a signal from the driver to the skier we drove in a gently turning curve towards the wall of coral. As the rocks appeared to be about to engulf the rapidly oncoming boat, a small diagonal gap orientated north-east to south-west materialized in the coral wall and the skier came into line directly astern. Dick showed us that at this exact point, a distant minaret and a nearby water tower were exactly in line along the white wake, and it became obvious that this important indicator would guide us safely back through the reef from the open sea. The clear water allowed us all to see the deep two-metre wide underwater path, but the close proximity of the multicoloured corals, complete with sizeable fish on either side of the rapidly moving boat, gave Lesley and me some concern. Trudi was oblivious to the danger and her bright eyes showed that she was enjoying every minute of the sights and excitement of this unexpected new sport.

Out of the shelter of the reef there was a slight swell, which Terry drove along, giving the skier a more comfortable ride. We traversed back and forth parallel to the coast about 200 metres outside the reef, with long straight runs and lazy turns in a race-track pattern, in unpolluted water averaging about 15 metres depth. As the boat sliced through the water, looking over the side gave an eerie sensation that we were actually 'flying' high over the incredibly beautiful multicoloured seabed. The occasional big fish appeared in the intervening gap, confirming the presence of water between the boat and the seabed.

Ten minutes later Ollie tired and indicated that she was releasing the rope. She threw the handbar to the side, sank slowly into the calm water and we circled the boat to stop alongside her. The discarded ski floated where it had been released. As Dick leapt over the side of the boat taking a spare ski with him, Ollie climbed aboard, over the boat's transom, stepping on the soleplate of the silent stationary outboard as she hauled herself aboard. I became the next driver and circled the boat to bring the handbar close alongside Dick in the water. As he popped up with the engine at full power, I reflected on the short time – only about two minutes – that it had taken to collect one skier and establish another on a single ski. It was a most impressive routine that Terry explained was essential in order to extract the maximum amount of exercise out of our only practicable physical sport, which was all too often cut short by external circumstances.

To add emphasis to his words, a large green flag fluttered to the masthead above our flats and I turned towards the reef looking for the minaret and the water tower. As they both came in line, Dick ceased his gyrations astern on the ski and settled himself into the frothy white wake. This exercise of penetrating the space through the reef had to be conducted at speed to enable the skier to stay upright, so as I lined up the two aiming marks I secretly crossed a couple of fingers and drove through the deep channel. Like every new skill, it was much easier to achieve than it originally appeared to a first-time passenger, but the first time did cause some trepidation. We sped down the lagoon, dropping Dick alongside the blue VW, which by then had been joined by a light grey Fiat 124 estate with Captain Stephen Sparrow at the wheel. Dick was apparently the duty engineer and was needed for an immediate flight to Calcutta in India with Major Kweldi el Hamidi, the Interior Minister, and two Libyan civil servants.

As they drove off the beach, on which by this time there were a few Libyan families relaxing in small groups nearby, we all jumped back into the boat and slowly eased out to recover the two discarded skis, still floating in the water. Outside the reef, where we found the second one, Terry took his turn on the skis and after a very active fifteen minutes indicated for me to turn back across the reef into the lagoon. As we stopped in shallow water, he skimmed onto the smooth beach and announced that it was the Atkinsons' turn for some exercise.

I remembered suffering a very unsuccessful attempt to waterski down the Bosphorus in 1952 behind a naval Gemini rubber boat whilst on an official visit to Istanbul aboard HMS *Plucky*, an Algerine class minesweeper. It had seemed to me then to be a black art that very few were destined to master. Terry assured us that I must have had a very bad driver because success largely depended on the expertise of the person behind the wheel.

Damn it, he was right! Careful instruction and judicious use of the correct engine power had all three of us skiing basically on two skis by 10 o'clock. Yes! We all fell in many times, sometimes quite spectacularly, but in the super-warm temperatures of that calm, clear, Mediterranean lagoon under a cloudless sky, that was all part of the fun.

The local Libyans, for this was a public beach, came up to watch the fun, especially when eight-year-old Trudi donned a pair of children's skis. Ollie swam alongside her holding her tiny body in the correct position and she popped out of the water at the second attempt. At the fifth try, she circumnavigated the lagoon in triumph, with the engine barely above idle revs. The small crowd of onlookers cheered and erupted into genuine applause as Trudi threw away the handbar and ski rope and executed a credible slow run onto the dry beach, remaining upright throughout. Some of those Libyans we met on that first morning became our friends and remained so throughout our entire time in their country.

They cheerfully helped us in many ways as we settled into the domestic life of Giorgium Popli, the suburb of the city where we lived.

Starting skiing at 6.30 in the morning seemed to us to be a good idea: the beach was deserted, which helped with our safety precautions, the sun was not too hot, the water beautifully warm and the surface usually flat calm. At that hour we were less likely to be interrupted by flying demands and, on completion, we all had sufficient time left in the day to do our work.

Tucking the boat securely back into its garage, we all bundled into Ollie and Dick's flat for a snack. Just as we were enjoying a cool fizzy drink and an early brunch, with me feeling fit but relaxed after the morning's exercise, Terry announced that he had booked the spare Falcon for the two of us to fly a local area familiarization flight. 'Great!' said I, wondering just how intense the instruction would be and quietly geared up the technical psyche for action.

All the roads in and around Giorgium Popli until you reached the main airport dual carriageway were soft sand roads, as yet untarmacked, and so anything but smooth. There were huge black holes everywhere where manholes into the sewerage system would be fitted. Driving after dark in those days was most hazardous – it is not common knowledge that a car wheel fits almost exactly into a manhole with no cover on it. When this happens the wheel and axle, complete with braking system, either separate with a great deal of noise from the car, or the car stops dead – depending on the speed of engagement with the hole.

Stoppages due to wheel spin were a normal driving hazard on the soft sand, but helpers to push the car always seemed available, day or night. Soldiers, police, shopkeepers, other drivers and passengers all helped spontaneously, but these hold-ups complicated travel around the city, making the keeping of appointments a nightmare.

The ready help was expected to be reciprocated when other cars stuck in the sand and a very dim view was taken of any superior being bowling past a stuck car without offering assistance. Even uniformed aircrew were not excused assisting and many long-term friendships were begun at these casual meetings. On one occasion we stopped to help the driver of a rather swish Mercedes, only to discover that the passenger was Libya's Prime Minister, Major Abdusalem Jalloud, whom we were expecting to fly to Casablanca half an hour later. He got out and joined the rest of us pushing his car.

On my first drive to the airport, not working to any urgent timescale, there were no hold-ups. Visiting the Air Traffic Control centre, we ran through the normal procedures for flight planning and met everyone, before being introduced to our Falcon 20, registration 5A-DAF. This was the identical twin of the second Falcon, 5A-DAG, currently leaving Cairo after refuelling and flying down the Nile to

*Our son Nigel at the northern end of the Forum at Leptis Magna,
a particularly well preserved roman city.*

The imposing Mediterranean Theatre at Leptis Magna.

Khartoum in the Sudan, where they would stay the night in the sumptuous Nile Hilton, a modern hotel strategically sited on an attractive spit of land with gently swaying palm trees at the confluence of the Blue and White Niles, before continuing to Calcutta the following day. (Transiting government ministers like Kweldi el Hamidi, who frequently flew with Special Flight, often used these necessary refuelling stops to oil the wheels of diplomacy with, apparently, casually convened meetings with the presidents or royalty of the host country. Such spontaneous meetings were often far more important than the original stated aim of the flight and could result in a level of secrecy in their political negotiations that would otherwise be impossible.)

But back to my familiarization flight around Tripoli. Special Flight's radio call sign when carrying VIP passengers was fixed as LN 999. If that call sign was in use by the other aircraft, the second aircraft became LN 888 and so on, but when we were training or test flying the side number of the aircraft became our call sign, so, that day, our training flight became Five Alpha Delta Alpha Foxtrot, by international agreement shortened to Alpha Foxtrot.

We drove to the Special Flight hangar via many airport offices and talked to the key people who normally assisted us with our overall operation. We were greeted at the aircraft by Mohamed, a swarthy Libyan who attended to the routine domestic normalities of the aircraft and speeded up our departures and arrivals. He leapt in and out of our official cars, collected the VIP catering from the French chefs and fitted the food boxes in their secure stowage on the aircraft. He cleaned, refuelled and oiled the aircraft; when needed took flight plans to Air Traffic Control and protected us from anyone who should not be near our aircraft. In short, he was an absolute godsend.

Terry supervised me carrying out an external inspection of the Falcon, as for a standard pre-flight, but en route he demonstrated all the nooks, crannies and compartments that could possibly house nasty inconveniences like explosives, best discovered whilst still on the ground. He showed me that a very bright electric torch and a suitable screwdriver were essential for examining the more unlikely small cavities. This level of security soon became routine.

On completion of the outside check, I sat in the captain's seat for the first time. It felt good. I knew, instantly, that the Falcon was destined to be a friend of mine, although at this time I did not appreciate just how good a friend, or how quickly. Perhaps it was better not knowing. The airspace around Tripoli was fairly familiar from my days in various aircraft carriers from which I had dropped many tons of practice bombs, and fired hundreds of various types of missiles and cannon shells into and onto targets cunningly hidden behind rocks in the desert around Tarhuna, south of the airport.

However these skills were no longer required and my concentration must now be dedicated to giving future passengers safe and comfortable flights, so I kept my previous exploits to myself. There had been changes since previous visits: the radio navigation aids were all working and reliable, and the voices of Air Traffic Control were now confident and professional.

Training lasted three flights on three consecutive days and ended with me taking Alpha Foxtrot to Basel in Switzerland, where Jet Aviation, our maintenance base, was due to carry out major servicing. After completion of this type of work by the factory, a full test flight was usually flown by the accompanying Special Flight crew, with the engineers actually responsible for certifying the work flying as passengers, sometimes in the cockpit, to enable them to take specific readings off the instruments as the test progressed. The more adventurous of the Swiss engineers usually liked the aircraft to be taken to some of its limits to check exactly how it performed just prior to losing control. We took great delight in satisfying their curiosity.

I was now a fully-fledged working member of Special Flight and very keen to do some real work. My first fully operational flight was organized through the Prime Minister in return for help from Colonel Ferjani, the C-in-C of the Libyan Air Force. The four-engined Lockheed Jetstar II executive jet that the Air Force used for communication was undergoing major maintenance in the USA and four Libyan pilots were needed at Le Bourget, in Paris, at the Marcel Dassault factory. They were required to test fly and deliver four of the very latest Mirage F-1s that had just rolled off the Dassault assembly line. Colonel Ferjani had been a great help to Special Flight over the years by using his transport aircraft to substitute our sick aircrew in various parts of the world or to transport vital spare parts for our Falcons when they were stuck in Persia, India or elsewhere, so requests for assistance of a non-military nature were given enthusiastic support, if at all possible.

The Air Force at that time predominantly flew French fighters – Mirages and Mystères – though the drive by the Soviet Union to replace France and Britain as the major supplier of military equipment to Libya was already under way. The lure of the almighty petrodollar eventually proved irresistible to the Kremlin and they pressed sophisticated military hardware onto the Libyan government, seemingly at less than their cost of production, so keen were they to enlarge their political influence in this part of Africa.

To pick up the pilots and equipment for Le Bourget, we flew from Tripoli International Airport to the Libyan Air Force base at Okba (the old American airfield of Wheelus Field) about ten miles to the east of Tripoli city. To my great surprise, parked next to us as we loaded the Falcon at Okba was a large Russian nuclear bomber, a TU-22 Blinder. This sophisticated supersonic aircraft, equipped with two exceptionally long reheated engines mounted on its tail, was one of the greatest airborne threats to the UK during the cold war which, in 1973, was still very much in progress. This impressive-looking beast was capable of carrying and delivering some very formidable stand-off thermonuclear weapons, which caused NATO's military planners a lot of sleepless nights.

Many of my later naval supersonic Sea Vixen days were devoted to learning different ways of destroying this huge, sleek, malevolent monster. British fighter pilots had only seen rather grainy, black and white photographs of it, taken at extremely long range, presumably by some poor sod risking his life in the depths of Russia. Here was the actual focus of our painstakingly practised fighter tactics, sitting right alongside me, with its crew milling around underneath between the main undercarriage bogies.

I remembered that our boffins at de Havillands even designed a new air-to-air missile, the Red Top, which was capable of being fired head-on at the Blinder. Previously all air-to-air missile attacks on enemy aircraft had to be executed from behind, but because we possessed a lower top speed than the Blinder – it could cruise into the attack at Mach 1.4 to a theoretical 1.8+, whereas our top speed in level flight was about Mach 1.25 – we developed this ability to attack from the front. But our troubles with the Blinder did not end there. It could fly on long-range attacks at 60,000 feet whereas our maximum permitted altitude was 45,000 feet, so we developed the 'snap-up, head-on attack', which I firmly believed at the time would have achieved some success for our fighters had it ever been put to the test.

This huge aircraft looked quite beautiful as it sat there in the unremitting sunlight, though its full camouflage – perfect for action over the rainforests of central Africa – was inappropriate for desert operations.

Eventually my curiosity overcame common sense and I wandered, unannounced, into the mill of people underneath the Blinder's fuselage to introduce myself to the Russian captain. International air traffic control regulations fortunately came to my help, as all pilots are required to communicate on the radio in English, and his grasp of the language was excellent. He commented on the oppressive heat so I invited him into my air-conditioned Falcon to enjoy a cool drink. As one aviator to another he could not resist asking to see our cockpit instrument layout. I agreed to show him round the Falcon if I could see round his aircraft in return. He agreed, but it did not quite work out like that.

Our engineer/steward, Pete Portland, offered my guest a choice of refreshments and we settled into the cockpit exploring the depths of French electronic ingenuity. He was surprised that many of our flight instruments were identical to his own, but almost had hysterics when he was shown that we possessed a braking parachute at the base of the tail for emergency stopping. We were probably the only civil aircraft in the world to be fitted with this normally military equipment. He asked what happened to the passengers when the braking parachute was deployed and I told him, truthfully, that if we failed to persuade them to keep their seatbelts securely fastened they all ended up joining the pilots in the cockpit, rather rapidly – but he did not believe me. As he drained his glass, he invited me to join him in the shadow of his fearsome Machine.

We walked round, beneath, examining the external bits and pieces of his Mk B version of the TU-22, with him answering my non-stop questions. There were no visible missile or stand-off weapons, but I could clearly see the hardened points to which external weaponry would be attached. An apparent recess and door under the wing root must have been an internal bomb bay. She really was a very beautiful piece of Machinery of which Mr Tupolev must have been very proud. I estimated that the fuselage was about 130 feet long with quite thin wings swept back in a dog-leg at approximately 45 degrees, and close to 90 feet in overall span. Its very long engines were quite narrow, so they were obviously straight turbo-jets without fan augmentation. I estimated that they would produce about 25,000 lb of thrust, but he corrected me – with reheat, and the clearly visible extendable front air intakes, they apparently each produced over 28,000 lb of thrust. The Falcon's very efficient fan-augmented engines produced just over 4,000 lb of thrust, so we were small fry by comparison.

The small rear-facing gun turret beneath the engine tailpipes harked back to the days of the Second World War and seemed strangely incongruous on a state-of-the-art supersonic thermonuclear bomber. I judged that it was too tiny to house a crew member so the single gun was probably radar operated by the co-pilot.

We climbed the almost vertical ladder into the cockpit. The crew of three had ejection seats which appeared very angular and lumpy when compared with the streamlined British Martin/Baker ejection seats that graced most Western military aircraft. My host explained that the captain's seat ejected the crew member conventionally, i.e. upwards, but that the other two crew members departed the Blinder downwards in an emergency, through what looked like trapdoors. Many of the instruments on the front panel were recognisable as rather old technology, but the armament switches were marked in Russian and the only one that I could recognize was the control to activate the rear gun turret radar. We were just discussing that the gun could be fired automatically on radar acquisition of a threat, or if preferred operated manually, when a very angry gentleman in plain clothes burst into the cockpit from below.

He was quite obviously beside himself with rage. His face was puce and when he momentarily stopped speaking in order to draw breath, I could see that his lips were trembling. He delivered a tirade of expletive at my pilot host in non-stop Russian and the marked bulge in the tailored jacket, just below his armpit, did not fill me with overmuch confidence. It appeared from the few further words that my host subsequently spoke to me that he was some kind of political commissar, though whether he had arrived with the crew or was based at the Russian Embassy in Libya, I failed to deduce. I thought at the time that he was most likely to be from the Embassy. Either way he was clearly a most unhappy bunny seeing me in the Blinder cockpit, and my exit stage right seemed appropriate. Fortunately Colonel Ferjani had just arrived at my Falcon with the diplomatic permissions for our flight to Paris so I made my excuses and walked as nonchalantly as I could over to the Falcon without a backward glance.

The Libyan Air Force eventually acquired twelve of these hi-tech bombers, equipped with conventional weapons only. The Soviet Politburo, despite their desperate need for petrodollars, obviously decided that they would keep the really dangerous nuclear toys locked away in the cupboard. They did, however, provide some sophisticated air-to-air missiles and rudimentary air-to-ground missiles to hang from the TU-22 wings a year later.

At the Dassault factory we were met by my recent ground school instructors who were hosting our stay. They came into the cockpit and suggested that our navigation equipment was very limited. They then led us to a very new Falcon 20-F that had just emerged from the assembly building and showed us the latest Omega satellite navigation system that graced all the new Falcons. After seeing this system operating we were full of curiosity, particularly as it was apparently inexpensive and very reliable. Omega enabled safe operation when ground navigation aids were unreliable and its information could be automatically fed into the aircraft's flight system and on to the autopilot.

The Air Traffic Control throughout Africa was acknowledged worldwide as poor. The local controllers meant well and if their radio worked they would do their very best to help overflying aircraft, but with malfunctioning or many times non-existent ground navigation equipment they did not have a hope of exercising proper control. To counter this inherently dangerous situation the pilots listened to every other aircraft on the same frequency and kept a written plot of just where everyone else was relative to themselves. When a conflict was detected the first pilot to recognize that collision danger existed would volunteer to climb or descend a couple of thousand feet or so to ensure safety. This probably sounds very amateurish to anyone without personal experience of trying to keep planeloads of passengers safe in such an environment, but I can only confirm that it actually worked very well. However the situation demanded one key ingredient – the ability to know one's own position accurately, without recourse to information deduced from unreliable ground transmitters.

Every pilot kept a course and distance (dead reckoning) line on his chart, but after three or four hours of uncertain wind effects that could in the worst case be blowing the aircraft off track at an unpredicted speed of over 150 mph in any direction, an error of anything up to 500-600 nautical miles was possible.

An example of this was the well-documented case of the Libyan Arab Airlines Caravelle (some accounts in various encyclopaedias state that the aircraft involved was a Boeing 727, but French pilot friends of the pilot assure me that it was a Caravelle) with 104 passengers and crew aboard, flying from Tripoli to Cairo on 21 February 1973, in bright sunshine. They encountered an unpredicted 200 mph easterly jet stream which blew them completely beyond Egypt and over the Sinai Desert. The first indication of any problem was when two F-4 Phantom fighters of the Israeli Air Force flew alongside the Caravelle with their pilots waving to the passengers and crew. Some passengers cheerfully waved back, not realizing the significance. The young Israeli pilots still appeared to be waving back, only 30 feet away. It was then that the French pilot suddenly realized his predicament and deduced his actual position. He broadcast to the world on three radio frequencies about his situation and instituted a 180-degree turn to fly back to Cairo. To the eternal shame of the Israeli nation, the fighters dropped astern of the scheduled passenger flight and fired several air-to-air missiles into it, exploding the Libyan Arab Airlines aircraft and killing everyone on board. Subsequent compensation from Israel for the atrocity did little to assuage the shock and horror that reverberated around the world at this appalling and unnecessary aggression against an unarmed passenger flight.

So the aircraft's actual position could be seen as all-important and the Prime Minister realized, when I explained, that everyone's safety would be greatly improved with an Omega on board. Within two months the factory engineers from Basildon near London were in Tripoli fitting the new equipment to both of our aircraft and we later flew back to Heathrow to have it calibrated by the makers. The system proved to be accurate, simple to use, and subsequently transformed the safety of our worldwide operations more than originally seemed possible.

Wherever in the world we landed, pilots of all nationalities asked for information about Omega and when it was demonstrated to them, actually operating, they were invariably very impressed. We should have been on the company sales team because many airlines bought and installed this new system in large numbers, due almost entirely to our enthusiasm and practical demonstrations.

Our hosts in Paris established us in a most civilized hotel on the Champs Elysées for our night's stay and later joined us, with their wives, for a taste of Parisian nightlife. Food really does taste better with lively company and a sophisticated floor show, especially as someone's guest, and we enjoyed our saucy entertainment at the Pigalle, ostrich feathers, high-kicking girls and all.

The following morning after shopping in Montmartre and the Latin quarter for those little nick-nacks that were difficult to find in an African environment, we stowed aboard the pre-ordered, extremely heavy aircraft parts for our Falcons and returned to Tripoli International. Just two and a half hours from Le Bourget and home in time for tea.

Lesley and Trudi had been busy settling in to Tripoli life in my absence. Ollie had introduced them to Omar Mousa, a young Libyan traffic dispatch officer with Libyan Arab Airlines. Omar was one of life's enigmas. A dark-haired gentleman, roughly 5 foot 8 inches tall, of very clean and tidy appearance, he was always helpful when any of the Special Flight families needed help. We frequently called upon his translating skills and sought his help locating the vital municipal offices haphazardly scattered around the city. His skill in procuring driving licences for the flight's wives was legendary and he knew the key immigration officials who provided exit and entry visas for trips home.

He did his best to explain the inexplicable Libyan bureaucratic systems. The government had modified (Arabised) the Italian procedures that the Fascists had brought across the Mediterranean with their conquest of Libya in 1910, although the British, who had administered the country since the Eighth Army days of Montgomery in 1943, only worsened the nightmare in their vain efforts to switch the bureaucracy to something that they, the British, could understand.

We were advised to take at least 50 passport-size photographs each with us, on arrival, for our initial documentation. We thought that this was somewhat excessive, but 50 proved to be woefully inadequate. Mandatory paperwork for a driving licence required nine photographs, my Libyan Airline Transport Pilot's licence consumed 12 and drawing up documents to rent our home from the landlord needed five more. Twenty-six photographs were used up in two days, and three days later all 50 had gone, but not to worry – Omar's photographer friend on the Istakal (Tripoli's Bond Street) organized more for us in batches of 100, as and when required.

Omar later suggested that we might like to consider taking a family membership at the Underwater Club, about a kilometre away, to help the family relax in comfort whilst I was away on extended flights. He took us to meet the Athenian, Mr Papadopolous, and his wife, who between them had been running the club for as long as anyone could remember. It was a very civilized and clean establishment that boasted surprisingly useful facilities. There were a couple of hard tennis courts, an attractive outside swimming pool surrounded by beautiful weeping tamarisk trees providing the right amount of shade, while behind the pool sat a mountain of soft drinks crates in front of the restaurant/snack bar. Individual sunshades arranged over small tables where the older generation played cards, backgammon and chess gave an air of relaxation and tranquillity, whilst two table tennis tables provoked frequent bursts of energetic activity from the younger members.

Across the car park lay a private stretch of coral rock on the edge of the clear blue Mediterranean with two diving boards and four stainless steel ladders leading over the edge of the coral into deep blue water, amongst shoals of multicoloured fish of every shape and size. Twenty-five or so small (two-metre square) platforms had been built in smooth cement over the sharp coral, about five metres apart, where members sunbathed and chatted under huge umbrellas shading them from the unrelenting heat of the midday sun. Mr Papadopolous welcomed us as his latest recruits, collected our 50 dinars and issued temporary documentation. We retained our membership throughout our time in Libya and were very grateful to Omar for his introduction.

Returning from Paris with a few goodies, as a full working member of the flight I dutifully trotted off to the Bank of Libya (formerly Barclays) the next day to open a bank account for my Libyan salary. The British part of my salary, which was almost identical to the Libyan one, was paid directly into a bank in the UK.

The Special Flight captains carried huge amounts of cash in US dollars or traveller's cheques to pay the aircraft's expenses whilst flying abroad. Record keeping was meticulous because the airline accounting system was very pedantic and every cent had to be accounted for when a top-up was needed. Finding places to hide the traveller's cheques and piles of $100 bills whilst staying in countries where the price of arranging an assassination was about $20, taxed the ingenuity mightily. We modified our casual clothes to permit some security zips and other fasteners to deter casual pickpockets. Mostly the precautions worked, because being fleeced of $10,000 or thereabouts would have been a very painful personal experience.

The aircraft carried fuel credit cards for all the main fuel companies, but inevitably in some African countries fuel bowsers would arrive at the aircraft sporting unfamiliar motifs. One such was Ouagadougou (pronounced 'Wagadoogoo') in Upper Volta. The fuel drivers complicated our problem even further by demanding only US currency, in $5 bills.

Flights to Benghazi, Libya's second city, soon became routine and sensing that government ministers disliked being lectured over the loudspeaker system, a personal touch seemed more appropriate. On reaching cruising altitude I handed over control to the aircraft's autopilot, supervised by the first officer, and walked back into the cabin to present the senior passenger with a route map of the flight annotated with points of interest and timings. This became a perfect opportunity to clarify the domestic arrangements, like length of stay, the availability of suitable accommodation and which refuelling airfields they would prefer to use en route. It was perfectly useless dropping in to ask for fuel in a country that may be temporarily unfriendly to Libya, when an airfield ten minutes' flying time away in another country avoided the problem completely.

Occasionally it was during these tête-à-têtes that surprising nuggets of information were divulged that were of supreme importance. Like me telling the Prime Minister the details of his flight to Cairo, when it transpired that he had only ordered a flight to Cairo as a security ploy. He really wanted to fly to Casablanca, in the opposite direction. 'Has nobody told you?' Such changes rarely caused serious problems because Libyan air traffic controllers assumed that our request would be on the instructions of their own President or Prime Minister and they would tend to reply as helpfully as possible. Our cockpit calculations on fuel flow, range, altitude and route were completed in a few minutes and we invariably managed to acquiesce to the passenger's wishes. Many of our regular passengers came up to the cockpit to listen to any new arrangements and some flew the remainder of the flight on the jump-seat between the two pilots.

On one unfortunate occasion the air traffic controller was less than co-operative and to make matters worse he was quite sarcastic about the crew and passengers. This was too much for a very tired and overworked Prime Minister, Major Jalloud. He asked for the microphone and tore the offending gentleman off a serious verbal strip, in quick-fire Arabic, most of which I understood. It certainly produced the desired result and our subsequent radio service on the flight over Libya, Tunisia, Algeria and Morocco was impeccable, but whether the young man involved is back from Siberia yet, I am not quite sure.

I settled into the routine of Special Flight during a period when Libya and Egypt were negotiating a merger to create a serious economic and military bloc between the Middle East and Africa. We, of course, were not included in any of the discussions, but from remarks made to us by the various Egyptian and Libyan government ministers who flew around the area, and by keenly reading the Cairo newspapers we could absorb the atmosphere of opinion prevailing in the two nations reasonably accurately.

A typical flight at this time consisted of us flying with a single passenger, usually the Foreign Minister, Major Abdul mun'im el Houni, from Tripoli to Benghazi. A quorum of senior Libyan dignitaries would join him during very lengthy waits in the sumptuous Benghazi VIP lounge and after prayers on the 100 square-metre, deep-pile, richly figured, silk carpets – a gift from the Chinese government – we would progress to Cairo, often landing at Tobruk[2] to embark yet more delegates to the merger conference.

---

[2] Renamed Gamel Abdul Nasser in honour of the late Egyptian President

34

The aircraft would be met at the Cairo VIP lounge by President Anwar Sadat of Egypt and Captain Hosni Mubarak, his then deputy, when our passengers were considered senior enough. Otherwise we were met by Colonel (later Brigadier) Shukri, the head of Egyptian intelligence services. Largely because of the frequency of such flights at this time and the fact that we flew these three senior Egyptians as passengers on several occasions, they became very friendly towards us. In private, both President Sadat and his deputy used my first name when imparting snippets of news that they thought would be useful or that were unusually humorous. I would have dearly liked a photograph of them walking on either side of me, each with a hand resting on my shoulder, their heads talking secretively and quietly into each ear and the three of us laughing out loud from time to time. Sometimes the hilarity was so extreme that we held each other up, all three laughing uncontrollably.

To avoid creating a false impression of familiarity with our senior passengers and their hosts, I should point out that as far as all crew members of Special Flight were concerned, the world's decision makers we had the honour to meet in the course of these flights were invariably addressed as *Sir* by us except for the female VIPs who clearly warranted *Ma'am*.

In fact, security was the bane of our lives and increased as time progressed, often because of the increasing influence of the Russian KGB on the Libyan government. I have already mentioned that we were sometimes given the wrong destination, supposedly in the interests of security, but during these merger talks in Cairo, we once flew President Gadaffi from Tripoli to Cairo where we were told that we would be informed of the details of our return flight. Meanwhile, we were to wait in our hotel with no estimate of the duration of our stay. We booked into the Shepheards Hotel in the centre of the city on the east bank of the Nile. They were used to our abnormal times of arrivals and departures and usually managed to find three comfortable rooms within an acceptable price bracket.

After three days of uncertainty, unable to stray too far from the hotel and being forced to leave one member of the crew behind (with whom we kept contact whilst indulging in a restricted form of tourism), we felt obliged to establish – with some probability – our proposed itinerary. The Egyptian telephone service at that time was very unreliable for local calls, although international calls could usually be made immediately. Unfortunately nobody of sufficient seniority could be contacted in Libya, so we devised a plan to shed some light on our situation. Packing our suitcases and dressing in full uniform, but being careful to retain our rooms – accommodation in Cairo was very difficult to find at that time – we took a taxi to the airport and started to perform minor routine maintenance on our Falcon. Whilst the engineer removed panels from the aircraft to access parts needing attention, we started the stand-by engine to activate the air conditioning system and cool the soft drinks. As anticipated, a familiar gentleman sauntered slowly over from the airport buildings in the searing heat of a Cairo midday to check on our unplanned activity.

This was the elusive Chief of Egyptian Intelligence, Colonel Shukri, who was perhaps the only person capable of finding out what was going on. Whether he could be persuaded to divulge that knowledge to us or not was uncertain and prising the information out of him was akin to playing a game of chess with a rattlesnake.

He consumed several cool Bitter Sodas – a drink that looks and tastes rather like a non-alcoholic Campari – and returned to his office in the VIP lounge, promising to establish the facts and let me know. Two hours later, as we were completing our work on the Falcon, his Land Rover pickup, with its two heavy machine guns mounted immediately behind the driver, stopped alongside our white and gold aircraft. With a conspiratorial air he spun me a most unlikely story that our passenger had left by car for a continuation meeting with various Egyptian officials in Luxor, 300 miles to the south. He suggested that we should return to the Shepheards where we would receive details of our eventual departure from the Egyptian Chief of Protocol. He confirmed, however, that we would not be returning to Tripoli for at least three days and that we could behave like genuine tourists providing the three of us went everywhere as a group.

It was highly unlikely that our President was in fact in Luxor, as this was the head of the country's intelligence services talking to us. Security was his top priority and a little white lie here or there would not bother him, but this gift of a few days' freedom was really appreciated and we were determined to make the most of the unexpected opportunity. The hotel manager organized a car for us and the driver picked us up after breakfast the next day.

Our driver was far too well versed in history to be a mere normal taxi driver. His knowledge was far-reaching and his use of the English language was impeccable. It slowly dawned on us that he was most probably a government agent, bodyguard and general chaperone, almost certainly under the direct instructions of Colonel Shukri. This was fine by us. He was a very pleasant young man and if he was under orders to keep us safe, which no doubt he was, then we concurred with these sentiments entirely. Ahmed, for this seemed to be his name, looked after us perfectly for over two days and the costs of employing him were ludicrously small. Once we were sure of his intelligence credentials we shamefacedly used him as a postbox to send messages that we wanted delivered to his masters.

So, for me, began a complete fascination with Ancient Egypt. Many much more learned authors than I have, in the past, explored and documented each intriguing element of over five thousand years of this, one of man's earliest civilizations. We were seeing it for the first time and I have no intention of trying to outdo literary giants like the ancient Greek, Herodotus, with his incisive grasp of the world that had preceded him, in 460 BC. He wrote his thoughts on Egyptology with only a sketchy grasp of hieroglyphics, the written language of ancient Egypt, which depicts grammar, names, titles and sounds as a series of pictures.

The Rosetta stone, a basalt tablet, eventually provided the key to accurately deciphering this language, carved and painted on most Egyptian monuments and still clearly visible today. The remarkable stone was found in 1799 near the town of Rosetta (in Arabic, *Rashid*) on the banks of the River Nile. One of Napoleon's soldiers is credited with its discovery, but it is far more likely that the soldier bought or stole it from the Egyptian who actually found it inside one of the tombs he was robbing. We will never know the truth with any certainty, but anyone who is interested can see the actual stone in a glass case on the first floor of the British Museum in London.

The stone is inscribed with a decree from the Pharaoh Ptolemy V in 196 BC. The decree is written in three languages, Greek, Ancient Egyptian hieroglyphic and demotic, so scholars familiar with either the Greek or demotic languages could, for the first time, with a little ingenuity, decipher the previously unreadable hiero-glyphics. To Egyptologists it was the equivalent of the Allies being given an Enigma decoding machine in 1940. It shone the searchlight of language on the whole of the ancient Egyptian world. The stories that the Pharaohs and their scribes had been trying to tell us for the preceding 5,000 years was suddenly unlocked and readable. My family and I even learnt to read a small amount of the language ourselves in due course.

In antiquity (3100 BC), Egypt was divided in half, with Upper Egypt stretching north from its borders with Nubia (modern-day Sudan) in the south up to Thebes (Luxor). Lower Egypt stretched north from Thebes up to the Mediterranean coast. In the east they were both bounded by the Red Sea – so named because the red mountains along the coast gave the sea the appearance of red ochre in the morning light – and the Gulf of Suez; whilst in the west their domains extended into the setting Saharan sun past a string of oases stretching from Kharga in the south up to Siwa in the north – or in practical terms, as far west into the desert as the Egyptians felt able to defend. Some one thousand years later, in about 2055 BC, Upper and Lower Egypt were united under one Pharaoh, Mentuhotep II, to form the Egypt that we know today.

Any exploration of Egyptian antiquity is immediately beset by some confident know-all, wittering on about this dynasty or that, and thereby causing great confusion. A dynasty is generally understood to mean the life in power of a particular family or group of related families, with a Pharaoh – or king – as its head or, sometimes, the span of a particular religion's sway over the people. The first dynasty started in 3100 BC and lasted 210 years until 2890 BC. The second dynasty lasted until 2181 BC, giving it a life of 709 years. The 31st dynasty is accepted as the last one and was graced by the kingship of the legendary Cleopatra I, who was noted for her drop-dead gorgeous body and her incisive mind. She is reputed to have had both Julius Caesar and Mark Antony as lovers, but unfortunately she did not survive an encounter with a certain snake in 30 BC.

Throughout these dynasties the years were further divided into three: Old Kingdom, Middle Kingdom and New Kingdom. There were other divisions of time into six Periods, but if the reader is interested enough to require knowledge of Egyptology in that depth there are plenty of books available to satisfy even the most avid investigator. Sufficient to say that this précis is only intended as an outline of the facts to help the reader understand a small part of this intriguing civilization.

Memphis, the ancient capital of Egypt, was the commencement of our enlightenment. This virtual living museum lay about fifteen miles south of Cairo on the west bank of the Nile. Now the size of an average British market town, it once, along with its funerary adjunct Saqqara, sprawled out as one of the major cities of the ancient world. It contained the Divine Court, where it was decided which of the mighty Pharaohs were Gods (and thereby elevated to receive eternal worship) and which had been evil enough to be for ever known as 'masters of the underworld' (and hence for centuries the focus of people's abject fear.)

The shrinking of this once mighty metropolis came about during the building of the present Egyptian capital, Cairo, when the need for prodigious quantities of limestone led to the dismantling of Memphis's grand buildings and their sites' subsequent obliteration by countless sandstorms from the surrounding desert. Many of the huge statues remain, but during the 65-year reign of Pharaoh Rameses II in 1250 BC, the Pharaoh's masons placed their master's cartouche (i.e. his name) on a vast number of existing grand statues. This led to untold confusion when the origins and ownership of the various monuments came to be catalogued. Rameses II was the Pharaoh credited with the expulsion of Moses and the remaining Israelites, though the story as portrayed in Biblical texts seems hardly credible.

In my opinion, and following some research, the Israelites (as the scribes of much later called them) were more probably the remnants of the Hyksos army that had conquered Lower Egypt and part of Upper Egypt during the XV dynasty, about 1650 BC. The origins of the Hyksos are open to question, but it is generally agreed that they came from an area covering modern-day Lebanon, part of Babylonia (modern-day Syria and Iraq) and stretching south as far as Jerusalem. The land they originally inhabited, along the coastal strip of the Mediterranean, was quite fertile and their agricultural methods were economically superior to those then employed in surrounding countries. Consequently they became rich and powerful and their young leaders grew acquisitive. Their army, though not huge by contemporary standards, exploited the very latest military technology from Persia – the horse-drawn two-wheeled chariot. No doubt the Hyksos generals had become envious when their traders returned from Egypt with exaggerated stories of a land festooned with gold and other treasures, a land of abundance that was regularly and reliably watered and fertilized by the beneficent River Nile each year.

The Hyksos single and two-man chariots were ideally suited to the flat desert terrain of Lower Egypt where they could attack the almost stationary Egyptian Army at high speed. When they attacked they struck with complete surprise and totally overwhelmed the unprepared defenders. Within a month they were established in Thebes and the country was under new management. In the interests of this narrative I have of course omitted a great deal of bloodthirsty detail, but the Hyksos had undoubtedly become the new power in Egypt.

The remnants of the defeated Egyptian Army and much of the nobility withdrew south with their portable wealth. Their old Pharaoh was killed in the fighting, but his name is not recorded – or more likely it was recorded but later obliterated by the new Hyksos rulers. Some believe that the survivors did carry their Pharaoh's body with them for suitable embalming and burial at a site to be chosen en route, but the site has never been found. After passing the second cataract of the Nile in their flight south, they encountered a more mountainous terrain, which provided safe haven from the pursuing Hyksos chariots, and here they set up a new home in what must have been northern Nubia. Decades passed as they licked their wounds, learnt from their obvious mistakes and slowly regained their legendary vigour.

If horse-drawn chariots won wars then the new Egyptian generals wanted them. They bred their own type of horse, for both speed and endurance, but with strong enough legs and ankles to cope with minor variations of terrain. This specialized animal became the Arab whose bloodline can still be seen in the modern racehorse. Meanwhile, their craftsmen designed chariots that could move at speed over variable ground without catastrophic failure. They had the benefit of an abundance of extra hard woods from the nearby forests for their wheels and axles, and when fitted with the superior, harder bronze that they had learned to smelt, they produced a serious fighting Machine.

It took nearly eighty years to perfect the stamina of the horse, because the animals readily became infected with a disease endemic in the surrounding wildlife, mainly the Wildebeests. The disease is believed to have been very similar to foot-and-mouth disease, though it could not have been quite the same as we now know it, because in its present-day form it only affects cloven-hoofed animals. Once contracted, as it was on an almost annual basis, it wiped out over 97 per cent of all their horses, but a clever breeder noted that if he bred solely from the few horses that recovered, their progeny and their progeny's progeny were totally immune – they were thus slowly able to breed an entire population of immune horses.

Meanwhile one of the keen young army officers experimented on groups of unprotected horses with diseased animals at their most infectious stage, by artificially infecting them with a view to disabling the horses of an opposing army. The tactics were soon demonstrated as successful and the generals realized that this could be turned into a war-winning strategy.

After almost 125 years of Hyksos rule, in 1525 BC the rejuvenated Egyptian Army returned from their enforced exile in the south and joined battle with the main Hyksos Army on the flat sandy plains of northern Thebes. Meticulous preparation ensured that groups of apparently healthy, but in fact infectious horses were infiltrated within the Hyksos overcrowded stables some days before the battle. The results were, as predicted, catastrophic for the defenders. The vast majority of the Hyksos chariots remained stationary, their horses dying, just when they were most needed. The Egyptian chariots with super-fit horses and well-trained archers rampaged unchecked amongst the enemy causing complete mayhem. Within two weeks the battles were won and Egypt was, once more, under the control of the Egyptians.

I believe that this is the first example in human history that biological warfare was successfully used to win a war. Make no mistake, this was pure biological warfare by any definition and a decisive tactic.

The Hyksos were driven out of the country, but the new rulers allowed those of the enemy who wished to remain to become Egyptian citizens. Most had already married into local families and were seen as potentially useful members of the workforce of the new unified nation. They were never slaves, just normal citizens and apparently subsequently lived without any aggravation.

For the next 235 years until about 1290 BC these good ex-Hyksos descendants and their families lived a normal life, fully integrated into local society. Then, it seems, from some of the later translated texts that subsequent supposed scholars recorded, along came Moses. It is significant that none of this story was recorded contemporarily, but only appears in religious texts many, many years later.

His origins are shrouded in doubt, but if (and I emphasize 'if') one of Rameses II's daughters did really find him as a tiny baby floating down the Nile in a basket, then I am very sceptical as to whether she or one of her maidservants had not launched him into the current a few minutes earlier a convenient distance upstream. Pharaoh's young daughter producing an unexplained child would have been a capital offence for both the baby's father and the daughter, so this little charade – if such it was – probably saved both of their lives. Nevertheless the baby boy seems to have been readily accepted into Pharaoh's family, but as he grew, for some reason he gravitated towards the company of some of these ex-Hyksos families and eventually persuaded them that they should attempt to travel to their ancestors' supposed homeland.

Self with the Rev Roddy Noakes at Trudi's Christening. He imparted his infamous roulette system to me later that evening.

They are credited with crossing a body of water en route or, according to recent BBC television coverage, maybe in fact an area of very wet ground called the Reed Sea in northern Sinai, and eventually after many years, when most of the wanderers had fallen dead by the wayside, the remnants arrived in what must have been the Gaza Strip on the western edge of the Mediterranean. Exhausted and severely disillusioned with constant travelling in hostile territory they decided to stay put and live where they had reached. It would doubtless have surprised them to know that later generations would refer to them, and call themselves, Israelites – up till then they had been proud that their ancestors were the Hyksos, the fearsome people who had conquered Egypt almost four hundred years earlier.

I have purposely refrained from too many comments about the various religions being practised over this timescale, in the interest of not causing offence. Many professed religious people of whatever persuasion are quite inflexible about their own religion's facts, fables and mythology and take each possible suggested variation to their accepted wisdom as a personal affront. One fact, however, that I discovered during my study of various Egyptian religious writing was that there is nothing new in apparent virgin births, where divine procreation is proclaimed. There are several reported accounts of such births during the 3,000 years of pre-Christian worship of the Egyptian gods. This is not surprising when one considers that in Egyptian and parallel religions throughout the region in those times, the punishment decreed for producing an unexplained baby was death – often by stoning. So had I been having some unauthorized hanky-panky with a lovely young princess in pharaoh governed Egypt, then claims of virgin birth may well have been at the forefront of my mind.

Memphis, as mentioned earlier, had deteriorated to a mere shadow of its former glory, but the statues and buildings still remaining had our enthralled attention, as an introduction to the mysteries unfolding every minute. Our small group of four were the only visitors to this once great city on a blisteringly hot and windless day. I remember an avenue of perhaps twenty or so small sphinxes, each set on metre-high plinths, lining the approach to some of the remaining huge statues, entrance columns and porticos of once great buildings. The stifling heat prevented our progress exceeding much more than a crawl, but this was a positive aspect because it provided an excuse for careful study of some of the wonderful stone carving that was everywhere around us. The older statues of long-dead Pharaohs and their chief priests showed the erosion of many millennia, but their features still betrayed the power that the original owners wielded over their subjects.

The art of stone masonry obviously improved over the centuries and perhaps the choice of the hardness of stone was better understood or superior quality stone or tools had become available, because some of the later statues had remained almost perfect. The facial features, sensitive hands and even the depiction of perfectly manicured toenails deluded one into a conviction that these colossal symbols of ancient might had only been completed a few years previously. The clearly inscribed cartouches and depictions of their prodigious deeds concealed the statues' actual age of some four thousand years.

To our great relief the afternoon saw each of us allocated a donkey, for a journey to some of the tombs, temples and statues of Saqqara. The oppressive heat was, if anything, even more intense. The little donkeys did their stuff admirably and received my boundless admiration and gratitude. Not sufficient, though, to persuade me to dismount and thereby lighten their load.

The step Pyramid at Saqqara is renowned as the first true stone building in the world. It was completed in 2613 BC for the interment of King Djoser (sometimes spelt and pronounced Zoser). We know for certain that the architect, builder and sculptor was called Imhotep, because he signed his work quite clearly as follows: 'The Chancellor of the king of Lower Egypt, the first after the King of Upper Egypt, Administrator of the Great Palace, Hereditary Lord, the High Priest of Heliopolis, IMHOTEP, the builder, the sculptor'. Well, he constructed the first stone building ever, without any instruction manual, and it is still standing 4,616 years later, so he had a perfect right to trumpet his achievement.

We welcomed the cool of the pyramid's internal passages and rooms, but I

Who says Donkey's do not need petrol?

must admit to being in awe at the hieroglyphics and other carvings depicting the life of the deceased king. They were staggeringly clear and sharp for their great age. Some of the paintings on plaster had suffered, probably with damp deterioration, but others were so crisp and clear and their colours so vibrant that I took a good deal of convincing that some recent artist had not touched them up in the meantime.

As we left the step pyramid and its associated temple complex, we all had an overriding feeling of relief that the history lesson in the searing heat was over for the day and thoughts of ice-cold beer, even litre bottles of Stella (the local Egyptian brew), loomed quite large in our thoughts. 'Forget it,' our guides insisted, 'remount those donkeys: there is much more to see.'

Like dutiful students, we did as we were told and en route to the next tomb about half a mile away, decided to have a little race. Not an entirely successful venture, it must be said. One donkey took off like the wind and threw its rider – me – into a pile of rocks; the second donkey stuck all four feet firmly into the sand like some petulant prima donna and refused to move; whilst the third moved about ten metres sideways, then decided it needed a five-minute pee. We were a somewhat dishevelled trio arriving at the next antiquity, the Temple and Tombs of the Bulls.

The name given to this area in antiquity was the Serapæum and was believed to be the place where the sacred Apis calf was conceived. According to the hieroglyphic scriptures the calf became the constant companion of the God Ptah. The high priest of Ptah claimed in the hieroglyphics at the entrance to the first tomb that the Apis calf's mother was subjected to a prolonged flash of heavenly light – perhaps lightning – and became pregnant with what was to become the sacred bull, her one and only calf. Here we go again, another virgin birth, and sure enough this one produces a god or something akin. This sacred bull was seen as the earthly manifestation of the God Ptah who is credited with creating Memphis and Saqqara.

Over the following centuries there were a succession of Apis bulls that conveniently seemed to arrive on the demise of their predecessors, but it is not recorded whether each one's conception was accompanied by a miraculous flash of lightning. Maybe I am possessed of a wicked sense of humour, but I can just imagine a sacred bull saying to its partner, 'Did the earth move for you, darling?' and the eager reply, 'No, but there was one hell of a flash of lightning.'

On their deaths these sacred animals were accorded the honours that befitted a deity. They were embalmed and mummified and after the religious rites appropriate to such a being, sometimes lasting more than a week, they were interred in huge sarcophagi for their journey into the afterlife. The first sarcophagus we examined in one of the bull tombs was awesome. It was hewn out of solid jet-black basalt rock, polished to a magnificent shining surface and was covered in hieroglyphics on every side. The huge structure, perhaps sixteen cubic metres, was reputed to weigh 80 tonnes. Unfortunately, when it was discovered, the top had been removed and the tomb was empty, but in AD 1850, a French archaeologist, Mariette, found a very large intact sarcophagus in a secret room nearby. His conventional efforts to remove the six-inch thick, heavy stone lid failed, so he resorted to dynamite. Inside he found a solid gold statue of the occupant, now in the Louvre in Paris, and the actual mummified bull, now in the Cairo Museum. The dates showed that this Apis bull had been buried in the 30th year of the reign of Rameses II, 1249 BC.

Herodotus tells us that one of the early Persian Pharaohs, Cambysses, stabbed the Apis bull with his knife in a fit of wild temper in 523 BC. The poor creature lay bleeding for two days in the temple before finally dying, whereupon it was buried with full honours. Such was the outrage of the Divine Court that the killing was taken as a sign of Cambysses' utter insanity, so he was officially deposed from office. He was replaced by the warrior Pharaoh, Darius I, who established a dynasty that was eventually terminated by Alexander the Great 200 years later in his famous battle against Darius III, the Battle of Issus.

As the bright red sun slowly disappeared seemingly into the distant desert, and the cooler evening wind blew in, our donkeys carried us back to the car where they were carefully groomed and fed by their owners. We stopped off at the Giza Pyramids in good time for the impressive *son et lumière*, which fortunately that night was taking place in the English language. Sir John Gielgud's sonorous tones drifted over to us from the Pyramids themselves and thanks to some clever lighting the Sphynx seemed to be narrating some of the history of Pharaoh Tutankamun's young life, the palace intrigues and his eventual cold-blooded murder. It was extremely eerie and a little unsettling, but perhaps we were over-affected by our recent experiences at Memphis and Saqqara.

Eating in Cairo in those days was fraught with danger. Undoubtedly there was wholesome food to be had in some of the restaurants in the souks and street markets of central Cairo, and the aromas of the spices of the Orient severely tempted one to risk a meal, but we had insufficient knowledge to differentiate between the good and the dodgy. Unless one was extremely careful a dose of neo-dysentery or cholera was a certainty and the last problem a pilot needed was to be throwing up all over the VIPs, or to spend four hours sitting in a pool of diarrhœa trying to look as if the smell was nothing to do with him.

Bottled beer and spirits were safe and in the Shepheards, Hilton and Sheraton hotels bottled water was used for mixers, without ice. Food was more tricky, but light meals served in the coffee bars of the Hilton and the Sheraton were usually safe, providing one avoided salads and doubtful meats like hamburgers. At the same time Egyptian salad vegetables – and I have no reason to expect that it is any safer now – were sometimes watered whilst growing with domestic animal or human excrement and the like, because of the shortage of suitable fertilizer and clean water. Furthermore, they were often washed before serving with water direct from the Nile, without the benefit of purification. This may seem reasonable but the River Nile has a high concentration of the liver fluke that causes the disease bilharzia and a fair amount of cholera and typhoid, none of which I can recommend. Hamburgers, however, could contain absolutely anything and, as an added bonus, may have been kept in a semi-warm condition for hours, the ideal breeding conditions for bacteria. Indeed they were quite likely to have developed into culinary time bombs, only suitable for those with pronounced suicidal tendencies.

Special Flight therefore evolved a system that, though not entirely foolproof, usually kept us healthy. Our usual Cairo food routine was: breakfast in the Shepheards, where the bread and toast tasted terrible, but was in fact safe; snack lunch in the Hilton coffee bar, half a mile walk on the same side of the River Nile; some afternoon activities; then back to the Shepheards to change for dinner before taking a refreshing walk across the main Nile bridge at Zamelek and a further three-quarters of a mile to the Sheraton.

If we decided to stay at the Sheraton for the rest of the evening – assuming we were not flying the next day – then it was a glass of beer for us at the bar and a wander upstairs in time for the floor show in the cabaret club. Dimly lit, with the sights and sounds of bustling Cairo in the background, the club was mostly outside in the relative cool of the desert evening under an array of twinkling brightly lit stars, seemingly close enough to touch, with soft evocative music from the small orchestra and usually a couple of celebrity artists. It was heady stuff after a couple of cocktails. To cap it off there was always Nagwa Faoud, the world-renowned voluptuous young Egyptian belly dancer. She arrived with her own Bedouin musicians and a wiggle of her scantily clad hips that drove some of the white- and gold-turbaned Saudi visitors in their usually white, full-length flowing robes completely wild.

She was a vivacious but quite normal girl to talk to, who had a lively mind and loved a drop of wicked gossip. In those days we were there so regularly that she thought we lived in Cairo and usually sat for a while at our table between her acts, much to the annoyance of the rest of the drooling audience. This caused us some trepidation because the formal dress of some of the Arabs incorporated a conspicuously displayed and vicious-looking curved dagger at the belt, with or without ostentatious precious stones. As they looked at the three British interlopers they fingered these weapons meaningfully and we certainly got the message, so did Miss Faoud, but she thought it hugely amusing and when she was next performing sometimes teased them further by dancing at us in a highly provocative manner.

Sooner or later a strategic withdrawal became appropriate so we would move down to the casino in the basement, trying to avoid the resentful eyes on the way. In this usually very busy establishment in the bowels of the Sheraton complex, fortunes were made and lost at the busy tables. As far as we could see, the operative word was mostly 'lost', but there were undoubtedly some who amassed a steadily growing pile of chips. Omar Sharif, the legendary film star of *Lawrence of Arabia* fame, could occasionally be seen sitting, studiously concentrating on the action of whatever table interested him, but it was usually a rubber of bridge that he preferred. He rarely left without a respectable pile of chips to cash in at the iron-barred cashiers' windows, but I was not privy to his financial arrangements on arrival. The look on his face, however, often clearly proclaimed 'I've won'.

We were of course in a different league, but were nevertheless made very welcome, so much so that despite our very careful betting habits some of the casino managers instantly recognized our arrival and welcomed us respectfully by name. They all knew who we were and what we did, and occasionally flying their President elevated our status considerably. There was a serious three-way conference between us outside the door where we would decide just how many chips we were each planning on losing that night. The average number of chips at the outset was usually about $50 US each. Occasionally one of us would be feeling lucky and decided to invest as much as $100, but that was rare. The financial strategy was always decided outside because inside there was a bevy of eager young ladies, dressed in their smart white cotton Roman togas, pressing free drinks on the newly arrived customers. Why they wore togas was a mystery, but they certainly did look very attractive on these nubile, slim figures. Perhaps Caesar or Mark Antony and their frolics with Cleopatra had something to do with the design. After a few visits it became quite apparent to us that these free drinks were strong, to say the least, and probably spiked.

Inside the casino we would separate and act independently, usually watching the talent operating round our chosen 'sport' for a while, before plunging in with our pocketful of chips. Each blackjack or roulette table had its own minimum and maximum stake, which had to be established before sitting down. It could be quite embarrassing to place a $2 chip on the table only to have the croupier push it contemptuously away and announce for all to hear that this was a minimum $10 table, 'Sir'. Very satisfying, though, to apologize and slowly place four more chips on top of the first and win. Nevertheless, a retreat to the lower value tables was inevitable if the quadruple-strength free drinks had not numbed the brain by then.

A friend of mine (a vicar no less) along with his many other words of wisdom had kindly warned me that roulette tables with double zeros should be avoided like the plague. By marking an extra compartment on the table with a double zero clearly embossed within, the management, at a stroke, doubles the odds in favour of the bank and hence, against the player. Playing on such a table can seriously damage one's financial health. If there are several roulette tables in the room, as found in quality casinos, one should either move to a single zero table, even if the minimum stake is slightly higher, or if not admit defeat and transfer one's attention to the blackjack table.

This same vicar, after consuming most of a bottle of my best brandy after we had both been thrown out of the Officers' Mess at a well-known Yorkshire RAF station, confidentially imparted a roulette system to me which has consistently assisted my financial well-being. He came with very good credentials because he had previously been the impecunious vicar of the British population in Monte Carlo and claimed that his system had ensured that he rarely paid for his lunches whilst in the principality. He admitted that he sometimes only covered a modest lunch and a glass of indifferent wine, but on average he lunched quite well, at times extremely well, without recourse to his own pocket. His system proved to be quite slow, the other drawback being that it requires a substantial pile of chips at the outset to ensure survival over the longer periods between wins.

At times, possibly due to the free drinks, I would grow impatient at the roulette wheel despite not losing and would decamp to the blackjack table for an increase in the excitement quotient. My $50 was cleaned out on many occasions, but it was worth that amount for the thrill of it all and the congenial atmosphere. About one visit in four was profitable to the tune of about $150, or if very lucky $200, but most of the time we all lost small sums overall. Nevertheless, it was enjoyable and there were often celebrities to chat to and a fair number of raving lunatics to watch throwing money at the tables, out of touch with reality.

It was unnecessary to take a taxi back to the Shepheards, which is remarkable as it was common knowledge that in those days Cairo was the espionage and corruption capital of the world. We all enjoyed the three-quarter-mile stroll after midnight back along the west bank of the Nile and over the Zamelek bridge, in the peaceful cool of the desert night – often lit by a huge moon and myriads of twinkling stars. We sometimes saw the odd policeman and occasionally a few Egyptian soldiers, but usually the streets were eerily empty, in stark contrast to their daytime chaotic activity.

Early the following morning, day two of our free time, our driver took us to the Giza plateau for a hands-on encounter with the Sphinx and its background pyramids. There were surprisingly few tourists around at that time and the sun was not radiating its full heat when we arrived, so when he explained that Cairo University students, before graduation, were expected to climb up to the pinnacle of Khufu's great pyramid and descend on the far side, the game was on. I was never convinced of the veracity of his story, but useful exercise was needed, so we decided to accept the implied challenge. A race could have been quite dangerous as some of the stone was crumbling, so we resolved to climb together and to help each other if necessary. After all, we were the crew of a VIP aircraft and one of us on a stretcher would have been seriously embarrassing.

The two and a half ton blocks of limestone were quite rough and the pyramid's 450-foot elevation slowed us considerably, but we were met at the desert sand of the far side with copious bottles of fresh water and congratulations. The sun's heat had been increasing as we descended and escape into the centre of the pyramid was appreciated. None of us succumbed to claustrophobia, and as we absorbed the words of wisdom from our Arab guide we were completely mystified – as are all new visitors who visit these immense structures: the mechanics of moving the 2,300,000 huge blocks with an average weight of 2.5 tonnes over great distances and propelling them up the 54-degree slope way back in 2600 BC are mind-boggling. No wonder it took the whole team of about 100,000 men over twenty years to build. I offer no theories, though many exist, but it is now certain that slaves were unlikely ever to have been involved. This mammoth task was undertaken by dedicated architects, masons and craftsmen with a religious fervour that has rarely been seen throughout man's long history. The secret chambers and passages are still being investigated and occasionally reveal some of their timeless secrets. Many of the cavities and passages are apparently orientated with reference to various constellations of stars, especially Leonides, as positioned in the heavens 4,600 years ago, at the time the Pyramids were built.

Our visit moved on to the Sphinx. This was constructed after Khufu's Great Pyramid by Pharaoh Khafre's team of masons, only about eight years later. It seems that the enormous amount of limestone infill excavated for the centre of the Great Pyramid formed a vast crater in the level ground, which revealed an outcrop of more dense rock. So Khafre ordered his masons to carve this denser rock into a statue for his continuing glory. They duly formed the sides of the outcrop into the body of a huge lion, the symbol of kingship and on it they carved the head of Khafre himself. Over a thousand years later in 1400 BC, during Pharaoh Tuthmosis IV's reign, the Sphinx was worshipped as the manifestation of the Sun God, Ra. Between its front paws the rock was carved into the Dream Stellar, a tablet that supposedly predicted the kingship of Tuthmosis IV when he was but a young prince and not in line of succession to the throne. As he did, in fact, later become Pharaoh it leaves me very suspicious as to just where this prediction fitted into the maelstrom of intrigue and violent death that proliferated prior to his enthronement.

In 1798 Napoleon Bonaparte arrived in Egypt with a substantial army and plans of African conquest. He was apparently sightseeing just like us, and standing in the same position in front of the Sphinx, when a distraught lieutenant galloped up to him, dismounted and in hushed tones broke the news that Admiral Lord Nelson had discovered Napoleon's mighty fleet at anchor in Aboukir Bay on the Egyptian coast west of Alexandria. Even with his inferior numbers of smaller British ships Nelson had sniffed victory in the air.

The superior fleet of larger French ships was close to the land with all guns facing out to sea for protection against any potential enemy. Sadly for the defenders the wily British admiral knew Aboukir Bay intimately. He had careened his ships on the shore years earlier before attacking Naples and so knew that the sandy beach shelved rapidly, leaving deep water behind the French fleet that would be navigable at high tide. As darkness fell, Nelson's ships formed line astern, shifted all their guns to the port sides and loaded them for battle. His flagship even scraped the bottom as it sailed between the coast and the most westerly French man-o'-war and on behind their line, but he destroyed the French fleet with minimal British losses and no further personal injuries. All the opposing ships that were not sunk were taken back to Portsmouth as prizes of war. Some of these captured French ships were renovated and seven years later fought in Nelson's fleet against Admiral Pierre Villeneuve at the Battle of Trafalgar, on 21 October 1805.

When Napoleon heard this disastrous news he was furious. He and his army were trapped without transport or supplies, thousands of miles from home. His dreams of an African empire were shattered. In a fit of rage against Egypt for seemingly forcing him into this ignominious position, he apparently ordered his artillery to blast the face of the Sphinx. During the bombardment its nose was partially destroyed and its face became somewhat pockmarked, but Pharaoh Khafre's likeness is still recognisable today on the famous lion body. What torments a poor Sphinx must suffer after 4,300 years of inscrutability, but this unique sculpture is certainly most impressive and still well worth visiting.

Exploration of the Giza tombs, temples and funerary chambers took up the rest of the day with most of the following day being spent in the Cairo Museum, although this fine repository of Egyptian antiquity needs far more than just a day to appreciate. When I returned to Cairo on future flights, and some time later with my family, I spent many days absorbing the exhibits. At every visit I started my study at the unwrapped mummy of Pharaoh Rameses II – probably the greatest of all the Pharaohs – trying to equate his legendary deeds, his incisive laws, his grasp of the stars in their courses, his successes in battle and the multitude of statues to him throughout the whole of Egypt, with his prone body, preserved facial features and hands with their long artistic fingers. Over three thousand years in the afterlife and we can still see him today. Hopefully the god Osiris, ruler of the underworld, eventually fulfilled his promise to sponsor him into their heaven with the falcon-headed Sun God Ra.

By the eighth day of this particular Cairo sojourn, I was determined to ascertain our passengers' plans. The Egyptian Chief of Protocol claimed to know nothing, but when I pressed him further he seemed uncertain whether President Gadaffi was, in fact, still in Egypt. My personal alarm bells sounded and to add to the mystery Cairo's daily English newspaper was printing anti-Libyan articles on its front page. Worries about our President's safety crept into my considerations and words like kidnap, abduction and assassination flitted across my thought processes, closely followed by fears for our own safety.

That evening, sitting in the Shepheards piano bar prior to our walk over to the Sheraton for a meal, a flamboyant new young barman appeared to serve our drinks. One look at him and I nearly fell off my chair. Although much younger, he was the absolute double of my own brother Gordon, who lived in Beverley, East Yorkshire. The likeness was uncanny – the same build, same height, same features, same way of walking and the same impish smile that I remembered on my brother's face when he had been eighteen. He even gave his older boss behind the bar some cheeky responses, typical of my brother at the same age. When he came over to our table to refresh the nibbles, I established that his name was Mohamed and that his family had moved up to Cairo from a village further south just after he was born.

Though I could not instantly recall the exact dates, I remembered that Gordon had been stationed with the British Army in Egypt, in Ismailia, on the Great Bitter Lakes of the Suez Canal, north-east of Cairo, in the late 1940s and early 1950s. There the coincidence ended. When I later quizzed him, Gordon denied any possibility of my insinuations being fact because contact with Egyptians was not allowed in those days. There was, he said, a mildly hostile atmosphere, from what he described as 'those clefty [thieving] Egyptians', one that was confirmed by several of his colleagues who accompanied him into Egypt. Four years later my wife and family stayed with me at the Shepheards and they too remarked on the likeness of Mohamed to my brother. To be accurate, Lesley could see a clear similarity, but my two children, Nigel and Trudi, who were not yet born when Gordon was in his early twenties, could see only a vague likeness to their 45-year-old uncle. Maybe my asking Gordon for his comments in front of his wife, Val, was not the most sensible course of interrogation.

A team from the RCC deep in the Sahara Desert, at Ghat, explaining new laws to the desert nomads. This group were closely related to the 'Tuareg'.

By the next day, the lack of reliable information began to cause us more concern, which was exacerbated when we tuned in to the BBC Overseas Service to hear the news programme discussing activities in Tripoli that implied that President Gadaffi was present. As we had flown him to Cairo nine days earlier and were waiting, as instructed, to fly him back again, confusion bordering on consternation reigned.

I took a taxi to the airport forthwith and persuaded Egyptair to send an urgent Telex to the chairman of Libyan Arab Airlines requesting government instructions. The reply the following morning instructed us to return empty back to Tripoli, so after rounding up the other crew we renewed acquaintances with the staff of the airport duty-free shop and returned home.

A subsequent confidential explanation by the charismatic Libyan Chief of Protocol, Mr Abu Shagour, for our unexpected stay in Cairo was that intelligence reports had been received – presumably from the KGB – that returning to Tripoli by air was likely to be 'dangerous' for the President. It seems that on receipt of this warning the Libyan Ambassador was summoned and in the interest of security, decided to borrow a nondescript small car from one of his embassy staff allowing the President to drive himself incognito back to Tripoli, over 3,000 km away. There were, of course, other security precautions taken, but they are irrelevant to this narrative.

Security at this level was our prime task, because keeping our passengers safe to the best of our ability automatically kept us safe. Their security was also ours. Who were we to complain about an expenses paid, ten-day, foreign holiday with interesting tours thrown in, even if it was not planned beforehand?

Tupolev TU22 – Blinder 'B' in Libyan colours.

CHAPTER TWO

Brotherly Love Turns Sour

The Egypt/Libyan merger talks progressed for the next month and we flew all the Libyan and Egyptian personalities involved. Most ministers of both governments were treated to our expert services and hospitality, but the most frequent users were the Libyan Prime Minister, Major Abdusalem Jalloud, the Foreign Minister, Major Abdul mun'im el Houni and the Egyptian minister responsible for the proposed merger, Hosni Mubarak who, since the assassination of Anwar Sadat in 1981, has been the country's President.

The underlying politics of the proposed merger were quite tempting to both sides. Libya had great wealth and a vast area of land, but a shortage of people, especially educated people. Egypt had lots of people including some highly educated ones in need of employment, but was financially and economically poor. The theory was therefore to combine both countries and sort out most of the problems at a single stroke. The devil, as usual with these good theories, lay in the detail and the details posed potentially insurmountable problems.

The major stumbling block was that though both populations were considered to be Arab with a common religion, the majority of the ordinary people in both countries disliked their neighbours. The average Libyan considered the average Egyptian to be unreliable, with poor personal hygiene and only fit to carry out menial tasks. The average Egyptian considered the average Libyan to be overbearing, pompous without justification and humourless.

As an outsider, I could appreciate that if one adopted a more positive approach there were enviable qualities clearly visible in both populations – though their backgrounds were very different, making it difficult for each to step back and even want to acknowledge the other's favourable attributes.

Egyptians are descended from an ancient ancestry with roots firmly established in their land since time immemorial. They might have been perched on the edge of abject poverty, and many had actually fallen off the edge already, but they could still muster peals of uproarious laughter on the flimsiest pretext. Yes, they would cheat you if you were gullible enough to accept their sales pitch, but if you smiled and tactfully pointed out the error in their calculations, as likely as not they would cheerfully return any overcharge, without taking offence. What else could be expected from them? The ordinary citizen was desperately poor whereas by comparison we were rich beyond their wildest imagination, as for that matter were the Libyans with whom they came into contact. If their hygiene lacked something on occasions and their whites were not as pristine as they should be, it was understandable. Clean water was not easy to find in the cramped living quarters of bustling Cairo. My generalization of course omits consideration of upper-class Egyptians, of whom Mohamed Al Fayed of Harrods fame is a prime example. There are, in fact, many sophisticated citizens of this intriguing country.

The single-decker buses that carry local Egyptians about their daily business are not very numerous. They are, however, very inexpensive to use, but are even cheaper if you do not go inside the bus and either sit on the roof or hang on the side or rear. The sight of these buses festooned with countless people was incredible and if the bus negotiated a sharp corner at high speed, those hanging on the outside were involuntarily thrown outwards by centrifugal force, in severe danger of flying off. I have no idea what kept them attached to the side, except their fingernails, but a bus with seating for thirty-five people seemed to be encased in a seething mass of humanity and we wondered just how many people were actually on the bus.

The answer was sadly demonstrated when a fully loaded bus plunged into the River Nile, whilst we were there. The *Cairo Times* proudly proclaimed that nearby boatmen saved 58 of the passengers, but that the other 65 had been drowned – 123 passengers on a bus designed for 35 looked about right from what we saw. The general chaos of modern central Cairo cannot be adequately described.

We found that Libyans have many enviable qualities and we enjoyed our life in their country for over ten years. With some exceptions they were quite slow to accept a stranger into their midst, appearing generally shy. They were noticeably extremely clean in their personal appearance and in their homes, but there was a certain lack of exuberance and spontaneous laughter was rare. However they had a generally loyal demeanour that was notably reliable in the conduct of personal relationships.

After some months in the country where, as a family, we were treated in a polite, but reserved fashion, an almost imperceptible change occurred. It was first noticed in our local shopping areas where, when shortages occurred, the owners of the individual shops would call Lesley's name and inform her confidentially that if she drew her car up to the back of the building, the item(s) in question would be loaded into the car with a 'Pay me the next time you are in town'. It seemed almost as though acceptance had to be earned and unfortunately some of the more brash and noisy expatriates were never accepted.

Libya's history explains much about its people's demeanour. This huge country was for millennia very sparsely populated and the majority of the people lived deep in the desert as nomadic families largely of Bedouins, self-contained within their own groups. The coastal strip was slightly more heavily populated with commercial traders and the Bedouin only came into these areas intermittently to replenish supplies or trade their products. They were suspicious of strangers, always alert for signs of aggression and were ready to defend their families with their restricted territorial interests whenever needed. The Berbers, descendants of the notorious Barbary Pirates, were a constant threat and even today Berber families resident in Libya conduct themselves in a haughty, ethnically superior manner.

A formal merger, therefore, between these two disparate nations of Egypt and Libya, with their own unique personalities, was always going to be fraught with difficulties, despite the desirability on economic and military grounds. The combined countries would indeed have been a mighty force in the region.

The merger talks stalled on a myriad of seemingly insurmountable details, then were resurrected when the heads of agreements were literally 'signed in blood', on television, for the world to see. It became apparent that the Egyptians had, through pressure from the people, eventually gone cool on accepting Libya. The Egyptian government feared for its survival if it had forced through the merger, despite the opposition, whilst Libya would not accept anything but complete integration.

The atmosphere grew so bad that we were even uncertain as to whether fuel would be provided for us at Cairo Airport when we flew the delegations there to prolong the talks. There was a further month of stop/start negotiations, mostly carried out by the press of both countries, each obviously expressing their own government's views; then bald statements were hurled back and forth. Egypt: 'We will not have a merger at any price.' Libya: 'We must have a merger, because it is in everyone's interest.' Then silence for a week.

It is impossible to say where the next move came from, but everyone at the time had his own suspicions. An announcement was made in Tripoli and Cairo newspapers simultaneously to the effect that there would be a 'popular spontaneous march of Libyans', walking from Tripoli to Cairo, to express their demands for the merger of the two countries. I had the impression at this time that President Sadat of Egypt envisaged a handful of Libyans, perhaps twenty or so, showing up to hand in a petition, or something similar. Libyans on the other hand had much more grandiose thoughts, that eventually came close to provoking a full-scale war between the two countries.

The time was July 1973 and the searing heat of the Sahara Desert was seriously life-threatening to people. Temperatures of 50-60ºC (120-140ºF) were not uncommon at midday and there were no trees to provide any shade. A 3,000-kilometre walk in these conditions would have been suicidal, so the Egyptians were very sceptical and quite complacent. Imagine their surprise, therefore, when it was suddenly announced on Libyan radio that the march had left Tripoli (in air-conditioned luxury coaches) and was expected to reach Mersa Matruh, a few miles over the Egyptian/Libyan border within two days. A small footnote revealed that there were about 36,000 Libyans on the march.

This was the height of Egypt's tourist season, with Cairo full to bursting with high-spending European, American and Japanese visitors, all soaking up the culture and spending heaps of the lovely money which single-handedly kept the cash-strapped Egyptian treasury solvent. The prospect of having Cairo disrupted at this time by what was feared to be an invasion of 36,000 inebriated Libyans – no alcohol in Libya, but unlimited alcohol in Egypt – was perceived as a nightmare scenario. President Sadat ordered his battle-hardened military Machine to stop this fiasco at Mersa Matruh, regardless of casualties. Though not an actual declaration of war, it was dangerously close.

Like the legendary 'knights in shining armour' we arrived at the main airfield of Mersa Matruh, just across the border inside Egypt, with Captain Mustafa el Karubi and Muktar el Qirwi, both respected members of the Libyan Revolutionary Command Council (RCC) and full ministers of the government. Captain Karubi, with his warm bubbly nature, ready grin and thoughtful diplomacy seemed to me to be the perfect choice to defuse this highly volatile situation.

At his request we were given Air Traffic Control permission to fly low before landing over the serried ranks of luxury coaches that had brought the unwelcome invasion across the border. Pushing my luck slightly, I widened the low pass over the Egyptian forces ranged against the Libyans and was horrified to see a stationary armoured troop train on the line straddling the east-west main road with about 30,000 fully armed troops taking up positions behind it, backed by a battalion of light tanks, all protected by batteries of anti-aircraft guns and portable ground-to-air missiles. This was indeed serious, but when we passed over the airfield there was also a full squadron of Russian ground-attack Sukhoi SU-21 fighters sitting at the side of the runway armed and ranged, ready for action. To make matters even worse, out at sea, ships of the Egyptian Navy were steaming parallel to the coast about two miles out, with the barrels of their guns traversing to and fro, seemingly flexing their muscles.

This scrubby desert had not seen such military might since Montgomery's British Eighth Army challenged Rommel's Afrika Corps at the Battle of El Alamein, just up the road, on the night of 23 October 1942. The impending bloodbath seemed unstoppable and a glance at the two peacemakers in the back confirmed the gravity of the situation. A halo of intense worry surrounded them and neither spoke.

Landing at Mersa Matruh, we taxied up to the control tower. Our passengers, dressed in civilian clothes, were met by a bevy of generals, air marshals and even an admiral, all resplendent in dress uniform.

Round one to the Libyans, I thought, as the engineer lowered the access stairs and our delegation descended the steps towards the power and the glory spread out before them.

Mustapha el Karubi made a brave attempt to defuse the tension by grabbing the one officer he recognized, a general, and enveloping him in a characteristic bear hug, complete with his characteristic guffaw. Muktar el Qirwi politely shook the hands of everyone and settled in to his diplomatic tasks with a quieter demeanour. He had been totally shattered at the mass of firepower ranged against the Libyans that our low fly-past had revealed.

As Captain Karubi was on the third step, leading the way up into the control tower, he turned, looked at the Egyptian senior officers following him, grinned, and in a loud voice clearly audible through my open cockpit window made a remark to the effect of, 'Where's the firing squad?' followed by another loud chuckle. My grasp of the Arabic language was not great at that time, but by the astonished look on the air marshal's face, his understanding of Captain Karubi's remark was similar to mine.

I parked our gleaming white and gold Falcon next to the silver Sukhoi 21s. Whilst Dick, the engineer, attended to the refuelling I made friends with the Egyptian fighter pilots, some of whom were familiar to us. Sufficient fresh coffee was brewed for everyone as we all relaxed out of the oppressive heat in our beautifully air-conditioned cabin.

Being of an inquisitive disposition it was not long before I was seated in the first Sukhoi cockpit with the squadron commander leaning in from the top step of the ladder. He explained some of the instrumentation and weaponry and everything else that former Fleet Air Arm pilots like to see. What I really wanted was a quick flight, but in the circumstances I did not have the cheek to ask. I formulated a persuasively reasoned argument in my mind and even contemplated an attempt at bribery, but with hostilities a hair's breadth away, it was obviously out of the question.

Just as the sun was setting over the horizon, a limousine drew up to the Falcon steps and the driver offered to take us to the hotel; so we put the aircraft to bed, threw our suitcases aboard the limo and left for the mighty metropolis of Mersa Matruh town. As we sped away in some style I remembered a previous visit, a few months earlier, when to relieve the boredom of waiting for our passengers the air traffic controller had taken our crew on a *tour de ville* in his car. There was, as I remembered it, no hotel or even anything looking vaguely like one. In fact there was only a handful of houses and what looked like a military hospital, so where were we going?

Every mile or so, we passed a heavy machine-gun position with half a dozen alert soldiers waving us onwards, but there were other, more relaxed soldiers everywhere – seated round small fires, they were smoking, drinking from grubby metal cups, skylarking, cleaning their rifles; some were even peeing into the road as we passed. We soon decided that an available bed in this town would be a complete miracle. Three rooms with three beds was certain to be an impossibility, however we had little option but to go through the motions, just to be polite.

We drew up finally alongside a house that was only slightly larger than all the others. The elderly man with a severely pockmarked face, who came out to see us wearing a dishevelled apron, laughed uncontrollably when we asked for three en suite rooms. Giggling quietly, he informed us that he only had five rooms in the whole place. When we explained what *en suite* meant, he erupted into more laughter. He said that he had one toilet only and that was at the end of his small garden, seemingly with no shelter whatsoever.

He also informed us that his five rooms were currently occupied by at least ten army officers in each one. We thanked him and returned to the limousine. Despite our driver being under pain of death to remain with us until suitable accommodation had been found, he had disgorged all our cases onto the dusty pavement and was preparing to leave. He seemed hell-bent on returning to the airfield and leaving us with our heap of belongings on the smelly windswept street as night established its grip on the chaotic scene.

I insisted that until we had acceptable lodgings he would stick with us and use his best efforts to care for our welfare. His reluctant second idea seemed crazier than the first – he proposed taking us to the hospital, an idea that confused us somewhat. We contemplated responding with, 'But we're not injured'; however we decided that his cantankerous reply was likely to be, 'Just wait until I get this Kalashnikov from under my seat and we'll soon correct that little problem!' and refrained from comment.

A fluky desert breeze blew zephyrs of sand-laden air round our legs as we dismounted with some solemnity outside a square mausoleum of a building, standing in its own litter-strewn grounds. The diminutive driver with unjustified confidence had our three cases out on the pavement before anyone had a chance to comment, picked them up and marched confidently inside. He slammed the great institutional wooden door behind us, but it bounced and swung wide open again as he prepared to drop our cases onto the floor. We rushed involuntarily towards him so fast that he stepped backwards, as if about to be attacked.

The reason that we all wished at all costs to keep the cases containing our wives' lovingly starched and pressed white uniform shirts off the floor was that even in the dim light emanating from the only electric lamp swinging from the high ceiling in the middle of the cavernous entrance hall, it was apparent that the floor was saturated with a great deal of unspecified brown liquid. The thought of the mess that would result from this vile-smelling stuff penetrating our cases and clothes was too horrible to contemplate, so we each grabbed our own case and clung on to it, keeping our belongings clear of the floor.

This entrance vestibule was like something out of a particularly horrific Dracula film and the insistent breeze coming down the various corridors did nothing to improve our confidence.

Seeing nobody there to welcome us, the driver ran around opening every door, shouting staccato, unintelligible bursts of Arabic into the apparently empty rooms. Eventually, when he had just about reached the end of a particularly long, unlit corridor and was becoming quite demented, a bright shaft of light illuminated him as he threw open yet another door. He seemed to grab someone he found inside and delivered a frenetic tirade, which apparently produced an unacceptable reaction, because he marched the poor soul he had found, almost dragging him at times, along the darkened corridor towards us.

As the now irate chauffeur and his reluctant captive drew slowly nearer, we were mortified to see that the reluctant Egyptian was quite clearly a surgeon. Worse than that, he told us later, he had been in the middle of a delicate operation on some poor car crash victim when our driver had burst into his operating theatre.

Dressed in his off-white operating gown, spattered with fresh blood, complete with white hat and facemask, he nervously shuffled his right hand into the pocket of his gown as he approached. Focussing on his hand in the dim light before it disappeared completely into his pocket, I was embarrassed to see that he was, in fact, still holding a dripping scalpel. This was growing worse by the minute.

He released one corner of his mask and spoke English with a cultured accent. We immediately offered our profuse apologies and urged him to return to his obviously more pressing task. The driver had seemingly apprised him of our needs as he was frogmarched up the corridor, because he ignored my pleas for him to continue his life-saving work and replied that there were beds available, but he did not expect that we would find them acceptable.

Still clutching our precious cases clear of the ground, and despite the aforementioned breeze we became aware of the musty, sewage-like, unpleasant odour permeating the whole building. As we dutifully followed our reluctant host along yet another unlit passage, at right angles to the first one, the smell intensified. He threw open a door and as he switched on the single 40 watts of electric light to illuminate the room, he pointed to a double row of beds in what was obviously one of the smaller hospital wards.

I had never seen such a dirty room in my entire life. Dick whispered in my ear that he was not keen on staying here, but I was still entranced with classifying the decay that met our eyes. There was a fair amount of livestock scurrying hither and thither, on the beds, floors, walls and ceiling, but my attention was taken up with the disgusting stains on the mattress covers and, in fact, every visible surface. Some was obviously long-dried blood, some was dried urine, but other marks seemed to be a variety of excrement – far from it being cleaned off, there were actual words clearly scrawled in it on the once cream walls.

I confirmed to the surgeon that he was quite correct in his assessment of our reactions to the quality of the available accommodation and stated emphatically that we would be returning to our aircraft forthwith. He looked very relieved and as he led us to the front door, now blowing lazily to and fro in the evening breeze, he confided in me that this had been a British military hospital, built for the troops in 1941 after the Battle of El Alamein, but that it was in urgent need of renovation. We wished him and his patient well, but he professed little hope for his unfortunate victim's survival. As we motored back to the airfield we all agreed that the only sensible renovation possible for this building would be a couple of well-aimed 1,000 kg bombs.

Returning to the airport was now fraught with unexpected danger for the way was littered with roadblocks and the routine, though very frightening at first, became absolutely farcical. At each roadblock an Egyptian soldier would rush straight at us, screaming like a demented banshee, his Kalashnikov AK-47 machine gun mounted high on his shoulder with his finger on the trigger, looking down the sights and aiming at the driver's head. To make matters even more terrifying, the sentry's two colleagues, with their faces plastered in copious amounts of charcoal, simultaneously screamed and rushed out of the darkness from either side, aiming at the driver as the car drew to a halt. We were not worried about them deliberately pulling their triggers, because it was quite obviously a game of bluff, but we were petrified that in the darkness one of them would trip on the rough stony ground and pull his trigger by accident as he fell headlong.

After we had passed three of these groups of comedians, it all seemed absolutely ridiculous so the other nine roadblocks had us closing our eyes and totally ignoring the crazy charade. It was a pleasant surprise when the airfield gates appeared in front of the car. We carried our cases up to the operations room in the tower to inform the senior officer where we proposed sleeping for the night. He was quite perturbed at our experiences in the town and shouted at the driver for his incompetence, whereupon we all sprang to the driver's defence, proclaiming that he had done his very best. The officer announced that he would not hear of us sleeping in our aeroplane and went through into an adjacent room where a row of beds, complete with sleeping occupants could be seen. He moved quickly along the beds, tipping the first three purposely on their sides, spilling the sleeping occupants unceremoniously onto the floor.

As the sleepers shakily stood up, blinking, after their surprise awakening from deep sleep, we could see that they were the pilots of the Sukhoi-21s. It was a ridiculous sight, these three intrepid young warriors shakily standing there in their underpants, rubbing their eyes disbelievingly. Seconds earlier they had been gathering their strength to enable them to carry out their duty at dawn, if ordered, to streak supersonically into the air and annihilate the marching Libyans. Now they were stood there like schoolboys in a dormitory roused from their beds for some minor infringement of the rules.

We apologized sincerely and urged them to return to their beds immediately, assuring them that there had been an unfortunate mistake. They thanked us, leapt enthusiastically back into bed and looked asleep before we left the room. We turned, and despite the senior officer's protestations marched purposely down the stairs, leaving the control tower. We were very choosy whose warm beds we climbed into.

Our driver was still in his car smarting from the officer's unjustified rebuke. He ferried us across to our Falcon, gleaming in the brilliant moonlight alongside the line of smaller Egyptian fighters – but relief turned to horror as we saw a blazing fire crackling away underneath the fuel mast of our beloved aircraft.

The fuel mast is the aerodynamic vent on the underside of the fuselage, out of which fuel is dribbled when the sun heats up the fuel in the tanks causing expansion. To avoid a pressure build-up that could rupture a tank the fuel sometimes becomes a continuous minor flow. Obviously this usually occurs during the day when the sun is at its hottest and here we had a situation where, if anything, the fuel should be contracting in the relative cool of the night air; but even in this benign circumstance I have sometimes noticed an internal valve suddenly click over, forcing a few ounces of fuel to be expelled down the external mast – which at the moment of our arrival was being licked by the flames of a substantial fire.

Around the fire was a group of about six soldiers totally engrossed in conversation and eagerly anticipating the boiling pot swinging from a tripod of sticks, over the flames. It was, of course, their lovingly prepared *chai* (tea). Alongside the group was a self-supporting pyramid of their Kalashnikov AK-47 assault rifles. As the car glided to a stop at the nose of the Falcon, completely unseen by this group of guards who were supposed to be protecting all the aircraft, my hand was on the door handle in preparation for a rapid disembarkation to deal with the obvious problem posed by the fire.

I was thinking fast, choosing words and rehearsing the Arabic to avoid a major diplomatic incident. My thoughts settled on an opening gambit of *Salaam Aleikum* (Peace be with you!) but I did not have the chance to speak. The door behind me burst open long before the car halted and Dick launched himself straight into the middle of the fire, kicking wildly with his legs and feet. Over went the teapot, accompanied by the burning embers of the fire sparkling over the hapless guards, who plainly did not know what had hit them.

Probably unwisely, Dick's final kick sent the Kalshnikov pyramid skidding across the concrete dispersal at high speed. There was a great deal of feeling in that kick for some of the guns skated off into the darkness for more than ten metres. If any of these lethal weapons had been set to automatic fire with the safety catch off, then the massive military Machine assembled nervously around Mersa Matruh could well have been launched into a major battle with horrendous loss of life.

Dick, however, had not yet quite finished with these unfortunate gentlemen. Standing with legs apart and arms akimbo, he launched into a verbal tirade combining Arabic and English, employing every known insult and swear word of both languages, some of which surprised even me. The guards, at first bewildered, were now terrified and fled into the shadows of the Sukhoi 21s, leaving their weapons behind. It was a fair bet that they would never light a fire underneath anybody else's aeroplane.

Dick announced that he thought the little problem had now been sorted, plunged his hand into his trouser pocket, extracted the aircraft keys and opened the fuselage door. We all dutifully trooped aboard. A few minutes later, as the throb of our auxiliary engine heralded three much-needed clean cups of hot bedtime cocoa, there was an almost imperceptible tap on the fuselage door. I opened it and at the bottom of the steps stood the sergeant of the guard. He had to shout to make himself heard above the noise of the engine, but his body language clearly announced that he had come to offer his sincere apologies for lighting the fire. I invited him to come up the steps and completely failed to keep a straight face as he asked if they could have their guns back.

We offered him a seat and after a quick word with his colleagues he relaxed and told us that they had been rushed from their barracks near Cairo that day, without having eaten. They were all very hungry. The chai they had been brewing, along with some survival biscuits, was to have been their only meal of the day. The mention of food reminded us that we had not eaten for quite a while either and I remembered that we had taken a full complement of twelve VIP meals with us from Tripoli. Our passengers had eaten two meals, which left ten still in the storage rack. These were no ordinary meals either, but were prepared by one of the top Air France chefs and would have done justice to the Georges Cinq in

Paris. If they were not eaten tonight they would probably have been ruined, so we decided to have a midnight feast to end all midnight feasts.

Such a meal needed a first-class wine to do it justice, but we had none so we made do with a cool bitter soda and used our imagination. The soldiers sat on their packs on the ground, grasping Dick's cups of tea, all grouped around the bottom of the steps, but the chauffeur had retired by then. Our guests were somewhat suspicious of the generous helping of Beluga caviar that surrounded the dressed lobster, but they ate it hungrily nevertheless. The hot *coq au vin*, when it arrived, was greeted with great enthusiasm by everyone and the expertly crafted parcels of steaming delicate vegetables were a source of some wonderment.

I forget the exact sweet we ate, but it was a typically French, fluffy, creamy brandy combination. Dick even served chocolate mints with the coffee. Our guests thanked us profusely as they left to resume their duties, but the confusion they felt at the evening's events clearly showed on their faces. How this whirling dervish of a maniac had materialized out of thin air, kicked them and their fire away and afterwards served them with a meal of superb quality, at no cost whatsoever, must have left them completely bewildered.

We subsequently saw some of these soldiers at Cairo airport and were quite embarrassed, in our smart uniforms, to be given full-blooded bear hugs with obvious affection by fully armed soldiers. It completely confused the ordinary passengers milling around the airport concourse, but we later received unexpected help in countless ways from these soldiers, so the gourmet midnight feast was appreciated and did us no harm whatsoever.

On the soldiers' departure to resume their duties as guards, we rapidly cleared up and converted the inside of our VIP aircraft into a three-person bedroom. First we drew the curtains, then the centre aisle became a two-person end-to-end bed with the cushions from some of the nine seats forming comfortable mattresses. The presidential double seat became a single full-length bed with the aid of more cushions, and the dozen soft, clean, monogrammed blankets that we carried for the passengers' comfort became our bedding. We even had soft pillows. Fortunately our Falcons had full toilet facilities. What more could we ask? It only remained for us to don our pyjamas, clean our teeth and retire to our respective beds.

As dawn broke over the eastern Sahara, a thundering cacophony vibrated the side of the aircraft. It took a few minutes for one of us to gather ourselves sufficiently together to climb over everything and open the door. On the tarmac stood our two Libyan passengers, briefcases in hand, for all the world like London commuters waiting for the 7.30 train into town, but in this case requesting to be taken to Cairo. As my befuddled mind gyrated, trying to muster a suitable response,

I unfortunately let slip an uncomplimentary expletive, but rapidly followed it with 'We'll be ready to take off in thirty minutes.' They looked quite sceptical, grinning at my striped pyjamas and bare feet, so I said that they could find a nice cup of tea in the control tower and promised to taxi there to pick them up in thirty minutes' time.

We triumphantly opened the Falcon door outside the tower exactly on time, and Mustafa el Karubi and Muktar el Kirwi embarked with cheery grins. Air Traffic Control cleared us to fly direct to the coastal town of El Alamein at 5,000 feet, turn south to Lake Qarun on the edge of the fearsome Qattara Depression, then east for Cairo Airport. The ultra-clear dawn views of Lower Egypt were stunning, but we had to turn our heads sideways to appreciate them because our course took us directly into the rising sun, which was just above the horizon. As we crossed over El Alamein at our low altitude, where even the cars on the roads were clearly visible, our minds pondered on the momentous happenings of 31 years earlier and I thought of some of my relatives who had fought in that critical battle.

Turning right towards the incongruous lake in the middle of the desert, we passed the obvious remains of the detritus of war. There were tanks, artillery pieces and various vehicles partially protruding out of the sand, but what dreadful sand. The Qattara Depression, feared by travellers for centuries, consists of a sinky, fine-grained, running sand that whips up into a sandstorm at anything above a gentle breeze – a survival nightmare. It persuaded me to have an extra close inspection of all the gauges to reconfirm that our engines were burning and turning normally, and that the tanks were full of that vital clear liquid. After all, we were less than a mile away from that fearsome quagmire and it looked like a burning cauldron even before the searing sun had fully risen.

Cairo Control called on the radio and welcomed us into their sphere of influence with instructions that we were the only aircraft in their airspace at that time, at any altitude, and they could give us permission to take a close look at some of their antiquities if we wished. I have never, before or since, been given such an invitation at Cairo and I would dearly have wished to take them up on their kind offer, but our passengers were anxious to land at the earliest opportunity, so we were forced to decline.

A high-powered reception committee met us at the VIP lounge, including the ubiquitous Colonel Shukri. After the rest of the entourage disappeared inside the building, he came up the steps and sat himself down in a seat. We offered him a coffee and sat with him for a while. He apologized for being misleading about our President's movements earlier that year. He assured me that there was a very real security problem at the time and said that if he had given us the true position... he paused and raised his hand horizontally and drew it across his throat in a cutting motion. I accepted his apology gracefully. To be honest, there was not much option. He could say exactly what he wished regardless of the truth and we had no way of refuting his story.

A message arrived from our passengers, somewhere in Cairo, to say that their meeting with the Egyptian government would last until lunchtime and they would like to return to Mersa Matruh in the early afternoon. They would probably have eaten a meal before arriving at the aircraft, but one could never be sure, so we dropped off our dirty meal containers at the catering unit and stocked up with another twelve fresh VIP meal trays. They were nowhere near the quality of the meals from the specialist chefs in Tripoli the day before, but they were quite presentable, so we stowed them on board and wandered off to the Duty Free shop for a browse around.

The shop was not the cheapest of the ones we visited, but it was run by an upmarket French company with Egyptian staff, mostly nubile young ladies who, because of our frequent visits, always seemed to be able to find some items under the counter that they kept as free gifts for their more affluent customers. Our wives loved the perfumes and cosmetics that we acquired this way, but it was sometimes more difficult when we wanted something special for an anniversary. Their designer boutique was a ladies' heaven, but first I had to find an assistant of the same shape as Lesley to model the chosen item. They were very good and entered into the spirit with great hilarity, although they drew the line at modelling the lingerie.

We retired to the Falcon a couple of hours later with our goodies, wound up the auxiliary engine, broke out three of the meals and enjoyed a leisurely lunch. Ironically, we now had a couple of crates of the finest Château Lafitte, courtesy of the duty-free shop, but we still could not partake. The rule that nobody consumed any alcohol of any kind within twelve hours of any flight was strictly observed for everyone's benefit, so once more we had to be satisfied with bitter soda.

As there was no sign of the passengers, we adopted the classic Special Flight pose of waiting. I am not being facetious about our typical passengers. They tried to keep us informed of their movements, but with the best will in the world it can't have been easy. They were usually travelling to destinations to have meetings of one sort or another. They tried to assess the length of the meeting, but there was often a problem to be solved; sometimes this was minor and could easily be assessed, but often it was important, with life and death ramifications.

In those circumstances meetings were as long as it took and delegates came and went as necessary. The players usually apologized for extended waits on their arrival. Occasionally they would confide the intensity of the negotiations that had transpired, but at times they would just slump on board, thoroughly drained, and one could only guess at their exhaustion by the fatigue showing on their faces.

We developed various methods of keeping ourselves ready to go whilst, in fact, relaxing. We read books and newspapers, we debated and our old stand-by was a protracted game of cards. 'Tail' was the favourite as it could be stopped at a moment's notice, should action be suddenly required. Of course, minor gambling was involved, just to make it interesting, but the usual stakes seldom cost anyone more than £1 in total and a £2 win was unusually high. The other advantage of Tail was that most of our usual passengers played it themselves so if they returned one by one, they would often join in until the remainder came aboard.

The Prime Minister was a very fine exponent of bluffing that he had a much better hand of cards than anyone thought. If he embarked prior to an unexpected Air Traffic delay, there was often a cry of 'Get the cards out' from the cabin and we would all join in a spirited session of Tail until we were cleared for take-off. We usually ended by paying him before leaving the table, but the very small stakes never upset anyone.

On this occasion our wait was of medium length, probably about seven hours. When the raucous motorcycle sirens and flashers eventually indicated the need for action, we plunged into the routine checks with some enthusiasm. Ideally we would reach the point of starting the engines just as the passengers embarked, but it did not always quite work out like that. This time our expected passengers arrived in unusually high spirits, which augured well for a relaxation of the tension around Mersa Matruh. They brought two extra passengers with them – Mr Hosni Mubarak and his secretary. Mr Mubarak came up to the cockpit, apologized for the delay and added, 'But we had to get it right, didn't we?' I nodded and informed him that we had flight planned for Mersa Matruh and he confirmed that after landing there they would all like to go to Benghazi.

We were cleared to fly at 4,000 feet to Mersa, but it was now quite dark and I was amazed, as always, with the dots of cooking fires deep in the desert below us. As we levelled off at cruising height Mustafa el Karubi tapped me on the shoulder and said that his meeting had gone very well. I asked him whether that meant that the 'spontaneous' Libyan march could now return to Tripoli and he replied that the coaches were probably even then loading up and would shortly be headed off westwards. I replied that he must have been feeling quite proud of himself for defusing this confrontation without bloodshed. He agreed. As he was obviously in a good mood I pushed my luck and said that he had probably earned at least a couple of extra virgins in Paradise. He laughed uproariously and returned to his seat. By the raucous hilarity emanating from the cabin as he sat down he must have shared my comments with his fellow passengers.

As we sighted our destination Mr Mubarak came up to the cockpit and asked if we minded him sitting on the jump-seat for the landing. I invited him to sit down and gave him the seat straps. As he put them on I commented that he seemed familiar with these kinds of straps. He agreed and told me that he was an ex-fighter pilot, just like me. That rocked me a little, not that he was a fighter pilot, but that he knew that I had been one. How much else does he know? I asked myself, but a landing was needed so I left the wondering for later.

As we circled to carry out a normal landing, even though it was dark, I could see that the troop train had gone and only a few tanks remained. The Sukhoi 21s were not on the airfield and some sort of normality had returned to Mersa Matruh in our absence. For no apparent reason I wondered whether the poor car crash victim whose operation we had so rudely interrupted was still alive, but I would never know. As I taxied up to the control tower, two Mercedes met us. Messrs Karubi and Kirwi leapt into one while Mr Mubarak and his secretary settled into the back seat of the second. I wondered whether they would encounter the same attacks from the sentries that we had experienced the previous night, but decided that those jokers had probably disappeared with the train.

Dick had just nicely finished refuelling and sorting out his domestics when the two cars and their passengers returned. Our flight to Benghazi was accompanied with serious good-natured discussions en route and we were met at the impressive VIP lounge by President Gadaffi and Prime Minister Jalloud. As they disappeared inside I followed them in and asked whether we were still needed. 'No,' said President Gadaffi, 'you can go home.' We did just that before anyone changed his mind.

When fuel consumption is irrelevant, as it was on the 1,000-mile journey from Benghazi to Tripoli, I felt that we could afford to open the Falcon up to full speed and with a straight-in approach and landing at base we were on the ground in little over the hour. Perhaps it was the prospect of a comfortable, cosy bed for the night, but the arrival duties, like refuelling the Falcon, were all conducted with an unspoken air of urgency and because all the crew lived in the same building, we were relaxing in our easy chairs with a mug of fresh tea in record time.

As I recounted the story of the flight to Lesley I wondered how different the stories being told to the wife and partner of my other crew members would be. Everyone perceives a set of circumstances he experiences very differently from others similarly involved. Sometimes the difference is because of a conscious or unconscious censorship conducted by the teller to save the listener any undue worry, but often it comes about because we human beings genuinely see tense situations differently from each other, and no two versions of shared events can ever be exactly the same. It must be hell for police taking witness statements following a serious incident.

During the flight my captain's cash float had dropped to being inadequate for an averagely long flight, so I spent a good part of the following day in town, justifying the expenditure of every last cent to the auditors and taking their demand for a fresh supply of US dollars to the Bank of Libya. There was usually at least an hour's delay in the crowded bank whilst authorizations were checked and a complicated security procedure was undergone, but it was invariably satisfactory and eventually I left with my deep zipped pockets bulging with a fresh supply of useable currency that, with care, should last me another couple of months of operations.

The Bank of Libya was in a building with a fascinating history. It owed its architecture to Roman architects in the time of the Libyan-born Emperor Septimus Severus who endowed it with impressive polished columns of a deep amber colour that held up a structure in the centre resembling a dome, which was further embellished with a series of what looked like gothic flying buttresses, further holding up a centrepiece. Tripoli was taken over in 1510 by the expanding power of Catholic Spain and in the 1530s was ceded to the warlike Knights of Malta, who converted the building into a very impressive Christian church. The Knights Templar and the Knights of St John were ousted from Tripoli in 1551 by the Turkish corsair admiral, Darghut Pasha, a renowned pirate who terrorized the southern Mediterranean for decades.

Under his control the building became the foremost Muslim mosque of the area with further modifications over the next two centuries until, in 1711, Ahmad Karamanli massacred all the Turkish officers and declared himself Pasha, independent of Constantinople. He was careful, however, to submit massive payments in salt, gold and slaves to Turkey to avoid retribution for his violent overthrow of the Turkish troops and administrators. The dome area of the building, at this time, was further improved with plain and coloured translucent glass allowing the sun's rays to illuminate what had hitherto been a relatively dark interior.

Slaves became a major trading commodity over the next century and the profits were considerable. By the early 1800s slaves were bought in Hausaland (modern-day Niger) for £2 6s 8d each and resold in Tripoli for £16-£20 each. It was unthinkable for anyone of substance at that time to actually marry a negro slave, but to avoid dynastic squabbles European slaves were frequently married into the major families. They were also used as skilled craftsmen and -women, galley slaves and manual workers. To satisfy this market, raiding parties of Barbary corsairs relentlessly attacked the Atlantic and Mediterranean coasts. In England the counties feeling the brunt of these lightning attacks were Cornwall, Devon, Dorset and as far inland as Somerset. A recent BBC TV documentary estimated that between 1600 and 1780 1.5 million English slaves were captured and taken back to North Africa. That amounts to over 8,000 a year, which is an enormous toll of people. When a titled English slave was ransomed in Algeria in 1650, the price was £1,400 – a prodigious sum in those days.

Returning to the building – it changed owners once more in 1911 when the Italians replaced the Turks in Libya as colonial rulers. There were proposals at the time to reinstate it as a Christian church. This must have been a tempting prospect to the successors of the Romans who had erected the building in the first place, but they decided instead to use it as a museum to house an impressive display of locally discovered Roman, pre-Roman, Libyan and Egyptian antiquities. In the aftermath of the Second World War, when a great deal of damage was done, what remained of the exhibits moved to a safer place in another building in Tripoli and this one was repaired and renovated to become the Central Bank of Libya, which it remains to this day.

With my captain's float re-established, I was available to fly anywhere we were required, but the aftermath of the failed Libyan/Egyptian merger still rattled around North Africa for a few more months and many of our flights were still in connection with the upheaval that had been caused.

About a week after the Mersa Matruh incident, the Prime Minister, Major Jaloud, asked me to take him to Cairo at about 9 o'clock in the morning. He embarked exactly on time at the VIP lounge along with Mr Hosni Mubarak and an Egyptian civil servant. The atmosphere seemed to be generally relaxed and both VIPs were in high spirits as we flew along the Libyan coast that lovely summer's day in absolutely clear conditions. Back in the cabin I could see that both men were avidly interested in the panorama that passed before their eyes.

Major Jaloud was pointing out the various oil facilities spread along the Gulf of Sirte with obvious pride and the Egyptian Deputy President was clearly quite impressed. The massive oil refinery at Marsa Brega 100 miles east of Benghazi looked particularly amazing, as we all enjoyed our eagle's-eye view from six miles above the huge industrial complex. It was totally self-contained with a small town of modern accommodation to house its workers who came from Libya, the USA, Britain, Italy and France. It boasted its own harbour, complete with five of the world's supertankers waiting their turn to load their precious cargoes of Libya's black gold, or maybe today's demand would be for gasoline for the automotive industries of the West. Whatever the requirement this industrial giant could supply it on demand.

Unusually, we had a substantial tailwind that our Omega satellite navigation system assured us was over 150 knots, so there was no need for us to land at Benghazi to refuel. Passing Libya's second city we flew over the area that appears in Greek mythology as the proverbial land of milk and honey – now known in Arabic as the Jebel Ahkdar. We could all see the Greco-Roman towns of Cyrene and Apollonia, some of which were underwater following a catastrophic earthquake a thousand years earlier. The water covering the collapsed Roman buildings was quite shallow and it only added to the interest as some of the beautiful columns protruded above the surface of the Mediterranean. I resolved to take my family snorkelling there at the first opportunity.

Passing just north of Tobruk airfield, I pondered on its past use as the British airfield of El Adem, which had provided sanctuary for me on numerous occasions in my earlier life as a carrier pilot with the Royal Navy. More than once I had been desperately short of fuel, alone in my Sea Hawk, somewhere out at sea, trying to land on a pitching/rolling deck when one of my colleagues had crashed on deck, for whatever reason. At that stage life became suddenly quite critical. To bring my aircraft down to landing weight I had previously ditched all the spare fuel overboard as instructed, but now the order rang into my earphones to go south and look for an airfield in the desert where all I could see was deep blackness wherever I looked.

With about fifteen minutes before the engine stopped, when I would be forced to trust my life to an ejection seat, my parachute and a very wet ocean, the confident voice of an air traffic controller announcing that he had me firmly on his radar and instructing me to squawk 2465[1] for positive recognition sounded like a voice from heaven. It injected unbelievable relief into a very tense situation. Minutes later the welcome lights of El Adem's main runway confirmed that I would be sleeping in a nice warm bed within the hour instead of the previous prospect of slopping about in a very wet rubber dinghy all night. That mile of lovely tarmac now just to the south of us had been a very welcome sight on a few occasions in my past, but my present passengers probably would not understand, so I kept all these thoughts to myself.

Mersa Matruh was clear of hordes of Libyans, troop trains, tanks, attack fighters and warships, but I noticed that the passengers chose to look out to sea as we passed – very diplomatic, I thought.

On landing at Cairo we were met by a very high-powered committee led by President Sadat, remarkable in colourful dress uniform, predominantly of a dark sky blue with gold and silver adornments. Colonel Shukri was hovering in the background, also in uniform, but his outfit was a light sand colour. He looked rather like photographs I had seen of his erstwhile leader, Colonel Gamel Abdel Nasser, and he also had the same build as his late President. They had even mustered some of the Cairo diplomatic corps in the reception committee.

---

[1] Meaning, select a specific transponder channel to enable him to track us more easily on his radar screen.

Had they, I wondered, been making their farewells to someone of more lofty rank, like King Faisal of Saudi Arabia, and decided to stay to welcome Major Jaloud, or were they turning on the full charm to cool fevered Libyan brows over the Mersa Matruh incident, or were they expecting Colonel Gadaffi himself? I never discovered the answer nor was there an opportunity to ask any of the decision makers. Whilst the Libyan Prime Minister was being introduced and was conversing with some of the ambassadors in the line-up, President Sadat peeled away and came over to the other end of the red carpet to give me their itinerary. He seemed to be in a jovial mood and told me that they were all going off to an important meeting in Cairo and expected to be finished before nightfall. We were to make ourselves comfortable in the VIP lounge and he would keep us informed of progress.

That was most unusual. For him to anticipate the duration of a high-powered meeting was unheard of and I felt sure that, with the best will in the world, we were more likely to be sleeping in Cairo that night than to be back in Tripoli as he implied.

When the wailing of the escorting motorcycle sirens reached its climax and the limousines glided serenely out of the airport, the co-pilot, engineer and I unhurriedly attended to the domestics of our Falcon, and elongated the process of refuelling in order to pass the time occupied with tasks we found interesting. The prospect of lazing in Cairo's VIP lounge for hours did not fill any of us with enthusiasm, so we dragged out the duration of the routine work for as long as possible. We could not render a flight plan ahead of time, because nobody had confided to us any likely destination and Major Jaloud had a good solid reputation for suddenly heading off in a totally unexpected direction, but in Air Traffic Control the co-pilot and I memorized the weather at all the airfields within our range and checked the Notams[2].

Eventually, sinking into the sumptuous, gold-braided easy chairs of the VIP lounge became inevitable so the three of us found our books hidden in the luggage, locked up the aircraft and behaved like bloated plutocrats. The manager of the lounge offered us a wide range of refreshments, boasting of his expertise with any cocktail we wished to try. He should have known better, talking to presidential aircrew on duty, but maybe he was trying to sabotage the opposition. We all settled for cool bottles of clear fizzy water, being careful to avoid his offer of ice. Reading the labels on the sealed bottles we were surprised to see that the water originated in a religious spring in the mountains of the Lebanon.

The heat from the searing Saharan midday sun, frying the tarmac and cooking our Falcon outside, was held at bay by an almost silent air-conditioning

---

[2] Notices to Airmen – written warnings of potential problems with airfields or airways on any routes that we might be asked to fly.

system inside the lounge. We all tried to relax, but it is never full relaxation in these circumstances. Nobody could anticipate the demands that could descend on us without any warning and each of us knew of examples where such a benign atmosphere had in the past suddenly transformed itself into mayhem.

About four hours later, a forlorn-sounding single motorcycle siren heralded a smart black Mercedes limousine drawing gently to a halt outside. A smartly dressed member of the Egyptian protocol department, resplendent in a gleaming white tropical suit, came inside and squatted on the arm of my chair. He said quietly that President Sadat would like us to join him at the Palace and requested that we take our luggage with us. That was quite clear and there did not seem to be any need for amplification, so we all gathered our own suitcases in the shadow of the Falcon and the driver carried them into his rather grand vehicle.

Being naturally inquisitive, as well as careful of my – and the crew's – security, I told the protocol official accompanying us that I was unaware of an actual palace in Cairo. He told us that there were, in fact, several palaces around the city, but that they were all situated in secluded places away from prying eyes. The one that we were being driven to was quite new, having been built by King Farouk a short while prior to his replacement in the 1952 coup d'état that brought General Neguib to power.

When we were sitting comfortably the motorcycle policeman eased away, followed by our black limousine with its tinted outlook and we resisted the temptation to wind down the windows and wave magnanimously to the citizenry as the busy midday traffic parted, at the behest of the police siren, to allow us unhindered passage. On the outskirts of the main city we branched right onto quiet roads that were unfamiliar to any of us. Gliding between open gates boasting polished stone columns on each side, surmounted by gilded eagles, we passed manicured lawns and flower beds enjoying the benefit of lavish irrigation. We swivelled our heads trying not to miss any of the opulent detail sailing serenely by outside the shaded windows.

The building that we stopped beside was obviously the palace referred to by our temporary host, but none of us could pinpoint where it lay in relation to the main city because the flowering trees and other substantial growth restricted visibility to just a few dozen metres. We left our cases in the car as instructed and climbed the five or six steps up to the building's main entrance. There we were met by one of the servants who led us across a large entrance hall which had about fifteen people predominantly in plain clothes, though a few Egyptian service uniforms stood out in stark contrast, all talking. They clustered in groups and paid us scant attention. I had the impression that they were delegates, secretaries and the like who were supporting the main conference being held elsewhere in the palace.

Doors were closed behind us and we realized that we had been shepherded into a medium-sized room with comfortable furniture, but no view of the outside world because the only two windows were too high up to see through. No worries, I thought, someone will tell us if we are expected to do anything, so we will just wait. About half an hour later a smiling, rather hassled, Hosni Mubarak came into the room and asked whether we were being looked after all right. I said that we were comfortable, but were starting to feel the pangs of hunger, as we had not eaten since breakfast. He apologized profusely and asked us to follow him. He led us into a large central room with an impressive high rococo-style plastered ceiling finished in pastel colours and a table in the middle that was simply groaning with dishes of food of every type imaginable. As none of the people in the room were actually eating anything I presumed that they had mostly partaken before and the dishes had since been replenished.

Mr Mubarak called over one of the organizers and we were invited to help ourselves from the array of delicacies before us. No second invitation was needed and we returned to the table many times, as instructed, to try as many different dishes as possible. I had just been handed a coffee when President Sadat came through a door at the side of the room and shouted 'Ah, Captain!' and attracted my attention with his white-gloved hand. Everyone else in the room immediately took notice and those who were seated stood up. Putting my cup on a nearby table, I joined him at the side of the room as he clearly indicated and listened to him attentively.

He apologized that progress of the meeting was not proceeding quite as planned and that our departure would probably be delayed. I assured him that this was no problem whatsoever and thanked him for his hospitality. He explained that he had brought us over here because he felt guilty at keeping us waiting for hours at the airport. 'Also,' he said, 'I have someone—' and he flamboyantly gestured with a sweep of his hand '—whom I know you would like to meet.' Trying to assess who, mysteriously, had suddenly materialized baffled me.

'Come,' he said forcefully. I obeyed and he led me through a labyrinth of clean airy corridors. As I was becoming lost in this maze he grinned knowingly, opened a door and announced, 'Here is someone to interest you.' Whether his words were intended for the benefit of the person inside, or for me, I was never quite sure.

The seated occupant of the room stood up and I immediately recognized him, but I was so flabbergasted that I was momentarily speechless. He made no attempt to extend his hand, nor would he, because this was the rather old and frail Mohamed Idris al Mahdi al Senussi, ex-King Idris of Libya. President Sadat informed him that I was the Chief Pilot of Libya's Special Flight, whereupon he commented in a rather croaky voice, 'My Special Flight.' No response was forthcoming from me, but as the President chuckled quietly I could not prevent a little smile from breaking out on my face. As if in mild rebuke the ex-King's right hand moved towards what looked like a small sword or dagger that hung from his belt. He later talked about 'my aircraft' whereupon I risked a comment that his aircraft had been American Learjets, but that the flight was now equipped with two French Fan-Jet Falcon 20s.

He asked whether they were reliable and I replied, 'Very reliable and larger than the Learjets.' I asked him whether he and his family were comfortable in Cairo and he confirmed that his hosts looked after them very well indeed, stating that he was eternally grateful to the President for his kind hospitality. President Sadat acknowledged the thanks and the conversation lasted a few more minutes. I asked the ex-King whether he had met my passenger Major Abdusalem Jalloud, the Libyan Prime Minister, and his response was negative and rather dismissive. Shortly afterwards the frail-looking ex-King excused himself and sat back down in his chair with an air of finality. We took this as an indication of mild fatigue, so we made our excuses and left.

Walking back to the central room, I thanked President Sadat for this most unexpected of meetings. I told him that it was a meeting that I would never forget and I apologized for my initial nonplussed reaction when I first realized exactly who was in the room, but was assured by him that I had come over as quite confident, which was not how I felt. He told me that the ex-King had lived in Egypt since the 1969 revolution, but that his health was quite poor.

What I had been told in Tripoli, but could only partially verify, was that his presence in Egypt was used politically by the Egyptian government in periods of tension with Libya. Apparently, to needle the Libyan government, the Egyptians were adept at producing the ex-King at high-profile events where photographs were certain to be taken and exhibited worldwide. He was prominent on the bridge of the first Egyptian ship transiting the Suez Canal on 5 June 1975 after the Royal Navy had cleared it of obstructions left by the recent war. He was rarely, if ever, seen as a major player these days, but rather he was kept in the background for his presence to be recorded. I know of no official interview with him at this stage, so his conversation with me was a surprising event all round. I suspect that it may have owed its origin to Anwar Sadat's impish sense of humour, but I can never be certain.

What nobody knew, and I preferred it that way, was that King Idris and I had crossed paths previously – with, for me, potentially disastrous consequences.

It happened about forty-three years ago, when as a young de Havilland Sea Vixen pilot flying from the aircraft carrier HMS *Centaur*, I was programmed as one of the most junior members of a practice strike on the weapons range at Tarhuna, 30 miles south-east of Tripoli, with live weapons. As Johnny Spear, my navigator ('observer' in the Fleet Air Arm), and I dutifully took our seats at the very back of the briefing room we worked out that, owing to our juniority, there was no way whatsoever that my aircraft would be called upon to lead this twenty-five aircraft attack on the Tarhuna range; so we would concentrate on delivering our weapons accurately on target, in sequence, when we arrived over the desert at the end of a planned thousand-mile tour of the Mediterranean. This was to be a realistic attack so Commander (Air) told us to pull out all the stops, whatever that meant. He further informed us that some pretty senior people would witness our efforts at a safe distance from the target, but that their actual position relative to the target was not known – quite a worry when we were delivering live bombs and other lethal ordnance.

Johnny and I scribbled as much detail on our kneepads as we would need including the weapons settings for when we eventually arrived at the massive wooden target that had been erected by the army engineers in the sand. We were to be catapulted off *Centaur* to the south of the toe of Italy, turn east to a position several hundred miles south-west of the Greek island of Crete and run in to the 'Initial Point' ten miles north of Tripoli. From there I had drawn a line 40 miles long straight to the target. The radar-equipped Sea Vixens were required to lead fourteen Supermarine Scimitars, which did not enjoy the luxury of inbuilt radar and had no navigator, onto the target.

Serious airborne opposition was to be provided by two squadrons of US Air Force Rockwell F-100 Super Sabres based at Wheelus Field, on the eastern outskirts of Tripoli city. They were to attack us en masse over the sea and split us up into a series of individual dogfights with the aim of preventing us delivering our weapons, or running us out of fuel, or both. Once we were over the land and established on the run-in to the target, the Sabres were to retire back to Wheelus. Everyone concerned imagined an horrendous low-level mêlée, with about 50 fighters rotating around the sky at high speed generating a multitude of dogfights, with the distinct possibility of flying into each other as the attackers tried to deliver live weapons onto the target. In actual combat, of course, the air battle would be pressed to its final conclusion, regardless of danger. Johnny, alongside me at the briefing, drew a passable cartoon on his navigation board, showing the resultant mayhem from a no-holds-barred air fight, with 100 parachutes floating down over Tripoli city, complete with hapless aircrew dangling from them. This actual drawing eventually found its place into the Squadron line book (the official record), so it must have been quite good.

Our little shindig was developing into just my kind of battle, but in my aforementioned advanced state of juniority I was unlikely to have any control of the tactics involved and prepared to follow my leader, as was usual when the big boys came out to play. We were squirted off the catapults as planned, but as the second-in-command (our senior pilot) left the ship behind me, his drop tank complete with 200 gallons of vital fuel exploded, so he fired his other drop tank into the sea, waited for the rest of the aircraft to launch into the sky and landed safely back on board. We assumed our planned loose formations whilst climbing and the leader set course for Crete at 35,000 feet. As we turned within sight of the island, the Air Weapons Instructor, who was number three in the chain of command, announced that his weapon circuits had failed so he would just 'tag along for the ride'. 'Maybe,' he said, 'I'll get me a brace of Yanks, and try to draw their main attack away from the rest of you.'

The leader acknowledged, but his radio was very crackly. I just sat in formation on his wingtip, watching for his hand signals. Radio silence was imposed from this point in accordance with the pre-flight briefing as we commenced the descent, several hundred miles north of the African coast. Halfway down the hill the leader turned to me and indicated that his radio had failed completely – transmit and receive. At first I expected that we would just carry on as planned, but then I realized that we could not carry on with a totally mute leader – it would cause dangerous chaos during the dogfighting stage if the leader were unable either to control the battle or hear evasion instructions.

The leader realized this and waved me into the lead position. I acknowledged and instructed him by hand signal to become my wingman (number two). He dutifully complied and took up position on my starboard wingtip. I continued the descent as planned meanwhile, formulating tactics as unplanned leader of this mighty attack.

Powerful American ground radar, which would be supporting the Super Sabres, had a major vulnerability – it could not see over the horizon. If I was to keep my lethal brood safe I must delay radar detection until as late as possible. We had a speed advantage against these old technology US fighters, but if they caught us before we crossed the coast this advantage would be nullified and some of our Vixens and Scimitars could well feature in the films of the Sabres' gunsight cameras. The US pilots were all battle-hardened veterans from their days fighting the Chinese in Korea, so they would be up to all the tricks that they had perfected in the heat of actual conflict. This would be no pushover!

We, however, had superior aircraft and a few advantages. We spent a good part of our aviation from the aircraft carriers, flying safely and very low over the sea and when required our Rolls-Royce Spey engines could give us a fair turn of speed – supersonic if necessary – so I decided to put these attributes to good use. I descended as low as I dared to keep all our aircraft below the radar horizon, giving,

I realized, some problems of control to the others I was leading into battle, but as they should have been capable of handling these problems I increased speed to 600 knots (about 690 miles per hour), marginally less than the speed of sound at sea level. Mercifully the air was unusually smooth and the low-level turbulence was minimal. As I caught sight of the sea breaking on a beach, the buildings of Tripoli town loomed into hazy view dead ahead.

To clarify, although we were equipped with the very finest of modern airborne radar, this phase of the attack had to take place with our radars switched to standby. Any active radar pulse would have given our position away to the ground detectors at Wheelus Field, so no radar and no radio transmissions were allowed until I gave the word. Navigating to this Initial Point was Johnny Spear, in the coal-hole (the observer's cockpit), with a compass, dividers and a pencil. He was good at his trade and brought us into the ideal spot.

In the clear bright sunlit sky above us I could see two flights of aircraft flying some sort of a lazy race-track pattern. There were about ten in each flight, at about 10,000 feet, and quite obviously they had not seen us. I knew that we would all be extremely difficult to see from above with the Mk I eyeball, because of our very effective grey camouflage almost exactly matching the colour of the sea in this part of the Mediterranean. Determined to maintain our anonymity for as long as possible, I was unfortunately forced to climb slightly in order to miss the minarets of the mosques that protruded into our path and hoped that the rest of the attack group would do the same. As we slid underneath the 'enemy' I was elated, because they could not catch us now before we reached the target and they had obviously still not seen us.

I broke radio/radar silence as we left the city heading south and formed everyone into a looser formation for the culminating action. As leader, it was my privilege to deliver the lethal weapons before anyone else, so I called 'Stand by live' to the range officer and pulled up sharply, extending airbrakes, throttling back the engines to slow down to attack speed. This was most unusual. We normally had to speed up from a slower cruising speed to reach attack speed, but this day things were different.

I was aware of the two 500-lb bombs leaving my wings, but it was a call from the Squadron Weapons Instructor who told me how close they exploded to the target. He had adopted a 'perch' position from where he could report everyone's fall of shot, which was just as well as he was unable to use his own weapons system and the settings we were using on the gyro gunsight were the result of his personal calculations aboard the carrier before take-off. In fact he had placed himself at about 6,000 feet, which gave him a grandstand view. Everyone fired their weapons in turn and when all had completed their first delivery I returned for a session with my 2-inch rockets. As I settled into the dive for the second time I could clearly see that the once smart wooden target was by now a splintered mess with small fires around and many craters close by in the yellow sand.

When all the aircraft had completed their various deliveries, I formed everyone into transit formation, checked fuel states, climbed to 12,000 feet and set course for *Centaur*. She had sailed due south in our absence and was now ready to recover us, east of the island of Malta. I was the last aircraft to land on, perhaps because I had more fuel than anyone else. The leader usually does conserve his fuel as he is not constantly required to alter the engine throttle to hold formation on anyone.

Climbing down from the cockpit I was feeling quite proud. I had led the entire attack successfully and eluded the American fighters with what would have been known during the second world war as a 'fighting wing'. We had all delivered our weapons as planned and everyone had landed on board without a problem. What more could anyone ask?

Unfortunately, the Squadron Commanding Officer was walking towards me with a very purposeful step, his yellow lifejacket in his hand and his white helmet gripped tightly under his arm. His body language exuded evil. When he arrived he gave me an aggressive push. I kept silent. He exploded.

'If you ever do anything like that again, Atkinson, I will personally court-martial you.'

I responded, rather lamely, 'But I avoided the American fighters and everyone dropped their weapons onto and into the target.'

'Yes!' he shouted. 'You did, but you led twenty-four Vixens and Scimitars with forty-eight Rolls-Royce Speys going balls out, slap over Tripoli at low level, at 600 knots. The noise must have been deafening. Somebody is bound to complain.' He was puce with rage.

'Sorry,' said I, weakly.

'Oh, go to hell,' he spat back. Having delivered that little broadside, he spun on his heel and walked away, but over his shoulder he could not resist one last parting shot, 'You're a blithering idiot,' he spat into the air before he disappeared off the flight deck and into the island.

That was most disappointing. Up to that moment, I had been very pleased. The rest of the pilots were, however, ecstatic with praise at my realistic attack and had all thoroughly enjoyed using the aircraft as they were designed to be used. Later that evening I glanced down the wardroom bar and actually caught the Squadron CO, smiling, not at me admittedly, but I took it as a good sign. Shortly afterwards Commander (Air), the senior aviator on board, came up to me and said, 'The ship's Captain would like to see you on the bridge.'

Now, I thought, I really am in deep shit! I climbed the ladder up to the bridge, dressed in my smart black doeskin monkey jacket, tight black doeskin trousers, stiff dress shirt and bow tie (our evening rig at sea), I rehearsed what my response would be in all the possible worst-case scenarios that life was likely about to throw at me. I practised obsequious apology, abject sorrow and every other ploy, as with deliberation I unlatched ten door catches on each of about fifteen en-route watertight steel doors, stepping over the sill and passing through the steel bulkheads, and of course carefully closing them on the other side. At last I pushed open the heavy door onto the bridge, which was almost in darkness as the Officer of the Watch guided the ship into a wild sea that had suddenly materialized without warning.

The four lookouts' voices were incessant as they reported the positions of dozens of small lights indicating the tiny Maltese fishing boats that dotted the sea through which HMS *Centaur* was attempting to steam. This was the lampuki season and these very tasty fish had arrived in massive shoals off the south-west corner of Malta, close to the tiny island of Filfla. It was a bonanza for the courageous gnarled old fishermen in their colourful *dghaijas* (pronounced 'dysos'), small slim boats about 20 feet long, with high prows and sternposts which when they were fishing for lampuki had outsized bright lights dangling at the stern. It was these lights that were periodically twinkling amongst the steep waves in front of us. There were also some larger boats called *luzzos*, catching the same fish, which were easier to see from *Centaur*'s bridge than the dghaijas.

The Captain sat in his high seat, surrounded by a gloom that my eyes were just starting to penetrate, from where he was available to authorize emergency manoeuvres of his huge vessel should it become necessary to avoid collision. I walked up to the side of his four-foot high chair and waited for my opportunity. Eventually, a lull in the intensity of activity provided a chance to speak.

'You sent for me, sir,' seemed a good opening.

'Aaaah, Atkinson, yes!' emerged pensively from his almost invisible mouth. I had the impression that he was studying me, though the dim light prevented me from being certain.

Leaping down from his lofty perch, he said, 'Come over here' in a not unfriendly voice, which gave me some hope. He led me over to an illuminated signals desk that was surrounded by a black curtain. The lights inside the curtains were red, as standard, to avoid ruining anyone's night vision. He opened a fat signals log and selected two sheets of paper. Looking towards me he said, 'There's good and there's not so good; we'll start with the good.' He thrust one of the sheets of paper into my hand with the instructions to 'Read that'.

It was a signal from the General Officer Commanding British land forces, North

Africa, to HMS *Centaur* (that automatically means 'to the Captain'), copied for information to the Admiralty. The gist of the message was:

This afternoon I saw the finest demonstration of accurate lethal firepower, professionally delivered, over long distance, that I have been privileged to witness in my long military career. I am given to understand that in striking the target your aircraft had first to evade the might of the US Air Force with all its sophisticated electronic equipment. Despite the opposition being warned prior to the attack of the exact time of the strike, your Vixens and Scimitars evaded the defences without detection. The accuracy of weapons on target was most reassuring. All air crew are to be congratulated, especially the strike leader. Thank God for the Navy.

I commented that he was very kind and the Captain said, 'Before your ego becomes too inflated, you had better read this other signal,' and he handed me the second sheet of paper. The signal was originated by the Admiralty, to HMS *Centaur*, and I noticed that it had been given a very high security classification, which I think was Secret. The gist of this message was:

This signal was received from the British Ambassador, Tripoli, Libya @ 1730Z [5.30 GMT] today. King Idris of Libya has complained to me that earlier this afternoon a great many British military aircraft flew in from the sea, simultaneously, very low, very fast and very noisily over his palace. He further stated that the thunderous noise caused the Queen to fall off her chair, resulting in her spilling hot tea onto her clothes. He was very angry and demanded that the officers responsible should be punished. When asked exactly what type of aircraft they were, the King commented that their speed made it impossible to identify them. In fact, he said that by the time he reached the window to look, they were all gone. Unfortunately, I cannot confirm or deny these claims because I was absent from Tripoli for the whole of the afternoon.

I tried my very best to look contrite as I handed the signal back to the Captain.

'There's no doubt,' I said slowly, wide-eyed, 'that must have been me.'

He snatched the paper from my hand and exploded, 'Of course it was bloody well you! Now you'd better consider yourself punished.'

'I certainly do, sir!' I responded gratefully. Whether he showed the last signal to my Squadron Commanding Officer or not, I cannot be sure, but he did show him the first one that praised our efforts on the strike.

It is perhaps not surprising that I was reluctant to inform ex-King Idris that it had been 'yours truly' who was responsible for the queen falling off her chair and drenching herself in hot tea.

We three crew members settled into our allocated room for the rest of the afternoon and were just finishing tea and sandwiches when Mr Mubarak came in to tell us that the meeting would now continue to the following day. He said that accommodation was very difficult to find in Cairo at that time because of several international conferences, and asked us which hotel we would prefer to try. I said that if we could have some transport we would first try the Shepheards which would usually find us three rooms, but that it was better if we actually went to the hotel and talked to the director personally rather than on the telephone.

He said that the transport was at the door and called for a servant to take our bags for us. We drew up at the entrance to the Shepheards and because of our prestigious transport, we were met with a well-known face grinning broadly and bearing a silver tray of cool drinks. It was the young barman, my brother's look-alike, in his smartest fawn and gold regalia. The director assured us that three en-suite rooms would be no problem, so we went through the time-honoured ritual of tipping just about everyone in the hotel as we disappeared inside to freshen up, arranging to meet in the bar prior to the usual walk over the Nile Bridge to the Sheraton for an evening meal.

Having done very little physical work all day, we were quite keen for some adrenalin-laced action, so we missed out on the cabaret after dinner and went straight down to the casino with rather more US dollars for chips than usual. As we stood together behind the players, sizing up the flow of numbers at the high-value roulette table, we quietly discussed the merits of the players, some of whom were building a fair pile of chips in front of them, while others seemed to be disposing of their wealth with gay abandon. The Co-pilot commented on one gentleman in white flowing robes who was losing rather a lot, suggesting that there was always the Nile to disappear into, if he lost everything.

When a chair became available I sat down and the other two wandered off to assess the blackjack tables. With my relatively small pile of chips in front of me I let the black ball fall into its chosen slot on the wheel twice before feeling confident enough to participate. The first five dollars' worth of chips fell to the croupier's rake before he rewarded me with my first win and from there on, for the next hour and a half, I steadily increased the pile of large value chips in front of me.

Although quite a few of my selections failed, on average I was winning at a rate that I had never before experienced. It felt good – in fact, if I'm honest it felt fantastic. Just enjoy it, Neville, I decided. The winning streak is bound to end shortly, so just be ready for it, I advised myself. Behind my chair, a circle of aficionados gathered, through which the lovely young girls in their white togas pushed to refresh my drink. For some reason, maybe the pile of chips in my slot on the green baize – each of my drinks was accompanied by a dish of blanched almonds. As my two neighbours – a young Saudi Arab to the left and a statuesque American lady aged thirty-something to the right – were not similarly favoured, I shared my tasty almonds with them both and did such a good job of chatting them up that they eventually stood up, rested their hands on my chair back and with what impressed me as indecent haste, sauntered out of the room together. Maybe she's a Muslim, I wondered, then I decided that by the look on the man's face, he did not seem to care whether she'd been a Buddhist or a primitive Methodist – his mind was probably not on religious matters just then.

My winnings increased steadily and as each top-value chip was slipped into a safe pocket, I mouthed a heartfelt 'Thankyou' to the kindly Church of England vicar who had passed on his system to me many moons before. I now saw his consumption of one of my best bottles of vintage brandy as a very sound investment indeed. In fact, at this rate I could well have afforded a barrel of the stuff without batting an eyelid.

After what seemed like about an hour, my other two crew members came back and regaled me with tales of their derring-do on the blackjack tables. They just could not go wrong, they said, then one of them saw the pile of chips on the green baize by my hand. You must have changed a lot more dollars, one said. 'No', I responded, 'the wheel has been very kind to me this evening' – and neither of them was aware of the pile of $200 chips sitting in my zipped pocket. The engineer said that he was feeling quite tired and was thinking of wandering back across the bridge. When I glanced at my watch and saw that it was 2 o'clock in the morning, I agreed, popped a sizeable chip in the croupier's box and we all left.

Cashing in one's chips was a very private affair. As we each stood in turn at the bank's steel-barred window, I did not watch either of the other two and they did not watch me exchanging the pile of coloured chips for dollars, but the wad of $100 bills that I folded into a roll and stuffed into my zipped pocket was very comforting, to say the least. The night outside the Sheraton was warm and the sky was alive with twinkling stars. The enormous moon lighted our way home, seeming to challenge the sun with its brilliance and we arrived back at the Shepheards without being aware of speaking to each other very much. As the Egyptian protocol department had not booked an early take-off, we agreed to meet for a leisurely breakfast in the Shepheards, take a relaxed stroll along the east bank of the Nile to the Hilton and after a snack and a swirl round the hotel shops, wander back to the Shepheards to await instructions.

Unfortunately, we could not get hold of anyone on the telephone to enlighten us on our return, so we made the fateful decision to take a boat ride in the early afternoon, to see this intriguing city from a different perspective. After enjoying a light lunch the boatman we chose offered to take us round the sporting island of Zamelek, passing in front of the Sheraton Hotel. It should take us about an hour, said our strapping young mariner as we boarded his scrupulously clean felucca, with its snow-white cushions. It was nice and cool on the water, beneath his white awning, despite the sun burning down from its lofty perch high in the heavens.

As we returned towards our original moorings, with both the Shepheards and the Hilton clearly visible ahead, I looked off to the starboard side and said, 'What's that?' Floating serenely down towards the Mediterranean on the fast current was what looked like a pile of rags. We all, unwisely as it turned out, insisted on going over to see what was floating down the river – this proved to be the body of a young man in his early twenties floating face down in the water. I rolled him over with the boathook and it was soon apparent that it had been no accident. A vicious gash high on the poor unfortunate victim's neck clearly indicated the probable cause of death, but the pristine features declared that we were not looking at a corpse that had floated 4,000 miles down the Nile from near its source in Lake Victoria. This man had probably been alive within the last twenty-four hours, so being three naïve Brits out of their own environment, we were adamant that the body be towed over to the bank for examination by the police.

The boatman resisted, but being full of investigative zeal, we stuck to our guns. It still required a dollop of bribery before he would agree to have anything to do with the body of the unfortunate victim, but eventually we moored alongside the jetty closest to the Shepheards with the body in tow. One of us grabbed the first Egyptian policeman we saw and steered him towards our felucca. After he had stopped being sick all over the concrete wall, he arrested the boat driver and was about to wheel him away when we insisted on giving our stories before anyone went anywhere. The whole incident became quite heated and at one time there was a distinct danger of us all being arrested.

Fortunately, for us, as we tried to reason with this gentleman in blue, a large black limousine drew up between us and the hotel, complete with two police motorcycle outriders and sirens. Hoping that their arrival may have had something to do with us, I strolled over – just as the Egyptian Chief of Protocol climbed out of the back seat. Sure enough, they did want us to fly immediately, so I apprised them of the incident with the body down on the jetty. The government whiz-kid professed no wish to gaze on a dead body and dispatched his two white-coated police escorts to sort out the problem. One of these outriders must have been quite senior, because he delivered a verbal onslaught at the original policeman who was still busying himself by the boat. The boatman was immediately released to return to his felucca and the corpse was secured by a rope to the side of the steps to await an ambulance.

83

Nobody was interested in our version of events. In fact, nobody seemed all that interested in the corpse. As our luggage was carried into the black Mercedes an ambulance drew alongside the steps and white-coated paramedics carried the body inside. On the way to the airport the Chief of Protocol informed us that bodies came down the Nile regularly and as the river passed through numerous countries it was rarely possible to establish their origins, so there was an established custom of ignoring them completely, hoping that the crocodiles or the sharks would save everyone too much bother. It may seem heartless, but this was Egypt and who were we to interfere? We resolved that the next time we would listen more carefully to the boatman.

Our carefully packed bags were hurried down to the limousine, complete with the ritual of tipping a never-ending sequence of porters and room boys. We regarded this charade as a wise investment in the future when we might arrive in Cairo, late at night, desperate for somewhere to lay our heads, with the city overloaded with tourists. In our crisp white shirts and smart lightweight navy blue trousers we were whisked to the Falcon in prestigious style, without the usual necessity of pushing through the crowds at the airport. It certainly is wonderful what a couple of police outriders with noisy sirens can achieve.

The Prime Minister rendezvoused with us just as we had completed the pre-flight inspections and the protocol department organized an Air Traffic Control clerk to collect our flight plan at the aircraft. Take-off was nicely expedited by moving us past the queue of passenger jets and we were levelling off at cruising altitude before we gathered our thoughts together.

Major Jalloud slid into the cockpit as we throttled back to cruising power and sat down on the jump-seat. He was in high spirits and we gathered that he had enjoyed a very successful meeting. He told us that he had seen us at the palace, the day before, but that by the time he had managed to break away from his group we had been whisked away somewhere else. We confirmed that we had been very well looked after and had spent the night in central Cairo at our usual hotel.

He responded by commenting on our bad habits of gambling in the Sheraton Casino, which gave us cause for concern, but we should have known better. Nothing is confidential in this city of intrigue and his knowing our movements was probably a very good sign. Our welfare was of importance to people of substance and that gave us a great deal of reassurance. So we were obviously followed, but as long as the followers were concerned with our safety, who were we to complain?

On the journey back to Tripoli, the Prime Minister talked a great deal on a wide variety of subjects, but he did not divulge the purpose of his meeting and in turn I did not reveal my introduction to ex-King Idris, as I was unsure of his reaction.

Because he stayed in the cockpit and his body language indicated that he would like to talk, I asked him about the revolution in September 1969 and he revealed details to us that, to my knowledge, have never been discussed before or since. He talked about the years leading up to the actual coup and said that the group of army officers who were eventually involved were outspoken critics of the then current administration. They had become frustrated that the policies being adopted by the existing government were not answering the obvious needs of the people of Libya.

Most of the ordinary people were clearly poverty-stricken and none of the economic indicators showed any improvement. Oil was discovered in substantial quantities in the early 1960s and by the mid-'60s the local industry was going from strength to strength, but despite this new money flowing into the country very little seemed to be improving. It appeared to this group of army officers that the country was relying on handouts from America and Britain, instead of standing proudly on its own feet.

They agitated in any way they could for improvements and were all thrown into Tripoli jail on numerous occasions, usually for relatively short periods, but at times for longer incarcerations and sometimes together, so that they came to regard the jail almost as a club. The warders were clearly largely sympathetic so treatment was generally benign, but not always. 'Here we go again,' was their general attitude as they saw who else was already occupying the spartan accommodation.

In 1964 they grouped together as a relatively secret society, 'The Free Unionist Officers'. At this time they all rated themselves as equal, with no one regarded as the leader. The government, of course, was not entirely unaware of the group, but there were no indications that they knew everyone involved, although they almost certainly did. They were dispersed as much as possible to avoid the group acting together and one of their main problems became communication. Remarkably this problem was solved in 1966 when one of the group, the promising 24-year-old Lieutenant Muammar el Gadaffi, was sent on a ten-month army signals course to the British Army signals headquarters at Beaconsfield in Buckinghamshire. When he returned to Libya he probably knew as much about radio and teleprinter transmission and reception as anyone in Libya. During his course he also acquired a thorough grasp of the mysteries of cryptography – coding and decoding messages – that was subsequently to prove invaluable.

This young, fully qualified signals officer now sat at the centre of the web. He devised a simple cipher, which enabled each of the group to communicate in relatively secret. To confuse their embryo plans in the later stages, King Idris, who was nearly eighty years old at the time of the coup, was growing tired with his responsibilities of state and had actively sought to abdicate in favour of his younger son. This decision infuriated his elder son who was then known as the Black Prince, a result of both his dark appearance and his fiery temper. The family was in turmoil.

There was a popular myth before and shortly after the revolution that it was the Black Prince who proposed the coup d'état against his father and asked the Free Unionist Officers to assist him in his takeover of power. After much consideration and discussion that scenario seems to me to be unlikely. The organization and planning that went into the minute details of the actual event could not have been the result of a casual whim of the prince, however greedy for power he had become.

By this time King Idris had strengthened his power base in Cyrenaica (the eastern part of Libya, with its capital Benghazi), the ancient Senussi heartland and had established the Cyrenaican Defence Force (the CDF), which was akin to his family's own Praetorian Guard. The CDF was a paramilitary body consisting predominantly of Saharan tribesmen and Bedouin Senussi loyalists. It was established as a counterweight to the regular army and great efforts were made to insulate its leaders from political contamination and Arab nationalism. Its equipment included helicopters, armoured vehicles and mobile artillery. It is interesting to note that when the Libyan Army re-equipped with British Centurion tanks, the CDF were immediately supplied with large quantities of various types of modern anti-tank weapons. The king also established a new palace and a virtually new city at Al Bayda, north-east of Benghazi, apparently as a bolthole in times of political anxiety.

The timing of the coup was critical and was altered several times. All senior army officers and government decision makers had to be in the country and the king needed to be separated from the CDF around Benghazi. In Tripolitania, the western part of the country, the army was balanced by an unusually strong and well-armed police force so they had to be neutralized early in the proceedings.

On the night of the coup Gadaffi was personally responsible for disarming the CDF. He and his men arrested the commander of the force at Barce (pronounced 'Barchy'), near Benghazi and forced him to summon his officers to an urgent meeting, where they were all arrested. Without the threat of the CDF he was able to swoop on Benghazi and garrison all its key points with his own people.

Simultaneously, the key points in Tripoli became the responsibility of Major (then Lieutenant) Jalloud, while other members of the Free Unionist Officers who were not actively assisting him became responsible for the garrisons at Sebah, Tobruk, Ghat, the Tunisian border, the Algerian border and Kufra. An efficient communications network was key to their remarkable success so that they had executed a daring and efficient coup d'état before anyone in the world realized what was happening. As each leader successfully secured the area of his personal responsibility, he reported the fact, handed over to his deputies and went to the Libyan radio and television offices on the edge of Tripoli, which became their base.

The twelve weary young officers[3] adopted the title of the Revolutionary Command Council, although amongst the foreign embassies and diplomatic centres they unfairly became known as 'The Dirty Dozen', after the Hollywood film of that name. Following the lightning efficiency of the bloodless takeover, as they gathered in the new building that was Libya's civilian communication centre the stark realization infiltrated their tired minds that they had to form a system for actually running the country. Everyone had his own idea of what was required, but up to that time the number one priority had been taking over – minimal planning had been devoted to the mechanics of national administration.

The requirement quickly became urgent and one of the RCC reminded everyone that they had not even formally chosen a leader. The revolution was subsequently presented to the world by the international news media as a single person directing and controlling all the action as his own personal brainchild, although I am assured that this perception was untrue. The reality until this momentous meeting in Tripoli's radio and television building on the morning of 2 September 1969 was that the whole affair had been carried out almost on a committee basis. – now a leader had to be formally chosen.

All present agreed, and it was decided, that the leader would be chosen by a majority vote with the person under consideration being ineligible to vote. Accepting that efficient communications had been the key to their astounding success and that the expertise had been provided by one officer – Lieutenant Muammer el Gadaffi – his was the first name presented for consideration, though who proposed him was, I believe, never recorded. A murmur of agreement rippled round the room at the mention of his name, and when a show of hands was requested, eleven arms were enthusiastically raised. As they had voted unanimously for the same man, they decided that he would become their leader and the country's President.

Though this account of the night of 1/2 September 1969 and its lead-up differs from the accepted version assumed in many foreign ministries and widely

---

[3]   In alphabetical order: 1. Kweldi el Hamidi, 2. Awad Hamza, 3. Bashhir Hawwa, 4. Abdul mun'im el Houni, 5. Abdulsalem Jalloud, 6. Mustafa el Karubi, 7. Omar el Mahishi, 8. Mehemed Migharief, 9. Mohamed Najm, 10. Muammar el Gadaffi, 11. Muktar el Qirwi and 12. Abu Bakr Unis – for practical reasons their ranks have been omitted.

disseminated by the world's media, I was assured by Major Jalloud on that flight from Cairo back to Tripoli that his recollection of events was accurate.

During many subsequent conversations in my cockpit with Colonel Gadaffi himself, I did not discuss these actual events directly with him, nor he with me, but some of his side remarks whilst discussing other topics appeared to confirm to me the veracity of the Prime Minister's story.

Subsequent to the leadership election the RCC remained in this communication hub for several days whilst the essential format of Libya's future government was decided. They debated at a table heaped with official papers and the odd machine gun whilst their identities were temporarily safeguarded from the outside world. Other Arab countries were just as baffled as the rest of the world as to the identity and allegiances of the new government and speculation was rife. Everyone seemed to want to establish contact with the new government and all were incredulous that this small group of patriotic Libyan army officers could have managed their earth-shattering achievement without outside assistance.

The world's press all claimed exclusive knowledge of the RCC's politics, outside financial and intelligence inputs, but without exception they were all wrong. They could not even agree on the spelling of the new President's name: Moamer al Kozafi (*The Times*, 9 September 1969), Maamer el Kadhari (*Guardian*, 9 September 1969), Omar Moammer Kazzafi (*New York Herald Tribune*, 9 September 1969), Moammer El Kadhafi (*Corriere della Sera*, 9 September 1969), Moammer el Kadhafi (*Le Monde*, 10 September 1969), Muammer Gaddafi (*Observer* 13 September 1969), Moamer al-Kazafi (*New York Times* 15 December 1969), Muammar el Qaddafi (*Sunday Times*, 11 January 1970). It was 21 September before the world had a picture to illustrate their speculative articles, but much longer before the papers published anything remotely near even the partial truth regarding Libya's new leader.

Following the coup ex-King Idris and his family fled to Cairo where he lived in modest comfort under President Sadat's protection until his natural death in 1982 at the age of ninety-two. The administration under the king had been supervised by the al Shalhi family. Lieutenant Colonel Abd al Azziz al Shahli was a senior army officer who at the time of the coup was manoeuvring himself and his brother, Umar al Shali, into pole position for assuming power on the king's expected abdication. They were apparently a ruthless couple, steeped in political intrigue, who confidently anticipated ruling Libya in the not-too-far-distant future, but their plans were thrown into sharp reverse following the events of 1 September. Umar al Shali, who was out of the country at the time of the coup, subsequently took up residence in Geneva from where he tried to organize a counter-coup which was described in detail in a book entitled *The Hilton*

Assignment by two ex-*Observer* journalists, Patrick Seale and Maureen McConville. His brother, Abd al Azziz, found himself inside the 'Tripoli Hilton', the popular name for the capital's major prison.

I am reliably informed that a rather swarthy gentleman who one day years later was swimming with my family at the Underwater Club was Abd al Azziz al Shali: apparently he was released from gaol in the late 1970s. We commented on the hot weather and shared some cool drinks, but apart from the assurance of a usually knowledgeable friend I could not confirm his identity.

CHAPTER THREE

Violent Death in Yemen

The background to part of this chapter started at a renowned sporting estate in the Highlands of Scotland, a year prior to my first flying in Libya. Lesley and I were invited by good friends to join them for Sunday lunch on a very snowy day in January 1972. Our hosts, Lynne and Sandy Taylor, lived in a baronial stone house outside the village of Tomintoul, where Sandy was the sporting factor for the Crown Estates Commissioners of Scotland.

A factor is, traditionally, a powerful local manager with extensive qualifications in all forms of land management who supervises the letting and local maintenance of sporting properties on behalf of the landowner. In this particular case the titular owner of the estate was the Queen whose responsibilities were carried out by the Crown Estates from their offices in Edinburgh.

Sandy was a very likeable and handsome fellow with a pleasant soft Scottish accent; he was an accomplished 12-bore shot at all the sporting birds and could execute a perfect 'Spey cast' when seeking the wily salmon. Apart from his professional duties, he had a first-class knowledge of most of the local malt whiskies and a fund of stories about his time in MI9 (Military Intelligence) during the Second World War, when he fought in Greece and Italy as an officer with the Highland Division, part of the British Eighth Army.

The occasion for this particular lunch was primarily to assess a new candidate, or group of candidates, who wished to take over the tenancy of a very large nearby estate under Sandy's control and Lesley and I had been invited along to provide a little light relief to the proceedings. We also knew that we would be asked to offer our balanced opinions on the prospective tenants when they finally departed.

Two of the candidates were very successful London businessmen who, along with their guests, had long-term interests in shooting high-flying pheasants, partridge and duck, roe and red deer and fishing for salmon in the local rivers. To increase their sporting clout, they had apparently teamed up with a renowned recently retired senior army officer who had become a Member of Parliament and was popular throughout the country.

The three men were a slightly incongruous group and the rather rough voices of the two main financiers seemed to be at odds with the very refined, cultured accent and meticulous manners of the new MP. To make matters more bizarre they were accompanied by two very confident, rather good-looking young ladies dressed in designer clothes, with expensive jewellery to match.

Sandy's wife, Lynne, who had a more developed view on the moralistic values of life than the rest of us, chose to regard the girls as 'friends of the family' and behaved perfectly towards them throughout the meal, but during the pre-lunch drinks I could not contain my curiosity any longer when, finding myself isolated from the rest of the guests and talking to a gently perfumed blonde lady, I perhaps ineptly enquired what the two girls were doing with these somewhat older men. Without a flicker of a pause and looking me straight in the eye she replied, 'Surely you can see that we are high-class call girls, living the life of Old Reilly and getting quite rich in the process.' That unabashed frankness took away any need for speculation at a stroke, and as we continued our conversation about the currently favourite London nightlife Lynne announced that food was about to be served.

This social occasion might seem to have nothing to do with the story that follows, but its relevance will become apparent.

On 17 June 1974 I was asked to fly without passengers to El Adem, the ex-British airfield at Tobruk – recently renamed Gamel Abdul Nasser – to take a delegation led by the well-groomed Major Ali Fitouri of the Libyan Army, along with a furtive smaller gentleman who was introduced to me as Ali Ahmed. They were accompanied by three Yemeni-looking young men, whose names I failed to register.

Apparently they wished to go to Sanaa, the capital of North Yemen, so we discussed the most favourable route and decided to refuel at Cairo in Egypt and Jeddah in Saudi Arabia before attempting to land in the potentially hazardous mountainous terrain surrounding Sanaa's international airport. The airport itself was very high at over 8,000 feet which could give our jet engines some problems, but the main hazards were the surrounding sharp fingers of vicious-looking columns of rock, some of which climbed up to nearly 2,000 feet above the inhospitable terrain and seemed to claw heavenwards to grab the unwary aviator out of the sky.

Our passengers' timing had ensured that we would be attempting our landing in these unfriendly conditions at the dead of night, but providing their radio navigation aids were working properly, we anticipated no insurmountable problems. How wrong we were proved to be, but in the event the dark of night, thankfully, became our friend rather than the enemy that had been anticipated.

Cairo in mid afternoon was as hot as hell and refuelling became an endurance test, as the air-conditioning needed to be closed down whilst fuel was being transferred. Colonel Shukri of Egyptian intelligence intercepted us as we strolled across the searing concrete to render an ongoing flight plan in the Air Traffic Control tower. He wanted to know our final destination and whom we were flying, so we told him all we knew as we waited for the lift to take us to the top of the very tall tower. Unusually, he stayed with us whilst we checked the weather en route and looked for any notams regarding Jeddah and Sanaa. There was only one, saying that work in progress at Jeddah Airport had rendered one of their parallel runways inoperable. What a pain, we commented – only one runway, about twice the size of London's Heathrow, to land on – how inconsiderate!

As we had enough fuel to take the scenic route, we were allowed by Cairo Air Traffic Control to fly at 5,000 feet, about halfway between the River Nile and the Gulf of Suez. As the most famous and ancient archaeological sites in the world passed under our starboard wing, I delivered a commentary to the passengers that would have done justice to a professional tour guide.

On take-off we turned 90 degrees to port to establish our southerly heading and as the wings rolled level we found ourselves smack on top of the Great Pyramid and Sphinx on the plateau of Giza. Having by this stage only climbed to 2,000 feet, we could all clearly see the afternoon tourists filing into Pharaoh Khufu's majestic funerary edifice, which had been constructed in an outpouring of religious fervour and with the dedication of some brilliant Egyptian stonemasons 5,000 years earlier.

The sun, still fairly high in the sky to the west, cast shadows towards us from every architectural structure, seeming to outline and emphasize them. The Step Pyramid of King Djoser, on the fringes of the ancient Egyptian capital of Memphis and Saqqara, built around 3000 BC, passed by as we continued the climb and I recalled the hieroglyphic inscription at the base of a statue at its entrance, to commemorate the builder, Imhotep, and his claim to fame at building the first stone building in the world. The Greeks later venerated Imhotep for his deep knowledge of medicine and placed him on a par with their own renowned healer, Hippocrates.

Sixty miles south of Cairo the monastery of Saint Anthony, and 12 miles further east the monastery of Saint Paul, could be seen on the port side, quite close to the Gulf of Suez. These monasteries were a testament to Egypt's Christian past. To the starboard side the town of Faiyum could be seen beside a small lake. Even in ancient times this had been the centre of Egypt's textile industry and the lake was a favourite with Pharaoh Rameses II who fished and shot the abundant wildfowl around its shores.

As the sun sank lower in the sky and the shadows lengthened we passed the temple of Abydos, where many of the first dynasty Pharaohs were found to have been buried. Most of the early excavations of this site were conducted by the Frenchman, Emile Clement Amelineau, who was apparently responsible for untold damage to the tombs in his search for valuable items. The work was continued in 1899 by the Londoner Flinders Petrie, who did his best to repair the damage caused by Amelineau and made many notable discoveries that had been completely missed by the Frenchman.

From our relatively low altitude we started to lose radio contact with Cairo, but before initiating a climb, I pointed out to the passengers the temples of Karnak and Luxor (formerly the ancient Egyptian capital of Thebes) on the east side of the Nile, and the Valleys of the Kings and Queens on the west bank. As we climbed, the massive Aswan Dam became visible under the nose of the Falcon, but before we reached our new cruising altitude of 15,000 feet, Cairo Air Traffic Control handed us over to Jeddah and we crossed the Red Sea under Saudi Arabian supervision close to Medina, Islam's second most holy site.

The visibility was perfect and they brought us further south along the easterly Red Sea coast towards Jeddah. Meticulously following their instructions, we were guided on their radar for a right-hand circuit onto the active north-south runway. Passing to the east of Jeddah International in the failing light, as clearly instructed, everyone on board had a clear view of Mecca, Islam's holiest site. The Muslims among them were somewhat surprised to look down on their sacred black cubic monument, the Kaaba,[1] at the centre of Mecca, because 'infidels' are not permitted to see it and we Christians were, by their definition, infidels. Nothing was ever said about this breach of religious etiquette, but the crew were aware of a difficult atmosphere on board the Falcon for about half an hour after landing.

The young Saudi air traffic controller came across from the control tower to see us and asked us if we had any problems with our landing. We assured him that everything was fine, to which he replied that he had been under supervision during his dealings with us and if we had no complaint about his guidance of our aircraft, he had thereby qualified as a full-time Controller. Nobody commented on our clear view of the Kaaba. He accepted our onward flight plan, assured us that there were no notams affecting a landing in Sanaa and promised they would contact North Yemen after we were airborne to inform them of our time of arrival.

The light was fading fast as we climbed out along the easterly Red Sea coast towards the North Yemeni port of Hodeida, which was the established run-in to Sanaa. The moon rose in the east as we levelled off at cruising altitude and it was the biggest, brightest moon I had seen in a long while. We all commented on its size and brilliance and even the passengers were impressed with its display.

Jeddah Air Traffic Control handed us over to Sanaa ATC an hour later and

---

[1] The Kaaba is reputed to contain the sacred black stone, said to have been given to Abraham (Ibrahim to the Muslims) by the archangel Gabriel and towards which the followers of Muhammad face when praying.

we made an initial call to Sanaa, which was acknowledged, but their instructions for descending to their airfield were hardly understandable and, for an aircraft frequency, very non-standard language was used. After talking for about five minutes, their transmissions ceased completely and Hodeida disappeared under the nose of the aircraft.

I called Major Fitouri up to the cockpit and discussed the problem with him. He assured me that he was not aware of any potential problems and urged me to fly closer to see whether communications could be re-established. His mission was, he said, very important and he would like to land at Sanaa if at all possible. I agreed to attempt to overfly the international airport at the lowest altitude of 10,000 feet – 2,000 feet above ground level – but only if I was positive about my actual position. If they had suffered a complete power or radio failure they could then guide us in to land by either Very light cartridges fired from the control tower or battery powered signal lamps.

I broadcast my intentions on their tower frequency and also on the emergency frequency 243.0 MHz, with no response from Sanaa, although another aircraft acknowledged my transmission on the emergency frequency. He informed me that he had also lost contact with Sanaa at about the same time as we had and intended orbiting at 25,000 feet for thirty minutes to assess whether communication could be re-established. I agreed to keep him informed of any progress.

The moon was an absolute godsend for it enabled me to see the mountainous surface of the ground from 20,000 feet, or 12,000 feet above ground level. When I saw the surface of the airport's unlit runway, with a completely darkened control tower, my first assessment was that they had suffered a complete power failure. My senior passenger agreed, so I asked him to remain in the cockpit whilst I carried out a low pass along the length of the runway in an attempt to encourage them to give me a light signal.

They gave us plenty of light signals, but not the kind I had anticipated. I announced to Major Fitouri that my first pass along the runway would be carried out at high speed, because I was becoming distinctly uneasy at the signs coming to us from the ground. Nothing specific, but something smelt very wrong indeed. Both the co-pilot and I saw a small vehicle speeding along the taxiway towards us at maximum speed. It looked like a short-wheelbase army Land Rover without lights. I lined up with the centre line of the runway at 1,800 feet above ground level, with my landing lights and navigation lights full on and broadcast my intentions to the aircraft overhead. Running in to overfly the runway, I noticed that the small vehicle had entered the runway and was then travelling in the same direction as we were.

As we crossed the airfield boundary, heavy calibre gunfire opened up from the top of the control tower, directed at us, the tracer shells passing overhead in a constant stream. Simultaneously, the Land Rover on the runway began firing at us with two heavy calibre machine guns in the back of the vehicle as the driver unsuccessfully attempted to keep up with our progress down the runway.

'Here we go again,' I shouted, as I extinguished all the aircraft external lights, slammed the throttles to full power, hauled back on the control column and thanks to our high initial speed we climbed like a rocket, passing 20,000 feet in an instant. We levelled off at 22,000 feet, because I did not know the exact position of the other aircraft orbiting overhead at 25,000 feet.

Without reference to anyone I announced that we would climb to 30,000 feet when we were clear of the other aircraft and divert immediately to Khormaksar International Airport at Aden, the capital of South Yemen. When I told the other aircraft of our unfriendly reception at Sanaa, he thanked me and announced that he was returning with his passengers to Nairobi, his point of departure. As he was currently over the Red Sea, we were well clear of him so we continued up to 30,000 feet on a direct course to Aden, at the southern tip of the Arabian Peninsula.

Levelling off at 30,000 feet was an opportunity for us all to relax and gather ourselves together. We had plenty of fuel for the 160-mile flight to Aden, the weather was perfect and Major Fitouri was profusely apologetic at having led the flight into such mortal danger. He was so contrite, I think that he even forgave us for looking down on his religion's holiest shrine whilst landing at Jeddah.

As he was claiming no knowledge of any reason for our potentially lethal reception at Sanaa, I interrupted him and said that I was pretty sure of the reason for the gunfire.

'It's my opinion,' I said, 'that whilst we were airborne from Libya, someone carried out either a successful, or unsuccessful, military coup d'état and one of their first actions would be to secure the airport.'

'Never,' he responded.

The next morning I was proved correct.

Khormaksar and Aden were a veritable home from home for me. I had flown night fighters from there for hundreds of hours as a Fleet Air Arm pilot and our times spent in the Air Force officers' beach club, the Tarshein, had been truly memorable on occasions. I just hoped that some of the more bizarre exploits of my younger days were not about to come back to haunt me. It was with some trepidation therefore that I taxied into the dispersal in front of the tower and climbed the steep steps to the controllers' platform to render an official report of the hostile gunfire we had encountered at Sanaa International Airport.

I need not have worried. Two of the four controllers on duty recognized me instantly and a cup of hot coffee was thrust into my hand within two minutes. I could conduct the official business only with great difficulty because everyone seemed to want to reminisce about old times. The Chief of Protocol was summoned and before I had gathered my thoughts together properly we were all whisked away in a government car to be given comfortable rooms in a government-owned complex, in cottages on a nearby hillside overlooking the Tarshein beach.

After a quick wash and brush-up, and change of clothes, we were on the move again to what used to be the Gold Mohur Club, formerly an exclusive, very expensive beach club reserved only for the very rich. It had cost a veritable arm and a leg even to join the waiting list, never mind the expense of becoming an actual member. The bay in front of the club was usually full of 40- and 50-foot big-game fishing boats that returned to harbour each day with huge marlin, tunny and every known species of shark suspended from their stern davits. A glance round the bay told me that now there wasn't even a rowing boat bobbing up and down on the wavelets.

This was my first time inside the Gold Mohur Club and I was about to revel in the experience. The rundown appearance of this once prestigious establishment was not going to put me off and I was determined to enjoy my evening, even though the place was, incongruously, now part of the only Communist Arab state in the world. We started off with a small bottle of imported Amstel beer each, which augured very well for the forthcoming meal and in view of our recent trials and tribulations was greatly appreciated.

We grew somewhat concerned when the chef appeared and went into deep conversation with the Chief of Protocol, but needn't have worried too much. Our host explained, apologetically, that because of the lateness of the hour, the chef could only provide one main course, and that was lobster thermidor, which would be prepared to his own recipe. He was taken aback by the enthusiastic reception his announcement received and when we sat down, the surprise showed on our faces as a very acceptable Muscadet was poured. Although the country was now Communist, Arab and Muslim, all of which were strongly opposed to alcoholic beverages on pain of the most severe penalties, the Chief of Protocol smiled and said, 'You see how the British corrupted us.'

The lobster was superb and wherever the chef learned to prepare food at that standard, it was unlikely to have been Moscow. When we commended our host on the quality of the food he was genuinely surprised and told us that the chef had learned his art in the Officers' Mess at RAF Khormaksar. These were coral lobsters – sometimes mistakenly called crayfish, because they do not have the two large claws at the front that cold-water lobsters possess. Prepared correctly, however, they can be just as tasty.

The Chief of Protocol explained that the government had huge supplies of large lobster tails in their deep-freeze storage, because the fishing had recently been leased to the Japanese government who paid the rental in boxes of 2 lb lobster tails, thirty-six to a box.

'Can we buy some?' we asked.

'No,' he replied, 'that would be impossible, but I will try to get you a box each to take back to Tripoli with you.'

'Thank you,' we said in chorus, never expecting that he would remember.

A member of the South Yemeni Foreign Ministry arrived as I was shaving the next morning and said that he had organized breakfast for us on the veranda overlooking the calm clear blue Gulf of Aden, with the hazy coast of Africa just visible in the distance. Immediately below and slightly in front of the balcony lay the beach and main building of the Tarshein Club, and whilst we sipped our coffee waiting for the rest of the crew to arrive I asked what the building was used for since the British left in 1967. With a touch of embarrassment he told me that after a short period when it was used as government offices, it had been converted into the Secret Police headquarters. I asked whether it was used to interrogate prisoners and he professed no knowledge of such things, but guessed that some 'questioning' was likely to be conducted in the basement.

Government offices in Sanaa – North Yemen.

97

'Would you like to go over there and see the place, as you know the building so well?' he asked.

'Never,' I replied. 'The sight would probably reduce me to tears with all my memories of the happy times that took place on the patio.'

I remembered that there used to be a tall stone pillar, in the Greek style, surmounted by the twin scrolls of an ornate Ionic capital, in the centre of the patio. It was about fifteen feet tall and perhaps half a metre in diameter. During one moderately riotous party, for no apparent reason, a diminutive lieutenant observer (i.e. navigator), whose name escapes me, threw off his shoes and climbed monkey-like up that column. With some difficulty he wriggled over the overhanging Ionic capital and stood upright on the very top, making some ribald provocative statement about one of the other squadrons onboard HMS *Centaur*, the aircraft carrier alongside in the harbour.

After experiencing something of a dizzy turn he sat down on the capital and gathered himself together before making the descent, slightly chastened by his own exuberance. Five minutes later, Lieutenant Pete Shepherd, a notable *bon viveur*, stood up and announced to the assembled company, 'Anything an observer can do, a pilot can do better;' whereupon he approached the stone column with the obvious intention of shinning up to the top. Unfortunately Pete was not small like the observer. In fact he was well over six foot and athletically built, but it was very late at night and the practicalities of the task of climbing this substantial stone column had been ignored.

Nevertheless he persevered and climbed almost to the top, but whilst grasping the Ionic capital, he was forced to lean backwards – which was his undoing. The off-centre weight of Pete's body leaning outwards proved too much for the column's centre of gravity and the whole stone edifice came crashing to the ground. The main bone of one of his legs was reduced to something resembling powder and the other one was also badly broken.

He spent a very long time in various hospitals and when I visited him on one occasion he said that his one aim in life was to recover his flying category and fly again for the Navy. Outside his room, the surgeon assured me that such an ambition was quite impossible and he would be very lucky to even walk. I lost touch with him at that stage and life became very hectic as I took over as Commanding Officer of one of the Naval Air Squadrons. The next time we met, I had just landed in a Sea Vixen night fighter at a flying display over an airfield in southern England, and the next performance was a Swordfish biplane with a huge torpedo between the wheels of its fixed undercarriage. Its display fascinated me because it was flown immaculately and they are quite difficult aircraft to fly, especially with an underslung torpedo – as the Fleet Air Arm Swordfish pilots found when they crippled the German pocket battleship, *Bismarck*, on 27 May 1941.

As the Swordfish taxied alongside me in the dispersal, I was amazed to see that the pilot who had given such a professional display was none other than Pete Shepherd. His broken legs had healed slightly asymmetrically, but he had regained his flying category and went on to complete a worthwhile naval flying career.

The stone pillar was no longer in evidence at the Tarshein Club, or what remained of it, and I felt sad to see the squalor into which this once-famous building had descended.

After a relaxed breakfast I asked the Chief of Protocol to establish the true state of affairs in Sanaa. He came back, all too quickly, with a verbal assurance that the airfield was now calm and that we were cleared to fly back into North Yemen. Fine, but we needed a much more formal invitation into the North Yemeni capital after our experiences of the previous night. I asked for a written signal from the government, stating that we were safe to land in Sanaa and that we were officially invited to use their airspace, without restriction.

Such a message was received two hours later and with that in hand, I informed our passengers that we were prepared to have another attempt to fly them to Sanaa. Not really being too confident as to the statements made in our written permission, I decided to transit the small distance from Aden to Sanaa at 30,000 feet, which was at least 15,000 feet higher than any known anti-aircraft gun could reach. Before we could taxi out to the runway, a black car rolled alongside the Falcon and the Chief of Protocol signalled to open our door and let down the steps. Mystified, we complied and his driver walked up the steps with the first of three large boxes, wrapped in thick polystyrene, to be neatly stowed in the front luggage compartment. Our lobsters had arrived as promised.

Sanaa's radio assured us en route that its airfield was fully open and we would be safe to land. Still nervous, we landed normally and taxied, as directed, to a parking slot almost in the middle of a vast area of concrete. We were the only aircraft to be seen on the whole airfield. Not requiring any fuel to reach our next destination, Jeddah, we kept our tanks closed and as Major Fitouri instructed us to prepare the Falcon for a take-off in about an hour, we sat in the aircraft cabin and relaxed with our latest reading books.

A bit later, having failed again to achieve any radio communication with the Sanaa control tower, I picked up my navigation folders and set off to walk to it to file a flight plan for our departure. There was not a soul to be seen anywhere on that 20 acres of this sun-drenched concrete. Having walked about 200 metres from the aircraft in the rarefied atmosphere at over 8,000 feet, a small boy sauntered out of one of the buildings towards me. The heat haze shimmering off the surface at first made his image indistinct, but as we came closer to each other I could see that he was carrying what looked like a very big gun, a double belt of heavy calibre ammunition strung around his neck. This little boy, I judged, could not have been more than ten years old, eleven at the most, and he made no response to my cheerful greeting to him in Arabic and English. He merely stuck the steel barrel of his gun painfully into my chest.

This left me with somewhat of a dilemma. He looked steadfastly into my eyes, spoke no words, but merely grunted and kept pushing the barrel of his AK-47 hard into my chest. I was fully prepared to comply with any wishes that he might have, especially when it was obvious that the index finger of his right hand was tightly curled around the trigger. Further examination revealed that the safety catch was off, the gun was set to 'automatic fire' and the magazine of 7.62 mm bullets was full. We stood stationary in that position with him looking up at me for what seemed like an eternity. I grew more frightened by the second as I noticed that his hands were shaking – it would only take a light pressure on his trigger finger for the weapon to explode in a paroxysm of rapid fire, blowing me to eternity. Who would have thought that a ten-year-old child could induce such stark terror in anyone? I can only confirm that he did to me that afternoon.

All I could think of doing was to remain absolutely still, keep a fixed friendly smile on my face, leave my hands visible to him and make comforting remarks in Arabic. He remained completely impassive, seemingly unable to understand me as the sweat coursed down my face, not daring to reach into a trouser pocket for a handkerchief in case the movement alarmed him. The lethal impasse continued.

Eventually, the sound of a diesel engine was heard behind one of the buildings ahead of me. A short-wheelbase Land Rover with two heavy machine guns mounted on swivels behind the driver turned onto the dispersal and came towards us. I wondered whether this was the vehicle that had driven down the runway, the night before, blazing away at our overflying Falcon. It was surprising to see that the weapons were British Bren guns; but the British had never been in North Yemen so they must have been captured during tribal warfare involving the British Army on the border with South Yemen.

The vehicle stopped about two metres away, alongside us, as we continued to play statues in the middle of the dispersal. The passenger door burst open and a moustachioed, senior army officer almost fell out of the vehicle as he rushed towards us. Ranting incoherently in a dialect that I did not understand, he grabbed the boy by his hair, pulled him sideways and removed the lethal weapon in a single movement. Whilst this was going on I shuffled away to remove my body from the potential line of fire. Still gripping the boy's hair, he handed the Kalashnikov to his driver and brought the flat of his other hand firmly across the boy's left ear. Looking slightly dazed the boy ran back to the building crying, dropping his belts of ammunition on the concrete as he ran.

It is impossible for me to describe fully the terror that this small boy had produced in me. As I had stood, petrified, in front of him, visions of me writhing on the ground with a huge hole blown in my chest had flickered before my eyes. Our inability for either of us to communicate with each other had only heightened the tension. My brain had feverishly grappled with finding a method of extricating myself from this ridiculous position. 'He's just a small boy,' I had kept saying to myself – but no feasible solution to my parlous situation had come to mind.

'Thank you,' I said with a great deal of conviction to my military saviour, who explained in almost perfect English that a military coup was still in progress elsewhere in the city, and that everyone was a little jumpy.

'Include me under that heading,' I told him, as I found a handkerchief and mopped the sweat from my face and neck.

'Your passengers will be with you in about two hours,' he said, as he turned towards his vehicle; but it was actually much longer before they finally appeared.

As the officer was about to remount his Land Rover, he asked me which direction I had come from that morning.

'From Aden, to the south,' I replied.

'That explains it,' he said.

'What does it explain?' I asked.

'We saw your aircraft on military radar as you crossed our border and because we did not know who you were we fired at you with heavy anti-aircraft weapons for nearly ten minutes.'

'That is exactly why I chose to fly at 30,000 feet, because there is usually a breakdown of communications in these circumstances and I anticipated problems.'

Without response, he roared off with small puffs of rubber smoke as his wheels tried to grip the hot concrete.

The glasshouse at the top of the tower was in chaos as I arrived and everyone seemed to be running hither and thither ineffectively. The man whom I took to be the senior controller took the flight plan, signed the back copy and pushed it back into my hands. Walking back down the stairs, I was convinced that by now he would have thrown the remainder of the plan into the waste-paper basket.

When our passengers eventually returned to the aircraft, they brought an extra person with them. He was the Libyan Ambassador to North Yemen who had decided that the middle of a violent coup was probably an ideal time for him to exit stage right, or to use the usual diplomatic language, 'return to Tripoli for consultations with the Libyan Foreign Ministry'. He advised me to leave as soon as possible and asked my permission to return with us to Tripoli. 'Certainly,' I replied agreeing wholeheartedly with his early departure recommendations. Being fully ready, we started the engines and were threading our way between the vicious-looking fingers of rock on the climb-out, before the passengers realized what was happening.

It felt good to be safely airborne again. There was a delay in refuelling at Jeddah owing to some accident in the fuel storage facilities that would take an estimated two hours to repair. Passengers and crew therefore decided to use the enforced pause to browse around the shops that had recently sprung up just outside the international airport gates. I had never visited these shops before, so it was with some surprise that the white-turbaned owner of the second shop greeted me as if he knew me well. Some sort of a sales gimmick, I thought, but I was wrong. Many of the shopkeepers were from the renowned shopping street at Steamer Point in Aden – when trade completely disappeared as the British left and parsimonious communism became established, most of the more affluent ones moved their families north to Jeddah to continue trading as their ancestors had done for centuries.

Trading conditions are very good here, he explained. The normal turnover was better than they had enjoyed at Steamer Point, where they had relied on the passengers from the ships that passed through the Suez Canal and the Red Sea en route to India and China, stopping in Aden for fuel. Here in Jeddah, the Haj pilgrimage to Mecca takes place once a year and millions of Muslims flood the whole area. Some of the pilgrims were quite rich and many wished to return home with souvenirs for their families, so trade became very brisk indeed. Better still, he explained, they were often full of religious fervour and forgot to haggle over the price, so profits were high.

'You wouldn't cheat an old friend, I know, Mustapha, so what products are best buys for people like me?'

'Cameras, binoculars, Swiss watches, telescopes, radio-controlled machines, Japanese hi-fi equipment,' he gabbled. 'We have everything in that line that you could possibly need and I will give you the best deal anywhere in the world.'

I was very sceptical of sales talk like this, but he was as good as his word and that night I acquired a top Canon camera and a pair of binoculars for prices that I would be embarrassed to reveal.

The fuel installation problems were more difficult than had, at first, been anticipated, so when we returned to our aircraft, they advised us to stay the night. It was lucky that we were carrying the Libyan Ambassador because he contacted his consulate in Jeddah and five-star accommodation was organized immediately. We even had smart transport to take us into the city. The misfortunes of the previous two days seemed to retreat into the distant past as crew and passengers tucked into a very acceptable meal of lamb couscous in a tasty, very spicy, onion, coriander and tomato sauce.

It made a change the following morning to have all our passengers, for once, in the same place at the same time, enabling us to retrace our track to Cairo in the early morning sunlight. Despite the fact that we were at 25,000 feet on the return flight, Major Fitouri flew with us in the cockpit, back along the River Nile to Cairo. He took great delight in naming the sights that I had pointed out to him at low level on our outward leg. 'You see,' he said, 'I was listening intently to your tourist commentary and I must take the opportunity to do some Egyptian sightseeing of my own in the near future.' I was delighted that my efforts had borne fruit and I had managed to convey to someone else my deep interest and curiosity in this awe-inspiring cradle of the human race.

Colonel Shukri met the aircraft as we taxied to the Cairo VIP lounge and was seen chatting inquisitively to our passengers as he led them into the air-conditioned room. It was then near midday and a merciless sun seared the concrete to an unbearable temperature as the year clicked on to the hottest day two days later. We were curious as to how our 108 lobster tails were faring in the baggage compartment in this intense heat, but no moisture leaked out of the boxes so we hoped for the best.

As the Chief of Egyptian Intelligence returned our passengers to the Falcon, he popped his head into the cockpit and wished us a good flight. The upper wind was over 100 mph from the east, so we were pleased to be able to make Tripoli direct without stopping in Benghazi for fuel.

Back at Special Flight, we carefully transferred our polystyrene-covered boxes of lobsters to the crew car. At home, we took off the polystyrene covers, checked the state of the lobster tails and found them to be perfect, still deeply frozen, so space was found for them in our own deep freezes – over the next few weeks we all enjoyed barbecued lobster, lobster salad, lobster thermidor, lobster Newburg and every other method of preparing them known to man. They were delicious, but it did not end there. Whenever I either flew Libyan government ministers to Aden, or visiting South Yemeni politicians back home after meetings in Tripoli, each time three boxes of lobsters were given to the crew. I once flew to Aden three times within ten days, which meant that I had to accommodate 108 lobster tails in the deep freeze. Pretty soon there was no cold space left despite eating them as fast as we could and inviting our friends round to help us devour these normally rare delicacies. We were very popular because lobsters were difficult to find in Tripoli, but we finally had to admit defeat and invest in an extra deep freeze to cope with this manna from heaven. Happy days!

When the new government was installed in Sanaa and the quasi-military régime had settled down we made a few relatively normal flights there with various people, both North Yemeni and Libyan. At the end of September 1976 it therefore came as no surprise when I was asked to fly the Libyan Minister of Natural Resources, more popularly known as the Minister of Agriculture, to Sanaa. His name was Dr Mughsi (pronounced 'Mugsy') and he was a small, capable, dapper young man who loved to chat about his country's history, geography and current affairs. He viewed the world with a great deal of enthusiasm and smiled all the time. His scholastic qualifications were said to have come from his studies at Manchester University, but that information came from his colleagues and I could not verify its accuracy.

Being treated as a VIP and a representative of his country's President appeared to cause him some embarrassment, so I always ensured that he was treated with the full solemnity due to his position. Libya's achievement in increasing agricultural production was phenomenal. In the fertile Green Mountains of the Jebel Akhdar, Cyrenaica, east of Benghazi, I had seen huge heads of wheat and barley leading to crops in excess of five tonnes to the acre on a regular basis. This was remarkable in a land with a tendency to be short of natural water.

This particular flight was being conducted during a period of very strained

Our Falcon at Sanaa in late September 1976 with the VC10 of United Arab Emirates on loan to UAE from British Airways.

relations between Libya and Egypt, so a landing to refuel in Cairo was considered inadvisable. A decision was therefore taken to refuel for our first stop in Larnaca, south-east Cyprus, leaving us a clear run to Jeddah, without bothering any of the Egyptian airfields. As expected Larnaca refuelled and refreshed us in about 30 minutes and sent us on our way with a new set of VIP meals.

It is perhaps worth noting at this stage that although we paid the bills for our regular services at Larnaca to a body calling itself 'Cyprus Airlines', we discovered many years later that the personnel refuelling us and carrying out all the other work needed to keep a modern jet aircraft flying were in fact Israelis on loan from their airline, El Al. When Libya was forced to adopt its hard political line throughout the 1970s over the 'Palestinian problem', it is probably just as well that we were blissfully ignorant of this fact, although it should be noted that no problems ever came from these connections and the people carrying out the work could not have been more efficient, helpful and courteous towards both us and our Muslim passengers.

Our next leg, to Jeddah, was uneventful – until we taxied into their main dispersal to refuel. A car arrived to carry Dr Mughsi and the other three members of his delegation, but as it approached the VIP lounge a troop of soldiers, perhaps twenty-strong and carrying sub-machine guns, marched out of the shadows, formed a cordon around our Falcon and refused to allow anyone out from the cabin or in from the usual servicing vehicles. At first I thought that someone had made a dreadful mistake, but studying the fixed looks on the soldiers' faces I realized that we were in for some serious trouble.

Eventually a very superior, tall, portly gentleman dressed in white and light brown flowing robes, trimmed with gold and sporting a white turban trimmed with even more gold, came up to me and demanded to know where we had come from and where we intended going next. His prominent black moustache moved sideways and up and down as he spoke and the more angry he became, the more it jumped about. I answered him politely and asked who he was and why did he need to know these things. He replied that he was the Commander-in-Chief of the Saudi Arabian Army and that they would not allow us to fly on to North Yemen as fighting between the two nations had broken out on the border. He further announced that we could not have any of their fuel.

We argued for some time and I showed him the official written diplomatic clearances that had been issued by his government for my flight, LN999, to pass through Saudi Arabian airspace and refuel at Jeddah. He then became quite obstreperous and seemed to be about to strike me. He shouted, 'I am the eldest son of the King, a royal prince, and as far as you or anyone else is concerned, I am the government. You will do as I say.'

That was a pretty unequivocal statement and it rocked me back, speechless for a few moments, so I changed my negotiating tack. 'Look,' I said, 'I am the captain of this aeroplane and I carry out the wishes of the Libyan President and his senior ministers. If you have any reversal of diplomatic policy to convey, you should not be speaking to me, but go to the VIP lounge and say these things to my senior VIP, Dr Mughsi.'

He almost jumped in the air at this little speech and shouted, so that everyone within 20 yards could hear, 'You...' then after a short pause he repeated, 'You,' even louder 'and your VIP can go to fucking hell.' Then his violent temper seemed to subside as he realized that a man in his position should not curse and swear at a mere pilot. He had suffered a grave loss of face and spun round on his heel before marching purposefully away, taking his men with him.

Two minutes later, a fuel bowser drew up alongside our Falcon and without a word the driver connected up the hose to our pressure refuelling point and filled us up. The flight plan to Sanaa was accepted and after gathering up my passengers from the VIP lounge, we were cleared for take-off. I had been warned that there might be fighting on the Saudi border with North Yemen, so I flew a little further out into the Red Sea than usual as we paralleled the Saudi Arabian coast, flying south to Hodeida.

Reflecting on my clash with the Saudi prince at Jeddah, I was at a loss to explain his violent reaction, but even today I consider myself very fortunate not to have experienced the inside of a Saudi jail after the fracas. Dr Mughsi appeared to be amused at the proceedings, but had no comment to make, having been blissfully ignorant of any contretemps whilst he relaxed in the air-conditioned splendour of the Saudis' lavish hospitality.

The delay at Jeddah had ensured that we were destined to land at Sanaa's unusually high death trap of an international airport at the dead of night, with the moon rising in the east over what desert explorers at the turn of the nineteenth century had called the 'Empty Quarter', only a pale substitute for the huge moon that had guided us on previous occasions. However, all was not negative. We had continuous radio communication with Sanaa and everything appeared to be normal this time, including all the radio navigation aids, so providing our Jeppesen navigation charts were correct, it should not be beyond us to ensure a safe landing.

The run-in up the North Yemeni valley from the port of Hodeida at 20,000 feet was exactly as anticipated and ten miles out from the airfield we could see the bright lights of Sanaa's single runway. The controller invited us to carry out a visual landing and gave us the barometer pressure setting on the surface of the runway, but being conscious of the many hazards around it, I chose to carry out a full Instrument

Landing System (ILS) approach and landing, which international aviation navigators had formulated to keep aircraft clear of all obstacles.

This time, a North Yemeni government representative met us and arranged all our requirements while I subconsciously scanned the corners of all the buildings to satisfy myself that a ten-year-old boy with a Kalashnikov was not about to frighten the living daylights out of me again. A junior army officer was detailed to look after the crew, whilst the passengers were whisked away elsewhere.

He took us through the main city, which looked very interesting, to the open country beyond, to what he called 'The Palace'. Though I can visualize this building even now without difficulty, I have never been able to adequately describe it. The whole edifice was constructed of what I would say was wattle and mud with a great deal of wood cladding that had been painted in various matt pastel colours, a very long time ago. It had been built on the top of a broad pinnacle of volcanic rock about a hundred feet up from the surrounding agricultural countryside.

It was about 50 to 60 metres square, with a strange type of neo slate sloping roof. From the gardens on the approach, it definitely appeared to be 'up in the air'. In fact, I was relieved to notice that servants were available to carry our suitcases inside, because the altitude of approaching 10,000 feet was causing us some physical distress from even small amounts of exercise. The internal rooms were of every conceivable size, with multitudes of doors everywhere. Some of the rooms were reached by flights of stairs from inside other rooms and the building had been constructed with a varying number of floors. One side of the palace had four floors of rooms whereas another side would only have two floors. There was nothing regular about it.

The whole place was intensely intriguing and the deeply worn wooden floors creaked and groaned at each footstep. Everyone we saw – although we really only saw the men – wore curved daggers in cummerbund-style belts. Some boasted ornate, short, bejewelled scabbards, but other daggers were bare-bladed and flashed menacingly when the owners walked past the lights from the abundant oil lamps. The overriding impression was that the owners were fully prepared to use their curved blades on the slightest pretext, so we all resolved to tip generously throughout our stay and smile sweetly when anything was offered to us.

The place inside seemed to be a cross between the *Arabian Nights* and *Lord of the Rings*, complete with a battalion of Hobbits. There were no locks on any doors – in fact you were fortunate if your bedroom door could actually be fully closed and the primitive bathrooms were invariably miles away from the bedrooms.

Food was offered at regular intervals in a cross between a normal restaurant and a school dining hall. It was generally quite tasty, but what we were actually eating was anyone's guess. There were rice and couscous dishes with various meats and fishes, but there did not appear to be any menu or choice. A plate of something was placed in front of us, completely different from the next person's. The whole thing was arbitrary, but there was a central table where various spices and other small additions could be selected.

One thing was certain – with those curved daggers, the evil looks on some of the servants' hairy faces and the doors that did not lock, nobody would consider complaining about anything. Surprisingly, we all slept soundly and on my one nocturnal visit to the bathroom, I managed to find the correct bedroom again. Walking inadvertently into some Yemeni lady's bedroom in the dead of night could have had disastrous consequences.

Whereas the evening meal had been somewhat unusual, the breakfast was entirely normal, with cereal, eggs cooked to order and a funny kind of spicy sausage. The coffee had a tendency to be very strong, but there were lashings of it. It was certainly very good and piping hot.

A young army officer named Zafir joined us after breakfast and I made the mistake of complimenting him on the high quality of the North Yemeni coffee. That innocent remark triggered a half-hour lecture from him on the intricacies of Yemeni coffee production, covering everything from growing the plants, picking the beans and on to the various methods of producing the different types of coffee. The only facts that I still remember is that the high mountain Yemeni coffee is the best, but very expensive.

He kindly brought a box about the size of a tea chest to the aircraft on our departure, which was full of the best high-grown coffee beans. The gist of the little speech that he made, as the box was stowed aboard, was that the coffee was to be shared amongst the three crew members. Unfortunately, the best-made plans often go awry and this gift was no exception. On our return to Tripoli, whilst all the crew were occupied on routine aviation matters the box was removed from the Falcon's baggage compartment by the Minister's chauffeur and the coffee was never seen again; so all we are left with is a pleasant memory.

During the forenoon Zafir took us on a tour of inner and outer Sanaa. It was a fascinating experience that we will never forget. The city was a maze of very narrow streets with many brightly painted mud and stone houses, some three storeys high, leaning perilously towards each other over the road below. The scene reminded me of very old pictures of Britain in the Middle Ages, centuries before. There were a few cars to be seen, but not along most of the streets where the buildings were too close for them to squeeze through.

People were working in the streets, outside their shops, sometimes sitting on three-legged stools as they hammered away at brass, bronze, steel, silver and gold, creating both practical and ornamental objects. The colourful dress for people walking around seemed to be a robe, covered with a waistcoat of varying colour and generally white pantaloon trousers with pointed soft-leather shoes. It all had a very 'Ali Baba' atmosphere with the prominent curved daggers. The only time that we saw anyone actually buying anything was when we came to the vegetable market, where very lively bargaining was the order of the day. At one end of the food area was a walled section where young and old Yemeni women, generally without veils, sat on piles of what looked like privet hedge cuttings, arranged in various-sized bunches.

Yemeni families spend, on average, about a third of their family income on these leaves, which when chewed produce a narcotic effect, apparently some way between the effects of cannabis and cocaine. These were the *qat* leaves produced from the high ground of the Jebel Sabir, in the northern part of the mountainous area. The trade was traditionally controlled by the women of this area, some of whom were remarkably pretty and dressed in very richly coloured robes and turbans, often in silk. The faces of the older ladies were tanned, with skin like deeply lined leather, perhaps revealing addiction to their own product.

Our guide bought a large bunch of the green twigs and leaves as a present for his mother. He offered us some to taste, but we respectfully declined. Flying aircraft whilst high on qat did not seem to be a particularly good idea and probably strictly against international aviation medical rules.

By the afternoon everyone seemed to be chewing away, with the green leaves protruding from their mouths. To us they looked like so many goats and the psychological effect of the plethora of lethal-looking curved daggers and a severe addiction to narcotics can only be guessed. Thankfully, we had an armed bodyguard.

As the sun slowly sank into the western horizon and the myriad of cooking fires and oil lamps provided an evocative flickering illumination, we returned to the palace, which, in the gathering darkness, seemed to be covered in twinkling lights. In our absence another plane's crew had arrived, much more numerous than the three of us. This was effectively the Royal Flight of the United Arab Emirates, but in fact was a British Airways four-engined VC 10 on loan, with its crew, to the Emir.

They were a very pleasant, outgoing bunch of aviators and the young captain announced that they had established a well-stocked bar in the biggest of their rooms and that after dinner we Falconers were invited to join them for a party upstairs. The bar was being operated, very efficiently, by three of the VC 10's air hostesses, and the other four girls were circulating with some tasty small eats.

James, the captain, called me over saying, 'Look what we are carrying' as he opened two shallow blue velvet boxes, just over a metre long. I was flabbergasted to see inside, on the pink silk padding, two beautiful solid gold swords and scabbards, encrusted in large red rubies, blue sapphires and with a spectacular green emerald embedded in each hilt. They twinkled tantalizingly in the light from the oil lamps, but from what I could see – and my family had all been watchmakers and jewellers – these two weapons were priceless.

'Let's have a duel,' he said, 'so that the crew can take some photographs.'

I thought that he was either drunk or had taken leave of his senses, but it sounded a pretty attractive idea. My last experience of handling this kind of weapon was as a boy wireless telegraphist at HMS *Ganges* near Ipswich in Suffolk, when I learnt how to use a naval cutlass. We flashed the Damascus steel blades at each other a few times and danced around the room like Errol Flynn. Having such a precious implement in my hand felt very superior indeed. Without making a mark on the valuable weapons we returned them to their scabbards and closed the velvet boxes.

'What's the story?' I asked him.

'They are gifts from the Emir to the new President of North Yemen.'

'Where were they made?' I wanted to know.

Everything with them was written in French, so he was sure that they came from some notable jeweller in Paris. The work was magnificent and Paris was one of the few places that had craftsmen who could have produced such quality. He said that they were a liability because he dare not let them out of his sight and there were no places of security in the palace. He was forced literally to sleep with them.

The party ended a couple of hours later when the drinks finished. We all dispersed into our own rooms and I slept terribly, with an unusually sore head and a terrible stomach. It was with some relief that I joined my crew at breakfast to discover that they both felt as terrible as me. Then the VC 10 crew came in and they were, if anything, worse than us. The girls looked like death on wheels and the men were not much better.

We eventually worked out the reason for our distress. It was all down to the altitude of our residence. At 9,000 feet there is insufficient oxygen in the atmosphere to allow one's blood to clear any alcohol out of the liver and kidneys, so it stays in the body for a long time, making the sufferer feel ghastly – and we did definitely feel ghastly. The female body is generally smaller and their metabolic rate is different from men, so the effects on them are amplified several times.

Well, we thought, we are at leisure all day whilst our VIP visits the Yemeni President and there is plenty of time for us to recover, so we will just relax. James had not been told their itinerary, so he sought out the guide to discover the plan.

Fifteen minutes later, he was back, saying that I would not believe it but the Emir was travelling to Taiz in the south of the country to visit the President and he had arranged for his crew to be taken there in two large government cars. The thought of 260 miles over unsurfaced roads, up mountains and along dry rocky river beds did not fill anyone with enthusiasm, but they had to go. As they left, we were quite amused and felt rather superior because we could stay in the palace and relax. We waved them off in two large pristine shiny black cars and shouted, 'Take care of the swords' as they slid out of the courtyard. We sympathized with them, looking so ill. James responded to our advice with a word that sounded like 'Bollocks', but it was drowned out by the sound of the car engines and the skidding wheels.

Ten minutes later a member of the North Yemeni Protocol Department stepped out of his car, asking for me. 'Your Minister would like to see you,' he said, 'please come.'

'We have just discovered that the new President is at his home in Taiz,' Dr Mughsi said. 'We would like to fly there as soon as possible to see him.'

That will teach us to laugh at the VC 10 crew, I thought. 'We will be ready at the airport in about an hour,' I responded.

Not knowing how long we would be in Taiz we decided to take our suitcases and having completed a thorough pre-flight check, we all sat in the cockpit, picked up the oxygen masks, switched the control to 100 per cent oxygen and breathed the life-giving gas for five minutes before our passengers drew alongside. The effects were like magic. The gas quickly washed the befuddled brains clear, helping us to return to our normally efficient selves.

The VC 10 convoy would be halfway to Taiz by the time we took off, so we looked out for them. All we saw was a single stationary car with its occupants running hither and thither, about 120 miles due south of Sanaa. It never occurred to us that the other car was down a steep embankment, upside down because a few minutes earlier the road had given way beneath them.

Taiz had a small but adequate airfield, quite close to the South Yemeni border on an arid, rock-strewn plateau where a few spindly olive trees were struggling to grow. Surprisingly, a car and chauffeur were waiting for us near the control tower, but there was no fuel available for the Falcon. The tanker was, apparently, due up from Aden in about ten days' time, so it was fortunate that we had sufficient fuel on board to return to Sanaa when required.

The drive from the airport into the town of Taiz was interrupted by our engineer, who had to ask Dr Mughsi to stop the car, as he was about to be sick. Resuming his seat, he explained that he only had one kidney and that if he drank too much black coffee his kidney could not cope. The problem with the altitude of 9,000 feet had exacerbated his distress, but nobody mentioned the further complication of the previous night's VC 10 hospitality.

The Taiz Hotel was a remarkably civilized stone building with ornate balconies and balustrades in contrasting shiny black basalt rock carved from a jet-black outcrop just outside town. A room each would be no problem, though water was only available in the taps for two hours a day, so along with our room keys we were each issued with plastic two-litre bottles of imported water.

The food was spicy, but pleasant. We were just finishing a very sweet dessert, dripping in fresh honey, when the front door burst open and a dozen or so dishevelled men and women, their clothes encrusted in a fine dust, spilled into the room. It was just like a scene from a western movie. We stood up to assess the problem and as we drew closer it became clear that these hobos were in fact the VC 10 crew. One car had apparently fallen off the road causing several torn shirts and trousers as it rotated, but miraculously there were no major injuries.

James told us that he had watched, aghast, as the chauffeur-driven lead car slid sideways off the mountain road and disappeared completely from sight. When they disembarked from their own vehicle they were unable to see any of the occupants of the first car, or even the car itself. Scrambling down the steep hillside they eventually found it on its roof, with people climbing out of the windows. There was a strong smell of petrol, so everyone left the scene as quickly as possible. As the RAC does not operate in North Yemen they were faced with the prospect of fitting everyone into a single, admittedly large, car for the remaining 150 miles.

His problems increased when he was told that there were only two rooms left available, so he asked us if we would forgo two of our rooms to allow his boys and girls to be accommodated separately. We agreed and persuaded the Minister's delegation to relinquish one of their rooms as well, so the five rooms enabled them to live with some kind of normality and it was a small price to pay in view of the unstinting hospitality that they had provided the night before in Sanaa. The Emir and his delegation were obviously travelling in greater luxury for their visit to the President.

'What happened to the swords?' I asked. It seemed that James had one and the co-pilot in the lead car had the other. Rotation in the crashed car had taken its toll on the precious weapon, but the box's catch had been securely fastened, so no serious damage was sustained to the blue velvet and after a few deft strokes of a yellow duster the sword was returned to its former beauty.

The following morning Dr Mughsi asked us to accompany him to the President's home and off-duty office, so that we could drive straight to the airport after his

Driving in Saudi Arabia towards Taif on the outskirts of Mecca
can be decidedly dangerous.

meeting, but before we left James came to see me, saying that 'these bloody swords' had become too much of a liability and asked me to take them off his hands and return them to Sanaa when we flew back.

'Certainly,' I replied, 'but to stop them disappearing completely you will have to send two of your crew back with us to take responsibility for them. Dr Mughsi may decide to leave the country as soon as we arrive at Sanaa airport.'

'Fine,' he said, 'take Jean and Maria back with you and that will also help with the logistics of getting the rest of us back to Sanaa. The girls can return the swords to the VC 10's safe and wait for us. There are beds on the aircraft so they can sleep on board.'

It was only after I had taken charge of his beautiful swords and left the hotel, complete with two of his stewardesses, that I realized that the swords were supposed to be presented to the President, so what had changed? I never found the answer to that question, but as it turned out our removal of these valuable weapons was probably their salvation.

At the residence, the North Yemeni presidential staff ushered our crew and the two extra hostesses into a small anteroom just outside the main meeting room. As Dr Mughsi was ushered into the presence, imagine my astonishment when two young ladies came out of the leader's office and exclaimed, 'Neville, what the hell are you doing here?' I knew the girls, but in what context, I was slow to recall. 'The north of Scotland – Tomintoul,' they both said, 'at Sandy Taylor's lunch.' Of course. They were the two high-class call girls with the prospective tenants that lunchtime, years earlier.

'What on earth are you doing in Taiz?' I asked. 'This is a very long way from the north of Scotland.'

'Don't ask silly questions,' they both said coyly, so I did not embarrass them any further.

'We are probably flying out of North Yemen tomorrow. Would you like a lift anywhere?' I enquired.

'No,' they replied, 'we are doing very nicely, thank you. We are being treated very well and will be staying about another week, with any luck.' It would turn out to be a great pity that they made that decision.

The Minister of Agriculture's meeting ended and we swept off to the airport to fly back to Sanaa with our delegation, plus the two swords and their escorts. On the way I went back into the cabin, borrowed the swords and showed them both to Dr Mughsi. He was flabbergasted and said that he had never seen jewellery so beautiful in his whole life; so I told him the story, assuring him that they were absolutely priceless. Clearly he was quite envious.

Anticipating problems at Jeddah Airport, we were pleasantly surprised to find everything sweetness and light. No soldiers, no prince and certainly no hassle. The Minister asked me to call in at Damascus, the capital of Syria, to refuel on the way back instead of Larnaca, so we happily complied with his wishes. At Damascus, the Libyan Ambassador to Syria met us at the international airport and told us that he was leaving his car and chauffeur to take us into the city when we had 'put the Falcon to bed'. He meanwhile left, amid much pomp and ceremony, taking our delegation with him.

We prepared our trusty aircraft, 5A-DAF, for its onward flight in a leisurely style. When we were fully satisfied that all the aviation and domestic arrangements were satisfactory, we sank into the back seat of the ambassadorial limousine and glided serenely along the wide dual carriageway into the city, recalling other much less serene journeys that we had made along this road in previous times.

Rooms had been organized for us in the recently completed Damascus Sheraton and as there was still some daylight left, we dropped our cases in the rooms, changed into more relaxed sandals, short-sleeved shirts and slacks to rendezvous by the opulent swimming pool a few minutes later. As I was passing my open wardrobe, I noticed to my surprise that there was a substantial door in the back of this fixed piece of furniture. Being acutely security conscious, I tried the handle and the door opened, so I stepped into the wardrobe, through the door and found myself in a pitch-black space.

Exactly at the same instant, my co-pilot in the adjoining room, dressed only in his underpants, opened *his* wardrobe door to find me standing, bolt upright, inside. He did a quick double take, leapt backwards and fell over onto his bed: his shock was so great that I feared he might have a heart attack. Imagine putting an adjoining door into the next room through two wardrobes and leaving the door unlocked! It hardly seems credible to plan such a glaring security risk in a new five-star luxury hotel such as the Sheraton.

The pool was an ideal temperature and the sun was very hot, so we swam for the next hour and enjoyed the exercise after being strapped into an aircraft cockpit for seven hours. Living in Tripoli, we all had respectable tans so the late afternoon sun gave us no problems. That evening we dined at the restaurant by the pool where our rather large co-pilot had his usual Chateaubriand for two people to himself. The engineer and I ate more modestly, but very well, so sharing a bottle of Bollinger champagne between the three of us rounded off the meal nicely.

The next day the Ambassador's limousine came for us just before lunchtime, so we returned to the airport to await our passengers. They arrived reasonably promptly, and Dr Mughsi was bubbling over with delight. He called me over to his seat where he produced a long velvet box, sprung the catches and there in all its splendour lay a gold-coloured sword and scabbard. 'What do you think of that?' he asked. I tactfully admired his purchase, which was certainly spectacular, but not quite on a par with the Emir's priceless gift. The gold appeared to be plated and the gems set in the scabbard were semi-precious topaz and tourmaline, but even that Lebanese work would have cost a lot of money. I wondered whether he intended to hang it on his wall at home or present it to his President, but I failed to discover its final destination, and it was really none of my business.

As we crossed the coast outbound over the Mediterranean, on the way home, the wind turned against us and dictated a landing in Benghazi for fuel. They were very efficient and it did give us the opportunity to telephone our families to warn them of our arrival home in two hours' time, so it worked in quite well. Lesley was at a social function with several countries' ambassadors at a villa 200 metres from our home when I telephoned, so I told her to stay at the party as I would be there shortly and could collect her and take her home.

This turned out to be a gross error. We were delayed two hours by a failed starter motor and arrived in Tripoli three hours later. As promised on the telephone I went round to the house of our friends and as I opened the door into their very big main room, Lesley stood up and walked towards me. Unfortunately, in the three hours that I was delayed, a great deal of drinking had taken place and instead of walking straight across the room towards me, she embarked on a seriously curved track to the right, eventually ending up halfway along the wall to her right where I rushed over and recovered her. It was clearly time to leave, so I made my excuses and the two of us walked home.

The sequel to this flight came a few days later when Lesley and I were listening to the news on the BBC Overseas Service. They reported a massive explosion in the Presidential offices in Sanaa, which had killed the North Yemeni President. Later amplifying broadcasts talked of two young ladies, thought to be British, also dying in the blast. It seems that a new, supposed ambassador from an unnamed country was presenting his credentials, in the customary manner, to the President. As he unfastened his leather briefcase on the main desk, ostensibly to remove some papers, the case exploded killing everyone in the room and other people in adjoining rooms. The suicide bomber could not be identified, nor could his country of origin.

I failed to discover any further details of the atrocity caused by this suicide bomber, but it is inconceivable that the young ladies referred to in the report were not our two from London.

The area that we had been operating in North Yemen was distinguished many years later by being revealed as the original family home of terrorist leader, Osama bin Laden. Perhaps the Saudi Arabian prince who had attempted to delay us in Jeddah that night of 29 September 1976 had information to which we were not privy.

CHAPTER FOUR

The Falcons of Ra

The 9th October 1973 was a beautiful day for flying. The autumn sun shone out of a clear blue sky and a mild anticyclone provided gentle breezes from the east that swirled flurries of fine yellow sand over the black tarmac of the road. I drove the other two uniformed crew members to Tripoli airport in one of Special Flight's grey unmarked Peugeot 404s. We cleared the built-up part of the city and settled onto the smooth dual carriageway of the recently completed airport road, which had apparently been provided by the politically interfering Chinese government of Chairman Mao, to ingratiate itself with Libya's new leader.

Alongside the road, for most of the 20 miles to the airport, grew a mass of fragrant small bushes, similar to the European broom, but covered in larger white flowers. They permeated the air with a powerful, heady, oriental-style perfume reminiscent of jasmine. These were the days before mandatory air conditioning, and as we progressed with the windows wide open the scent was all-pervasive and unforgettable.

Our progress was momentarily slowed by a heavily overloaded Peugeot pickup truck driven by an ancient gentleman dressed in the sparklingly white robes and black trimmed turban of a desert Bedouin, making a rare trip into the mighty city. He had obviously struck an advantageous deal with the breeders at Tripoli's fascinating walled camel market and was taking the results of his dealings back to his home farm.

To confirm this observation two fine-looking camels were installed in the body of the pick-up, pressed close together and facing backwards. Their long erect necks were surmounted by haughtily superior heads, which sported big brown eyes surrounded by long dark eyelashes that would be the envy of most young ladies. They gazed imperiously down on us as we waited our opportunity to overtake. The newness of the vehicle betrayed the fact that this was probably the owner's first drive into the big city and nobody had explained to him the complexities of dual carriageways and their traffic rules.

Though his 25 miles per hour was slowing us down badly in the fast lane, I was reluctant to beep the horn because the sudden sound could well have panicked the camels and none of us fancied them jumping out of the back of the pickup on top of our 404. We decided that there was plenty of time so we just stayed safely behind the camels until an overtaking opportunity occurred. To while away the chronically slow speed we speculated on what exotic destination our chief passenger, the Libyan Foreign Minister and Head of Intelligence, Major Abdul mun'im el Houni had in store for us today. Paris or Rome, both his regular destinations, was our hopeful first guess.

Egypt had, three days earlier, set the Middle East aflame once more by declaring war on Israel, in what became known in the Arab world as the October War, so we were fairly confident that easterly destinations would be entirely out of the question unless the route took us north of Turkey or south of Sudan. How wrong could we be? If only we had known what lay in store for us, it would certainly have wiped the smiles off our faces. Life itself was destined to swing perilously in the balance that day, but as we progressed in our enforced stately fashion along the airport road the overriding air was of blissful ignorance.

At the airport, Special Flight's ground engineers had towed the gleaming white Falcon 5A-DAG, with its opulent gold lateral stripe, out of the hangar and were busily polishing the paintwork until it sparkled in the bright sunlight. They had already confirmed its full fuel load, both visually by looking in the tanks, and on the cockpit instruments. The two catering boxes, containing twelve trays of delicious, lovingly prepared French gourmet meals, were securely stowed in their compartments in the galley, and the self-contained auxiliary jet engine was gently purring away as its air-conditioning system cooled the hot cabin interior and heated the water for our first coffee of the day.

The waiting documentation confirmed that Alpha Golf had been fully inspected and was ready to fly, so I signed the acceptance and discussed all the work that had been completed on the aircraft since its last flight with the chief engineer. When everyone was completely satisfied, our own flight engineer and I conducted a minute external visual inspection. The myriad of locked panels were unfastened for inspection and after each examination, carefully refastened. Signifying complete satisfaction by signing the onboard documentation, the crew embarked and we started the starboard engine.

It was decided that as we had not yet been entrusted with the proposed destination we would taxi to the VIP lounge and await instructions. Stopping by the end of the red carpet, I closed down the one engine and as the cabin was fully cooled and the beverage water nice and hot I also dispensed with the auxiliary engine. Experience dictated that waits outside the VIP lounge to collect passengers could be of unpredictable duration and the incessant noise of an aero-engine running immediately outside could be infuriating to anyone conducting important meetings inside, so in the interest of fostering good neighbour relations we silenced the engine.

Inside the ostentatious main room, with its golden curtains and furnishings,

I was met by the government's Gaffir[1], who professed no knowledge of any flight whatsoever. This was unsurprising and indicated that the flight was being conducted with a high degree of security precaution, so we locked the Falcon and settled into the sumptuous easy chairs and deep-pile Chinese carpets of the lounge, to await events. It must have been about two hours, measured in games of cards and various cool drinks, when the peace of the airport was shattered by the wail of dozens of police motorcycle sirens leading a line of black Mercedes limousines towards the airport.

We galvanized into activity. I stood up, smoothed my uniform and prepared to meet the passengers, whilst the other two crew members activated the Falcon for its impending flight.

A mass of people seemed to burst into the large room, led by the stocky, muscular figure of the Foreign Minister. He marched towards me past the tastefully arranged groups of chairs and tables to the window, where I stood looking at the flight preparations being conducted outside on the tarmac. 'Captain,' he almost shouted, grabbing me warmly by the hand, 'come and meet the rest of the passengers.' He led me towards the centre of the room, still grasping hands tightly, and proceeded to list the names of eight Palestinian men in their late twenties, with ready smiles, each of them shaking my hand in turn. I noted that about half of them sported closely cropped designer stubble like their leader, Yasser Arafat.

Palestinian men can, quite legitimately, have three entirely different names, by a mechanism I will explain later. I had therefore fallen into the bad habit of forgetting Palestinian names given to me on introduction because the same person usually assumed other names later on, thereby causing utter confusion to everyone. As a result, I have been unable to recall the names of the men introduced to me that day.

Major el Houni enquired whether we were ready and, trying desperately to keep the sarcasm out of my response, I said, politely, that we would be ready if only we could be told our destination, thereby enabling us to file a flight plan. Looking furtively around the room he pulled me conspiratorially towards him and said that they would like to fly to Cairo.

'Cairo!' I blurted out, shocked by the suggestion. 'Surely you're aware that Egypt and Syria declared war on Israel three days ago and that Cairo is now in the centre of a war zone. People are killing other people in large numbers and I have no wish to swell the statistics with my crew and passengers.'

'No, no!' he countered. 'We have full permission.'

'From whom?' I demanded. 'Has anyone contacted the F-16 fighter pilots of

---

[1] Pronounced 'Gaffeer', a cross between a messenger and a housekeeper.

the Israeli Air Force who would shoot down anything of whatever nationality flying over the whole of Egypt with cynical delight? We are a relatively slow civil aircraft with no weapons and no protective systems to warn us of impending attack. We would be a very easy target for any aggressive military fighter and a flight into this area would be foolhardy in the extreme.'

He grasped my right elbow and silently led me into a small anteroom. When the door was tightly closed he delivered a lengthy speech on the importance of his flight to Cairo and applied abnormal psychological pressure to persuade me to reassess my negative views. We were both at this stage pulling no punches in our arguments and I told him about a lengthy statement made personally to me, three weeks earlier, by President Gadaffi. During a relaxed conversation with him, I had stated to the President that there was an apparent danger of some of the flights demanded of us carrying a quasi-military overtone and as purely civil pilots, flying civil aircraft we were ill equipped to carry out such flights. We could, under no circumstances, carry explosive materials and it would be extremely unwise for us to fly into areas of active military conflict. To personalize the warning I emphasized the safety of the passengers being in jeopardy, should we agree to such requests.

The President seriously considered my statement for some minutes then responded that he agreed and gave me authority, with immediate effect, to refuse any flights with which I was not completely happy on the grounds that I had stated. This permission, he emphasized, applied to me personally and any other member of Special Flight with operational misgivings must express those reservations directly to me – my decision would be supported by him, unreservedly. Sometime later this presidential approval was confirmed to me in writing by the Chairman of the National Airline, Mr Ahmed A. Zawi.

When I informed the Foreign Minister of the President's statement, he looked a little perplexed and paused for several minutes before sending the Gaffir to find some cool soft drinks. As we subsided back into the chairs, cool drinks in hand, he asked whether there was any way that I could agree to this flight to Cairo. After a short while I responded that I was prepared to fly as far as the Egyptian border, but would go no further without personal assurances to me from President Sadat himself that he would accept us into Cairo airport and that there was absolutely no danger of enemy air activity in the region that day. He made several telephone calls in very rapid Arabic and assured me that all my stipulations had been agreed. He said that we would land at Mersa Matruh, just over the Egyptian border and that President Sadat in Cairo would speak to me personally on the telephone when we arrived at the Egyptian control tower.

After agreement from the other two members of the crew, we left for Mersa Matruh. Passing Benghazi at 36,000 feet on our easterly track I called the airfield and confirmed the weather for Mersa Matruh, which was still perfect. Shortly afterwards we gazed down on the ancient Græco-Roman coastal cities of Cyrene and Apollonia, where many of the massive buildings could be seen under the clear blue Mediterranean Sea. This collapse had been due to a catastrophic earthquake a couple of hundred years after the time of Christ. Dick, the flight engineer – now steward – announced that he was serving meals to the passengers and offered us food if we were ready. The co-pilot and I settled for another cup of coffee and decided to eat our meals on the ground at our destination.

Half an hour later Tobruk airfield (named El Adem by General Montgomery in 1942, but recently renamed Gamel Abdul Nasser in the Egyptian leader's honour) slipped slowly over the horizon towards us as we approached the Egyptian border. A lurking wish for the details of our flight to be universally known and the time noted by as many recording Machines as possible encouraged me to call up the Tobruk tower, establish exactly who was on duty in Air Traffic Control and appraise them of our intentions – knowing full well that our every word would thereby be etched, for possible future reference, on permanent tapes in airport control towers and even some of the larger aircraft.

Fifteen minutes later the small town of Sidi Barrani came into view on the coast and I knew that we were then overflying a country at war. Mersah Matruh control verified our position on their radar and invited us to commence descent into their airspace. They confirmed that no other aircraft was closer than 100 miles from our position, but requested that I remain to the west of the centreline of their runway as anti-aircraft defences were active to the east.

At the mention of anti-aircraft defences the hairs on the back of my neck prickled and I resolved to stay west of that runway at all costs. It was then that a realization slowly seeped into the brain that I had automatically changed modes. I had become a fighter pilot once more, with eyes examining every part of the sky in an ever-moving search pattern. The unforgettable dictum ingrained into my subconscious over twenty years as a night fighter pilot of the Royal Navy was 'find the enemy before he finds you, or die'. I even set up a slow weave and periodically strained my head behind so that I could check that the Falcon's tail was clear of any possible threat and consciously informed the young co-pilot, partly to reassure him, but mainly to teach him the lessons learned in the hot fire of actual combat, that might just keep him safe one day. Overdramatic maybe, but a sixth sense nagged me and refused to be ignored.

As we landed, quite normally, at Mersa Matruh we became aware of a solid cloud sheet covering the desert east and southwards as far as we could see. It appeared solid from about 16,000 feet up to about 35,000 feet, and would completely obscure sight of the ground from above, but by now I was concentrating on the promised discussion with President Sadat, as I mentally rehearsed the questions that needed to be answered and the assurances that I must be given before this flight would continue any further. It is not considered good manners to actually swear when talking to presidents, so I had to choose my words carefully.

The Foreign Minister preceded me up the steep steps to the glasshouse on top of the tower and after preliminary greetings with the staff, he was given an important-looking red telephone, whereupon he announced his identity to the person on the other end, liberally using the words 'Sadat' and 'President' and periodically pausing. Eventually he seemed satisfied, announced triumphantly, 'President Sadat,' smiled and handed the phone to me.

The disembodied voice on the other end was Arab, throaty, quite guttural in fact, just like Anwar Sadat, but the crackly line and the speed at which this now very important and busy man was produced, gave me considerable misgivings. I searched my mind for something that only he and I would know the answer to and eventually remembered that President Sadat had introduced me to King Idris, the ex-King of Libya, in a closed room in his palace with no one else present. He even kept it private from Major Abdusalem Jalloud, the Libyan Prime Minister who at the time was in another room in the same palace.

I respectfully explained that it was necessary for me to confirm that I was, in fact, talking to the real President and he assured me that he completely understood. When asked by me to say exactly who he had introduced me to in his palace about three months earlier, he responded without hesitation, 'King Idris'. How could I doubt further? I must now be convinced, so I rapidly explained the position and requested his personal assurance that we would be entirely safe flying to Cairo, that the Libyan Foreign Minister was coming for a meeting with the Egyptian President himself and that the current fighting was a long way away. He gave me adamant assurances on all three points.

Lastly, I made the observation that due to the cloud sheet obscuring a good part of Egypt from above, and because it was in a war situation, all the normal civil radio navigation aids would be switched off, so how were we to find Cairo? He replied almost without thinking, that his radio navigation aids were still functioning and we could approach normally. I asked him to confirm that his ground-to-aircraft navigation beacons – ADF, VOR, DME and ILS – were radiating normally and he confirmed that they were, but before I could clarify this surprising statement further the line went dead and no further conversation was possible. All efforts to re-establish the link failed.

As soon as the phone was returned to its cradle a cacophony of voices demanded to know my intentions. I refused to commit myself to a decision until I talked to the rest of the crew and faithfully relayed to them everything that had happened up in the tower, except for the reference to ex-King Idris, because I had given my word not to reveal the meeting to anyone. I shared my nagging doubts about the response regarding the radio navigation aids as, in my experience, nobody at war leaves a radio beam transmitting that could guide enemy bombers directly onto their targets. It would be crass stupidity. I suggested to myself that perhaps President Sadat had not been directly informed of the true situation about these beacons, as those decisions would be taken by lesser military officers, but I was still wracked with doubt.

The co-pilot and engineer confirmed that if I was prepared to proceed to Cairo, they were happy to continue, so I informed the Foreign Minister accordingly and we re-embarked all the passengers. Leaving the northerly facing runway, we headed out to sea, climbing to join the official civil airway, along which we would normally be expected to approach Cairo. This track also avoided any nasty accidents with land-based anti-aircraft defences.

As anticipated, every Egyptian radio navigation aid was silenced and my nagging doubts grew worse, but as we turned right, in the middle of the airway and crossed the coast above the cloud sheet, a firm voice identifying itself as Egyptian military radar, called Lima November 999 – our call sign – and confirmed our position as crossing the coast. He guided us to overhead Lake Qarun in the Qattara Depression where a small break in the cloud enabled us to confirm our position visually and asked us to 'squawk 2350'. We switched our own weather radar off to prevent its inherent radiation being used by any potential enemy aircraft to home in on us.

The controller's ordered turn over the lake to Cairo aimed us much further south than usual, but one does not argue with military radar, only follow their instructions. I informed him that we were still at 40,000 feet and that we would have to descend to be in a position to land at Cairo. He confirmed our altitude and immediately ordered a descent as rapidly as possible to 16,000 feet.

'We've got a right cowboy here,' I announced to the rest of the crew. 'He doesn't seem to know his arse from his elbow.'

We descended through the slowly decaying cloud into bright sunshine and a large part of lower Egypt stretched out in all directions. It was a breathtaking sight, seemingly with Cairo and its airport at the centre of the view.

The guidance from military radar ceased and we were left passing eastwards south of Cairo towards the Suez Canal with no reply on the radio and no further instructions. Cairo airport steadfastly refused to answer on any of its known frequencies and I was about to institute the civil radio failure procedure when the first missile snaked up towards our Falcon, closely followed by a second.

I was mesmerized. Surely someone must have made a tragic mistake. Did they not realize that we were full of passengers? Of course they did. Egypt had been at war for three days and this was no accident. Whoever ordered this atrocity on an unarmed civil aircraft probably knew the name of everyone on board. Any of our deaths would be completely incidental to the main aim of terminating the target passenger. My mind flooded with emotions from stark terror, through disbelief to the reluctant realization that, as captain of this aircraft, I had to take immediate action if life was to continue beyond the next five seconds.

Then, surprisingly, time appeared to be running super-slowly, despite the violent explosive destruction speeding unerringly towards us at many times the speed of sound. Ridiculously, I ran through a list of excuses for the person holding us in his sights: he thinks we are an Israeli fighter aircraft, after all we look like a fighter at first glance; he's brushed against the big red 'Fire' button and the missiles were launched accidentally; perhaps he's gone insane.

All, of course, total nonsense. There could be no confusion about any of the details regarding LN999 – we were guided to this rendezvous with death by Egyptian military radar controllers and these missiles were clearly fired from Cairo Airport, our destination.

The £2,000,000, ultra hi-tech Russian SAM IIs, called the 'Chariots of Death' by American F-4 Phantom pilots in Vietnam, were authorized for use only on the highest authority. Someone wanted us dead and this was no casual error by a trigger-happy minion, but naked aggression backed by complex politics; we had been deliberately funnelled into the ambush.

But – and the contemplation of that 'but' sent a tingle of excitement along my spine – the radar controllers, anti-aircraft gunners and missile battery commanders had all made a glaring error. Sure, they had lured us to the right spot on their radar screens, but to get the Falcon there they had brought us far too close for a normal descent to the optimum SAM II killing altitude. They were obviously not aviators. No aviator worth his salt would have made such an error. To obey their quite clear instructions forced me to set both engines to 'idle' power, extend the airbrakes and make a very rapid descent, building up speed in the process. The aircraft was literally 'gliding', technically converting potential energy to kinetic energy or, more simply, exchanging height for increased speed. Consequently, when they fired the first two missiles, initially directed by the crew's ground radar, they presumed that I was a 'dead duck', but when they handed over control to the missile's own inbuilt infra-red homing system to finish the battle, it should be a very different story.

Our rapid descent from 40,000 feet (about eight miles high) down to their ordered 16,000 feet, meant that the whole of the aircraft retained the temperature of the cruising altitude and that temperature was close to –60°C – at least 40 degrees colder than the coldest deep-freeze. I retracted the airbrakes and prepared to use that lovely excess speed as a useful weapon. It enabled me to manoeuvre the Falcon without the use of any engine power for a short while so our infra-red signature would remain almost zero – and without this heat source these evil chariots of death should not be able to continue to home in on us.

That at least was the theory according to Neville Atkinson, but would it work in practice?

Frantically searching for every scrap of information about these missiles in the furthest recesses of my mind, I remembered a February Friday of filthy snowy winter weather at the naval airfield of Yeovilton, seven years earlier....

Brian Young, our youthful Squadron Commander, bounced into the instructors' crew room shortly before lunch, proclaiming that all flying was cancelled and that the last man to the bar of the *Lamb and Lark* at Lymington, three miles away, would buy the first round of drinks for everyone. 'Don't forget to bring all your wives and girlfriends. My wife's already halfway there,' he shouted as he closed the door.

The resultant departure from the squadron car park on this foul, damp, sleety Somerset day was more like a racing start at Le Mans than a group of responsible naval officers going to lunch. Well, it was serious stuff – a round of drinks for such a gathering of at least twenty-five people could, even then, amount to a lot of money and naval officers were anything but rich. In fact, when I look back to those days of early 1966, young pilots were permanently hard up and the struggle to settle monthly mess bills on time and thereby avoid a one-sided interview with the Commander was a serious consideration.

Lesley and I, in our stylish cream MG TD, turned into the beautiful country pub's car park just feet ahead of Ralph Magnus, our tame Major from the US Marine Corps, in his swanky red Cadillac. Not for him the tight financial constraints of fighting the family budget. He was with us for two years as a staff navigator on exchange, and by our standards he was rich beyond belief. His salary alone was several times ours and his overseas allowances for having to live with us peasants of 766 Squadron bought him a relatively opulent lifestyle. He readily shared his good fortune with us, but we never quite accepted his habit of smoking a huge Churchillian Havana cigar during student debriefing following every long Sea Vixen flight.

Strolling into the bar we gravitated towards the massive inglenook fireplace and noticed that we were among the earliest squadron arrivals. As the blazing logs, the size of small tree trunks, crackled beneath the huge chimney, warming the entire room to a rosy glow we quaffed the local scrumpy, chatted to Ralph and perused the food menu, anticipating the last arrival with childish humour.

Remembering that he had recently returned from four years combat in Vietnam, I was keen to discuss the actual weapons that his F-4 Phantoms had used against the Viet Cong and the weapons that had been used against his supersonic fighters. He warmed to his subject, concentrating most, as he seemed to be chewing lumps off his gigantic cigar in quite nervous contemplation, on the infamous Russian surface-to-air missiles known as the SAM IIs.

He listed the Phantom's onboard countermeasures that were routinely employed to defeat these hypersonic killers, which his squadron had nicknamed the 'Chariots of Death'. F-4s were fitted, he said, with very effective 'wide-band homers' that listened to the SAM IIs' homing systems and warned of an impending attack with urgent high- pitched tones in the earphones. Some of his colleagues confided to Ralph that the noise of these bleeps in actual combat had the tendency of producing an instant set of soiled underwear. These persistent missiles were very difficult to avoid at this stage, but several devices and counter-tactics had been devised with good effect.

Firstly, the F-4 was equipped with small rocket-type heat generators that could be fired behind the aircraft to give alternative infra-red sources to attract the missile's homing head away from its original target.

Secondly, consideration could be given to shutting down both jet engines to reduce the inherent heat output to nearly zero, but gliding along without power over severely hostile territory was not something any fighter pilot contemplated lightly and it demanded a great deal of trust in the built-in relight ability for the jet engines. The few 'aces' eventually went even further and whilst gliding without engine power they led the enormous terrifying beast on their tail round to face the sun, the giver of all heat, and hopefully a more attractive target than the rapidly dying heat from the engines' tailpipes. Sometimes, this tactic worked and the aircrew had the rewarding sight of seeing the evil monster speeding past, heading to self-destruction when its fuel was exhausted, and sometimes even watching the missile plummet back to earth.

The third evasive tactic really appealed to me and I can recall his actual words, complete with Ralph's pronounced southern Louisiana drawl, whenever my mind is allowed to dwell on this life-saving conversation. He explained to Lesley and me that if the exhaust gas wake of the SAM II, and presumably most other anti-aircraft guided weapons, was seen as a line in the sky, then usually, though not invariably, the missile will miss or is homing on another target. However, if the first view of an attack is a shimmering circle of white smoke, small at first, but growing in diameter, then 'Boyo, it's coming at yer' and the pristine condition of 'yer trollies' (underpants) is definitely at risk. In fact, if your entry through those pearly gates is not to be marred by an unattractive odour, there is one split second left to you for evasive action and your nerve has to hold until the right instant. Precise judgement is the key to survival. Action early or late is invariably fatal.

During this intense lecture Ralph's hands were moving around repeatedly to illustrate the missile's position relative to its target and the attitude of the aircraft in its attempts to escape. He was, in fact, living the battle and spoke and acted with such feeling and intensity that the hairs on the back of my neck prickled incessantly. I was to all intents and purposes up there with him, and as good as flying his fighter.

Conspiratorially, he rested his left hand on my shoulder, with beads of sweat breaking out on his face, not entirely due to the heat of the fire. He had a slight tremor in his voice and his right hand had become the aeroplane as he moved its position in relation to the missile, which in his mind's eye he could obviously see quite clearly.

'You see, Neville, this circle of pulsating energy, with wisps of what looks like steam curling off at regular intervals, is rapidly increasing in size until you realize that a black dot has appeared at its centre. That black dot is the nose of the actual missile and the time for extreme action has arrived. Throw the aircraft on its back or its wingtip without any attempt at finesse and pull maximum G towards the SAM. Pull for your life, you bastard. Haul-arse that airplane round the sky like there's no tomorrow, because if you cock this up, there *is* no tomorrow, for absolute certain.'

He then annunciated the theory backing his instructions. If you lose your nerve and turn before the black dot appears in the centre, the missile's onboard computer merely alters course a few degrees in the new direction and hits you, regardless. If you become mesmerized by the little black dot in the centre of the circle and delay the extreme turn, the aircraft will not have changed its position in the sky relative to the missile before collision occurs. Whereas, if you throw an extreme turn towards the bastard at exactly the optimum time, the missile is presented with a control problem that it is incapable of solving.

Relative to the missile your position in the sky is changing very rapidly, so its onboard computer is telling its control surfaces to follow – i.e. change its course – but the missile's extreme speed and huge weight prevent it following the target fast enough because of its own massive inertia. The control surfaces are simultaneously thrown into a stall condition so making them ineffectual and incapable of turning the missile.

This effect was originally explained by Daniel Bernoulli, working in a small workshop in Basel in 1750, but it is just as relevant today in modern space flight.

Ralph continued to update us on the guidance and homing systems of the SAM IIs and eventually showed how the missile's warhead was exploded when it

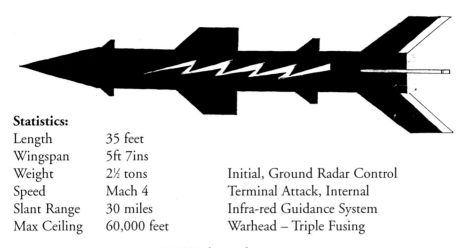

Statistics:

Length	35 feet	
Wingspan	5ft 7ins	
Weight	2½ tons	Initial, Ground Radar Control
Speed	Mach 4	Terminal Attack, Internal
Slant Range	30 miles	Infra-red Guidance System
Max Ceiling	60,000 feet	Warhead – Triple Fusing

SAM II drawn from memory

was close enough to its target to ensure destruction, but more of this later. Realizing that his very understandable information could have some important use in the future, and as in any case it had been most entertaining, without regard for the cost I bought him a pint of scrumpy. If I had realized then that his vital tactics and good solid detail would one day save not only my life but the lives of my crew and passengers, I should have been thinking in terms of giving him a hogshead (54 imperial gallons) of the stuff – if not buying him the entire pub. Meanwhile, we were nice and warm, in enjoyable company, the cider and food were outstanding and we had a free afternoon. What more could we wish?

When asked how many SAM IIs he had actually faced in anger, in his anti-missile-equipped, super £25 million hotrod of latest technology, the F-4, Ralph replied that he had survived five separate attacks by individual missiles. I was horrified.

Little did I know what the future held in store for me.

Amazingly, in what must have been an instant, that detailed conversation in the *Lamb and Lark* came back to me over the Great Pyramid that October day in its entirety. I clearly saw Ralph Magnus's face as I organized my mind into battle mode. Things were very bad for us and deteriorating rapidly, but were not entirely hopeless. The Russians/Egyptians had picked on probably the only civil pilot in the world who knew the intimate details of the SAM II and with luck it should be possible to evade at least some of their missiles. The worrying fact that in a confrontation with these rockets no civil aircraft had ever managed to avoid destruction, I forced to the back of my mind. It perturbed me that my life was about to end in a smoking heap on the edge of the Sahara, and that someone would assuredly announce that I had committed some basic aviation mistake, thereby causing this disaster. There would be no mention of missiles, just the ubiquitous 'pilot error' epitaph, with all my fellow aviators saying, 'What a pillock!'

'Right, you bastards,' I said out loud, with only the other two crew members in earshot, 'if it's a fight you want, let battle commence. This is Neville C. Atkinson you are trying to kill. I know a thing or two about your fucking missiles and I'm not dying easily.' I remember being frightened and very angry at this blatant atrocity and my concern shifted from the threat to 'us' changing into a more personalized attack on 'me', very much in the singular. Not that it changed anything – if I died, we all died – but somehow it helped me to get the enormity of the predicament into clear focus.

During this seemingly protracted build-up, with all the personal mental turmoil involved, my eyes were glued on the two missiles hurtling towards my beautiful white Falcon 20. I detected that the missile controller had directed them perfectly in the azimuth plane (i.e. horizontally), but had misappreciated the vertical plane. In other words he allowed for us to be lower than the level 16,000 feet that I held, immediately the missiles had been sighted. Unless he made a drastic correction within the next two seconds the missiles' mesmerizing flight would take them underneath me.

No correction was made, but as they passed a few hundred feet below I could clearly see that the first missile was travelling somewhat faster than the second, and that the rather smart right echelon flight that they had seemingly adopted on launch had become rather a ragged tail-chase. What would happen, I hopefully pondered, if the gap increased and the second missile started chasing his leader? After all, in the final stage of attack these evil sods needed lots of heat to attract them. My engines were at minimum revs so the tailpipes were cold and my airframe was still at $-50°C$ or thereabouts. The lead missile was burning its solid fuel at something between $2,000°$ and $3,000°C$ and if that huge infrared plume ever came within the 2.5 degrees activity angle of the second missile's homing head, things might become very interesting. The thought of one missile attacking the other really appealed to me.

Wishful thinking, unfortunately. They both passed cleanly underneath and to my acute dismay executed a smooth 180-degree turn to make a second attack. Their manoeuvre was significant to me in two ways. Firstly, it confirmed conclusively that it was certainly LN 999 that they were endeavouring to kill and not some other unseen target. Secondly, as they turned towards my tail they commenced their characteristic 'damped phugoid'[2] search pattern, looking for

---

[2] *See* Diagram on p.129

my, hopefully, non-existent infrared output. This positively aggressive action by them forced me into my first, considered, countermeasure.

As they rolled out dead astern of me I turned quite rapidly to port, from a roughly easterly heading to fly directly at the sun which was slightly south of due west (about 240 degrees), still without the use of any engine power in order to keep everything nice and cold. I even asked Dick to check that the coffee machine was switched off. The missiles could now only look at my tail whilst squinting into sun and the sun over the Sahara around midday in late summer is unbelievably hot.

Having completed the turn, I felt slightly drained. I had no further countermeasures left to use. After what seemed like an eternity, but could not have been more than two seconds, my heart did a somersault as the nose of the first missile streaked past, closely followed by its colleague, heading inexorably at the sun. Almost immediately their white plume of exhaust gases ripping through the sky petered out, restarted, coughed and ceased altogether. Simultaneously both their noses slowly arched over towards the ground and we last saw them heading for the south-western edge of Cairo city, travelling at phenomenal speed, accelerating with the inexorable pull of the earth's gravity.

The feeling of elation when the first two missiles faded from sight against the dusty gloom of the desert was intense, but very short-lived. I was still in the middle of the Egyptian/Russian war Machine and they had just spent about £4,000,000 to achieve my annihilation. It would be unthinkable that they would just forget about the whole thing and watch me escape. They had expended a great deal of financial and military effort in this deliberate attack and would obviously only be satisfied with our complete elimination.

Compounding their dishonesty, the radio crackled into life from a source that identified itself only as 'Cairo Area Control'. The voice was not that of a normal air traffic service. The words used were heavy with official military overtones and the short staccato terminology clearly came from someone used to giving orders and being unprepared for any contradiction. I was surprised that anyone actually spoke on the particular frequency we had selected because earlier, when I had broadcast to the world that we were a civil passenger aircraft under unprovoked missile attack, no response had been forthcoming – except from a fellow passenger airliner over the Mediterranean who acknowledged my plight and wished me 'Good Luck'. Normally, a change of frequency would follow any lack of response, but with salvos of hostile military hardware hurtling past my ears, I was rather preoccupied with staying alive, so the radio had stayed on this apparently dead frequency.

He almost shouted into his microphone, 'Lima November 999, you are to return to Cairo immediately.' I responded that I was under lethal attack by

Egyptian SAM II missiles and was not prepared to attempt a landing at Cairo in these conditions. Astounded at my non-compliance, he barked back that this order came from President Sadat himself and reiterated that I was to return to Cairo immediately. Unconvinced, I replied that having been attacked twice in the last few minutes, it would be foolish for me to continue my approach. He spat back, and I could hear the droplets of spittle hitting the microphone, 'You have two MIGs on your tail and if you do not return to Cairo, you will be shot down.' This made me angry, but not so angry that I ignored the threat. I reasoned to myself that we were clearly in a missile environment and no air force risks its own fighters in the air when they could be shot down by their own missiles. There are two types of war. Firstly, there is a fighter war – aircraft versus aircraft – and secondly, a missile war – where fighters are grounded. This was definitely a missile battle, but just to check I weaved from side to side to look behind to assure me of a clear tail.

I was very tense by this stage and my reply threw politeness out of the window. I said, in a very firm voice, 'If I have two MIGs on my tail, which I very much doubt, then by your present performance you would probably shoot down three aircraft instead of one. I am returning to friendly Libyan airspace.' He did not reply!

A mental review of our situation removed any cause for complacency. We were deep in Egyptian airspace. Their hostility was clearly confirmed. I was heading west towards Libya, flying level at about 12,000 feet, directly at the ball of the sun, rapidly running out of airspeed, but reluctant to increase power on my still cold aeroplane, because of the heat-seeking missile threat.

As if to compound my dire position, the Foreign Minister, clearly shaken, pushed past Dick and enquired whether I was aware that anti-aircraft shells were bursting behind and underneath the fuselage. It may seem complacent, but I thanked him for the information and asked him to return to his seat and tighten his straps. I ignored this conventional weapon threat as we were 2,000 feet higher than their maximum effective altitude of 10,000 feet; but we were slowly descending. Could I afford to increase power and climb for the heavens?

In answer to the unspoken question, my next glance astern and beneath the Falcon to the left showed a very bright light, followed about two seconds later by a second. Missiles 3 and 4 had just been launched from very close indeed and we were at the ideal killing height. I forced myself to forgo engine power and commenced a gradual descent to keep sufficient airspeed to enable me to manoeuvre safely.

The crew later told me that I gave them very little information at this stage and for that I was sorry, but in truth I was near petrified and almost speechless. Engine power was needed to stop me drifting down into anti-aircraft gun range, but opening the throttle would result in certain death from the SAM IIs. As they were underneath us I could only see them intermittently, but the missile operator had made a remarkable error: he had fired his two chariots of death directly into sun. My aircraft was still cold and if I could manage without power to reduce heat output a little longer, they might just go for the sun. My gut feeling, due to the long tails of exhaust gas I could see, was that they were shaping up to miss, but vision was difficult due to a dusty desert haze and nothing was certain.

With pounding heart, sweating palms and a vice-like grip on the control column I was immensely relieved to see the nose of the first missile, underneath and slightly left, cruising past, closely followed by its evil partner. They pulled ahead, but quickly disappeared from view into the ball of the sun, never to be seen again.

To avoid the dreaded gunfire zone we urgently needed engine power, so I slowly eased open the throttle to avoid causing a thermal shock to the cold power units. The power surge of our two General Electric CF 700s gave a most reassuring pressure on the spine as the airspeed indicator rapidly rotated clockwise. At the optimum climbing speed of 300 knots the Falcon settled smoothly into its max rate climb as I coaxed extra power out of the motors by selecting the 105 per cent power setting and watching the exhaust gas temperatures like a hawk for signs of stress. Emergency power, it was called, and few people encounter situations loaded with more emergency than our present predicament. Height would give any other missiles more problems and I wanted them to have as many problems as possible, so we clawed our way upwards and westwards, gazing at the ground and around the sky for any more threats.

With a partially relaxing mind, during the climb my concentration wandered onto an earlier visit I had made inside the great Pyramid of Cheops, above which this attack had commenced. There was a statue and many paintings inside the Pyramid of the falcon-headed Sun God, Ra. We were flying a Falcon for the battle and the sun had been our eventual saviour from four missiles, so far, all of them undoubtedly intent on our violent destruction. Could Ra possibly be fighting in our corner? Was he sitting with us here, on the jump-seat in the cockpit? I glanced over my right shoulder, but no, it was definitely Dick, with his fixed grin, sitting on the jump-seat – maybe some being somewhere was guiding my moves to help us stay alive. The vision of this ancient deity subsequently came back to me many times. And the next time I stood beside Ra's statue I did say a profound 'Thank you', just in case.

Back to the battle, which did indeed seem to be increasing in intensity. It was now clear that a high-level decision had been made that an immediate explosive end to our lives would enhance Egypt's military/political position, for whatever reason. Another worrying aspect was that the voice that had ordered me back to Cairo on the radio was remarkably similar to that on the telephone in Mersa Matruh control tower, claiming to be President Sadat giving his full authorization for the Libyan Foreign Minister to fly to Cairo – the voice that had lulled everyone with its assurances that the flight would be safe. My mind in these relatively quieter moments swirled with the confusion of probabilities, possibilities and suspicions. I became clear, as I concentrated on the whole picture, that the actual target was the Foreign Minister himself – but it took me years to work out the actual reason.

Meanwhile, I stuck tenaciously to a westerly heading in a desperate attempt to escape to the Libyan border. My best speed whilst climbing away from the most likely threat was just over Mach 0.8 (about 8 nautical miles a minute). Unfortunately we were more than 350 miles into Egyptian territory and it did not take a genius to see the seriousness of the predicament. Time for some mental arithmetic. Distance divided by speed produces time, so 350 divided by 8 produced the appalling fact that we could not escape in much less than 44 minutes. Did we have enough fuel to keep this high power for that length of time? More mental arithmetic confirmed that if we maintained our present altitude of 35,000 feet or higher, the fuel was sufficient – but if we descended too early or called upon extra power for manoeuvring, we would make the border but have insufficient fuel to make it to the nearest Libyan airfield of Tobruk. Careful judgement would be needed.

The co-pilot and engineer searched the ground on the starboard side of the aircraft for any signs of further attack, and as I intermittently weaved from side to side they strained their beady eyes astern to watch for enemy fighters. The strain was now showing on both their faces and I tried to minimize the problems and sound reassuring – probably unsuccessfully. Looking down on the port side, towards the south I picked out the ancient cities of Memphis and Saqqara, with the shadows on King Zoser's step pyramid clearly visible. Moving my gaze westwards, a group of newer buildings in a distinctly military layout slowly became visible out of the shimmering desert haze.

I will never know what possessed me to super-concentrate on this barrack-like area, but it held my piercing gaze for perhaps a minute, before I forced my attention on the surrounding airspace for a second or two, seeking the first view of attacking fighters before they saw me. The sky was clear; nothing was on my tail so I glanced back at the ground.

My heart seemed to somersault and the brain almost seized up into numb inactivity as the now familiar double-delayed explosions of light illuminated those buildings nearly eight miles underneath the Falcon. Had Ra done his stuff once more in allowing me to see the actual launch, or was this a case of basic Fleet Air Arm fighter tactics paying off? Early view of an attack is all important in air warfare and I had been incredibly fortunate to see the actual launch of the first four missiles,

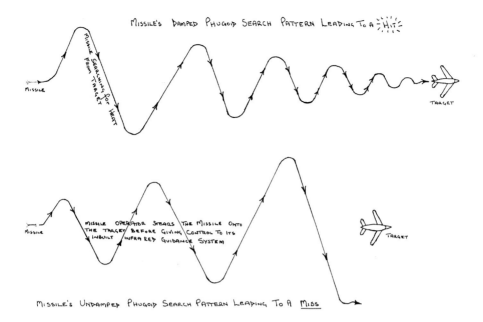

MISSILE'S DAMPED PHUGOID SEARCH PATTERN LEADING TO A :HIT:

MISSILE'S UNDAMPED PHUGOID SEARCH PATTERN LEADING TO A MISS

but seeing the terrible puffs of flame once more as missiles 5 and 6 started their lethal streak towards their hapless target was almost beyond belief and certainly gave me the edge in the game of death that was about to commence.

Whether guidance came from God – the crew was Christian of various intensities – or the almighty Allah – the passengers were all Muslim – or whether Ra was fighting on our side after 5,000 years of rest, was immaterial. The battle shortly to be forced upon me would probably be decisive and I would eagerly accept all the assistance and guidance that came along, from whatever source.

Things were now developing very fast indeed, but I was not aware of actually praying, as might be expected. There was too little time, but as my mind clarified into icy cool assessment, it seemed to become part of the aircraft. I lost awareness of making actual control movements and instead thought in terms of up, down, port, starboard, more power or less, and reacted automatically to each snap decision. I was part of that Falcon, just as if Mr Marcel Dassault had built me into it at the factory as yet another of the thousands of components. I knew the hydraulic pressures, fuel state, flight instrument indications, aerodynamic capabilities and everything any pilot needs to keep his flight in an ideal condition, without consciously checking. It was a unique experience, probably driven by abject fear.

The missiles closed inexorably, both of them shimmering circular masses of wispy white exhaust gas, the circles expanding in diameter very slowly. This was a different quality of attack altogether. This operator knew his missiles as well as I knew my Falcon. Probably hands-on by a Russian instructor; certainly not an Egyptian trainee, as with the other missiles. This was a true experienced professional, undoubtedly the 'Premier Division' I was facing this time, and either he lost his job by failing to sell any more very expensive SAM IIs to Egypt or I would lose my life in a very violent explosion in a few seconds' time. We were both super-concentrating for very different reasons, but I think that I had the edge on desperation. Not for him the error of initially firing into the sun or ignoring the target altitude. He was using perfect technique.

My response was to close the throttles on both engines to reduce infrared output, but at nearly 40,000 feet the rarefied air, containing little oxygen, was a problem that General Electric had solved by preventing the rpm decreasing too much at altitude, thereby discouraging a flame-out with resultant total loss of power.

I even considered shutting down both engines entirely, but the resultant loss of services like flying controls and major instruments would be too great a sacrifice as the missiles came nearer, so closing both throttles to minimum revs, which at this altitude was about 70 per cent was my compromise. Still, the muscles on my backside tensed as I considered all that heat attracting these two deadly Machines up our jet-pipes.

Uniquely, the operator kept radar control of missiles 5 and 6 for much longer than their predecessors. He really did know his stuff. When he switched over to the missiles' internal infrared homing system, he obviously thought that they could not possibly miss. For that matter, so did I. The point of changeover was clearly signalled by their phugoid wiggle[3] as they first searched and almost immediately found our 'scent'.

The visual difference I detected was infinitesimally small, but to me nevertheless, terrifying. Whereas when the operator had control Missile 5 seemed to be pointing at the Falcon's nose, with Missile 6 pointing somewhere amidships, after giving them both control of the final stages 5 still pointed at the nose but 6 shifted to a new aiming point, which appeared to be my head. Something would definitely have to be done about that, when the time was right.

I remembered Ralph Magnus's tactics imparted around the inglenook fireplace of the *Lamb and Lark* a long time ago, but he always talked of single missiles. Facing a salvo of two missiles close together compounded the tactics considerably. As Ralph's *moment critique* of the black dot drew ever closer, Missile 5's aiming point lifted imperceptibly. 'It's tracking to go above us,' I announced – which meant

---

[3] *See* Diagram on p.135

absolutely nothing to the other crew members, who could see nothing of the deadly threat. I had manoeuvred us into a relative position where only I could see the evil beasts.

Ready to do some of Ralph's 'haul-arsing round the sky' to avoid the now more deadly Missile 6, my inbuilt cerebral computer indicated that during the manoeuvre there would be a possibility of the Falcon's relatively sluggish flight manoeuvrability at this altitude ballooning me into Missile 5.

Milliseconds before the time for life or death action arrived, I resolved the dilemma of the proximity of Missile 5 by deciding to ignore it completely. I reasoned that it was now probably destined to miss and the chances of arranging a mid-air collision with a hypersonic telegraph pole at 37,000 feet were negligible, but Missile 6 was now definitely shaping to hit and would need exactly the correct response for anyone to live longer than the next couple of seconds. By now I had descended down to 37,000 feet by sacrificing height for speed, without any engine power. Speed would be needed for the aerobatic manoeuvre that I intended to use in the final analysis.

My thanks should go here to the Marcel Dassault factory test pilot who demonstrated to me exactly what the Fan-Jet Falcon could do if pushed, and I proposed to push – or more accurately 'pull' –the old girl into the tightest positive-G vertical turn that any Falcon had ever done at 37,000 feet, even risking an involuntary spin[4] in the process.

Missile 5's track took its climb angle ever higher relative to us and it was quite clear that my reduction of infrared by throttling back as soon as the SAMs were identified had paid off. However, Missile 6 was tenacious and its plume of exhaust gas angled towards my head with any small change of relative position, as its shimmering circle grew larger by the second. I was quite clear as to my next action and icy cool in its contemplation. My whole world hinged on judging the proximity of that rocket with absolute accuracy. There is no textbook available to help, no rehearsal or practice to perfect the tactics, just Ralph's pictorial description of 'Haul-arse towards it as if your very life depends on it.' His smooth Southern drawl rang in my ears as my eyes were transfixed, seeking out that dark centre-spot in the circle of angry gas.

Ralph's F-4 Phantom could do the haul-arsing at 10 or 11 G, but my Falcon was designed for more sedate usage and would be lucky to reach 4 G even *in extremis* – which was where we surely were. Even 4 G would be tricky at 37,000 feet. My speed was now .85 Mach and too harsh use of the elevator would

---

[4] The flight condition of an aircraft in a nose-down, spiralling, stalled descent.

produce an unstable supersonic shockwave on the top surface of the wing leading to a 'Mach stall'; this would be tricky to handle and slow the rate of turn, leaving us a sitting duck. The doubts jostled round the brain interminably, but eventually I realized that I would feel the buffet signifying the onset of the shockwave and should be able to guide the Falcon round the tightest possible turn by riding the burble just prior to full buffet. I was ready.

As predicted, the white gas plume grew to about ten times its original diameter and the dreaded black dot appeared in its centre – very small at first, perhaps no bigger that a pinhead, but rapidly becoming more positive. This was the Semtex warhead that contained the means of our destruction just beneath its carbon fibre covers and it was as close as I needed it. Missile 5 was still above, but very near.

My brain directed my muscles to move, but for a millisecond I seemed to be paralysed. A supreme effort eventually broke the frozen arms and to my great relief they functioned normally. Down went the port wing and back came the control column. Careful to maintain positive G, I felt the pre-buffet burble quite early, but found that I could ride it without inducing the full stall, and our angular movement across the sky was most impressive. We really were 'haul-arsing' towards the missile at a high rate of knots, but the rocket seemed to be starting to cut the corner on our maximum-G turn. Now I could see the whole missile, or certainly its small wings, when – wonder of wonders – a small sonic shockwave jumped up and was clearly visible in a mid position on one of those wings. Its turn towards us immediately stopped.

I was elated at the sight. This small shockwave indicated clearly to me that the missile's control surface – the wings – had either stalled, or was about to, thereby preventing the SAM changing its direction rapidly enough towards us to activate any of its three different fuses. Meanwhile we were turning beautifully out of harm's way, albeit vertically downwards – but that could be corrected all in good time. Things were happening in microseconds now and for a split second I had the vision of the nose of the missile to the starboard side of the cockpit simultaneously with its tail on the port side. Just as I realized that it was therefore very close indeed, an earth-shattering explosion rocked the Falcon and I momentarily lost control. Everyone aboard except me thought that the missile's warhead had exploded, but I knew otherwise.

If the Semtex had been activated at that close range, we would all have been descending earthwards, feeling quite chilly (if any feeling still remained – the air outside the Falcon was −50°C), but more probably in small pieces. No, what had actually happened was that as the missile passed close to us the hypersonic shockwaves from the rocket's main body had hit the fuselage an almighty swipe and had given us the full benefit of its thunderous hypersonic boom. I regarded the massive explosion as a most welcome last goodbye as Missile 6, the most dangerous Chariot of Death, disappeared to heaven knows where in an instant.

As I extended the airbrakes to arrest the dive earthwards and regain control, my search of the sky produced no sign of the unholy twins – the sky was eerily clear of any threat. I wanted to relax, and remember feeling exhausted, but relaxation was impossible. Now I had to anticipate the reaction of the brains of those who were determined to terminate us. They had expended a fortune, perhaps as much as £12 million sterling, to achieve our violent demise and had, so far, failed. I could not believe that they would just give up and let us escape after all their efforts, so I had to devise a survival plan.

It was possible, even probable, that I had just eluded the last missile battery to the south-west of Cairo; after all, these were very expensive toys and Egypt's finances were quite limited. Their major concentration of SAM defences would be central and to the east, between the capital and Israel, because the Israeli F-16s suffered from short range, without flight refuelling, so the cover on this back-door sector would be a lesser priority. Having used the Egyptian Air Traffic Control facilities on numerous occasions I was fully aware that their detailed radar coverage of this south-westerly area was very patchy.

In fact some areas of this part of the Sahara enjoyed no radar coverage whatsoever. Just as important was my knowledge that the minimal radar they did possess was never, or very rarely, able to detect an aircraft's altitude with any accuracy. To add to their problems of knowing our exact position I pulled the circuit breaker on the Falcon's squawk box[5], which was already switched off, as I wanted to ensure that nobody in the cockpit made the error of accidentally switching it back on again.

Anyone seeking to destroy us would, I was sure, expect us, as a civil aircraft, to fly along the normal airways that civil passenger aircraft almost invariably use, but the nearest airway back west to Libya was over a hundred nautical miles north of our actual position. We were approaching the Qattara Depression, a morass of soft fine running sand where, as Generals Montgomery and Rommel found during the Second World War, vehicles and machinery disappeared without trace. I resolved to avoid contact with this dreaded area, knowing that my erstwhile enemies would love to bury the evidence of flight LN999 deep in its inaccessible wasteland.

Allowing for our dire circumstances and using the dictum that the shortest

---

[5] The device used to assist ground controllers follow an aircraft's track on their radar screens.

distance between two points is normally (but not always) a straight line, I decided to hold a course direct for Tobruk, the nearest friendly airfield, now about 300 nautical miles away. Throughout these mental gymnastics my hand and brain were automatically adjusting the power to give us best speed without running out of fuel. I was hurtling westwards towards escape and away from the mighty military machine intent on my destruction.

Threat evaluation was difficult with no outside intelligence assistance available, but being familiar with this area I could work on several probabilities. If they had any more SAM installations to the west, they would certainly use more SAM IIs to attack us, but at our current altitude of 40,000 feet I would hope to pick them up, as before, with our keen visual lookout. Anti-aircraft fire would be useless at this altitude so could be completely ignored.

However, one threat that could not be ignored was the airborne fighter threat. If I was correct and there were no more Egyptian ground missile batteries between us and Libya, the hundred or more Egyptian MIGs and Sukhois within range would be free to operate against us. I was fully aware of the quality of this aspect of the threat, because I knew some of their senior pilots and respected their undoubted capability of removing us from the sky with the minimum of fuss. Naïvely I hoped that our past friendship would be strong enough to prevent them launching their air-to-air missiles up our jet pipes, but in truth I was fully aware that if the generals ordered our immediate destruction, the young pilots would have no option but to carry out the execution. If I could have found their fighter control frequency I might have pleaded for my life, but the chances of us stumbling on such a secret frequency by flicking through the channels would be infinitesimally small.

Hopes for our survival hung on three things: firstly, complete radio silence on our part, to avoid giving away our actual position via their many radio direction finding stations; secondly, by avoiding the civil airways we were giving our hunters a massive area of sky in which to find us visually; thirdly, most of their MIGs and Sukhois would undoubtedly be loaded with bombs destined for Israel at this aggressive stage of the war, so removing the bombs and replacing them with the air-to-air missiles that would be needed to kill our high-flying Falcon would take time, perhaps enough time for us to make good our escape.

I could just visualize the chaos they would be suffering. Some senior genius back in Cairo would have to guess our actual position. When he had decided where we might be, based on my last transmission, and that we were returning to friendly Libyan airspace, he would need to contact the commanding officers of all suitable airfields with the right type of fighters, ascertain their squadrons' readiness for flight and their weapon loads, and order the bombs to be removed from the 'ready use' aircraft.

Then, the one man with the key to the armoury where the air-to-air missiles were stored would have to be located – he might even be enjoying an afternoon siesta. When located and transport was found to take a team to the armoury, it might be discovered that the only suitable missiles for this type of action were still in their locked storage containers, as they had arrived from Moscow. Fifteen minutes later, when the packaging had been removed and the fuse covers taken off, there might even be a cry of dismay as everyone realized that all the weapon trolleys needed to transport the heavy missiles to their latest state-of-the-art fighters were full of bombs just taken off the aircraft – by which time we could be across the Libyan border. This was all, of course, wishful thinking, but interlaced with banks of experience absorbed in many hours working around the Egyptian military organization.

As my mind was becoming more embroiled in this 'What if' stage, I felt a sharp tap on my right shoulder and quickly looked round to see the Foreign Minister's face half an inch away from my nose. He seemed to be in some distress and kept repeating, 'Thank you, thank you!' As I half-turned round to make some response he grabbed my shoulders and gave me a peremptory hug. It was not a totally successful manoeuvre as I was still firmly strapped into the Captain's seat, there was little space and he was a stocky man. However, I understood that he was pleased to be alive, so far – as indeed were we all.

He discussed the explosion that had occurred as the last missile passed our Falcon and questioned why we had not disintegrated and fallen out of the sky. I told him that the warhead had not exploded. When I explained that we had been struck by its hypersonic shock wave he seemed reluctant to believe that such a massive explosion could be caused without activating the Semtex. He enquired what fuses the SAM II possessed to activate the warhead and I explained that its primary fuse was positioned behind two strengthened glass windows about three metres apart along the missile body. When the target's image passed the first window its computer noted the time until it was seen by the second window. If the time was short enough to indicate that the missile was near enough to destroy its target, it activated the full force of the warhead. Alternatively if the time interval was too great, the missile would realize that it was out of lethal range and the warhead would fail to detonate.

The second and third fuses I explained were both contact operated. The leading edges of all four of its wings were fitted with a type of pyrotechnic chord which caused the warhead's explosion with the slightest knock and its nose-cone had a similar arrangement, so if the missile physically struck the target, which was its prime aim, the collision would activate total destruction of the combined machines. By this time he looked bewildered and somewhat terrified so I neglected to explain that the visual fuse behind the two windows was highly sensitive to sunlight and its critical chemical coatings were destroyed by prolonged exposure to the sun's rays. The Russian manufacturers, therefore, constructed covers to keep these windows in the dark when the missiles were in their ready-use positions out in the field, or in this particular case, the desert. These important covers were held in place by substantial rubber straps, but unless these straps were regularly checked and religiously changed when faulty, they simply fell off when the elastic perished and this part of the fusing mechanism rapidly became inoperative.

It was my firm belief that Missile 6 was, in fact, close enough for this primary fuse to have operated, but it failed to explode. I believe that this failure was caused by premature sunlight penetration onto its sensitive surfaces, probably as a result of malfunctioning or non-existent protection whilst in the outdoor readiness state – or perhaps Ra had intervened again!

I continued to outline the actions that I was attempting to take in the hope of our eventual survival, and quickly covered the potential remaining threats to our continued enjoyment of life. He understood most aspects pretty well and exhorted me to be most careful, as my proposed track would take us over three Libyan SAM II sites en route. I assured him that I would avoid overflying them until we had been given full clearance from Tobruk. He returned to his seat and told the other passengers of our situation in rapid staccato Arabic that betrayed his acute concern.

On normal flights we occasionally listened to the news programmes of the BBC Overseas Service, because they often provided us with amplified details of the actual flight that we were undertaking. The senior passenger would always tell us our destination clearly, but sometimes this was merely the first stop in a more complex long-distance flight. It needed some detective work on our part to deduce the ramifications of the whole flight. The BBC often filled in the details for us, which was helpful to enable us to plan our domestic arrangements and deduce the security problems that we were likely to face. At this point the Co-pilot reminded me that a news broadcast was about to commence, so we listened to the words of wisdom. These BBC news broadcasts also enabled our families back in Tripoli to follow our progress when official details were somewhat sparse.

One of the headlines announced that the Israeli Air Force had mounted an air bombardment of central Cairo. Later it amplified this statement by stating that its Cairo correspondent had reported that a series of six huge rockets had hit central Cairo, resulting in massive damage to buildings and substantial resultant loss of life. These enormous explosions occurred at the exact time that the SAM IIs and anti-aircraft fire were being directed at our Falcon and were obviously our six SAMs, their fuel exhausted, returning to earth at high speed under the pull of gravity. We later discovered that no Israeli aircraft was involved in hostile activities over Cairo that particular day. These days, the incident would be reported as 'friendly fire', or blue on blue, but in the 1970s nobody was that specific.

The clear blue sky still remained empty as we powered towards Tobruk from the south-east, at 40,000 feet, the pristine yellow sand of the Sahara seeming to ripple like wavelets on the surface of the sea, almost eight miles below. As the Libyan border and salvation grew ever nearer – now less than 100 nautical miles, or about ten minutes' flying time ahead – four contrails appeared in the sky about 100 miles to the north, and quite close to the civil airway. The angle of the contrails indicated that they were climbing rapidly on a westerly track and their position was almost exactly where we would have been had we been flying in or towards the airway.

With very good cause, I assumed that these came from four Egyptian fighters, probably looking for us, and if I had seen them from their contrails it was essential that I was not producing any myself. An immediate wide weave confirmed that my tail was clean so I decided to maintain altitude to avoid revealing my position with a contrail.

The meteorological entropy needed to produce a contrail from an aircraft's exhaust is quite specific to particular altitudes, which alter throughout the day. During wartime this absolute giveaway of position is so important that it is covered daily at the Met briefing prior to all military flights, and pilots write the details down on their kneepads for reference throughout the flight. Civil pilots ignore their contrails as unimportant, but today was an exception for me. If a contrail escaped from my jet pipe, I would be a dead duck.

My speed was now .9 Mach, whereas the fighters whose contrails I had just seen were likely to be moving supersonically at about 1.4 Mach. Any faster – they were capable of 2.2 Mach – would burn their fuel too rapidly and they would have insufficient range to reach me. They, therefore, had a realistic closing speed of about .5 Mach, allowing for the angles involved. Their airborne radar was useless at this range, while their ground radar, I knew, was very patchy and without height definition in this area.

If they anticipated my tactics and turned south to intercept a possible position, they could only close at about five miles per minute, so for them to arrive within air-to-air missile firing range would take a minimum of 18 minutes.

However, there could still be other fighters closer to my position that had been clever enough to remain outside the contrail layer and could catch this particular rabbit before it reached its burrow. No time for complacency. I must remain invisible for as long as possible, so no use of the radio and no descent into the contrail layer were, for the moment, vital.

Another important decision point was approaching and had to be faced within the next few minutes. My efforts, so far, had been directed to reaching friendly Libyan airspace, and that was now a realistic possibility, but could I be certain that pursuing Egyptian fighters would not continue over the border in hot pursuit? If the roles had been reversed and I had been the hunter instead of the hunted, I would have been very tempted to continue a few miles over the border, despite the possibility of diplomatic and military repercussions.

As the seemingly unattainable border eventually drew closer my heartbeat increased rather than the expected decrease. I suddenly remembered a visit to the Tobruk radar installation months before where one of the proud technicians boasted to me of its hi-tech capabilities and superior range, and I realized that these facilities were actually on my side, not against me, and could provide invaluable help at this moment. With that in mind I broke my self-imposed radio silence on Tobruk's main frequency.

It gave me intense relief when Mustafa, an old friend, answered loud and clear and called me Neville. That was nothing really significant, but somehow it succeeded in bringing tears to my eyes. I outlined our predicament, probable position and altitude, asked for radar assistance and requested clearance to overfly Tobruk's missile batteries en route to the airfield. He seemed surprised by my multitude of requests and replied something like 'As Lima November 999, you can do anything you wish at a Libyan airfield. We're ready for you to land immediately.'

Radar came on the same frequency and assured me that the sky in the immediate area was clear of any other aircraft. I said that we would like it to remain that way and asked him to pay particular attention to my tail and the positions of any Egyptian fighters. His response was significant to me. He told us that the nearest Egyptian Fighters, four Sukhoi 22s, were 78 nautical miles north-east of us near the coast and that they appeared to have set up a search pattern of some kind at 35,000 feet. I was incredulous when my request for the Libyan radar operator to watch those four attack fighters, and report any indication that they were closing our position, brought the response that LN999 was now in Libyan airspace and therefore safe. I commented that although we were 15 nautical miles inside Libyan territory, following our recent experiences I could take nothing for granted. At max speed these aircraft were three minutes' flying time from our position and my turn north, towards Tobruk, served to decrease that separation – with their air-to-air missiles boasting a kill range of over 20 nautical miles I would be vulnerable until touchdown.

An army officer who identified himself as the Commanding Officer of ground-to-air missiles made a brief appearance on the radio with the assurance that all Libyan missiles were set to safe and that we were clear to transit the area to the south of Nasser airfield. As I glanced at the ground 20 miles north, the runways of Tobruk came into view.

I had first landed on that main runway as a new aircraft-carrier pilot in a Sea Hawk of 802 Squadron, Fleet Air Arm, in 1959, having earlier been catapulted off HMS *Eagle* north of Crete. One of the pilots in our sister Squadron 898 distinguished himself that day by bursting a tyre on landing, whereupon he shot off sideways into the sand at great speed. All efforts to recover the hapless fighter out of the deep sand only succeeded in pulling more pieces off its exterior. First the nose-wheel and oleo leg parted company with the aircraft, followed by the port main wheel assembly, and after one of the RAF recovery vehicles skidded into the side of the fuselage, it was decided to remove all the useable components and leave the remainder of the plane to the tender mercies of the desert winds. Today, a mound of sand marks the spot, between the two runways where she lies and if the sun is not too hot and one is feeling energetic, it is possible to collect a memento or two from the discarded body of one of the Royal Navy's first carrier jet fighters. I remember the crash pilot's name very well, but to save his blushes I will keep stumm as 'there, but for the grace of God, go I', or to be truthful, any of our merry band of aviators. It is worth noting that this particular young man eventually went on to become one Britain's top test pilots, responsible for pushing the frontiers of aviation forward and preparing the way for eventual space flight.

With life promising to return to some sort of normality shortly and with precision radars and their operators watching my tail for a change, I felt secure to surrender the relative safety of our lofty perch eight miles up in the heavens and make a dash for the tarmac. Throttles closed, airbrakes out and down we went, careless of the contrail position and with a modicum of confidence seeping back into my sinews. A glance at co-pilot and flight engineer proclaimed two very happy bunnies, each smiling uncontrollably from ear to ear. At 10,000 feet and ten miles out, lined up with the runway we were given clearance for a straight-in approach. A short burst of engine power confirmed the health of both engines and after thorough pre-landing checks we slid onto the long runway and taxied to the control tower.

As the engine noise slowly subsided I was aware of more people than usual for a desert airfield walking towards us out of the control tower. At the bottom of the Falcon's steps the Foreign Minister made to shake my hand, but pulled me bodily towards him for a sincere bear hug and kisses on both cheeks. There followed words of appreciation and thanks, but in all honesty they were lost in the overwhelming relief that was flooding over me. The rest of the passengers lined up to shake my hand in turn and everyone else seemed to be talking at once. With difficulty I broke free from the babble and slowly walked round the outside of Falcon 5A-DAG, half expecting some signs of damage, but there was none to be seen. I had asked these engines and this airframe for 110 per cent of its maximum capability, and it had delivered without a quibble. Without their extra performance, we would all surely be dead. I wanted to give it a hug, but it was too big so I settled for an affectionate stroke on its gleaming white body and when nobody was able to see me, a heartfelt kiss!

Subsequent detailed examination of the engines and other sensitive elements of 5A-DAG showed that no part of the aeroplane had suffered any stress damage whatsoever. This was, to me, an amazing result because I had asked that beautiful Machine to perform beyond most of its design parameters and if it had not answered my call in full, the stark truth is that we would not have survived. The Falcon's performance during the battle spoke eloquent volumes testifying to its superb design and manufacture. I could not have wished for more, except perhaps for one of my old Sea Vixens to enable me to fight back effectively, while a touch of supersonics would have been very useful at some of the critical stages of the conflict.

After a short pause for breath Dick dropped the engine panels to check all the oil levels as normal, and eventually conducted a minute examination of all critical components to satisfy himself of 5A-DAG's fitness to carry us safely back home to our families in Tripoli. Meanwhile, Major el Houni and I climbed up into the glasshouse on top of Tobruk's control tower where we found that our fame had spread and every radio seemed to be demanding attention. I left the diplomatic questions to the Foreign Minister to debate with the great and the good, seemingly from every known ministry, embassy and country one could imagine. I dealt with the technical details, mostly in answer to the authorities of the Civil Aviation world, but the Libyan President and Prime Minister's offices demanded answers to a multitude of detailed questions.

As the questioning was showing signs of moderating, a Libyan Air Force Lockheed C-130 called for permission to land. He parked alongside our Falcon and the young Libyan Air Force pilot arrived in the control tower with more than average agility. I was astonished when he told me that he had orders to collect my passengers and take them on to Cairo. I expressed my severe misgivings, saying that he must be very brave, and advised him to check first with the Foreign Minister, who impressed me as having the look of a man who had experienced more than enough excitement for one day and perhaps for his entire lifetime.

He proceeded to quiz me about the actual details of the Egyptian military's efforts to blast us out of the sky and I gave him the details as truthfully as I was able. He became quite agitated and his eyes seemed to grow wider and wider as the facts were revealed. I told him that I was an ex-fighter pilot, that my Falcon was infinitely more manoeuvrable than his heavy Hercules transport and that if he had faced a similar attack he would certainly be dead by now. He became visibly worried and quite shaken and asked me for my opinion on what action he should take. I advised him to contact his superiors at headquarters to inform them of the severity of the current threat and ask for a reappraisal of his orders.

He lifted the red military telephone and somewhat heatedly informed whoever was on the other end, using both Arabic and English, of the relevant facts. Surprisingly, he suddenly handed the telephone to me and I found myself talking to Colonel Ferjani, the head of the Libyan Air Force. He understood the situation quite quickly, confirming my assessment of the severity of the battle and sending his heartfelt congratulations at our survival. Half jokingly, I think, he offered me a job at many times my then current salary to become a weapons instructor with his air force. I politely refused his offer, but the thought of getting my hands on the latest Russian MIGs, Sukhois and Tupolevs was extremely tempting for someone who was always a rip-shit fighter jockey at heart.

When the young C-130 pilot returned to the telephone to talk respectfully to his commanding officer his face changed and he looked visibly relieved, but I was baffled when he left the tower saying that he was still going to Cairo. It did not make sense. I watched as he and my ex-passengers climbed aboard his mighty, ponderous beast. When his voice confidently requested take-off clearance I could not resist taking the microphone and wishing him the best of good fortune – he responded with his thanks for all my information.

It was time for us to go home. Fuelling complete, we filed our flight plan and LN 999 was cleared all the way to Tripoli International, with no restrictions. As we settled onto the civil airway at about 42,000 feet, I detected a slight catch in the voice of Stu, our young co-pilot, as he talked to Tobruk control. When I glanced at him he seemed to be quite stressed, which surprised me at the time, but on reflection that assessment was unreasonable. He had had to endure extreme trauma over the past two and a half hours, with imminent violent death zipping past our aircraft at intervals and a seemingly demented captain wopping the controls around as if he was flying a single-seat fighter. To make matters worse, the captain had hogged the radio and navigation duties, which would normally be the co-pilot's prerogative when the captain was flying the aircraft, so he had been left with very little responsibility or activity to occupy his mind. Of course he was stressed. In the circumstances it would have been surprising if he had not been.

A Falcon 20 on a ferry leg without passengers, fitted with Omega navigation coupled to the autopilot, must be the easiest civil aircraft to fly – having a crew of two experienced aviators was a total luxury. It could easily be flown safely by the captain alone so I told the co-pilot that he could go and relax in one of the comfy armchairs back in the cabin and enjoy one of our excellent VIP meals that Dick had been saving for an opportune moment. He agreed and after settling him down with his meal and a fresh coffee, Dick came up to the cockpit to keep me company. As we approached Benghazi, far below us, their control tower asked me to call the C-130 which had left Tobruk with our former passengers, as all radio contact with them had been lost.

I did as requested. Because VHF radio is line-of-sight, if there is ever any radio-range difficulty the highest radio station always manages much longer ranges than fixed installations on the ground. Considering my recent conversation with the young Hercules pilot, and visualizing him getting the same reception as me, fighting his way into Cairo, I called his call sign with some trepidation in my voice. He cheerfully replied immediately to my transmission and I informed him that radio contact with him had been lost for the previous twenty minutes. He responded that I should tell Benghazi that his radio had failed; he had decided to return to Tripoli and would be landing at Okba in about thirty-five minutes.

I relayed his message and then it dawned on me that he was talking a heap of rubbish. If he had indeed had a radio failure, how on earth was he talking clearly to me – if he had flown east to Cairo from Tobruk, as stated, how had he managed to travel nearly 1,000 nautical miles west to Tripoli instead? Then I recalled the smile on his face as he finished talking to his headquarters. Something had obviously been cooked up on the telephone, to which I was not privy, but it was very reassuring to find him and his/our passengers still alive and cheerful.

Flying the Falcon back empty from Tobruk to Tripoli was very routine and not especially demanding, so I failed to stop my mind trying to figure out the reason for the attack upon us. A decision to kill the Foreign Minister of a neighbouring country could not have been taken lightly and would certainly not have been a spur-of-the-moment whim. I was now fairly certain that the person speaking to me on the telephone at Mersa Matruh had not been President Sadat as he claimed, but that a complex deception was in progress culminating in our unwanted rendezvous over the Great Pyramid of Pharaoh Khufu at 16,000 feet, with the first two deadly missiles.

The best theory that I could come up with on the flight home went back to a flight that we had made to Luxor in southern Egypt with a very astute Libyan Minister of Communications, Mr Sharif Ben Amer, accompanied by Mr Hosni Mubarak, the Egyptian Deputy President, about a month previously. On the ground at the military base was a recently delivered squadron of Libyan Dassault Mirage F1s. Their pilots, many of whom I knew, told me that they were on a combat evaluation exercise with the Egyptian Air Force carrying out mock attacks, opposed by the Egyptian MIGs and Sukhois. It was significant that they were operating from Luxor because it was out of range of Israel and could therefore not be construed as aggressive posturing.

Though these highly effective and expensive Libyan fighters were never used in the October War then in progress, they were in fact effectively trapped by the surprise declaration of war by the Egyptians, on the wrong side of the Libyan border, and at some stage may well have become an inadvertent target of the Israelis' longer-range bombers.

Libya did not agree with Egypt's rationale, nor indeed the tactics being employed in this risky conflict and wanted no part of it, but Colonel Ferjani could see that his fighters, though not active in the war, could nevertheless be at risk of violent destruction. At over £25 million per Mirage F1, Libya's eighteen aircraft sitting at Luxor represented more than £450 million worth of Libyan property, a sizeable part of its inventory – not to mention the thirty or more highly trained aircrew which the Air Force Commander- in-Chief could ill afford to lose.

It is my considered opinion that Major el Houni's mission to Cairo that day was to engineer the release of Libya's valuable fighters trapped at Luxor. I also believe that Egyptian intelligence had somehow been informed of this fact and some military genius possibly reasoned that if the Libyan Foreign Minister inexplicably disappeared en route, the Egyptians could subsequently make use of Libya's fighters, should it become necessary, later in the war. I have no proof of this theory whatsoever, but it is not entirely speculation, rather it is the result of my piecing together many seemingly disconnected scraps of information remembered from conversations with senior Libyans, both civil and military, and some Egyptians over the preceding few weeks.

About two months later, after the war, I was strolling round the Cairo airport dispersal outside the VIP lounge, with President Sadat, who was looking resplendent in his official finery. I took the opportunity of asking him why the Egyptians had fired six SAM II missiles and various anti-aircraft hardware at me during the recent war as I tried, with full permission, to land at Cairo airport. He stopped abruptly, turned to face me, placed his left hand loosely on my right shoulder and looked me straight in the eye. He said, 'Captain, please accept my sincere apologies for that regrettable mistake. The situation here, at the time, was very complicated and very political. I promise to tell you the full truth, but it is too soon for me to talk about the complex military position that led to that incident. I repeat, I do promise that you will be told the full story.' I thanked him, and confirmed with him that he did not, in fact, speak to me on the telephone whilst we were at Mersa Matruh that day. As I suspected, that was a hoax, and hence part of the original ambush. He grinned afterwards and said words to the effect that he and his senior officers thought that I had been a very skilled aviator that day and deserved to survive. My response was to confirm that I very nearly did not escape; unfortunately, I could not produce a smile.

President Sadat was assassinated on 6 October 1981, whilst reviewing a huge military parade, without having the opportunity of divulging to me the real reason for the notorious missile attack. My only hope now of discovering the real truth behind that horrendous day lies with the present Egyptian President, Mr Hosni Mubarak, whom I must try to meet again if at all possible, before any chance of confirming the truth disappears.

As we approached Tripoli International Airport the radio frequencies we used were full of other pilots congratulating us on our escape from Cairo, though I had no idea how the information had been publicized or by whom. It was evening by the time we taxied into Special Flight's dispersal and the warm desert night that enveloped us as we stepped down from 5A-DAG seemed the sweeter with the recollection that despite everything they had thrown at us, we were still alive. The feeling of well-being was accentuated by the knowledge that the three of us would shortly be home with our families and able to relax and forget the horrors of that particularly grim day.

As Dick busied himself with his tasks of post-flight inspections and topping up the various oil levels, I realized that he was talking almost incessantly, asking permission to carry out tasks that would normally be automatic and needed no permission. The dreaded stress had set in once more. As I drove home along the dual carriageway from the airport I decided that there was very little that could be done by me to lessen my two compatriots' severe tensions. That was, most definitely, their wives' prerogative. I did my best to relax the atmosphere by pointing out to them the clarity of the brightly lit stars, naming the ones with which I was familiar and the ones that were useful for celestial navigation. Whatever they may have thought, it was the only neutral subject I could muster and provided a constantly changing picture to contemplate.

We arrived at the captains' small block of four flats almost automatically, and

I invited my other crew members to join Lesley and myself for a quick drink. It seemed the natural thing to do after the intensity of our recent experiences. A little inadequate in retrospect, but intended to appear as a small 'thank you' for accompanying me to the fringes of death without complaint or comment. As I turned to open my front door at the top of the first flight of stairs I could see Lesley was actually coming out to invite us all in – she stood in front of a table spread with liquid hospitality and her body language was clearly welcoming. Before I could enter, however, the Chief Pilot's door opposite burst open and Terry Danby grabbed my arm and hauled me inside his flat. 'Tell me all,' he said, once I was over the threshold.

It seemed that the Foreign Ministry had contacted him and stated that a dreadful incident had befallen us en route to Cairo, but that no details were then available. So calmly – or as calmly as I could – I related the events of the day. As the story unfolded his face became as white as a newly laundered sheet. Without any words he handed me a nicely chilled brandy and ginger ale and we sat there for a while. I think it would be described as cogitating. After a few minutes I excused myself and walked across the hallway to my own flat, still grasping Terry's half empty libation in my right hand.

Lesley's reception as I walked through the open doorway was especially enthusiastic and took me by surprise, but I had the clear impression that she was very pleased to see me, which was nice. My other two crew members were a good way through their second drink when I arrived and the speed that Dick had related events – was, in fact, still relating events – had left Lesley quite confused. As I closed the door behind me Dick announced loudly, evidently for the third time, 'If we had had any other pilot but Neville, we would all now be dead,' and a small tear rolled down his cheek. Seeing that tear really affected me and for the first time I could feel my throat choking up – I think that the enormity of what we had all endured had finally sunk in.

Lesley could see the signs of stress and topped up my drink as normally as possible, tactfully hinting that the other two wives would be anxious as some warning of serious problems had been given to them earlier. They agreed, finished their drinks quickly and descended the marble stairs still talking loudly to each other.

As the door closed behind them Lesley asked, 'Is it true?' Not having had the benefit of Dick's dissertation, I replied, 'Probably.' It sounded dreadful, she said, and for some totally incomprehensible reason the tears started to run down my cheeks in a deluge. I attempted to speak, but the words refused to come out in any intelligible order, so I sat in my favourite armchair and just stared into the middle distance for a while. Eventually as we picked at a buffet supper, I related the day's events as casually as possible. Lesley later told me that I was obviously still 'stressed off my little twig', whereas I had the impression that I was handling the whole drama nonchalantly.

In the circumstances an early night seemed to be in order and lots of TLC formed a large part of my anticipation, but sleep intervened all too quickly and I awoke late to find my aviation services were needed once more.

CHAPTER FIVE

Straight to Jail – Without Passing 'Go'

Tucking into a healthy breakfast of iced sugar melon and fresh peaches, for which Libya is justly famous, followed by toast and a soft-boiled egg, Lesley related the activity that had transpired whilst I slept. Evidently she had taken a telephone call earlier from the President's office requesting that as duty captain I fly to Uganda in the late afternoon to collect President Idi Amin and take him to Riyadh in Saudi Arabia for a meeting with King Faisal. Shortly afterwards Terry had come in from his flat across the hall and volunteered to take this flight to allow me to relax and play some tennis.

'No, no!' replied Lesley. 'This flight would be perfect for Neville.' Similar to falling off a horse, the sooner one gets back on again to recover one's confidence, the better. Terry replied that she could be right, but that I should be left to sleep as long as possible as the late start probably meant us flying most of the night – little did they know that by midnight the crew and I would be incarcerated in prison cells in one of the most vicious countries in the whole of Africa. Thanks a bunch!

The Chief Engineer said that we should take the second Falcon, 5A-DAF, to allow them to carry out a thorough stress test on DAG after its previous day's pounding over Cairo. I suggested that he might like to 'stress test' the aircrew at the same time, but the remark fell on deaf ears.

It was a very pleasant prospect, flying deep into equatorial Africa, with the aircraft to ourselves and without a party of VIPs needing to be mollycoddled en route. These flights usually took less time because they could be completed without any involvement with diplomats and their inevitable protocol. The huge orange ball of the sun was balanced on the western horizon as we slid smoothly into the evening sky to the first refuelling stop at the desert fortress of Sebha. Climbing up to our allotted 30,000-foot cruising altitude we again noticed a strange phenomenon that always intrigued me – seeing the sun rising in the heavens as we climbed and by the time we throttled back into the cruise, returning to its afternoon position. The sun appeared to be rising in the western sky in the evening, whereas everyone expects it to behave conventionally and rise in the east in the morning, setting in the west in the evening. This apparent reversal of established fact was simply due to our increasing altitude, as any smart mathematician would readily appreciate.

The scene below us, though entirely familiar, was nevertheless fascinating. As the panorama of the brightly lit Sahara Desert unfolded before us in all directions, the position of the sun exaggerated the surface irregularities with heavy brushstrokes of shadow and the visibility appeared to be almost limitless. To the west, on our right, lay the escarpment of low hills stretching out past the fabled city of Timbuktu (known to the Bedouin Tuaregs as *Tombouctou*, the City of Gold) towards the Atlantic Ocean. This land was historically occupied by the Berber, Tuareg and Tebu peoples.

The Berbers were the direct descendants of the feared Barbary Pirates who terrorized the seas as far away as Cornwall, Devon and Dorset, where they raided the coastal villages for centuries, capturing thousands of English slaves for the harems and slave markets of Tunisia, Algeria, Morocco and Mauritania. This unholy terror was inflicted on European coastlines in the sixteenth and seventeenth centuries, hundreds of years before African slaves started to be transported across the Atlantic to America and the Caribbean, and is frequently overlooked by commentators on the savagery of later African slavery.

To the south, which was our route, lay a veritable ocean of sharp-topped yellow sand dunes interspersed with ripples that could easily be mistaken for the surface of a calm sea, with occasional gentle breezes ruffling the surface. Irregular patches of nasty stones, about 200 to 400 mm in size, occasionally appeared to litter the ground in groups of about 200 square metres. These were the natural traps that had ensnared Rommel and Montgomery's light armoured vehicles in 1942, as they grappled for supremacy during the Second World War.

To the left the sand, generally flat, could be seen to be interspersed with a low-growing scrub, rather like the tumbleweed beloved of the cowboys and Indian movie producers. The dead clumps rolled over the desert until they eventually gathered against some obstruction, but the live patches generally seemed, from 30,000 feet, to be an organized crop of something or other. Experience had, however, warned us that these apparent 'crops' were nasty prickly little things, of use to nothing except possibly the desert goats. These hardy creatures seemingly ate anything they found littering the ground, with apparent pleasure.

As we progressed steadily southwards the terrain underwent a subtle change. Amongst the sand dunes, interspersed with rippling flatter areas, large rocks protruded out of the desert floor. Far ahead of the Falcon, on the horizon, it was just possible to make out a substantial building on top of the biggest of these obviously volcanic remnants. Alongside, to the west of the construction, was an incongruous-looking massive straight line of lights, orientated in a north-south direction. As we got closer it became clear that the line was the long runway at Sebha, which was almost three miles long and so wide that some light aircraft could take off comfortably across its width.

The building that first attracted our long-distant attention was actually a substantial fort that had been expanded by the French Foreign Legion from an old Turkish construction in the late nineteenth century and was intermittently garrisoned by the Legion up to the various battles with the Italians around 1911, prior to the commencement of the desert war in 1939. It was a very imposing structure that clearly commanded a huge area of relatively flat desert. The impressive castle-like building, whose twinkling lights emphasized its dominance, instantly reminded all who visited it of the French Foreign Legion hero Beau Geste, which is hardly surprising as it was the actual building used for some of the scenes by the film company when they were making the film of that name. It was also famous for being the picture on Libya's 10 dinar note, the most popular unit of currency in the 1980s.

As we taxied up to the control tower, with the fort etched against the sky above us in the gathering gloom of the early desert evening, it was easy to imagine the total subjugation that this building and its occupants exercised on the Bedouin, who peopled this vast land when the castle was built. Its position astride the major trade routes from equatorial Africa to the ports of the Mediterranean coast and from Sudan westwards to Mauritania and the Atlantic, was then seen as an emphatic statement of superiority by the French. As Europeans jockeyed for territory and influence at the turn of the eighteenth century onwards, they were a force to be reckoned with in this part of Africa and would not easily be dislodged. In the event the fort was never seriously attacked, mainly because in its heyday nobody else was interested in acquiring these vast areas of inhospitable sand. The importance of uranium, bauxite, oil and all the other minerals sleeping quietly beneath its surface was yet to be appreciated.

That evening we were only interested in the purified oil product from the coastal refineries and designated all over the world as Jet A1, which we preferred to have in our tanks, although we could use other designations of the clear liquid – petrol for instance – if it became absolutely necessary. The fuel bowser crews were automatically given ice-cool bottles of soft drinks by the engineer during the refuelling process, a perk that encouraged them to attend to the needs of Special Flight aircraft as quickly as possible. This small investment in the future paid off handsomely when there was only one fuel bowser serviceable and a jumbo jet landed at the same time as one of our Falcons. Mahmoud, the fuel supervisor, always knew whom to attend to first.

Members of the flight learned very early in King Idris's day that the established manners of the Saharan Bedouin, the Tuaregs and the Berbers must be absorbed if any kind of friendship was to be established in this roasting cauldron of intrigue and death. Unwritten signals from strangers in their land, sometimes inadvertently given, were instantly interpreted in established formats.

For instance, human life itself in these conditions depended heavily on adequate supplies of that valuable commodity, water. A ready offer, on first meeting, of a cool drink is always taken as an overt statement of friendship and hospitality. To accept such an offer is tantamount to replying that the offer of friendship is accepted and reciprocated. Acceptance also carries an overtone of equality – it makes a statement that you regard the person offering the gift as equal in status to yourself.

However, to refuse such an offer, on whatever pretext whatsoever, instantly proclaims hostility in varying degrees. Overtones of 'I will not accept your hospitality because I do not like you', or 'I wish to do you some kind of harm', or 'I consider myself superior to you' ring out from such refusals. Modifying the refusal with excuses like 'I have just finished a drink and am not thirsty' does absolutely nothing to lessen the implied hostility.

I was once present at a meeting in Tripoli, Libya where a high-powered delegation from British Aerospace were attempting to sell the national airline more than £25 million (at 1978 prices) of civil commuter aircraft. The aircraft on offer were perfect for the task, but there was intense competition from Russia, France, Italy and the Netherlands for the business.

The head of the British Aerospace delegation and some of his team had spent the previous night dining and sleeping at my villa, causing considerable disruption for Lesley and me, because they had been unable to find hotel accommodation in the city. As I drove them to the meeting the next morning, I offered advice on the protocol that would be expected during the discussions, concentrating on the inevitable preamble where polite enquires would be made about the family of each team member. I explained that this would take quite some time, perhaps about ten minutes, and an offer of a cup of tea or coffee, I emphasized, was sure to follow and must at all costs be accepted for the reasons I have already mentioned.

In the event I was the first person to be offered a drink and chose tea, but I nearly fell off my chair when I heard the head British Aerospace negotiator refusing to accept the airline Chairman's kind offer of a drink, with the excuse that he had recently had a drink at breakfast. I tried to make eye contact with him, but he was shuffling his presentation papers around and avoided my piercing gaze from across the table.

Further detailed discussion about the aerodynamic detail of the aircraft under offer, the British Aerospace's four-engined BA146, and its performance parameters, maintenance options and price never really proceeded with any interest from the prospective buyers, and the meeting concluded with transport being provided for the delegation's journey to the airport for their return flight to London. They had originally intended spending several days in Tripoli, but they took the hint and left.

The Dutch aircraft firm Fokker was eventually awarded the valuable contract, but I was not involved from then on, so cannot comment on the Dutch manners or negotiating prowess.

This may seem, at first, irrelevant to the story, but it is quite important for the reader to absorb some of the atmosphere of life in our working environment in order to appreciate the outside influences affecting the efficient Special Flight operation and impinging on the background of many of our decisions.

So we continued our journey by filing an official flight plan over the radio for our next leg to Fort Lamy (called Ndjamena from 1976), the capital of Chad, on the edge of the equatorial rainforest of Central Africa. It was early evening when we were eventually cleared for take-off and launched our Falcon 5A-DAF, Call sign LN 999, into a magnificent African sky of perfect weather, with the moon illuminating the ground and myriads of stars twinkling overhead. The air itself was very smooth with no turbulence whatsoever and we glided into the heavens with feelings of neo-serenity.

The Falcon levelled at 40,000 feet and, as usual, three sets of eyes took stock of all the parameters that needed attention in a modern commercial aircraft and reviewed the requirements for the remainder of this medium-range leg – fuel more than sufficient, engine oils, temperatures, pressures and rpm[1] optimum, hydraulic systems up to pressure, electric generators at the correct voltages and producing normal amperage readings, batteries fully charged, oxygen systems operating and ready for use if required, and radio navigation systems performing correctly.

As mentioned earlier the Air Traffic Control facilities became less reliable over this part of Africa, especially at night, so a moving plot was instituted to keep track of all other aircraft, civil and military, as they periodically made their routine position reports on the radio. Many a potential accident was avoided by listening and taking note of other aircraft positions, courses and altitudes within two or three hundred nautical miles. It eventually became second nature and all nationalities were involved for their mutual safety. Useful information was repeated at these times to interested pilots regarding potential hazards.

I was once warned by a Russian airliner's captain of an inordinately large number of vultures, at very high altitude, above the planned destination airfield. Fortunately it was midday with perfect visibility and we spotted the lethal hazard early and managed to avoid these huge birds by modifying our landing pattern.

---

[1] Speed of rotation of the compressor and turbine.

A collision with a single bird of this size would almost certainly have been fatal for all concerned.

The night was so clear that a glance towards the ground revealed literally thousands of twinkling lights, rivalling the stars above with their numbers. They were the cooking fires of the people below and seemed to be only a short distance apart, but that was an illusion. I once had the experience of travelling in this area by Land Rover and on foot, and extended walks along established pathways produced no sight of even a single soul for days. Yet here was proof that people did exist in this sparse land where the yellow desert sand reluctantly surrendered its grip and the first meagre signs of green plants eventually showed themselves at the start of the equatorial rainforests.

My mind drifted onto the abundant life that tumbled over itself down below us in the jungle, fighting for its individual place in this verdant environment that inevitably caused wonderment to everyone who found himself in this veritable paradise for the first time. Then I considered the less-than-nice creatures, like the multitude of venomous snakes that could be encountered anywhere and the huge crocodiles that inhabited most of the waterholes. Some very unpleasant creatures crossed through the imagination and I eventually pondered on the voracious soldier ants that could swarm all over a person, even on the move, biting and injecting their irritating formic acid anywhere they could reach.

Like a bolt from the blue, I suddenly remembered mosquitoes. Heaven knows, how could I have forgotten the dreaded malaria until we were this close to one of the worst infected places on God's earth? This part of the jungle was renowned for normal malaria, which was bad enough, but recently a new form of the killer parasitic disease (cerebral malaria) had been identified which concentrated on attacking the human brain with catastrophic results. We had not yet taken our anti-malarial tablets so I interrupted the engineer's evening meal to ask him to open the aircraft's medical chest and bring us a dozen Paludrin tablets and a glass of water.

Ten minutes later he arrived in the cockpit to announce that owing to some regrettable oversight (better described as a cock-up), there were no anti-malarial tablets on board. This was a very serious problem that needed careful consideration. The moment we stepped out of the Falcon under the arc-lights of Fort Lamy's dispersal, surrounded by coconut palms, date palms and huge mahogany trees, in our nice, crisp, bright, white, short-sleeved uniform shirts every mosquito within a mile would make a beeline for our bare arms, faces and even up our trousers. The prospect was not good so we considered our options and decided that the most promising was to keep the aircraft door closed as much as possible whilst refuelling, and bribe the bowser driver to find us a taxi to take one of us into the city to buy the requisite drugs from the local pharmacy. Having made our decision we concentrated on the details of actually finding this, the second ex-French Foreign Legion fort of the night, and landing there safely.

Leaving the radio frequency at the limit of Fort Lamy airfield's control, we called the control tower, but to no avail. Having tried to communicate on every published frequency without success, I made a short transmission on the emergency frequency and was immediately advised by a French airliner that Fort Lamy's control tower had suffered a total power failure. They advised trying a totally new frequency, not published in any of the flight manuals, so we thanked them and complied with their advice.

To our great relief the airfield's controller replied on the new frequency, but his voice confirmed that none of Fort Lamy's main transmitters were working and that he was talking to us using a battery-powered portable walkie-talkie from the roof of the tower. His voice was quite faint, with some interference, but utilizing three sets of ears we managed to make out his instructions. He advised that his runway lights were illuminated, but that the light was provided by smoke pots every 50 metres, not electricity. His southerly runway was in use, but we should be aware that there was a large, deep, unlit hole in the tarmac to the left side of the landing run stretching almost to the runway's centreline. We should use maximum landing lights and be on the right side of the runway during the braking run. He also informed us that we were the only aircraft airborne for the next thirty minutes, so there was no confliction in his airspace.

These instructions may sound alarming when contemplating landing an aircraft at 150 mph on a damaged runway in the black night of the equatorial rainforest, but none of the instructions caused overmuch concern. I had not seen smoke pots illuminating a runway for nearly twenty-five years and in those days our aircraft had no onboard landing lights, but the pots were quite adequate then, so I had no reason to suppose that they would cause any problem now, especially with our two million candlepower onboard landing lights to assist us. Smoke pots are galvanized metal containers shaped rather like old-fashioned watering cans with wide spouts. They contain about ten litres of kerosene each and have a robust piece of absorbent rope teased out to form a wick, hanging out of the spout soaking up the fuel. When the wick is lit, it burns with a yellow flame and a great deal of thick black smoke.

Considering our predicament of having no anti-malarial protection, they were an absolute godsend. Their flames would attract any insects in the area and as the varmints flew close the flames would singe their wings – indeed, if I was any judge, the flickering smoke from the pots would almost eliminate our mosquito/malaria problem over the immediate area of the airfield.

We navigated to the extended centreline of the runway using the onboard Omega system and picked up the double line of smoke pots visually at about nine miles. The whole area was in complete darkness. Perhaps not quite complete, for occasional swarms of jungle fireflies seemingly in loose balls about 12 feet in diameter swirled around the trees below us, looking for all the world like wraiths, as we flew over the roof of the dense jungle a few feet under the Falcon's belly. Fort Lamy's controller squatting atop his control tower, clutching his walkie-talkie, burst onto the frequency at unusually high volume to inform us that he had our landing lights in sight and we were clear to land with no opposing traffic. He added the small proviso that we should remember the hole in the port side of the runway and avoid it at all costs.

The touchdown was one of those greasing contacts with the ground that usually happens when there are no passengers to appreciate the excellence of your abilities. We sailed down the runway, as near to the starboard edge as I could manage and even though we had been adequately warned, the size and apparent depth of the chasm that had opened up surprised us all. The controller later informed us that a UTA jumbo jet, fully loaded with freight, had caused the hole earlier in the day when the tarmac had been as hot as hell under the influence of a

Some of the enroute accommodation could literally be described as palatial, but a small shift in political fortunes, as with our occasional visits to Moundou in Southern Chad, caused a distinct deterioration in the quality of beds available.

relentless Chadian sun. He had engaged maximum reverse thrust after landing and decided to turn off the runway at the halfway point. Bringing the huge heavy Boeing to a complete standstill on the runway the pilot proceeded to rotate it on the spot. The effect was that of an outsize, left-handed corkscrew boring itself right through the tarmac and into the ground. Realizing his predicament, the pilot applied full power, or so it seemed, in order to climb out of his self-made hole. Unfortunately the enormous thrust that he employed completely flattened about an acre of banana trees on the starboard side of the runway, the intense heat converting the ripe fruit into a couple of tons of banana fritters before he managed to leap his aeroplane out of the hole.

As we taxied into the dispersal the Chadian marshallers parked us alongside another jumbo jet that was loading up with passengers and the engineer remarked that he expected they would have plenty of Paludrin tablets on board their flying hotel. As begging the necessary prophylactics was probably the easiest way of acquiring them at this time of night, I dashed over to see the French captain before the cabin doors were finally closed. After a monumental climb up to his cockpit I found him very helpful. A prolonged press on his cockpit alarm buzzer brought the harassed chief stewardess zipping up to the cockpit to assess the emergency. She was not amused to find that it was for some impecunious Brit who could not afford his own anti-malarial tablets. She rather tetchily confirmed to her captain that they had an almost unlimited supply of Paludrin tablets on board and that if I cared to follow her she would find them for me.

Wishing to return to her onerous job of embarking the passengers in an orderly and hopefully legal manner – correct documentation would have been paramount – she moved along corridors and up and down flights of stairs like a spring gazelle until I was hopelessly lost. She finally threw open a door with the revelation that we had just entered her bedroom. The concept of there being an actual bedroom on an aircraft rather surprised me, but she explained that they often cruised around Africa for weeks and that as their crews were not keen on overnighting in mud huts the airline had modified some of their 747s to enable the crew members to sleep on board, although it appeared that only the senior members of the crew qualified for an actual bedroom. The rest had to slum it on rearranged passenger seats and some of the bedding from the first-class section.

Having relaxed somewhat and curious to know what brought me to darkest Africa, she opened a cupboard, sat on the end of her bed, smiled sweetly and offered me a drink. From the contents of her drinks cabinet I could see that she was implying something a bit stronger than orange juice. In fact her demeanour had undergone a complete volte-face and it slowly dawned on me that this pert young mademoiselle was doing a very good job of chatting me up – or maybe I was just being optimistic. I accepted the kind offer of a drink and asked for some cool fizzy water, explaining that I was on duty and unfortunately could not partake of anything stronger. She poured herself a vodka and coke and pulled out a dish of blanched almonds. It was all getting a bit ridiculous as we sat on her bed together. My crew would think that I had been hijacked, so I manoeuvred the conversation back to the Paludrin tablets. She said 'Oh, yes' as if the prime reason for me being in her bedroom had been forgotten. Kneeling on the carpet she pulled out a black box with a large red cross emblazoned upon the top from underneath the bed and, opening it, fished out a box clearly marked 'Paludrin' in large letters. There was a plastic envelope inside the box and she filled it with the small round white tablets. I remember remarking that they would be sufficient for the rest of the flight and thanked her profusely.

The 747 Captain's voice with a classic French accent boomed round the corridors, requesting the chief stewardess's presence at the top of the gangway. I leapt up, finished the fizzy water and opened the door. Saved by the bell, I thought, as we left to perform our particular duties.

Fortunately the young lady led me to the top of the gangway before shouting a lively 'Bon voyage'. I contemplated that, left to my own devices in that labyrinth of corridors and ladders I could well have been still on board the jumbo when it arrived at its next airfield. Normally when taking Paludrin tablets as a prophylactic for the various forms of malaria one starts with four tablets on the day before departure into an 'at risk zone' and continues to take two tablets a day thereafter, until eventually leaving the danger area. To make absolutely certain of achieving full immunity the medics recommended continuing the two tablets a day for two weeks after leaving the zone.

Back at the Falcon, the crew were full of ribald comments about the length off time it had taken me to collect a few tiny tablets, especially as they had noticed a preponderance of eligible young ladies amongst the 747's cabin staff. If I had mentioned the incident of my sitting on the chief stewardess's bed with her whilst she poured us drinks and nibbled almonds, I would never have lived it down, so I decided to reserve the story for another day and place.

As I walked over to the relatively diminutive Falcon I could see that refuelling had been completed, but the fuel bowser driver obviously had some problem, which he was announcing at maximum volume to the engineer. It seemed that he would not accept our fuel carnets (credit cards) issued by Mobil, Exxon, Shell, BP, or any of the others that we carried. He only took Elf carnets which were, in fact, fully covered through Mobil, but he could not be convinced. The driver had called on the air traffic controller to mediate on his behalf and everything was bubbling away like a bomb about to explode. The driver's problem was that he had put the fuel into the aircraft and would have lost his job if he had not received payment. The sweat cascaded down his face in the heat and 100 per cent humidity and his skin seemed to adopt a shiny jet black appearance in the dim emergency lights illuminating the concrete dispersal. He looked the colour and shine of the old advertisements for Cherry Blossom boot polish. It was fair to say that he was extremely stressed.

I listened to the proceedings for a second or two, then asked, 'Do you accept cash?' The atmosphere relaxed as if somebody had thrown the 'happy' switch. Everyone was smiling as the account was produced in CFA (Central African Francs) and I enquired whether he could accept US dollars. Beautiful, he replied, as I unzipped my secure pocket and produced a wad of $100 bills. Rapid conversions produced the exact equivalent of the cost of the fuel in US dollars, which I counted out and produced with a flourish, like a magician. There were, of course, a few dollars extra for his family. His face beamed with gratitude. He disappeared behind the fuel bowser and reappeared almost immediately with a huge vicious-looking spear sporting a thick red shaft with decorative leather trimmings. This latest turn of events severely worried me because he was obviously heading in my direction at speed, with this lethal-looking piece of weaponry. He grasped my hand and thrust the shaft of his spear into my open palm. It took a few seconds to realize that he was, in fact, presenting me with a gift, rather than manoeuvring into position to impale me straight through my pristine white shirt, as at first seemed imminent.

Everyone present then went through the inevitable routine of hugging and kissing. Everyone, that was, except the experienced co-pilot, who had read the signs earlier and withdrawn inside the Falcon in order to avoid the ritual performance.

Before the air traffic controller left the scene, I handed him a flight plan to cover the next leg of our journey to Bangui, the capital of the Central African Republic. He signed my copy, jumped on his bicycle and happily pedalled away to the control tower. As if to reassure us of his arrival on the balcony outside the glasshouse, he waved enthusiastically to us in the cockpit and gave us a cheery greeting on his hand-held radio. Completing the pre-start checks, the engineer arrived in the cockpit with a fistful of small white Paludrin tablets and a glass of cool fresh water. Both pilots carefully selected six of the malarial prophylactics each and swallowed them with a gulp from the proffered tumbler.

I could see that the Boeing 747 doors were being closed and the steps wheeled away, and not wishing to take off behind its four huge engines at full power, we completed the remainder of our pre-flight checks with a greater degree of urgency. My reluctance to follow the jumbo into the air sprang from a knowledge of the numerous accident reports where smaller aircraft taking off behind these

Boeing giants had inadvertently flown through their massive slipstream, produced both by their high-powered engines and their very powerful wing-tip vortices. Known together as 'wake turbulence', the force of these disturbances, which can exist invisibly in the air for as much as 20 miles behind the offending machine, are particularly hazardous in calm conditions and have frequently flipped following smaller aircraft completely upside down. This particular hot, moist, jungle atmosphere was absolutely calm and the prospect of being unintentionally inverted close to the ground, at night, with some of the majestic mahogany trees protruding as much as 200 feet from the roof of the jungle, perturbed me greatly.

As we called for permission to taxi for take-off, the controller cleared us and advised that the jumbo would be held until we were airborne. The French captain's voice, heavy with sarcasm as he gazed down on us from his lofty perch, volunteered, 'Be my guest.' Reminders of the smoke pots, the hole in the runway and air traffic hazards were still being delivered as we lined up for take-off. As we hurtled past the pit at the left side of the runway immediately prior to separating from the ground I wondered how the jumbo would avoid the hole without squashing the smoke pots or clobbering the coconut palms with its starboard wingtip, so I ghoulishly remained on the radio frequency to await events.

The 747 evidently left the ground safely, but according to the controller a dozen smoke pots had either been squashed or overturned in the process and the fire brigade was dealing with the resultant kerosene fires. That sounded quite exciting so we turned round to have a look. The sight was quite spectacular – just as if the airfield had been attacked by enemy dive-bombers. A string of substantial fires were blazing along half of the runway's length and the diminutive fire engine was trying to douse them with foam as quickly as possible. The jumbo captain apologized profusely and offered to bring the controller a case of champagne at the end of the week. Perhaps the controller was a Muslim because he sounded singularly unimpressed with the offer. His response, whilst not actually an expletive, was certainly very derogatory.

Leaving the excitement of Fort Lamy, we climbed to 42,000 feet, changed to our en-route frequency and announced our presence to the world at large. We might just as well have saved our breath, for nobody answered our calls and it began to appear that we were entirely on our own above this massive continent… until, that was, following about my tenth transmission, a voice came through the ether asking whether I was Neville Atkinson.

A question like that, in the middle of darkest Africa, I found quite spooky. 'Who's asking?' was my guarded response.

He replied, 'Eric Oldfield, see you on 123.45' – the radio frequency used for informal chat. He was an ex-Sea Vixen pilot who had formerly flown with me from the Royal Naval Air Station at Yeovilton in Somerset. Eric was one of the world's true characters who conducted his life in myriads of unconventional ways, usually designed to better his personal financial position. His schemes were rarely totally successful, but that did not deter his efforts to succeed.

He was currently flying a Hawker Siddeley 125 from an airfield in Southern Rhodesia, just north of the Limpopo River, to Heathrow, with a small party of tourists who had chartered the business jet from his employers. He was as buoyant as ever and still as optimistic as I remembered from our navy days. Talking to him after all those years awoke a guilty recollection about our time with 766 Squadron.

In those days he had developed a market for fresh eggs, which he supplied in large quantities to just about everyone in the area – a commercial activity so successful that it started to interfere with his official work. He never seemed to be available for his primary duties, which were of course flying supersonic fighters and instructing the younger generation on the mysteries thereof. To facilitate his egg venture he drove a large van loaded to the gunwales with stacks of trays filled with eggs housed in racks in the back.

One Monday morning, Eric found himself on the early launch at six o'clock, for a land away flight to somewhere far off. Whilst he was absent the remaining squadron officers hard-boiled all his eggs in the five-gallon squadron coffee water boiler in the crew room and returned them to the back of his van where they cooled by the time Eric returned. The numbers of eggs involved seemed to be about a thousand dozen, but nobody actually counted.

Secrecy was maintained and the incident was just about forgotten when, at the early morning briefing about a week later, Eric (who was quite tall) stood up, called for silence, turned slowly round looking at everybody and announced with some feeling, 'You are all a bunch of bastards.' A tumultuous uproar rocked the normally sedate proceedings as we all fell about in uncontrollable laughter. His customers, evidently, had not been amused and the market had collapsed overnight, which was a pity, although it was subsequently noticed that he was more available for his primary duties.

On this occasion I found it interesting to compare notes with a pilot who also had a naval carrier flying background and was now flying a similar aircraft over Central Africa, both of us in the middle of the night. He confirmed that he still had a distinct allergy to hard-boiled eggs.

It was about this time that the co-pilot and I remarked on feeling an overwhelming weariness that could not be accounted for by any strenuous activities since leaving Tripoli. We both tried the aviator's routine pick-me-up of breathing 100 per cent oxygen for a minute or two, with only marginal improvement to the fatigue factor. The engineer brought us a routine cool drink each and we discussed the problem with him. He decided to rummage into our medical cabinet to compare the pills that I had acquired on the ground in Fort Lamy with several others that we carried for routine use whilst away from base. He returned to the cockpit minutes later with alarming news.

Evidently, when he examined the remaining small white tablets that the kind UTA stewardess had given to me half an hour previously, he found that they were all branded with an indented cross. Examination of the pills that were routinely carried in our own medical supplies revealed tablets of the same size, similarly marked. Unfortunately, the label on their container proclaimed not the brand name Paludrin, but the information that they were, in fact, high dose sleeping pills. Having taken eighteen of the supposed malarial tablets between us we discussed the possible effects that could be expected, and pondered on just how intense the fatigue could become over the next half hour.

Our engineer suggested that we resort to the tried and tested cure for extreme weariness – strong black coffee. In the absence of a better suggestion it seemed to be a sensible course of action and within about a minute the steaming mugs of the blackest coffee any of us had ever consumed arrived in the cockpit. It did produce a small improvement in our awareness, but whether we were functioning on all four cylinders or not was quite another matter.

The radio crackled into life to inform us that we were passing Ombella-Mpoko and should commence our descent into Bangui, the capital of the Central African Republic. Carefully reading out each pre-descent check from the book we adopted the correct settings and complied with the controller's instructions. Losing altitude as the prospect of a touchdown in one of the cruellest countries in Africa grew nearer, we all considered our likely reception on the ground. We expected problems, but there were always problems to be dealt with in this part of the world. We all had the odd shiver traversing our spines as we contemplated the stories of extreme cruelty that periodically leaked into the world's media. Could they be true? Did the President (Bokassa) actually carry out executions on condemned prisoners personally, in the main square of Bangui, using a 12 lb sledgehammer as had been reported? Little did we expect that we could really be about to find out for ourselves.

A short résumé of the little-known Central African Republic and its then President may be helpful at this stage. The landlocked country is appropriately named as it is indeed in almost the exact centre of the continent, bounded on the west and south by Cameroon, Congo and Zaire, on the north by Chad and the east by Sudan. It has tribal links with all its neighbours, which accounts for its many languages. The country was formerly divided into numerous individual kingdoms, but these were all amalgamated into a single entity in the late 1700s, the 1800s and 1900s under the overbearing influence of foreign slavery. Indeed, by the early 1800s the country was one of the major sources of black slaves in the whole of Africa.

They were sought after for their outstandingly skilled craftsmanship. For centuries they had been designing and making superior weapons, ornaments and musical instruments, and apart from the pygmy tribes around the border with Cameroon, were generally well built and intelligent. It is recorded that by 1800 the Arab slave markets of Egypt were selling 20,000 slaves from there per annum and an equivalent number was being driven westwards to the coast for shipment to the West Indies and Brazil.

In the mid to late 1800s when the slave trade was starting to wane, along came the French and Belgians to squabble over what became known as French Equatorial Africa. They developed coffee and cotton plantations and started a thriving diamond mining industry. The European administrators indulged in the slavery trade at every opportunity, though public opinion in Europe had by this time become very anti-slavery. The French fought outright wars against the Baya people from the western half of the country, who resisted their occupation with great determination.

Mission schools were established by the French in 1949, and one notable product in the early 1950s was Barthélemy Boganda, a courageous and far-sighted young man who demanded basic political and economic rights for Africans. He won the first democratic elections allowed by the colonial French, despite numerous attempts on his life throughout the process, and later won overall supremacy in 1958, which proved to be too much for his former overlords. In March 1959 he died in a plane crash, popularly believed to have been 'arranged' by local accomplices of his French enemies.

Various political parties allowed by the French jostled for position in the early 1960s. The most noteworthy of these were MESAN (Mouvement d'Evolution Sociale de l'Afrique) and MEDAC (Mouvement d'Evolution de l'Afrique Centrale). They were either permitted or banned in equal parts. Sometimes their leaders were arrested, but eventually David Dacko of MESAN emerged as puppet leader. In 1962 the French, for whatever reason, established a Central African Republican Army with Jean-Bedel Bokassa, one of its own French Army sergeants, as its Chief of Staff. Because of French incompetence and Dacko's blatant corruption the economy was soon in ruins and in 1965 a general strike was called. The French response was to direct Dacko to hand over the presidency to Jean Izambo, but on 1 January 1966 Bokassa, having won meteoric promotion to Colonel, seized power.

He changed the country's name to the Central African Empire with himself as Emperor. It was a complete disaster and within a year he turned the entire populace against him by his dictatorial, erratic and incompetent administration. He was singularly cruel, grossly corrupt and made himself immensely wealthy, protecting his power by executing those thought to be responsible for any opposition whatsoever. The French continued to support him, largely it is thought because they held the uranium mining concessions. Only when Bokassa ordered a massacre of children did the French move to bring him down – it was just prior to this despicable massacre that we, unfortunately, came onto the scene.

In view of our inadvertent consumption of sleeping pills everyone performed his landing duties meticulously and after a careful touchdown we taxied into one of the biggest aircraft reception dispersals in all of Africa. There were about a hundred acres of flat concrete and we were the only aircraft on the whole parking lot. A scantily dressed marshaller directed us to park on an exact spot about a kilometre from the control tower and about the same distance from the airport buildings. Having parked us as he wished he leapt into a beat-up khaki-coloured van and hurtled away into the black night. Not a word was spoken to us and the vast concourse was quiet on his departure except for the usual chatter of animals in the surrounding jungle.

Whilst the engineer was checking and topping up the engine oils the co-pilot and I decided to wake ourselves up with a steady jog around the aircraft; after all, we were only planning to be on the ground for a few minutes to refuel, but still felt drowsy from the effects of the half-dozen sleeping pills. If anyone had been observing us – later events confirmed that they were – they must have concluded that the aircraft was crewed by a bunch of raving lunatics, but as far as we could tell, we were totally isolated on this vast dispersal area. As we waited a decent interval for the fuel bowser to roll alongside, the lights surrounding the hardstanding were systematically extinguished one by one. An interrogatory call on the radio produced no response whatsoever and we started to feel alone and unloved.

Preparing for the next leg of the flight to Entebbe seemed to be the most productive occupation, so whilst the engineer carried out a post-flight inspection outside, the co-pilot and I extracted the correct charts from our Jeppesen holdalls and absorbed the information that they contained. We may have started the auxiliary engine in order to use the full lighting in the cabin and activate the air-conditioning. That would have been entirely logical, but none of us can accurately recall this particular detail – after all we would hardly disturb the neighbours from this distance.

Five minutes later, the engineer poked his head through the open cabin door and announced, 'There's a big black chap out there. Says he's the Chief of Police and by his agitated state, I think he wants to give you a parking ticket.' Jumping up dutifully, I walked deliberately down the steps where I was met with a most incongruous sight. In the all-pervading darkness stood a huge, rotund, black gentleman, wearing only a pair of off-white shorts and battered rubber flip-flops. He was an ox of a man, in excess of 6 foot 4 inches tall. His chest was covered in dense, sweaty, coarse, black hair and a beer-belly-type stomach flopped over a wide brown leather belt which sagged forward as it struggled to convey a semblance of modesty. He was flanked by two very tiny wizened guards sporting Kalashnikov AK-47s. The guns seemed to be as big as the people carrying them so I could only presume that these were representatives of one of the pygmy tribes. They sported long camouflage trousers, which in this oppressive humid climate passed as a sort of uniform and were barefoot. Standing alongside them later, I looked down on the tops of their heads and guessed that they were about 4 foot 6 inches tall. Contemplating the group of three aggressive representatives of Central African Republic's officialdom gave me a barely controllable urge to laugh, but experience had taught me to control such urges and I adopted the dictum of always being notably respectful when dealing with gentlemen toting automatic weapons, however ludicrous they may at first appear. Bullets can be very painful, whoever fires them.

Arriving off the last step in the tropical darkness I misjudged my forward motion and found that I was much closer, just a few inches, to the angry looking gentleman than I would have wished. Burbling an almost incoherent introduction I grasped his right hand and shook it enthusiastically. Retrieving his arm tetchily he unleashed a tirade of words, mostly in French, but interspersed with native dialects with which I was unfamiliar. I invited him to come on board the Falcon in my best French and without replying he pushed past me and marched aggressively up the steps, cracking the top of his head on the stout metal door frame in the process. On board, he glanced left into the cockpit and proceeded to march purposefully up and down the centre aisle, seeming surprised to find nobody else except the three crew. As if to satisfy his curiosity further, he grasped one of the rear seats and shook it energetically from side to side. My offer of a cool drink was met with a derisive response and he marched down the steps, being very careful to duck his head before it struck the door frame again. Arriving down on the concrete he spoke briefly to his two pygmies, but seemed to ignore us and the aircraft completely.

Striding off towards the main airport building he disappeared into the darkness with his two diminutive guards in tow, whilst the three of us discussed the encounter and decided that we were probably free to go on our way. The co-pilot and I decided to walk over to the darkened control tower to render a written flight plan and ascertain the whereabouts of the fuel compound, to enable us, hopefully, to refuel. Our purposeful tropical moonlight walk in the direction of Bangui's Air Traffic Control tower took us across the dispersal on a track that diverged from the last observed path of our three-man welcoming committee by about 60 degrees, so after five minutes of brisk walking we must have been between 500 and 600 yards apart. At this point a monumental bellowing seemed to emanate from the large policeman's approximate position and as we squinted into the darkness we convinced ourselves that we could see the trio silhouetted in the lights from the airport building. The view was not clear because of the distance and the clouds of night insects filling the air, but it was quite obvious that something in that direction was very angry indeed and as the shouting was obviously aimed in our direction we discussed our most appropriate course of action. There was some small relief that the noise was not emanating from a rampaging bull elephant hurtling across the dispersal towards us, as we had both feared initially.

Remembering the armament that we had already seen, a tactical decision was unanimously taken to look keen and jog over to see exactly what the irate gentleman wanted. Our decision turned out to be a wise one because as we closed the distance we could see that each of the pygmies seemed to have become even smaller. This illusion came about because both guards, presumably on direct orders from their leader, had dropped forward onto their right knees, thereby decreasing their stature even further, to take careful aim at us with their automatic weapons.

I was careful to stop a good two yards away from him this time, as he did a very good imitation of a seriously angry silverback gorilla. All it needed was the odd grunt and he would have qualified for an Oscar. He gabbled away rapidly in several languages mixed together. The words were totally incomprehensible to me, so as he paused to draw breath for more verbal onslaught I slotted in a quick '*Je ne comprends pas*'. This seemed to infuriate him even more. He took a step in my direction, which unfortunately forced me to smell his rancid breath, his hands grabbed my shirt collar from both sides and he seemed to be about to lift me clear off the ground. Instead, he relaxed the pressure slightly, bent down until his mouth was half an inch from my face and spat at me in perfect English, 'You'll fucking well *comprends* before I have finished with you. Now collect your engineer and follow me.' These were the first English words he had used, but they gave me no confidence, as our situation seemed to be deteriorating by the minute.

We turned as instructed and returned to the Falcon to collect our remaining crew member, this time escorted by the two guards. It took us less than two minutes to button up and securely lock our precious aircraft, but this appeared to be too slow for our escorts who had, by this time, adopted an annoying habit of prodding us with the barrels of their Kalashnikovs at regular intervals. They spoke no French, only the Hausa and Sango languages, and professed to understand nothing of my admittedly basic Swahili, so communication between us was impossible except by rudimentary sign language. Whilst they were quite aggressive with us, they were obviously terrified of the Chief of Police, if that was his true title. Before leaving the cabin we picked up a 75 cl plastic bottle of cool fresh water each and walked off towards the angry black gentleman who was by this time pacing a hundred-metre stretch of the hardstanding, apparently immersed in deep thought. The heat and humidity surrounding us appeared to be almost liquid in its cloying oppression.

About fifty metres away he launched into another noisy verbal onslaught in our direction. This time apparently aimed at his guards for not showing more alacrity in herding us towards him. Their response was to prod the co-pilot and me once more, very painfully, in the ribs with the points of the barrels of their guns. I loudly shouted 'Stop!' Everyone stopped instantly. The now stationary group of unlikely characters, on this huge area of concrete, listened without comment whilst I explained in forceful tones just what I would do to the next person who jabbed me with his gun. Of course, they understood not one syllable, but the sign language that accompanied my tirade was clear to all. The ox muttered something to his guards as he turned to resume his march and they managed to shepherd us the rest of the way without any further physical contact.

Approaching the brightly lit airport concourse I pondered on what the airport staff would make of our unlikely group crossing their half-acre of polished marble. Maybe, I thought, this was not an unusual sight in this country of corruption, cruelty and terror and would not give rise to undue comment. In the event I needn't have wasted my imagination. As we approached the brightly lit entrance, the party turned right a few degrees and seemed to be heading for a solid block wall. A few feet away from the wall, a darkened doorway became evident one floor lower than the main entrance. It was at this stage that the engineer offered his opinion that the two guards would have been perfect for film roles in the African film *Saunders of the River*.

We entered the narrow and dimly lit passageway beyond with some trepidation. There were dim lights embedded in the concrete of the walls, but only about one in three was actually glowing with nothing more illuminating than about 15 watts. The atmosphere was dank, humid and very unfriendly and the heavy door clanked shut behind us. One wondered how many poor unfortunate souls had traversed this way en route to a violent death. As if to emphasize the whole evil charade we could see that the floors and some of the walls were festooned with various forms of unpleasant wildlife. The fact that some of these creatures were more than just unpleasant was confirmed when I saw that our barefooted guards were doing all in their power to avoid actually standing on or touching any of them.

As my eyes grew accustomed to the foreboding gloom, I searched the walls and floors for any sign of snakes. This country is renowned for being home to some of the world's most deadly – even quite small ones are known to carry the gift of instant death in their venom. All the creatures moved very quickly and one could easily imagine all sorts of nightmare scenarios, but I saw no actual snakes. There were many different lizards, some upside down on the ceiling, as were spiders that were bigger than any I had seen till that night, centipedes and millipedes of every shape, size and speed of travel. Eventually it all coalesced into a blare of horror. We could even have imagined crocodiles, we were so twitched. It was like something out of a Tolkien novel, steeped in malevolence.

My new shoes afforded basic protection, but not against anything seeking sanctuary by scurrying up the inside of one's blue uniform trousers. It was not pleasant to contemplate. I was bordering on mild panic, but just when it seemed that we would be going round this labyrinth all night, our *de facto* leader flung open a door into a cleaner, lighter, corridor, off which he ducked into a room which to anyone who had lived through the Second World War, could immediately be recognized as an interrogation cell, owing its origins to the time of the Nazi Gestapo. There was the obligatory large leather-topped desk behind which a black swivel-chair rotated to allow easy seating for the interrogator. The surface of the desk appeared to be covered in high-powered spotlights on stands, strategically positioned to shine directly into the eyes of those being interrogated – likely to be us shortly, if I was any judge.

The floor was smooth concrete and the desk appeared to be slightly elevated on a small plinth, forcing the victims on our side of the table to look upwards into the lights when listening to questions directed at them from the other side of the desk. There was a slightly humorous aspect to the Chief of Police, as viewed from our lowly position, who appeared to us to be completely naked, and because the room did not benefit from air-conditioning, he was sweating profusely as he glowered down on us. Maybe a naked interrogator should have worried us even more.

Not a word had been spoken when I became aware of a small window behind and to the right of the interrogator. Squinting past the light that was supposed to be directed into my eyes I could clearly see that there was no glass in the window – although it was barred thousands of mosquitoes were flooding into our room through the opening, as if somebody had rung the dinner gong.

The reason for us having taken the sleeping pills by mistake on leaving Fort Lamy was an attempt to give ourselves malarial protection, but because the tablets later proved not to be Paludrin, we now had no protection whatsoever. As these facts resurfaced from our now dulled senses I analysed our situation. The mosquitoes flocking towards us were of the large variety, whereas the dangerous ones carrying malaria were smaller ones of the anopheles variety. Academically it may be useful to know that it is only the females that carry the dreaded plasmodium protozoan parasite, but it becomes irrelevant when it is realized that nobody has ever been able to differentiate between the sexes, except under laboratory conditions. It was whilst these facts were rotating round my head that I clearly saw a much smaller mosquito fly into the room towards us.

The almost certain anopheles headed towards the nearest light and, wishing to pre-empt its expected attack, I leapt out of my chair with the intention of travelling towards the creature's position and crushing it between the palms of two hands. Unfortunately I had not appreciated that the two pygmies had followed us into the room and were standing silently, the nearest one being behind and slightly to my left. It is possible that the lights that were intended for our benefit were actually blinding them as well – the cells were, after all, only designed for interrogating just so many people at any one time.

The action of pushing my chair violently and unexpectedly backwards and rushing at the mosquito caused me to run full tilt into the poor unfortunate little man who was invisible to me, knocking the guard completely onto his back, and sending his Kalashnikov skidding across the floor. I only became aware of my mistake when I found myself walking up the prone body of the upended guard, eventually standing, quite painfully I imagine, on the poor man's head. Even then I could not see him as he lay moaning on the floor because of the shadows cast by the lights and my partial blindness.

The dreaded mosquito had by now completely disappeared, so being a basically decent chap and wishing to make amends for the disturbance caused, I stepped over to the corner of the room where his Kalashnikov had come to rest and picked it up to hand it back to the badly bruised dwarf. This was probably an error because our three tormentors obviously presumed that I was about to kill them all. As I was in the process of handing the gun back to its keeper, the Chief of Police apparently thought that I was about to aim it at him. He dived horizontally at the concrete floor and hit it with a sickening thud. When he nervously rose to his feet again, the gun had been restored to the pygmy and I was sat back down in my chair looking as innocent as a child and apologizing to everyone. The other two members of the crew could hardly contain their laughter, so I forced myself to adopt a deadpan expression. The policeman was, by this time, very angry indeed and appeared likely to resort to physical violence without further provocation.

To make matters worse I could just discern by squinting through the bright lights, a trickle of blood running down his face from a small cut on his forehead that he had suffered in his spectacular dive to the floor. As he mopped the blood with a piece of dirty white cloth his temper seemed to bubble over and he snapped at me, 'You're a bunch of bloody mercenaries!'

'No, no, no!' I shouted back. 'You've got it all wrong. This –' pointing over my shoulder in the approximate direction of our Falcon '– is the President of Libya's aeroplane. President Gadaffi has asked me to fly it to Uganda and take the President, Idi Amin, to see King Faisal of Saudi Arabia.'

He studied me with somewhat evil piercing eyes for some time, obviously trying to absorb the ramifications of my little speech, stood up, pointed at me menacingly and before sitting down again said, 'You're fucking mad!' Just then, what I judged to be another anopheles mosquito flew by, quite close. I stood up, clapped my hands together and squashed it, revealing a large blob of someone's red blood. He was obviously not too pleased so I attempted to walk round the desk to show him that I had killed the beast.

As the guard pushed me back down in my chair the interrogator said, 'If you get out of that chair once more, I'll bloody well strangle you with my bare hands.' I really believed that he meant it.

Next, he challenged me to produce documentation regarding our flight. I responded with 'You've brought us here without our papers. There's plenty of documentation in the aeroplane, but you did not ask for it. Come over and you can see all the documentation that you could possibly need. What's more, if you let me use your Air Traffic telex machine I can produce for you anything else, direct from Libya, so that you can see it coming in from the Libyan government itself.' All bluff on my part, because we had very little documentation aboard regarding this particular flight, it was then 3 o'clock in the morning in Libya and any message would arrive into empty offices, not likely to be seen for at least another six hours.

Seeing a perplexed look on his face, I decided that attack was probably the best form of defence, so I challenged him to contact his Minister of Communications and ask him whether 5A-DAF had permission to refuel at Bangui en route to Entebbe. 'Go on,' I insisted, 'ask him, or give me a telephone and I will ask him.' Clear signs of worry showed on his face because the whole thing had now moved up into a bigger league. The Minister of Communications of the Central African Republic was only one down from President Bokassa himself – disturbing him unnecessarily in the middle of the night was likely to be tantamount to suicide and totally out of the question for a policeman, even the Chief of Police, if that was in fact his title as he claimed.

Got you! I thought, you have to let us go now because you're manoeuvred into a severely dangerous position. I was feeling quite pleased with myself, when he stood up, looked slowly at the three of us and said, 'You lot bother me. I am putting you in prison.' With that he walked out of the room.

This is an edited version of the actual interrogation, which actually took in excess of two hours, was conducted in many languages on both sides and was therefore quite slow, but his decision to send us to jail was astounding when it came. As he left the room we looked at each other and said in chorus, 'The bastard!'

Three new larger escorts, obviously from a different tribe, entered the interrogation room and applied the customary handcuffs, surprisingly fastened with our hands in front of us, before taking us outside to a dirty, camouflaged, short-wheelbase Land Rover for our short journey to incarceration. The jail looked like no other prison any of us had ever seen, even in the movies. It was a large building that from the outside had all the presence of a low-grade African hotel of about three floors. As we were ushered inside much irrelevant detail was recorded and my small Swiss Army knife caused unusual interest, but our shortage of currency of any type was regarded with distinct suspicion. All we had between us were a few Libyan coins, as we had locked our serious money away before leaving the aircraft.

We were allotted an entire corridor on the second floor about 30 metres long with cells directly off it on one side only. Each was about three metres square with a single barred window about half a metre square. I occupied the first cell, which I presumed was similar to the others. Our guards removed the handcuffs as we entered the cells. The windows must have been covered with fine netting of some kind because I have no recollection of any flying insects bothering us. The wall at the right side of the corridor had been removed and replaced with substantial steel bars about an inch in diameter, at one end of which swung a large door into the corridor, constructed of the same bars. Inside the cell was a complete cage constructed of slightly smaller gauge steel rods, with a second door of bars just inside the outer door. The only furniture was a single wooden bed with some kind of relatively clean cloth covering.

I pulled both doors closed, but there was no lock in either door, which we found strange. Preparing to lie down on the bed, still dressed in trousers and shirt, I was quite surprised when both doors were pushed wide open and a classic French Foreign Legion machine gun mounted on a tripod was moved into a position in the open outer doorway, from where it was lined up to be pointing directly at my head as I lay on the bed. Two other similar guns were trundled down the corridor to be installed outside the other crew members' cells. These machine guns were unbelievable – they could have come straight off the set of the film *Beau Geste*.

The barrels consisted of a ribbed metal cover, either of bronze or brass, about four and a half inches in diameter and about 2 foot 3 inches long, that appeared to contain about nine smaller barrels inside. At the opposite end of this ribbed tube was a two-handed grip and a backsight, with the whole thing mounted on a substantial metal tripod. There was a four-inch horizontal slot forward of the handgrip through which a belt of ammunition was fed, with one operator pulling the belt through on one side and another guiding the bullets into the slot as the belt progressed. To complete the picture a soldier in camouflage fatigues squatted on the floor in a determined firing position, whilst his two similarly dressed colleagues squatted either side of the barrel, grasping the long belt of heavy calibre ammunition in their hands and preparing to feed the bullets into the breech of the gun. These evil-looking weapons were positioned in the corridor, aiming through the two open doorways at the person inside the cell.

I looked at this arrangement with suppressed amusement, rolled over onto my side and surprisingly, despite the bright lights slept soundly, wishing afterwards that I had a camera to photograph this obvious charade. If they had decided to kill us it would have been done in a much more efficient manner than this play-acting. It was clear to me that my talk of presidents and telex communications had caused serious doubt which could not be ignored, in this country of extreme cruelty. In such surroundings it might only take a small shift in political emphasis for the hunters suddenly to become the hunted.

About 0630 I was awakened by an authoritative black gentleman wearing a smart grey pinstriped suit. He sat down on the end of my bed and was most apologetic. He explained in cultured English tones that he felt that all our problems of the night before had been his fault.

'Pardon my asking, but who are you?' was my first response.

'I am the Central African Republic government's Minister of Communications,' he replied, 'and all your permissions to refuel in Bangui en route to Entebbe were left on my desk but after I left for an unexpectedly urgent meeting yesterday afternoon, my staff failed to copy them to the airport.'

When I informed him of our reception and interrogation he said, 'Everyone involved has been dealt with, including the Chief of Police.'

I replied that the poor man had not been too bad and that only pride had been hurt, but he responded by pointing his foot at the machine gun and its crew and shook the bars with his hand. 'This is not the kind of reception that we aim to give to our guests, or pretty soon we will have no guests. Is it possible,' he continued, 'that you could stay with us for a day so that we could fly you up to one of our game parks in the north? You would find that our hospitality is quite genuine and I am sure that you would all enjoy the experience.'

I thanked him sincerely, because we would genuinely have enjoyed such an expedition, but I explained that we were needed in Kampala as soon as possible on presidential business and that our schedule did not allow undue delay. He promised to arrange breakfast and insisted that his limousine would take us on a *tour de ville* (city tour) on the way to the airport. As he was leaving he turned, with eyes sparkling, and announced that he would personally see us at the airport to ensure that there was no untoward interference this time. He continued that he appreciated our understanding of the night's difficulties, which he found a complete embarrassment, and that if I and my family would like to spend a couple of weeks in his beautiful country some time in the future, I must contact him beforehand and he would ensure an enjoyable welcome.

He was obviously a kind, considerate man, but my mind's eye conjured up a vision of Nigel and Trudi, our children, being boiled in a steaming, missionary-style spherical cooking pot over a fire, often depicted in children's comics at that time, somewhere in the dense jungles of equatorial Africa. However I thanked him for his kind offer. As the Minister departed he issued firm orders to the machine-gunners to remove their equipment from the corridor. The engineer's cell was at the end of the corridor, some distance away and it became obvious that the message to remove that particular gun had been misunderstood. I walked up to the soldier grasping the aiming handles of this last gun and tried, in vain, to explain that he had been instructed to 'go away'. Finally, the engineer's patience ran out. Having satisfactorily donned his trousers, he opened his cell door wide, looked deliberately at the three men and their ancient weapon, carefully placed his foot on the stout gun barrel and pushed the gun over. The aimer fell over sideways with one of the ammunition providers on top of him and the gun almost upside down. The soldier looked totally perplexed. Glancing up the corridor from where his colleagues had disappeared, his mouth opened as if to speak, but no words came. The three of us left in search of the promised breakfast.

Considering our situation of the night before, the food was remarkably good and as we finished our second cups of coffee the promised Mercedes limousine glided to a silent halt by the outside door. The lack of guards by this time mystified us, but we picked up our suitcases and walked out of the unlocked door, admittedly with some relief. Walking out of the open door of a prison and being assisted into a spotless limousine had an air of complete unreality about it, but this was the Central African Republic and we had long since resolved just to 'go with the flow'.

The driver glided around the seemingly unremarkable, dusty, rather squalid town and did his best to commentate on each building as we passed, but he had severe language difficulties and we only really understood him when he reverted to his few words of French. We noticed a pronounced French aspect in the layout of the various churches and municipal erections. Eventually, we persuaded him to cut short the *tour de ville* and head for the airport where we were somewhat relieved to find our gleaming white Falcon, with its ostentatious lateral horizontal gold stripe, in good condition. Two unusually smart soldiers, who were apparently standing guard on our precious aircraft, snapped to attention and saluted as we disembarked from the shining black limousine.

The driver removed our three suitcases from the car and when the fuselage door was opened, insisted on carrying our bags up the steps, carefully placing them in the luggage stowage before wishing us '*bon voyage*' and driving his opulent monster over to the airport building. The fuel bowser arrived shortly afterwards followed by an Air Traffic Control officer who volunteered to take our flight plan to the tower for processing. I bent down to pull out our pack of official flight plan blanks when the efficient messenger produced the pristine book of flight plans that he happened to have with him. This was all going too smoothly, in marked contrast to the night before, but similar changes in fortune had an all too regular habit of happening on this intriguing continent. The Minister arrived, as promised, to assist with our departure and I thanked him for his invaluable assistance. He reiterated his invitation for my family to visit the CAR, but practicalities prevented us ever taking up his kind offer.

It was a great relief, emotionally and physically, to climb serenely heavenwards and separate ourselves from the implied threats of Bangui and its evil Head of State. The coolness of our air-conditioning system bathed us in a sense of well-being and it was good to feel wide-awake rather than drugged into near-sleep as we had been on arrival.

The flight to Entebbe went exactly as planned. Landing in Uganda we all commented that the efficiency of the whole aviation operation improved by at least ten notches. As the marshaller guided us neatly into the slot reserved for the VIP lounge, a smart green and white BP fuel bowser glided into the perfect position for refuelling and without fuss the driver drew off a sample of his fuel for our engineer to test for purity. When this was accepted he returned from his machine with a metal static line to bond our Falcon safely to earth, thereby avoiding any unwanted static electricity sparks during the movement of fuel along the pipes. Whilst we completed our usual domestic chores and made tentative plans for onward flight, a smart uniformed chauffeur came up the steps to say that cool drinks had been prepared for us in the VIP lounge and when we were ready he would drive us to State House to meet the President. He emphasized, with a beaming smile on his face, that there was no urgency as Idi Amin Dada was at an early morning meeting and it would be nearly lunchtime before he was available.

Two limousines in one day was just too much. We were in danger of suffering from inflated egos at this rate, but something would surely bring us down to earth before too long – sure enough, it did, but not before we had enjoyed even more pampering for a short while. The early morning in Entebbe was a truly invigorating experience. Here we were, standing on the actual Equator, surrounded by luxurious growth with myriads of colourful birds flitting from tree to tree all around us. The sun shone out of a clear blue sky, but the temperature was comfortable owing to the stabilizing influence of the nearby massive Lake Victoria (the largest lake in Africa and the second biggest area of fresh water in the whole world). The 5,000 feet altitude, and the last of the early morning mists left tiny wisps of white vapour ascending from the treetops of the surrounding jungle. The whole effect bordered on the magic – an almost ethereal prospect.

It was difficult to tear one's attention away from this idyllic scene to deal with the more mundane practicalities that demanded attention. To inject even more surprise, the refueller refused to take any payment for his plancload of Jet A1 fuel. This may seem reasonable, as we were preparing to fly the country's President, but it was almost unique in our experience.

Within half an hour of touching down we sauntered into the VIP lounge and partook of the proffered hospitality. Glancing back, our shiny white Falcon looked resplendent against the jungle background, with its bright red engine blanks in place to avoid any native animals or birds choosing the jet pipes or air intakes as attractive nesting sites. Red flags fluttered from each undercarriage leg to remind us that locks were in place to avoid inadvertent operation of the hydraulic retracting gear in our absence. As we glided away in the luxurious transport, a smart army Land Rover equipped with two heavy calibre machine guns behind the driver's cab and accompanied by three uniformed soldiers, took up position alongside the cockpit to guard our precious bird during our stay in Uganda.

On the way to State House the driver thoughtfully broke the short journey at the Lake Victoria Hotel, a colonial-style single-storey building with grounds sweeping down past lawns and terraces to the water's edge. It is worth commenting at this stage that Uganda was never designated a British colony – Queen Victoria declared it a protectorate in 1894, which it remained until 1962 when it became independent within the Commonwealth.

We were led onto the terrace facing the lake where a table, with a pristine white, hand-embroidered tablecloth had been prepared for our second breakfast of the day. As we scooped out a tasty sun-ripened mango each, we were taken by surprise when a huge giant tortoise ambled onto the lawn immediately in front of us, about six feet away. It was followed by a second, slightly smaller. The bigger one was about four feet from head to tail and stood about 1 foot 8 inches high. The smaller one was nearly a foot shorter.

The director of the Lake Victoria told us that they had been part of the hotel for as long as records had been kept and they just wandered around as they wished. They were regularly fed with salad vegetables by placing suitable offerings a couple of feet in front of them and retiring, but they cropped the grass if it ever became long enough, and seemed to have an affinity with most small children, allowing some to ride on their shells. They took instant dislikes to others and would raise themselves six inches off the ground and face them menacingly with their powerful beaks. People generally took the message and kept clear, but they had been known to attack noisy dogs with their six-inch razor-sharp beaks and were rumoured to be capable of severing most small animals' legs when provoked. I certainly had no intention whatsoever of finding out, by allowing any part of my anatomy to be in range of those formidable creatures.

The age of the larger one, the Director claimed, was about 250 years and the smaller one about 200, though how they knew remains a mystery. He quoted the Kampala veterinary college whose giant tortoise expert called by on a regular basis. If these ages were anywhere near accurate – and I remain very sceptical – we were in the company of two animals that were alive when Kings George II, III, and IV were on the British throne, and over 150 years old when Queen Victoria placed their home under her protection in 1894. Long may they continue into this nuclear age, though I failed to discover how long their life expectancy might be.

Eventually the chauffeur ushered us back into his palace on wheels, with its smart Ugandan flag fluttering at the side of the bonnet and no number plates, evidently indicating the status of its presidential owner. We drove into the grounds of State House and were accorded polite recognition by the smartly dressed guards. Inside, the furnishings were smart and functional, but not opulent. The butler invited us to relax whilst he contacted His Excellency to ascertain his wishes, and cool soft drinks appeared on the tables by our armchairs as if by magic. There did not appear to be any noisy air-conditioning but the soft breeze seduced into the rooms by judicious use of louvred doors and windows kept the temperature at a very comfortable level.

The world's newspapers had recently made the wild claim that Idi Amin Dada was a practising cannibal and kept human body parts, especially heads, in the State House kitchen refrigerator. The whole story struck me as being ridiculous, but on my way to the toilet, I could not resist opening the two refrigerators in the kitchen to have a peek. They contained normal healthy food and some of the shelves were stacked with cans of beer and soft drinks, as one would expect. It is amazing what the normally sober press will publish when instructed to blacken someone's name by the powers that be. None of these bizarre stories were ever credited to any known source which was surprising and more than a little sinister.

After we had a couple of hours of relaxing inside and wandering out to see the lush gardens with their beautiful show of tropical flowers, the chauffeur drew up to the front door to say that we were required to meet His Excellency in the Command Post. He drove us to Number 29 in a row of substantial, detached, red brick houses down a street in Kampala called Prince Charles Avenue. Seated at a desk festooned with telephones, in a room that occupied most of the ground floor, was the unmistakable figure of Idi Amin. If anything he was even larger than I had expected. He jumped up with amazing agility for a man of his size, came round the desk and grasped my hand, pumping it up and down in welcome. His hand was one of the biggest I had seen and I am sure that he could have inflicted very painful damage to my comparatively much smaller fist if he had so wished, but as a one-handed pilot would not have been much use to him he settled for what in his terms must have been a gentle grip, along with a warm smile.

The room was remarkably large for the apparent outside dimensions of the building. Its walls seemed to have been draped with many tea towels so, opening the conversation, I asked what was the significance of the wall hangings. He beamed with enthusiasm at my interest in his artistic display and shepherded me over to the nearest wall where, as I came closer, I could see that they were indeed tea towels, each one depicting different Scottish regiments and divisions. I remember seeing colourful pictures of members and barracks of the Black Watch, the King's Own Scottish Borderers, the Gordon Highlanders and many more. Pride of place seemed to be occupied by the 51st Highland Division and its Second World War onslaught on the monastery of Monte Casino in Italy. After talking to him for a short while it was obvious that he appreciated tartan and swirling kilts with an almost obsessive enthusiasm.

Idi Amin had been a senior NCO in the British Army, fighting against the Japanese in Burma (1943–5) and the Mau Mau in Kenya (1952–6). By 1962 he was an officer in the Ugandan Army, becoming its Commander-in-Chief in 1966. Another claim to fame that I was aware of was his boxing prowess – he had been heavyweight champion of the Army and then the country, a claim that I decided I would not challenge under any circumstances.

Although one now hears very little of Milton Obote as President of Uganda, corruption had flourished under his patronage and members of his Acholi and Langi tribes had been promoted in the administration, often far beyond their capabilities. As Prime Minister, he had jealously opposed the Kabaka (King of Buganda), Mutesa II, who had been a benevolent President, and in 1966 assumed the presidency himself, driving the Kabaka into exile. He further promoted members of his and associated tribes to positions of power and brutal massacres became commonplace in other tribal sections of Uganda. The Kakwa tribe, from which Idi Amin came, was particularly badly treated.

In 1970, when Obote attempted to sack his Army C-in-C, Idi Amin – who was popular within the army – Amin staged a successful coup d'état and drove Obote into exile in Tanzania. Idi Amin Dada is reputed to have been guilty of various excesses during his rule but when I spoke to various Ugandans in shops, hotels and on the streets of Kampala, they were quite keen to express views about their leadership. These were a wide cross-section of ordinary Ugandans and their comments about the country's President were largely positive. If the perceived terror that prevailed in the country – according to the Western press of the time – had been fact, then the people I spoke to would have been too terrified to express an opinion to a stranger. Those same people hated Milton Obote and were at great pains to inform me of their reasons for such a view, which usually involved violent deaths of family members.

I have been in countries where terror stalks the streets, before and since this visit to Kampala, and where the atmosphere was oppressive, almost evil. The terror affects everyone and even a casual visitor is soon aware. Nobody in such conditions is brave enough to express any opinion of any kind, pro- or anti-. In fact conversation on any subject is avoided in case the secret police see anyone just talking to strangers.

Uganda was not in this league. Odd complaints about schooling, health care, public transport and the like surfaced in my conversations but then they surfaced when talking to strangers in Britain and, if I am honest, the same type of views still surface here today. There was no indication to me that the population were anything but jovial, bubbly, well-fed people. I therefore put the bad-mouthing of Idi Amin in the world's press down to Foreign Office pique that he had ousted their anointed Ugandan leader Milton Obote.

Following the tour of the tea towels of most of the Scottish Regiments, we discussed our unfortunate treatment of the night before and the surprised President resolved to take the matter up with President Bokassa at the imminent meeting of the Organisation of African Unity in Libreville, Gabon, where they would both be present.

Having made polite conversation for more time than intended I asked the President what he actually wanted us to do for him in the way of flying. He outlined his wishes, including a visit to Riyadh, and made vague references to Amman, the capital of Jordan. I responded with discussion of some of the potential practicalities of his route. Firstly, we discussed the limited range of the Fan-Jet Falcon 20 and I led him to a large map of Africa and the Middle East that took up most of one wall. Indicating an arc on the map of our practical range, he looked very thoughtful for a moment.

Eventually he stuck out his enormous right thumb and plonked it on the surface of the map, proudly declaring that we would refuel just here. The map indicated an unbroken area of dense jungle immediately beneath his thumb, so I asked what was on the ground at the point he was indicating. 'It's an airstrip,' he replied. From my briefcase, I produced a current Jeppesen air navigation chart, which showed no such airfield in the position indicated, about two hundred nautical miles north-east of the northern Ugandan town of Gulu. Further enquiries elicited facts about this landing-strip which sent shivers up my spine.

I explained that although we were a civil aircraft our tyres were very thin, which gave us a high LCN (Load Classification Number) – in other words our wheels pressed on the ground with a high number of tons per square inch, so if the ground underneath the tyres were not thick concrete or load-bearing tarmac, the aircraft would sink into the ground and subsequently become immoveable. He responded that his aircraft landed there without trouble, but he did not know what type of aircraft used the airstrip.

I insisted on ascertaining more details before confirming that a landing there was a practical consideration for our Falcon. He sat on the top of his desk, which visibly bent under the strain of his weight, leant over and picked up a telephone at the extreme of his reach. 'Send in de Foreign Minister,' he bellowed authoritatively, to which the poor unfortunate soul on the other end must have replied, 'Which one?' The President erupted with frustration, 'The new one, you bloody fool, the new one.' He slammed the receiver back on its cradle with some force, causing some of its inner components to fly out of the telephone and pitter-patter onto the wooden floor. Whereupon, perhaps unwisely, my crew and I erupted into uproarious laughter. Fortunately, Idi Amin Dada saw the funny side of the telephone's demise and laughed loudly with us, breaking any tension that might have been created by his secretary.

About five minutes later, as we sipped a second cool drink, the hapless replacement Foreign Minister arrived to face a barrage of questions from his leader that left him totally perplexed. It appeared a complete revelation to him that there was an airfield of any kind in the position under discussion.

Fortunately, I had taken the opportunity whilst waiting for the Minister to arrive at the Command Post to assess the distances involved in flying from Entebbe to the capital of Saudi Arabia. I ended the hapless Minister's discomfiture by announcing to the President that his airfield was too close to Entebbe to be of any use to us, whatever its surface.

We needed somewhere to refuel about 1,200 nautical miles, generally north-east, in order to reach Riyadh with only one stop. Two airfields were obvious contenders so I gave the President and his Minister the choice of Djibouti on the African coast or Aden on the coast of South Yemen. They both have very long runways, the correct fuel and were comfortably within our range, but we would need to obtain prior diplomatic permission, I emphasized, to refuel in either country. The Foreign Minister seemed heartily relieved that the subject of his cross-examination had shifted into an arena with which he was both familiar and comfortable.

He advised his leader in Swahili that Uganda's relations with Djibouti were first class and that the French Embassy in Kampala could be relied upon to produce the necessary documentation quickly, in writing, without any problem. Aden on the other hand was unreliable because South Yemen was involved in a shooting war with North Yemen – furthermore we were unlikely to be allowed into Saudi Arabia if we had already landed anywhere in Yemen, North or South, because Yemen and Saudi Arabia were at daggers drawn with each other over some unexplained assassinations on their joint border.

Appearing to give the problem serious consideration and meanwhile doodling in his desk dairy with a gold fountain pen, the President suddenly looked up and announced that Djibouti would be his choice to refuel and instructed his Minister to make all the necessary arrangements for a take-off from Entebbe early the following morning.

Having satisfactorily established the proposed route, refuelling stops and diplomatic complexities en route to Riyadh, I returned to a throwaway remark that the President had made earlier, that he eventually expected to fly on to Amman in Jordan. As calmly and tactfully as I was able, I explained to His Excellency that Egypt, Syria and Jordan were currently at war with Israel and that as a civil aircraft we were prevented from flying into the active war zone. 'Indeed,' I said, 'I would be putting your life in severe jeopardy by flying over the Saudi/Jordan border towards Amman, regardless of any permissions that may be obtained. It must be remembered that Amman is, in fact, only about fifty miles from Jerusalem itself – about three minutes' flying time for an Israeli F-4 Phantom to be in a firing position on our relatively slow-flying passenger aircraft. If that happened we could not hope to avoid being blasted out of the sky.'

I thought that I could see that my remarks had been absorbed and appreciated, because the whites of Idi Amin's eyes had grown larger and larger, indicating concern as he considered the implications of 'being blasted out of the sky'. Perhaps I should have underlined the seriousness of the proposal by relating my experience with the SAM II missiles over Cairo less than three days earlier, but decided (wrongly as it turned out) that he satisfactorily understood the gravity of his proposal and would make other arrangements if he really did wish to enter the war zone. Subsequent events showed that he was in fact relying on being able to place me in an impossible diplomatic position from which I would be unable to refuse his wishes. This was an embarrassing error on his part, but all that was yet to come.

The Foreign Minister was dismissed with instructions to produce the necessary paperwork for the flight by early evening. He seemed relieved that nothing impossible had been demanded of him and almost scurried towards the door. Just as his hand secured the brass doorknob, His Excellency shouted, 'Wait.' The Minister reluctantly released the shiny brass sphere that promised an end to his potential torment and walked very slowly back to the desk. Idi was writing, head down, on a message pad with his fountain pen, totally engrossed in his authorship, eventually tearing off the missive with a flourish. Before handing over the words of wisdom he had produced, he read them once more, with a smile.

'Send this to King Faisal in Riyadh,' was his almost barked command.

'Certainly,' the Minister responded, as he finally escaped through the door.

Seeming in buoyant mood our host stood up and invited us to join him for lunch. We thanked him and followed him out of the Command Post. His chauffeur held open the rear door of yet another shiny black Mercedes limousine, which was purring away across the wide pavement as the four of us left the building. The President cautiously gazed up and down the empty avenue before emerging and acknowledging his two uniformed guards. He quickly climbed into the vehicle and sat in the middle of the wide leather seat with the engineer and co-pilot being invited to sit either side of him. I was duly shown to the front passenger seat and enjoyed an uninterrupted view of Kampala as we swept past the commercial district, pausing for a short while outside Makerere University whilst the origins of this famous seat of African learning were explained to us. Evidently it is one of Africa's oldest universities, being established in 1921, with a current population of 7,000 students. Its history is scattered with examples of brutal suppression of political activists and some student demonstrations had developed into absolute bloodbaths, but this information was not imparted to us that day.

Very little in Africa is exactly what it seems on first contact. The honour, given to me, of sitting in the prime position in the presidential limousine for our journey to lunch through the centre of Kampala was possibly a back-handed compliment. About a year earlier whilst driving through Kampala in a similar vehicle, a well-organized assassination attempt was made by supporters of Milton Obote on the life of Idi Amin Dada, who was that day riding in the rear of the vehicle. His Head of Security, sitting in the front passenger seat on that occasion, was riddled with bullet holes. His driver was shot, but survived and the President remained unscathed.

Blissfully ignorant of these events my ego grew as we cruised through downtown Kampala in the company of Uganda's President. At times I was almost tempted to wave serenely at the citizens as many of them dutifully acknowledged their leader with his flag of state fluttering over the front of the limousine's bonnet. Our tour of the city complete, we drew under the portico of the Kampala Hotel, a rather grand establishment on about five floors, in a vaguely colonial style and with a cream stone façade. Senior staff were out in force to make an opulent show of welcoming their leader and his guests. Four doors, including the chauffeur's, were opened simultaneously by uniformed staff as we were invited to disembark. The chauffeur had to become most insistent to avoid being dragged out of his own vehicle by the over-enthusiastic hotel staff.

Leading us into a private dining room, the director of the hotel group showed us to an extravagantly appointed table, set for six people, with an extra large chair at one end. The Ugandan Minister of Intelligence and his colleague the Minister of Education were waiting to join us, and after introductions a rather nice bottle of Vintage Moët et Chandon was broached and politely sipped. I was fascinated by the tall-stemmed crystal glass in Idi Amin's enormous hand. It not only looked incongruous, but the glass almost disappeared in the folds of his huge fingers and seemed to be in danger of shattering in his fearsome grip. Conversation was easy with the two ministers, but when I found myself in a small circle with the President, my mind blanked and a suitably light topic of conversation escaped me. As I gazed into space trying to give the impression that I was considering matters of great pith and moment, a Pakistani member of staff walked by and I was reminded that Idi Amin was reputed to have expelled most Asians from his country. It was possibly not the most tactful of topics during pre-lunch drinks, but for want of a better idea, I asked him if it was true that he had deported the entire Ugandan Asian community from the country, as had been reported recently in the British press.

He raised his eyes thoughtfully to the ceiling, lowered his gaze, looked me in the eye, sipped his champagne and said that he had regretfully been forced to take such a step, but not all Asians, as he pointed with his glass to the gentleman who was serving us. He went on to state that the Asians were very good businessmen and that he had had many good friends amongst the Asian community, but in protracted discussions with his ministers of Finance and Defence, it became glaringly obvious to him that the Asians had a complete stranglehold on the financial workings of his country. They prevented normal discharge of international obligations and blocked commerce at every level. He had talked, he said, to the heads of the various departments of government and there seemed always to be a key Asian who was fouling up the wheels of progress. Eventually he decided on the drastic step of banishing a high proportion of them from Uganda. Almost all, he said, decided to resettle in the UK. I asked him if they were thrown out with or without their Ugandan assets. He denied that anything had been confiscated from them and quoted their subsequent success in business in Britain, claiming that such immediate success would have been impossible without them arriving in Europe with all their funds. He said that the withdrawal of their assets over a very short timescale had given the Ugandan economy a severe jolt from which it took nearly a year to recover.

I was mustering my thoughts in order to establish exactly what had been the process of expulsion when the *maître d'* announced that lunch was served and the topic died. I subsequently thought of many questions on the subject which would have been interesting to have asked, but the opportunity, unfortunately, never reoccurred, so no further answers were forthcoming. It should be noted that I present these presidential statements, on what must be a deeply upsetting subject for many of the people directly involved in this deportation, without any guarantee for their veracity. It is a version of events that had recently taken place, which up to that time had never been blessed with an official Ugandan justification, but which seemed to me to go some way towards stating their view of the expulsions – presented to the world by the British press as an intensely wicked act. Perhaps there was more than one interpretation of these events that needed calmer consideration.

During lunch, I was seated between the President and the Minister of Intelligence and the conversation was light and jovial, bordering on the hilarious at times. Our host's comments about his predecessor, Milton Obote, were largely derogatory. He described him as a typical 'union man', whatever that meant. I was later told that Obote had been the leader of a Ugandan workers' union before becoming Prime Minister. In an attempt to appear relatively knowledgeable about Uganda's recent history, I commented that the press had reported that shortly before being deposed, Obote had expelled the hereditary King of Buganda (a major part of central Uganda), Mutesa II (known as the Kabaka), who had up to that time been the President of the new republic. Idi Amin's eyes lit up at the mention of 'the Kabaka'. He said that the King was indeed expelled by Obote to Britain, but that he was currently visiting the country with his son Prince Ronald who was living with his mother and the Kabaka's other wives. 'You must visit them this afternoon and they will tell you how well they are being treated,' he proclaimed. Sure enough, as we finished our coffee a black Mercedes, complete with a furled Ugandan flag on the bonnet and the number plate conspicuous by its absence, drew up under the hotel's portico and the three of us were ushered aboard by the President. The chauffeur had obviously been pre-briefed because he needed no further instruction as we glided out into the sunlight of a tropical Kampala afternoon.

We travelled generally south-west, and about twenty miles past Entebbe turned due west until we reached the town of Mubende in the foothills of higher, thickly forested ground. A few miles outside this small town we turned abruptly left and stopped in a compound surrounded by many mud buildings with roofs largely covered with seasoned palm fronds. With a sweep of his hands the driver announced triumphantly, 'This is Buganda.'

We found ourselves in the reception area of the residence of the Kabaka of Buganda, although he apparently no longer enjoyed his royal title. We were introduced to many older female members of the palace, who all seemed to be either wives of the Kabaka or blood relatives. A single younger man, dressed formally in a light-coloured safari suit, introduced himself as Prince Ronald. Everyone knew the reason for our visit and after a great deal of inconsequential chatter we were invited to sit. The furniture consisted largely of various heaps of comfortable silk cushions into which everyone subsided with little problem. Everyone, that is, except me! I attempted to descend gracefully onto my allotted pile of cushions, but owing to the constant babble of non-stop information being fired in my direction, I completely misjudged the density of the material that would support my weight. The cushion that I intended to sit upon ended up halfway down both legs and as my weight compressed it further I tipped gracefully backwards, executing a manoeuvre that must have looked like a backwards somersault. The Kabaka's wives erupted into peals of raucous laughter which never really subsided, collapsing intermittently into groups of uncontrollable jollity until tears streamed down their cheeks. I made matters worse by laughing with them and as they rushed over to rearrange my cushions and seat me more comfortably two of them actually fell on the floor and rolled about, consumed with unrestrained mirth.

The situation was only brought under control when more sober members of staff arrived with refreshments. It takes a semblance of organization and control to balance a glass of cool fruit juice with a plate of cakes and eat, whilst sitting on a pile of wobbly cushions.

The Kabaka's extended family declared themselves comfortable in their present circumstances and expressed no animosity towards Idi Amin, who, they declared, provided them with a very comfortable living. They had no wish to leave Uganda, except to visit friends in neighbouring countries, which they could do without restriction. They did, however, express some apprehension when Milton Obote's name entered the conversation. He was no friend of the Kabaka's family, they declared, though I failed to establish the specifics of their fear of the President's predecessor, as they changed the subject each time his name was mentioned.

We were later honoured with a tour of the royal residences and they were very proud of the ancient carvings and artefacts from their past, some of which they claimed were more than a thousand years old. The state jewellery, which was quite extensive, was carefully preserved in secure storage with guards to ensure its safety. Though not enormously valuable, the gold and precious stone ceremonial pieces showed notable artistry and some were of great age. After our reverent examination, each crown, bangle and necklace was lovingly returned to its place of safekeeping.

During a tour of the beautiful tropical gardens surrounding the Kabaka's ancestral home, our chauffeur reappeared and ushered us back to the limousine for our return to Kampala. The departure was a ceremonious occasion and the outbreaks of involuntary laughter amongst the King's wives reminded me that my unplanned aerobatics on arrival would be remembered long after our names had been forgotten. Our driver's sedate progress towards the capital was temporarily interrupted by a very large wild bull elephant that emerged from the jungle and nonchalantly strolled up the road towards us, carefully examining each vehicle as it passed. For some inexplicable reason it turned off the road 50 yards behind us and carried out an unprovoked attack on a lone coconut-palm. As the substantial palm crashed to the ground under the unexpected onslaught, the elephant gleefully ran along its length to what had been the crown. Ignoring the actual coconuts, it broke off the top of the tree with its feet and tusks and ate the soft kernel, before trotting off back into the jungle, for all the world like a naughty schoolboy on a scrumping expedition into the neighbour's fruit orchard. He obviously liked the soft, sweet heart of this particular tree very much indeed, for there was very little of it left when he chose to depart.

Back at the Kampala Hotel we were met by the Ugandan Chief of Protocol, who discussed the preferred programme of flights with us. The President wished to depart from Entebbe very early the following morning and twelve VIP meals had been ordered for 4.30 a.m. We told him that the aircraft had already been prepared for immediate take-off so there would be no need to make any further preparations. We asked for transport from the hotel to be arranged for 4 a.m. and I said I would telephone the control tower from my room to arrange for up-to-date weather forecasts for landings at Djibouti and Riyadh to be ready for us before take-off.

He kindly offered to arrange entertainment for us for the evening, which at the Kampala Hotel usually consisted of a gourmet meal in the rooftop restaurant, accompanied by his nubile young wife and her friends. This would be followed by a descent into the Leopard's Lair, the basement night club, where live music, high-class cabaret performances and dancing would eat the hours away until we were all unfit to fly. With as much tact as we could muster I declined his kind offer and said that in view of our early start with such an illustrious passenger we would take the opportunity of a light meal and an early night.

He seemed disappointed that our refusal forced him to forgo an expenses-paid evening for his family and himself in the highest-quality tourist establishment in the whole of Kampala, but said that he understood our decision and reiterated that all our meals and drinks were to be signed to our rooms, for his attention. We sincerely thanked him and he departed, saying that he would see us at 0400 with our transport.

Room service provided an attractive snack and we soon dispersed to our individual rooms for an early night. I spent an hour preparing plans for every conceivable requirement that anyone could unexpectedly throw at us. Diversions to every airfield within range of our proposed track were covered and the facilities available noted down. When confident that every possibility had been considered, I surrendered to a comfortable night's sleep and a 3 o'clock alarm call.

The sharp tap on the bedroom door at a quarter to three was accompanied by a most welcome cup of tea that got the day off to a fine start. The three uniformed figures, complete with suitcases, exited the lift as the government car and Chief of Protocol drew up underneath the hotel's portico. Our journey alongside Lake Victoria to Entebbe was slightly marred by the driver's eagerness to propel the car at breakneck speeds along the dark roads that, even at this early hour, were littered with every kind of animal and human obstruction imaginable.

This phenomenon of drivers presuming that aircrew in uniform travelling to an airport to fly must automatically be in a tearing hurry was one that we frequently encountered, to our eternal distress. Quite often requests to slow down would go unheeded or even convince the driver to actually speed up in a futile attempt to impress us with his driving prowess. In this case we were fortunate to have the Chief of Protocol in the car with us. He translated the stark terror showing on our faces into angry Swahili, which persuaded the driver to proceed at a more sedate pace – just as well because round the next bend a sleepy rhinoceros was lazily ambling across our path on the way to his early morning drink.

It was a real relief to draw up alongside our shiny, white, floodlit Falcon without further mishap. Each crew member slipped into his normal role of preparing the aircraft for flight without the need for too many words. The control tower accepted our flight plan and gave us written permissions for every aspect of the remainder of the flight, as far as those details were then known. The engineer started the auxiliary engine and made us our first cup of coffee, just in time for the completion of all our pre-take-off checks and as we were speculating what time the 'big man' would appear an alarmingly numerous fleet of cars arrived on the dispersal and parked around the aircraft.

Before the growing piles of luggage being disgorged from the vehicles grew too high I found the Chief of Protocol once more and explained the capacity of our small plane. He grinned at me and said, 'There must be some confusion; he obviously thought you had brought a 747 jumbo, not a Fan-Jet Falcon.' More uproarious laughter followed and eventually seven ladies and gentlemen filed up the steps with their suitcases, and when each person's relative seniority had been established everyone was appropriately seated.

In the pre-dawn darkness around us groups of government ministers and their staff, as they turned out to be, vied with each other for the President's attention. They received and imparted information and instructions with solemn expressions until everyone seemed to be satisfied. The Foreign Minister, the same one we met in the Command Post, climbed aboard and took his seat, followed five minutes later by Idi Amin himself, who stood on the top step and waved magnanimously for the benefit of a group of photographers below.

The climb-out from Entebbe was quite spectacular. As we passed 5,000 feet the huge ball of the sun ascended over the horizon, and as we climbed up to cruising altitude the yellow fluorescent disk moved up ever higher. Who said that I was not a magician? I had caused the African dawn to occur two hours early. Some of our passengers were intrigued at the phenomenon and the engineer, who was now acting in his other capacity as chief steward, tactfully explained to them the principles involved.

An hour later the sun had risen far enough to illuminate the ground directly underneath the Falcon and below us unfurled the mysterious land of Ethiopia, its undulating mountainous terrain, with each high ridge seemingly separated from its neighbour by a deep valley and associated streams eventually merging together to become the Blue Nile. Fifty miles to the left lay the capital, Addis Ababa, on its high plateau, clearly visible in the early morning light. The smoke from half a million cooking fires mingled freely with the morning mists to form a ghostly countenance to one of Africa's oldest Christian countries. Its legendary leader, the diminutive 81-year-old King Haile Selassie was still in power, but a vicious communist holocaust would shortly destroy the advanced civilization that he had painstakingly achieved for this impoverished country during his dynamic 45-year reign. He had stoutly defended Ethiopia – or Abyssinia as it was called in 1935 – against Mussolini and his land-hungry Italian Fascists who stooped to the depths of using poison gas against the primitive population of this sparsely populated country.

Abeam Dire Dawa (pronounced 'Deradawa') 50 miles to the right, we contacted Djibouti, who assured us that they were expecting us and that the weather was perfect for our landing. This tiny country of 8,000 square miles, formerly French Somaliland, was the ancestral home of two small tribes, the Afars and the Issas who numbered less than half a million in total. The air traffic controller revealed that a visiting Head of State had thrown their diplomatic capabilities into complete chaos. The most senior person that they had been able to muster to welcome the President at such short notice was the French commandant of a battalion of the local army. When I assured them that he would be perfectly acceptable to His Ugandan Excellency he relaxed and even joked with us. He invited the passengers to disembark and make use of any facilities they may require. He offered hot or cold drinks if anyone wished. I thanked him and accepted his kind offer, saying that they would all, probably, appreciate a stretch of their legs whilst refuelling was in progress.

In this atmosphere of co-operation we landed and were hooked up to a refuelling bowser very efficiently. The Commandant in full white tropical uniform smartly saluted everyone as they walked down the steps and clicked his heels together as only the French Army can. The President and his Foreign Minister chatted amiably with him in the cool of the early morning and he asked me if he could see the aircraft's cockpit as he was an aviator himself. I sat him in the captain's seat and explained the instruments that I thought would interest him.

He was very keen on hearing about our Omega navigation system and wrote down the details with a view to having it installed in their communications aircraft. He said that they were usually lost from take-off to landing as none of their ground radio aids remained serviceable for very long and a satellite system would be an absolute godsend, whilst admitting that it might be quite frightening knowing the aircraft's position with absolute certainty. As it was they drifted over everyone else's territory with gay abandon and hoped that they would eventually find their way home before the fuel ran out. Knowing where they were at any time would be most unusual and make them very nervous of being attacked. I assured him that knowing one's position accurately without the need for ground radio aids was a most reassuring feeling.

Our Falcon's pressure refuelling system had been newly fitted in Switzerland

and we were experiencing some problems in balancing the fuel in the port and starboard wing tanks. On this occasion there was a discrepancy of over a thousand pounds between the two wings, which amounted to nearly half a ton and could produce a tendency to rotate the aircraft at an alarming rate on take-off. The Commandant, who by this stage was much more relaxed, suggested that moving that big chap, pointing to Idi Amin, from the heavy side of the aircraft to the light side would make all the difference. We noted his comments, but decided to open up the over-wing fuel cap to balance the fuel visually, with a refuelling hose from the fuel bowser. When we were absolutely satisfied that the fuel levels were equal, the engineer and I completed the pre-flight inspections and prepared to leave.

Our proposed track took us up the middle of the Red Sea until well clear of Yemen and then turn directly north-east for Riyadh, if the Saudi Air Traffic Control system permitted us to fly off the civil airways. In the event they were quite happy with our proposals and offered to advise us when they could see that we were clear of North Yemen. In order to be sure that we would be beyond the threat of any possible anti-aircraft activity and to conserve fuel we elected to fly at 44,000 feet – which gave us a marvellous view of the legendary Empty Quarter (in Arabic, 'Rub al Khali'), the world's largest continuous area of sand, as we were about to turn towards Riyadh.

The Saudi air traffic controller at Jeddah informed us that we were abeam the Yemeni port of Hodeida and should shortly be sighting the Farasan Islands dead ahead where we could turn right towards Riyadh. The sea around these islands was the site in the Red Sea where Captain Jacques Yves Cousteau, the co-inventor of the aqualung (later renamed Self-Contained Underwater Breathing Apparatus, or SCUBA), encountered the greatest concentration of sharks of nearly every variety on his first diving expedition to this prolific sea.

Peering into the mountainous terrain beyond Hodeida to the east, we could just make out the country's capital city, Sanaa – an intriguing place with its buildings frequently wreathed in clouds, because it is built on a plateau 7,250 feet (about one and a half miles) high. The low-lying Farasan Islands came into view a short time later, about five miles offshore, and in accordance with Jeddah Control's instructions we turned north-east towards the Saudi capital. The islands were roughly one third of the flight time from Djibouti, but the remaining two thirds were over unbroken sand and rock. The word 'inhospitable' is probably overused in modern literature, but the majority of this parched desert of Saudi Arabia can reasonably be described as truly inhospitable. The chances of us being forced to survive in the blisteringly hot terrain below our Falcon were remote indeed, but I involuntarily found myself making lists of the amounts of fresh water

MILES

KM

BAY OF BISCAY

PARIS

SWITZERLAND

BASEL

FRANCE

SPAIN

MADRID

PORTUGAL

LISBON

ROME

MEDITER—

GIBRALTAR

TANGIER

ALGIERS

TUNIS

SICILY

MALT

CASABLANCA

ORAN

SFAX

RABAT

OCCOROM

FES

TRIPOLI

LEPTIS MAGNA

MARRAKESH

MISRATAH

SIRTE

GHADAMIS

ALGERIA

SEBHA

LIB

TAMANRASSET

GHAT

SAHAR

WESTERN

SAHARA

NOUADHIBOU

MALI

NIGER

NOUAKCHOTT

MAURITANIA

TIMBUKTU

LAKE CHAD

DAKAR

NIAMEY

FOR

ND

THE GAMBIA

SENEGAL

UPPER

VOLTA

SENEGAL

KANO

GUINEA BISSAU

BAMAKO

OUAGADOUGOU

NIGERIA

CONAKRY

GUINEA

MO

FREETOWN

SIERRA LEONE

IVORY COAST

GHANA

CAMEROON

AF

MONROVIA

LIBERIA

ACCRA

DOUALA

YAOUNDE

B

ABIDJAN

EQ GUINEA

LIBREVILLE

GABON

194

ODESA

BLACK SEA

ISTANBUL

ATHENS

CASPIAN SEA

CRRTA

TURKEY

RANEAN

CYPRUS

SYRIA

DAMASCUS

TEHRAN

PERSIA/IRAN

LEBANON
BEIRUT

BAGHDAD

IRAQ

ISRAEL

MERSA
MATRUH

EL ALAMEIN

PALESTINE

AMMAN

TOBRUK

EL BARANI

SUEZ

JORDAN

KUWAIT

GULF

STRAITS
OF
HORMUZ

CAIRO

QATTARA
DEPRESSION

EGYPT

LUXOR

RIYADH

SAUDI
ARABIA

BAHRAIN

QATAR

U.A.E.

MUSCAT

KUFRAH

ASWAN

MEDINA

JEDDAH
MECCA

THE EMPTY QUARTER

OMAN

RED
SEA

OMDURMAN

KHARTOUM

ERITREA
MODEITO

NORTH

SANAA

SOUTH

YEMEN

TAIZ

ADEN

GULF
OF ADEN

SUDAN

DJIBOUTI

ADDIS ABABA

SOMALIA

PUBLIC

ETHIOPIA

MOGADISHU

UGANDA

KENYA

LAKE
KIVU

KAMPALA

ENTEBBE

LAKE
VICTORIA

CONGO

RWANDA

and other survival requisites as the arid landscape rushed by nearly nine miles below us. I patted the structure of the aircraft affectionately and whispered to it to keep those engines burning and turning nicely, and to be 'a good girl'. I am pleased to say that she obliged beautifully.

As we were preparing to descend towards Riyadh an authoritative voice enquired whether we were carrying the President of Uganda. As I answered in the affirmative it was obvious to me that we were about to undergo a dose of full ceremonial, as one rarely experiences it in lifetimes of flying kings, queens and other assorted Heads of State.

Sure enough that assessment became all too apparent as we taxied across the acres of concrete dispersal towards the conspicuous red carpet. This one was shimmering, almost fluorescent, in the deepest of blood-red silks. I glanced up at the massive airport buildings, the flat roofs of which were silhouetted with soldiers, each one conspicuously armed with an automatic weapon – not a single rank of soldiers, you understand, but two ranks, back to back. One line was turned towards the airport whilst the other one was quite clearly facing towards the city itself. As we extinguished our trusty engines at the end of the red silk carpet, a line of artillery pieces close by fired an immaculate 21-gun salute.

The noise of the guns was ear shattering. As the explosions died away the unmistakable figure of King Ibn Abdul Aziz al Saud Faisal, no doubt accustomed to feeling silk carpets beneath his feet, strode confidently towards the Falcon's steps. Fortunately, with the warning radio call before landing, we had had time to ensure that His Excellency Idi Amin Dada was bedecked in his very finest of uniforms before lowering the steps, though how he managed to manoeuvre his huge body into his finery in the cramped confines of the Falcon's tiny cabin is anyone's guess. He must have been rolling about the floor to achieve the unbelievably smart appearance that he had assumed as he stepped towards the king. The usual hugs and kisses were given and received, and with a beaming smile he was led up to the obligatory immaculate guard of honour, which had as its commander one of the king's own sons. Father and son were bedecked in snow-white robes that were edged in pure gold. A great deal of pure gold.

Sitting in the cockpit of our stationary aircraft, we were doing our best to look ceremonious. Whilst the welcoming show was in progress, we tried to assess the actual numbers of troops involved in this show of force, ringing the rooftops. As the furthest soldiers were on very high buildings off to our right, some of which were at least a mile distant, an actual count was impossible. The best we could achieve was a guesstimate of the number of soldiers within view at well in excess of 2,000, but then we noticed further armed soldiers standing in a line on the ground within touching distance of each other, facing the airfield, who had not been visible earlier. Some of them were obscured from us by items of ground servicing equipment so accurate counts were impossible. Our final assessment of the overall number of soldiers in the protection unit was 2-3,000. A truly impressive show.

Eventually King Faisal and his guest strolled into the VIP lounge, the carpet was rolled up and the guard of honour marched away with much flashing of swords and barked commands. This was the signal for our engineer to emerge from the Falcon rather like a greyhound coming out of its trap at the start of a race. He needed to complete his aircraft after-landing checks before the time limits for such maintenance had expired. He moved so fast that the flurry of activity alarmed one of the Saudi security officers, who sprinted over to check that everything was OK.

When satisfied, he waved a fleet of white limousines alongside for the President's entourage and their luggage. The king's Chief of Protocol appeared and sat on the jump-seat in the cockpit from where we had some difficulty in untangling his robes as they snagged on the protuberances found inside the working places of even the most modern aircraft. Sitting comfortably at last, with only a few small aircraft grease marks on his brown robes, he outlined our programme.

Evidently the Saudis were uncertain as to the reason for the President's visit, but they estimated that he would be staying a couple of days, so arrangements had been made to accommodate his delegation, including the three of us, within King Faisal's palace in Riyadh. One of the white limousines was specifically for our use and would stay with us throughout our visit. A glance to my left showed that it was already in attendance two metres away from our port wingtip. A similar distance away on the starboard wingtip was a gentleman with a fuel bowser, obviously trying to offer us fuel.

We told the protocol supremo that we would prepare the Falcon for departure before coming to the palace, and that if we could refuel in this position it would take us about thirty minutes to be ready. He confirmed that he would wait for us in the VIP lounge and urged us not to hurry. Air Traffic instructed us to refuel in our current position, but asked us to taxi to a secure area close by to leave our Falcon overnight. The chief of the VIP lounge took our used food boxes for cleaning and gave us his telephone number for us to order fresh meals when take-off details were known.

As we completed our post-landing chores, the scream of motorcycle outriders sirens confirmed that the king's party was leaving the airfield with maximum ceremonial. The royal chauffeur stowed our three suitcases in his vehicle as we activated our own security systems and walked to the VIP lounge. It was noticeable that the Chief of Protocol had relaxed considerably now that his royal taskmaster was on his way to the palace. We leisurely sipped cool fruit juices before being seated in the cream leather upholstery of the capacious white limousine. Even our relatively lowly status entitled us to four immaculate and very noisy police outriders to escort us to our upmarket residence. The city's traffic police were still blocking more ordinary vehicles away from our route to the Palace.

As the limousine approached the walls of the palace, impressive gates swung open as if by magic and we drew up beneath a Romanesque white marble portico, the roof of which was supported by four robust columns surmounted by ornate Ionic capitals. We were entering the royal palace through the main entrance, not, as expected, some lesser door reserved for more menial souls. We were suitably impressed and the cooling burble of clear water trickling along a dozen picturesque miniature streams soothed the senses as we crossed the inner hall.

The major-domo led us up an impressively wide staircase to a suite of rooms on the first floor. Each room had drapes of material suspended from the centre of the ceiling and secured two-thirds of the way up the walls so that the pleats of the material clung to the walls in the style of a tent. A chandelier suspended from the central point within the material gave an almost bizarre appearance. The main bathroom of several available had floors, walls and ceiling covered in mirrors, with numerous lights spread around the corners. Seeing reflections of oneself wherever the eyes fell was quite unsettling and whether the mirrors were two-way or not posed intriguing questions.

A servant appeared at the door to announce that food would be served in an hour's time in the dining room off the main entrance hall. The places at the very large table were all named and uncannily all the waiters seemed to know everyone's name without being told – they had been very well briefed. As we sat in our allotted ornate, high-backed, dark wooden, leather-upholstered chairs, a waiter stood rigidly behind each chair and I noticed that five of the chairs were unoccupied – though each chair still had a servant stood behind them as if the chairs had been occupied. When the first course, a spicy soup, was served, each waiter held the plateful until, without any obvious signal, the plates were placed simultaneously in front of each guest and eating commenced almost immediately. To my great surprise, as I spooned the last of the tasty soup into my mouth, the plate and spoon were removed by my waiter and immediately another plateful of soup was placed on the table in front of me and a fresh spoon appeared on the white tablecloth. Not knowing what was expected I looked around the table and saw that the other diners were taking a single spoonful of the second plate of soup and leaving the spoon on the dining plate beneath the soup plate. I did the same and when everyone ceased eating, the full plates were taken away by our respective waiters, again almost simultaneously.

The meal progressed at a relaxed pace, each course being treated in exactly the same way, so that we ended each course with full plates. The male diners on each side of me were dressed in the white gold-trimmed robes of the nobility and spoke perfect English. They were of a younger generation, probably aged about twenty-five with lively conversations and ready smiles. When I remarked that finishing a course with a full plate was unusual, they laughed and said that most guests found it slightly perplexing, but the food, when we had finished with it, was given to the families of the servants, so the more we left, the more food their families received. They said that if I found anything unusual I should just watch them and do the same, but that if they anticipated a problem they would warn me beforehand.

Seeing me trying to read the names in front of them on the table, they introduced themselves and I was not surprised to find that they were both the king's sons and therefore royal princes. They knew London quite well, but only the more genteel aspects, they claimed, as they were chaperoned by the Saudi Embassy whilst staying in the city.

Around the fifth course of the meal, the occupants of the empty chairs arrived having obviously been present at the meeting, until then, between King Faisal and President Amin, complete with his entourage. They were somewhat dismissive of the Ugandan President's proposals and indiscreetly proceeded to discuss what had been suggested. It appeared that he had a scheme to stop the war (the October War already mentioned) with his 'girl soldiers'. The precise details of his tactics were not clear, but the fighting qualities of his girls seemed uncertain and how these young ladies were to be deployed into the war zone was quite vague.

I could well appreciate that if, as these probable eyewitnesses stated, a suggestion had been made to employ tactics of questionable decorum in this conflict, King Faisal would have been horrified. This male-dominated Muslim country that routinely covered its women in order to conceal their female attributes would never condone such a proposal. Presumably our visit here was to achieve an element of financial assistance through the offer of such proposals. If this was the case, I reckoned that we could anticipate leaving the king's palace sooner rather than later.

The newcomers to the dining table took their seats and commenced the meal at the stage that the rest of the diners had already reached so they accepted missing the first four courses.

In the early evening we were treated to a tour of the city starting with an obligatory viewing of 'Chop Square' where most Fridays (the Muslim Holy day), in front of a large crowd, a man with a vicious sword or axe separated items of adjudged criminals' anatomy from their persons in accordance with Sharia Law. Having seen the marks of dried blood liberally splattered across the ground always convinced me to be on my very best behaviour for the duration of any stay in the city. A year after our first visit to this gruesome site, the assassin of King Faisal, our current host, was decapitated in this very square with a golden sword. According to the world's press of the time, the assassin was his nephew.

Browsing around the shops could be difficult because every time the muezzin called the faithful to prayer from the nearest minaret, the shopkeepers herded all their customers outside into the street and closed the shop. Presumably the shop staff were answering the call to prayer in the mosque beneath the minaret. These interruptions to normal commerce occurred five times a day, so anyone shopping for much more than an hour was bound to encounter at least one and frequently two breaks which generally lasted about twenty minutes, although it was more like half an hour before the shops opened their doors again.

Strict observance of these religious requirements was enforced by the Religious Police, who were armed with stout sticks or staves to enforce the law as they saw it. We witnessed ordinary people walking down average streets receiving arbitrary punishment with a whack from a stick for no apparent reason. Surprisingly to us, the victims of such punishment rarely complained and we were not involved. Expatriates with whom we came into contact assured us that they were never bothered by these quasi-official religious law enforcers, but some had witnessed severe treatment of shop owners who were slow in closing their shops when required.

We spent two days enjoying the privileges that living in the royal palace provided. We assumed the meetings were continuing, but were given no further insights into the mechanics of the discussions. The princes were very hospitable towards us, so when two of them asked to see our Falcon I had no compunction in providing an official tour of the aircraft, which they thoroughly enjoyed.

Back at the palace, the Chief of Protocol told me that we would be leaving in the early evening. He could not tell us what destination had been chosen so we emphasized the difficulties we would have with planning the flight without knowing where we would be going. He assured us that he was doing his best to find out the details, but that he was not in direct contact with the Ugandan President at that time, the implication being that Idi Amin was on the move somewhere and therefore incommunicado.

Our best efforts proved fruitless in discovering the proposed destination and I became distinctly suspicious. We manned the Falcon and taxied it to the end of the red carpet to await developments. The troops assembled on their respective rooftops, so the full ceremonial works appeared to have been put into gear once more. The auxiliary engine kept us cool and heated the coffee water, but when the guard of honour marched towards us we closed down the unnecessary noise and waited in silence. About an hour later the wailing of motorbike sirens announced the arrival of the main players. Giving them a little time to settle down in the VIP lounge, I walked up the red carpet into the lounge to establish the important missing details.

King Faisal and the Ugandan President were seated at the far side of the room so I had no alternative but to walk directly up to them. About two metres away from the king, one of his security guards took hold of my right arm quite forcibly. King Faisal instructed him to release me and asked, 'Is there a problem?'

'Yes,' I said, 'nobody has divulged the destination and I need to submit a flight plan to the Saudi authorities before they will allow us to taxi.'

Idi Amin intervened and announced, 'We will be going to Amman, the capital of Jordan, to see King Hussein.'

Trying to speak with equanimity in almost deferential tones, I turned to face the Ugandan President to make it absolutely clear, without stating the fact, that I was not contradicting the king personally. 'Jordan,' I said, 'declared war on Israel three days ago. The two countries have joint borders, and in fact Amman is only about fifty miles from Jerusalem. They are shooting and killing each other at this very moment. We are an unarmed civil aircraft and as such are not permitted by international law to fly into this or any other war zone. If you would like us to fly you anywhere else, we will be only too happy to oblige, providing it is outside an active war zone.'

The king was very angry indeed and looked as if he was about to explode. Anticipating that they would like to confer in private, I made my excuses and withdrew back to the calm of the Falcon cockpit. Fifteen minutes later we were asked to vacate the end of the red carpet and move to a new spot about 50 metres away. We complied as instructed and, avoiding blowing over the guard of honour with my jet blast, taxied in an arc to the new spot. As we vacated the carpet, our place in the prime position was taken by a Lockheed Jetstar, a four-engined version of an aircraft similar in size to our Falcon. It was an identical machine to the Libyan military communications aircraft, but this one was in United States of American colours.

As the Jetstar engines shut down, its door opened and two obvious Americans in plain clothes ran down the steps, across the dispersal to us and up our steps. The spokesman, probably the captain, introduced himself and said that he had heard that we had refused to fly to Amman. I confirmed his information and asked for their identity.

He replied, 'We are the American military advisers.'

'What are you doing here,' I asked.

He replied in a relaxed southern drawl, 'Well we have *advised them* that

Amman is over there.' Pointing in a north-westerly direction he continued with a deadpan expression, 'We have further advised them that if they need us, we will be over there' – pointing due east. 'We ain't flying into no war zone for nobody.'

This was perhaps not the most grammatical sentence ever created, but was nevertheless a great relief to me that an independent aviation adviser had come to a conclusion identical to my own. If anyone was contemplating heaving us into jail for insubordination, then at least we could anticipate some humorous company.

Both aircraft remained on the dispersal as if awaiting some important management decision; the guard of honour fidgeted with their rifles and exercised their feet, and a general unease permeated the whole proceedings. Eventually the guard of honour was marched away, the rooftop troops dispersed and the red carpet was rolled up. The main players left the airport to a greatly reduced ceremonial and the two aircraft crews played cards in the back of the Falcon for the princely stake of a dollar a hand. Half an hour later the Chief of Protocol came up the steps saying that the Jetstar could return to its hangar and we could return to our normal overnight position.

He told me that the king was 'not best pleased', but that we were still welcome back at the palace. He asked whether it was true that the Ugandan President had failed to divulge his routeing until he arrived at the VIP lounge. When I confirmed that this was the case, he expressed amazement. 'What a buffoon!' He told the king, he said, that I had agreed to fly to Amman that very afternoon. The king had been very surprised, in view of the worsening conflict, but he had been assured. The Chief of Protocol did not anticipate a response from me, so I let the matter drop.

The arrival of our limousine at the Falcon as we shut down the engines was very reassuring. I had pictured us walking up the road carrying our own suitcases and knocking on the palace gates, but I need not have feared. No one, I was assured by the Chief of Protocol, blamed the crew for the debacle and we were as welcome as ever, but he did not anticipate that our stay would be a long one this time.

The next morning I was woken quite early to be told that we were required at the airport and would be flying as soon as possible. I was informed that the destination was Baghdad, the capital of Iraq. I telephoned the VIP lounge to organize the meals as instructed and was told that they were already at the aircraft. They really did want rid of us as quickly as possible, it seemed.

Arriving at the Falcon just as dawn was breaking, the engineer swung into his familiar pre-flight routine, so in the absence of any further routing information the co-pilot and I took the limousine over to the flight planning room to render a flight plan. From the outset, something was strange. The walls of any international flight planning room are festooned with weather reports that are constantly updated, and most importantly, notams. These warnings cover everything that could be of interest to anyone landing at the named airfield, listing relevant times and activities to be noted. It would be most unusual to find no notams on the board for a neighbouring capital city.

I asked the Air Traffic Control officer in charge of the planning room and he said that all notams for Baghdad were 'out of date' so they had been removed overnight. I asked to see any current notams and he stated that there were none in force. We had to accept his assurances, but it was with a great deal of unease.

Our flight plan was accepted with undue haste, stamped as official, and returned with a beaming smile, but the officer had not checked the details as if he knew what it contained before we rendered it. Something would appear to be wrong, but we had complied with every regulation, both international and local. Nothing indicated a particular problem so we proceeded with organizing the flight. The weather en route and at our destination was perfect. We had plenty of fuel to divert to at least six different international airfields at any stage of the flight. Everything seemed to be organized to reassure us, but I was still cautious.

The ceremonial was noticeably lower key – no guard of honour, no troops on buildings but King Faisal did stand on the end of the red carpet as I started an engine to taxi clear. His body language clearly indicated a distinct lack of enthusiasm for anything Ugandan and he retreated back into the calm of the VIP lounge at the first rotation of our wheels.

The flight proceeded normally in line with the flight plan, until our first radio contact with Baghdad control. They requested us to squawk 2346 and turn 90 degrees right onto due east. After a minute they confirmed that they had us in firm contact at Flight Level 420 and we should resume our previous course. This was pure military, not civil control. We were instructed to avoid flying over Baghdad city and to commence a slow descent towards the runway and stand by for further instructions at 10,000 feet. I checked whether we would be carrying out the standard Instrument Landing System (ILS) approach to Baghdad International and was told in no uncertain terms that all ground navigation systems were out of operation. They were intending to guide us down the extended centreline of the runway until I could confirm that I was visual with the airfield.

It was all very intriguing until I looked underneath the Falcon at the desert floor – every 500 metres along the extended centreline of the runway, an enormous gun pointed straight at us. Below 2,000 feet they did us the kindness of turning the barrels of their guns 90 degrees away from us, first one left, second one right and so on, so that we were not looking immediately down the barrel of each gun as we flew over it. I was very impressed, because such a manoeuvre would take a great deal of organizing. At about two miles range, the barrel of each gun swung rapidly sideways and as we passed above, they swung smartly back in reverse line of the runway. This was not a normal military requirement and was being done solely to give us confidence that there was no intention of firing those guns at us.

But why was this massive concentration of guns there in the first place? With a little thought it became glaringly obvious. Sometime during the last few hours, Iraq had apparently joined its Arab neighbours and declared war on Israel. It could not have been a long time ago because the news had not yet appeared on the BBC Overseas Service. So that was the reason for the subterfuge in the planning room at Riyadh airport. We had been completely hoodwinked. I wondered whether our star passenger knew the true situation, but decided not to put it to the test. Our main priority now was to land the Falcon safely at Baghdad airport – any other considerations were completely superfluous. There's an art in knowing when to back down.

Iraq military radar remained with us until our wheels touched the ground and we taxied to the front of the airport building. We were instructed to close down our engines and remain in our present position, but our passengers were not to disembark until instructed. As we silenced our noisy motors, the concrete dispersal became alive with activity. A large military band with magnificently burnished brass helmets was assembled immediately and a resplendent guard of honour marched immaculately into position alongside a hastily produced red carpet leading to our steps. They might have been at war, but they were not intending to let their protocol slip in any way. The rendition of the Ugandan and Iraqi national anthems was excellent and as President Bakr of Iraq and President Amin of Uganda inspected the guard, the band played some splendidly chosen music for our appreciation.

I really had not expected such pomp and ceremony, but then I had not expected to be in Iraq at all 2? hours previously, so I resolved to play the hand as it was being dealt and not to over-concentrate on the ramifications. The Iraqi Chief of Protocol ran up the steps and with a cheery grin pushed his face into the cockpit, between the two pilots. 'Anything I can get you,' he enquired.

'Yes!' I replied, 'some information would be quite useful. Firstly, has Iraq joined Egypt, Jordan and Syria in declaring war on Israel?'

'Yes,' he responded, 'about twelve hours ago.'

The subterfuge of hiding all the notams in the Riyadh flight planning room now made sense. Not nice, not friendly and with dangerous overtones, but understandable.

'Where would you like us to park?' I enquired and he suggested that we could stay exactly where we had come to rest. 'Where are the rest of your aircraft that would normally be all over this dispersal?'

'They must all be in the hangars undergoing maintenance,' he guessed.

'Is there no room in any hangar for our small Falcon, because I feel very vulnerable with our white and gold aircraft sitting out in the middle of all this concrete on its own in the burning sun. You can just imagine an Israeli bomber pilot seeing us and selecting the Falcon as the perfect target. He could hardly miss. Surely there must be some cover that our Falcon could use whilst we are staying in Baghdad?'

He volunteered to enquire.

It may seem to the casual observer that I was being somewhat pedantic about my Falcon's security, but the co-pilot, on this occasion Steve Sparrow, had been sent to Damascus in the days of the Kingdom of Libya Airlines, shortly after the revolution, flying one of former King Idris's Learjets. Syria had recently declared war on Israel and its air force was fighting a violent air-to-air battle with the Israeli air force over Syrian and Israeli territory. Steve's Learjet was loaded with £4.5 million in gold bars for the Libyan Ambassador in Damascus.

When he landed he taxied to the VIP lounge to await the expected diplomatic activity. Eventually the Embassy sent a messenger to say that the Ambassador would collect the cargo the following morning and he was to securely lock the aircraft and stay the night in the Damascus Airport Hotel. He complied with his instructions, locked the Learjet and the Embassy car took him to the hotel, which was very close and overlooked the airport dispersal. Fancying a cool beer in the bar, he unlocked his suitcase and was changing into plain clothes when he decided to draw back the room curtains to check on the view of the airport.

He found himself looking directly down on to the Learjet about half a mile away. It was perfectly secure and undisturbed so he walked towards the room door, but before he left the room something made him take another look. He scrutinized the entire area around his aircraft and, being perfectly happy, was about to turn away when there was the first of four massive explosions. When he shook his head and refocused his eyes again he could not believe what he saw. Where his Learjet had stood seconds before there was a huge hole in the concrete, with tiny white pieces of what could have been aircraft parts scattered over about 100 metres. Other craters could be seen near the main runway and a small fire had started close to one of the fuel stores.

He changed back into his uniform, gathered the rest of the crew and leapt into a taxi to go to see the damage. He cannot remember what they hoped to achieve but whatever it was, when they arrived at the airport buildings he was prevented from achieving anything. Soldiers with both heavy and light weapons were running wildly in all directions. Officers in vehicles were everywhere, but none of them seemed to be actually doing very much. He was blocked from even entering the airport buildings by soldiers who seemed to be about to open fire without quite knowing what they should fire at.

After about an hour of trying to persuade somebody to allow them to return to where their Learjet had been, they gave up, found the same taxi that had brought them to the airport and returned to the Damascus Airport Hotel. Failing a better suggestion, they retired to the bar and cogitated on their poor position over a couple of glasses of cool beer. Nobody contacted them that night and all the telephone lines were dead so they ate, had a game of cards and went to bed.

The following morning, the hotel director informed Steve that the Libyan Embassy had been vacated in the night and that all the diplomatic staff had crossed the border into Lebanon. The airport was closed until further notice and he suggested that exiting stage right, in the direction of Beirut, might be a wise move in the circumstances. With some major worries about the welfare of the £4.5 million of gold they were carrying on the aeroplane before the Israeli bomb had dropped on it, they persuaded the same taxi driver to drive them to the Lebanese border.

At the border the immigration officials refused to allow the Syrian taxi to cross into Lebanon, so they paid his quite reasonable fare and set off to walk in the direction of Beirut. In uniform, carrying a suitcase each, the three of them were quite conspicuous walking through the Lebanese countryside and it was not long before an entrepreneurial agricultural gentleman drew up alongside and offered to drive them to the Libyan Embassy – at a price. Terms were soon agreed and life improved beyond measure when they walked into the Embassy. The international airport was closed due to aggressive military air activity, so they spent a pleasant three-day break in Beirut whilst a suitable course of action was decided.

Eventually the Ambassador organized a ship to take them to Larnaca in Cyprus, from where Libyan Arab Airlines found them three first-class seats for their return to Tripoli. The £4.5 million of gold was never recovered, or if it was, someone became very rich. Perhaps there is a patch of tarmac in Damascus airport's dispersal containing a misshapen heavy blob that will be discovered when the diggers are brought in to improve the hardstanding.

By the time the Chief of Protocol returned, we had refuelled, the guard and band had marched off and our passengers had disappeared in a flurry of wailing sirens. He proudly announced that he had the perfect solution to our vulnerability. Two soldiers would be out shortly to stand guard on our Falcon whilst it was at the international airport. This gave us no consolation whatsoever, but it was obvious that nothing better could be achieved by negotiation, so we nervously accepted his arrangements.

Expecting a limousine to appear at any minute and hoping that it would whisk us off to Scheherazade's Palace for the perfumed delights of *A Thousand and One Nights*, we waited, suitcases in hand. Unfortunately the Chief of Protocol had other ideas. He had been outside the airport and grabbed a beat-up old taxi for our transport. Not only that, but we had to carry our own cases through the empty airport buildings and were just stowing the three cases into the taxi's boot when an angry immigration official ran screaming to drag us back into the building. What next? we wondered, as we re-enlisted the aid of the Protocol office. It would appear that this little official was hurtling into a paroxysm of anger because we were leaving the airport without having our passports stamped. What a difference from Saudi Arabia. We really had come down a peg or two.

The taxi took us to the Baghdad Hotel in the middle of the city, close to the River Tigris, where the driver demanded his fare. That would have been reasonable but he would not accept any of our currencies and kept the other crew members hostage on the pavement whilst I walked the 15 metres over to the reception desk and changed US dollars into sufficient Iraqi currency to satisfy his demands. Looking at the state of his vehicle we must have paid him enough for a new taxi. It was some relief to find that our three en suite rooms had been ordered and were ready for us. As we completed the inevitable hotel paperwork a smart Iraqi army officer in uniform sought us out and announced in perfect English that he was our liaison officer for the duration of our stay, and – surprise, surprise – he had his own official car, so it was difficult to see why we were messing about with beat-up taxis.

A walking tour of the city in the cool of the evening was very interesting. The mosques, of which there were dozens, were each surmounted by gold, turquoise or pale green bulbous domes, exactly as one is led to expect from the tales of *The Arabian Nights*. They are unique in the Muslim world, unlike the domes on the mosques of neighbouring Syria, Persia, Saudi Arabia or Turkey.

Meandering through the Silver Souk, or market, as we slowly made our way back to the hotel we were suddenly in the centre of violent action. Whilst intently haggling with a shopkeeper for a silver cigarette box I was aware that all was not well when a rather swarthy, overweight, bareheaded gentleman, dressed in mixed colour Arab robes, passed horizontally over my head at some considerable speed and smashed with a sickening thud against a nearby wall. As he lay dazed and groaning on the ground a black wallet could be seen in his right hand. Our liaison officer, who by now was in plain clothes, took a step forward, pulled the wallet from the man's grasp and gave it to our engineer. It seemed that our chaperon, looking after our better interests, had seen this rogue with his hand in the engineer's pocket and being somewhat of a wrestling champion decided to demonstrate his prowess. In an instant he had somehow taken this rather large gentleman round the waist and heaved him bodily skywards to the miscreant's grave discomfort. He was bleeding profusely by the time our protector handed the thief over to a nearby policeman.

I regretted that my attention had been elsewhere whilst the action had quickly developed behind. The shopkeeper too was most impressed, capitulated to my lowest offer and seemed keen to be rid of us as quickly as possible. Perhaps he thought that police involvement would get his establishment a bad name, or maybe the local mafia were his worry. Whatever the reason, it helped me secure a beautifully made solid silver box for US$10 less than I had been prepared to pay.

We wandered back nonchalantly to the Baghdad Hotel where we decided that our guard had truly earned a bottle of beer for his heroic efforts. He stayed with us for our evening meal and we found him very pleasant company. It was quite comforting whilst we were in somewhat of an involuntary limbo in the middle of a country at war to have a companion prepared to protect us as spontaneously as he had just proved.

Before retiring for the night he suggested a stroll by the river to stretch our legs. The action by the side of the Tigris was fascinating, with dozens of teenage boys fishing by the light of intensely bright lanterns. Their lines, on the end of rudimentary fishing rods, had coloured metal spinners, which they deftly pulled across the beam of the light with notable success. A steady number of fish averaging about a kilo in weight ended up on the bank where the anglers' sisters, usually younger sisters, bargained with passers-by to sell the fish. Scales were suspended from bank-side trees to ensure fair play and each sale was accompanied by good-natured bargaining. Because there were so many boys fishing, it was difficult to assess the success rate, but each one appeared to be catching at least a fish an hour. The girls were achieving about two dinars a pound, so the income in Iraqi terms was substantial.

I gathered that the season for these migratory fish, which looked rather like bass, was very limited and as these were the last few days, maximum effort was being directed at the task. When we later tasted these fish in the hotel they had a pleasant flavour, although their flesh was more dense than Mediterranean sea bass, possibly because of their obvious predatory lifestyle. They were usually served in portions rather than a whole fish to one person.

Not knowing the duration of our stay in the country, we decided the next morning that some unavoidable routine maintenance must be carried out on our Falcon, so we dressed in uniform and our guard took us to the airport. He obviously carried a reasonable amount of clout, because the immigration apparatchik who had been so officious on our arrival was forcefully told to 'Go away'. I suppose that in this war situation the military reigned supreme.

As we approached our aircraft we were all horrified to see that someone, probably one of the guards, had pulled our high-frequency fixed copper radio aerial out of its anchorage point at the back of the starboard wing. There was absolutely no way of repairing the damage away from base, so the other end of the wire had to be cut off the starboard engine intake cowling to protect the aerodynamic integrity of the airframe. Needless to say, before the engineer removed the dangling wire I photographed the evidence and made sure that everyone in Iraqi authority was aware of this unwanted damage.

It's only a wire, was the initial reaction of generals more involved with executing the war, so I was forced to explain to them that such damage had far-reaching consequences. Without our HF (long-range) radio we were not permitted to fly over areas not covered by line-of-sight VHF radio coverage because no communication with the ground would have been possible. We therefore could not fly directly back to Uganda with President Idi Amin.

When the senior officers realized that they had a presidential problem on their hands and not just a small broken wire, their first reaction was to find the culprit and kill him. I dissuaded them from this course of action but emphasized that I had never been happy with the Falcon's lonely and vulnerable position on the international airport's dispersal and something would have to be done to improve its security. The head of the Iraqi Air Force agreed and within an hour we were instructed to fly to the main military airbase at Muthena, in the centre of Baghdad.

The flight of 20 miles was almost instantaneous; however, I was not actually sure whether our new position was any more secure than the international airport that we had just left, but need not have worried. A small tractor towed us into our own small hangar, totally out of sight.

I thanked the Air Force Commander for our improved security, but insisted that I must have discussions with the Iraqi President on the problems created by our damaged Falcon. He agreed, but said that such a meeting would take a while to organize in the present circumstances. We wandered around the aircraft hardstanding discussing all the ramifications of taking the President of Uganda home, when a young pilot came up to the Air Force General, saluted smartly and said, 'Excuse me, sir, I would like to introduce you to my British flying instructor.'

'Where is he?' the General replied.

The young man turned to me and said, 'Right here. This is Lieutenant-Commander Neville Atkinson, my combat jet flying instructor from Linton-on-Ouse in Yorkshire.'

Sure enough, the young man was Omar, my first foreign student on Mk III Jet Provosts, by coincidence now based at Iraqi Air Force station Muthena, flying Sukhoi 20 interceptor fighters.

The General suggested, with a grin on his face, that I could have done a better job with him. 'He's a lousy pilot.' The senior officer then excused himself and disappeared to talk to the President's office, leaving me to spend the next couple of hours in the Sukhoi 20 crew room with Omar and three other pilots from the same flying course, to whom colleagues of mine had taught the mysteries of air-to-air combat ten years earlier. It seemed strange to look at these faces from the past, smiling away and bubbling with enthusiasm, on the brink of leaping skywards to fight to the death with other young pilots, as we sat there sipping coffee in friendship, laughing over incidents of a decade earlier.

The ex-students reminded me of their arrival at the RAF station at Linton-on-Ouse. It was an occasion that I had completely forgotten. A tradition had sprung up whereby on each new course's first night, a social function was organized for them to meet the wives and girlfriends of the station's senior officers and all their instructors. These functions could often be quite boring affairs and this one was likely to be no exception, especially as most of the students would be Muslim and probably would not drink any alcohol.

The younger instructors decided to liven the proceedings up by telling the Iraqis that the training course ahead of them was Israeli and that they would be meeting them at the bar. The truth was that the preceding group was, in fact, another Arab course from Kuwait. The Iraqis arrived expecting some kind of confrontation, but would have none of it when we introduced the Kuwaitis as Israelis. They knew instantly that these were fellow-Arabs with whom they had great affinity, so there was joy all round. These four students told me, in their Sukhoi 20 crew room, that they had, in fact, all armed themselves with makeshift weapons before coming to the bar that evening. They were prepared for dead bodies on the floor before the evening was out. It could have gone horribly wrong.

I can't help wondering now and then how these young men coped with the actual furnace of all-out warfare which was about to engulf them, especially in view of their country's chequered subsequent history.

Just before dinner our chaperon rushed into my room to say that President Bakr wanted to see me right away in his office. He would accompany me, but we would travel in style as the President's car was waiting downstairs. The palace was a high white stone building of many parts, including a small central dome and a recessed entrance area. After the normal protracted wait in outside anterooms, I was shown into his presence. He was a serious middle-aged man, slightly stooped, with a stocky build and prominent dark moustache. He sat in a substantial central golden-coloured chair about three metres from the wall – not a throne, but quite similar – surrounded by about five senior military officers, some in uniform. Two of his advisers sat in chairs on either side of the President, but the rest were clustered round, standing. The large room had a high ceiling, surprisingly with no windows or desk, so it must have been a major reception room outside the President's main office.

I was offered a chair slightly to the side of him towards his front, about a metre away. We discussed the damage to the Falcon and its consequences and I explained that there was no real problem as we could still fly His Excellency Idi Amin back to Uganda, but, because of the loss of our long-range radio, we would have to fly via our base in Tripoli to repair the damage en route. I added that there was also a second Falcon in Tripoli that could be used if we were unable to repair the damage quickly enough. President Amin would not be detained very long and if he preferred the work could be carried out without him leaving the aircraft.

'That seems reasonable,' President Bakr replied, 'but Idi Amin has driven to Amman to see King Hussein. He will be back tomorrow and we can confirm all the details with him when we see him.'

On that co-operative tone, the conversation ended and I returned to the hotel for dinner with the rest of the crew. In a fit of exuberance during dinner our guard announced that we would all go to a nightclub later. The idea of relaxing in a nightclub when the country was newly at war struck us as rather strange, but who were we to refuse spontaneous hospitality? The venue was the top floor of another of the city's hotels. Despite the fact that it was very brightly lit the music was pleasant, the cabaret acts were enjoyable and the belly dancer entertaining to watch. Having said that, someone in charge must have been warned of our presidential connections, because whereas all the other tables, as far as we could see, were visited by hostesses from time to time, our table received no such provocative attention. Also, when we stood up to leave just after midnight, the air of relief on the part of the management was obvious.

The following day we relaxed by the swimming pool and after a light lunch walked around the commercial district, taking care this time to avoid pickpockets. Holding ourselves in readiness for departure we spent the hot part of the afternoon in our rooms. Early that evening the same car arrived to take me to the President's palace, but this time I took the co-pilot along to witness any instructions that we might be given.

The meeting was in the same room and similar to the previous discussion, but an air of aggression hung in the air, which I had not felt on the previous visit. This time Idi Amin was present and gave the impression of being somewhat agitated as President Bakr announced that President Amin did not wish to return to Uganda via Tripoli, which surprised me considerably. I explained the aviation problems that the damage to the HF radio had caused and the flight times that the new route would take, but he was adamant. He refused to return via Tripoli under any circumstances and was not interested in the danger of flying most of the way back without any radio communication whatsoever. He became furious and I was very doubtful whether he understood the difference between HF radio and VHF radio ranges at all.

We had a complete impasse – I was not allowed by the terms of my civil aviation licences to fly several thousand miles without radio communication over hostile terrain and Idi Amin refused to fly any route that resolved the problem. The party around President Bakr discussed solutions and eventually a rather unpleasant, taller Iraqi gentleman in plain clothes, standing to the left, turned and was quite aggressive – almost abusive. I answered him in a friendly tone as calmly and factually as I could, but large beads of sweat stood out on his face as he almost barked his words at me, until eventually the discussion was terminated by the Iraqi President's intervention. He said that they would consider the position and let me know. We were obviously dismissed.

As we left the room I asked our guard for the name of the angry gentleman giving me a hard time. 'That was Saddam Hussein,' he replied. I made a note of it on my aeronautical chart with a large exclamation mark.

Reflecting on the discussion, I decided that Idi Amin was probably very tired, having just been driven nearly 1,500 miles over very rough roads in searing heat. Air-conditioning was in its infancy in those days and could never cope with desert temperatures. He was obviously not thinking too clearly.

On a later visit to Amman, after the war, one of King Hussein's ministers told me that he had been in the Army Headquarters at the time that Idi Amin crossed into Jordanian territory, when a messenger burst in and told the king that President Amin of Uganda and party were on the outskirts of Amman, having driven from Baghdad, and was coming to see him.

He picked up his cap, placed it thoughtfully on his head, walked towards the door and as he passed the Army Commander, announced that he was going to inspect his tank regiment. When the Army Commander expressed surprise the king said that Idi Amin would be arriving any minute and asked the hapless general to see what the president wanted. 'But I don't know him,' he said.

'That's all right,' King Hussein replied, 'you'll soon recognise him. He's a big black man,' and without further ado he closed the door.

The minister did not know what subsequently transpired but the Ugandan President did arrive shortly afterwards and was privately hosted by the Army Commander.

The following morning I thought that it prudent to be on hand at Muthena, so we sat in the Falcon's cabin and planned our return route. Just as we were discussing which refuelling stop would extricate us from the war zone the quickest, Saddam Hussein came up the steps and announced the President had decided to return President Amin back to Uganda in one of their Iraqi Air Force aircraft. He still appeared to be quite aggressive towards us so I politely acknowledged the presidential decision and offered him a coffee. To my great surprise he accepted the offer and sat down in the cabin. I could see that he was quite harassed so I chose positive, lighter subjects for conversation and I flatter myself that he was actually starting to relax before he left the Falcon.

Ten minutes later he returned in a Tupolev 134A which taxied alongside the Falcon. This Russian transport aircraft had obviously been designed originally as a medium-range bomber, because the bombsight and the bomb aimer's glazed nose were still quite apparent. In its Iraqi configuration it was an 80-seat passenger plane, typically Russian, without a great deal of comfort, but it would be adequate for a flight to Entebbe.

We transferred as much of the Ugandan baggage as we could find into the Russian aircraft and whilst on board I took the opportunity of sitting in the bomb aimer's seat. The compartment was terribly cramped, but the view forward and downwards was superb. The top of the aimer's head was about half an inch below the pilot's shoes, so there was no room for a floor in that part of the cockpit. From the Falcon, the Tupolev 134A looked very similar to the French medium-range, 100-seat airliner, the Caravelle, but internally the French aircraft was finished to a much more comfortable standard.

When the Ugandans boarded their utility transport a short while later, it was noticeable that President Bakr's farewell handshake with Idi Amin was very lukewarm indeed, and Saddam Hussein was nowhere to be seen.

Saddam bin Hussein al Takriti, to give him his full name, was a leading member of the Baath Party of Iraq and after a great deal of political intrigue he succeeded President Bakr as President and dictator in 1979. It is a strongly held belief in Baghdad and outside the country that he personally killed President Bakr.

I cannot confirm this, but considering my minor dealings with the man, I think it quite likely. He seriously worried me during our short acquaintance and an air of evil seemed to surround him. Iraq's political history is littered with the assassinations of the leaders and members of one regime by the next. Killing one's predecessors seems to have become almost the accepted method of succession in this beautiful desert country, once home to the Hanging Gardens of Babylon. Yet, on a personal level, they are as a whole very likeable people, relatively well educated and with a good sense of humour.

Nevertheless, with our passengers now gone it was clearly time for us to leave the war zone with all speed, before anybody thought otherwise, or any unfriendly bombs started raining from the heavens. Despite having no diplomatic clearances for overflying or landing in any other countries, we filed a flight plan to fly north into Turkey, which was not fighting anybody, and to land in Istanbul to refuel. Istanbul was chosen because Libya's airline flew regular scheduled flights to the country and there was an airline office at the airport to help us if necessary.

Remarkably, there were no problems whatsoever. The Libyan Arab Airlines station manager met us on landing, took care of all the paperwork and sent his fuel bowser to replenish our fuel. We were airborne for home within forty minutes, complete with three VIP meals – and flying in airspace a thousand miles from the war zone was very reassuring indeed.

We arrived back in our hangar at Tripoli International in the early evening. The broken HF aerial was replaced within an hour, so Idi Amin would not have been inconvenienced for very long if he had been with us on his return to Entebbe. It would certainly have been a lot more comfortable than thousands of miles in a shaky old Tu-134A, and probably safer.

As we stopped our car outside my first-floor flat, Trudi, my daughter, was standing on the balcony that ran round the outside wall, shouting for everyone to hear, 'There's Daddy! There's Daddy!' Then she started wagging her finger at me. 'You have been into the war zone and Mummy is very cross with you.'

'How do you know?' I asked.

She replied that it had been on the BBC Overseas Service.

Was nothing private?

CHAPTER SIX

Some of the Middle East's Intractable Problems

In order to avoid being accused of anti-Semitism, I should explain the background that formed my early opinions on the Arab-Israeli situation during the Second World War and in its immediate aftermath.

As schoolboys, our only knowledge of the Jewish religion came from having two Jewish boys in our class, various oblique references to 'the Jews' in passages read to us occasionally from the Bible and short news items that were heard on BBC radio broadcasts during the war. We had no knowledge whatsoever of what was happening to the Jews in Nazi Germany, although anything that the Germans were doing during the war was judged by my family to be evil. The two young Jewish boys at school seemed to me to be as normal as any of the rest of us, except that they were allowed by the headmaster to walk out of morning assembly whenever prayers were said at the end of each morning gathering.

I completely failed to notice that these two boys only ate certain items of the school lunches, because several of my Christian friends were picky about their food and we all made our preferences known to the 'servers' as we progressed along the queue, without any comment from anyone. Everyone was given exactly what he requested from whatever was on offer. The two of them played games like anyone else, except that one of them was a particularly good swimmer and was always the one I tried to pass whilst racing up the swimming pool.

It therefore came as a complete shock to me – as it was to most of the British population, at the end of the war – when our daily papers featured photographs of the horrors of Bergen Belsen, Auschwitz, Dachau, Buchenwald and all the other Nazi extermination camps. Although it made me feel completely sick to look at the pictures, my boyish mind tried to make some sense of why anyone would wish to treat their fellow human beings in this barbaric way. My parents were not much help. Mother responded to my questions with 'Don't talk about such things as it makes me cry,' and father declared that all Nazis were animals. My response that I knew of no animals capable of throwing members of their own kind onto bonfires only succeeded in producing a painful clip round the ear.

Killing on such a vast scale had been proposed before in human history. Kublai Khan – renowned in Samuel Taylor Coleridge's poem for his 'stately pleasure-dome' of Xanadu and probably the most famous of the Khans after

Ghengis Khan – was, in about 1250, so offended by the northern Chinese people's betrayal of his trust during his absence from the country, that he set in place a system to execute and dispose of the bodies of the entire Chinese population – perhaps as many as thirty million.

Fortunately he was dissuaded from his declared aim by his skilful Chinese treasurer who persuaded the Great Khan that the resultant loss of tax revenue following the proposed extermination would be catastrophic to the Mongol economy. The Russian people, at almost the same time as the Holocaust, were less fortunate than Kublai Khan's Chinese. It is reasonably certain that Stalin, in his supposed Communist Utopia, managed to exterminate in various devious ways upwards of 25 million of his own people to further his crazy theories.

A major problem for me, trying to understand the very visible brutality presented in the international newspapers of the time, was that I did not know any Jews or Jewish families to ask for their views, and I was further confused when our compulsory reading at school included Sir Walter Scott's classic tale *Ivanhoe*, which implied that there was animosity towards the Jews even in Britain in the Middle Ages, but nothing on the scale of the Holocaust. I remained confused, but confident that the Allied armies had done their best to stop the Nazi's diabolical endeavours and had eventually prevailed.

My next real knowledge of any of the related facts of the problem was when my older brother, Gordon, joined the Army and was sent to Palestine. His regiment's prime task, he said, was to stop Israeli illegal immigrants killing the native Palestinians, a people who had been fighting alongside us against the Germans during both of the last world wars. Palestine was, he said, a British protectorate and it was our country's duty to stop its citizens being killed and their land being stolen from them.

'Who are these Israelis?' I asked, and he replied that they were Jews who had decided to leave their sometimes comfortable homes in Europe, America, Russia and elsewhere and live in Palestine.

'Why?' I asked.

'They apparently claim that it is their ancestral homeland,' he explained. 'Their holy book claims that their ancestors once lived in this area and, because of what was done to them by the Nazis during the last war, they claim that they have a God-given right to return.'

'How long ago do they say that their people lived in this area?' I asked. 'About two thousand years,' he replied.

'Does that mean that because our ancestors were Vikings from Norway at about the same time, that we should be allowed to cross over to Norway and lay claim to houses and land in Bergen or Oslo?' I asked.

'Don't ask me,' replied Gordon, 'but in my opinion, the Norwegians would have a great deal to say on the subject. I cannot make any sense of the mess.'

'You'll be all right,' I pointed out, 'because you're in the Regimental Band.'

'Think again,' said Gordon. 'In Palestine, I lay down my musical instrument and become a real soldier, with a .303 Lee-Enfield rifle and pockets full of ammunition.'

When he returned to Jerusalem in July 1946 one of the Israeli militant groups, the Stern Gang, placed milk churns full of explosives in the basement of the King David Hotel, the British Army Headquarters, and blew the place sky high. He wrote to me saying that other Israeli groups, which I believe he called the Irgun Svie Liumi and the Haganah, were killing British soldiers and Palestinians on an almost daily basis.

This was standing logic on its head, it seemed to us. First, the Jews are treated diabolically by the Nazis, and then a few years later, under their new title as Israelis, they are rushing around the Middle East, misappropriating land owned by other people and forming themselves into groups, that the world calls terrorists, to further their infiltration of the country. Meanwhile, the displaced Palestinians, it seemed, were being transferred from their own land into refugee camps in the Lebanon and the Gaza strip. Nothing made sense to the simple mind of a fourteen-year-old boy.

But when I studied my current affairs curriculum, I found that the actual infiltration of these Biblical lands by these people had been in progress for perhaps forty or fifty years before the start of the Second World War. Legally, at first, wealthy Jews bought land from Palestinian owners who were prepared to sell, and sporadic settlement started – primarily in the more fertile parts of Palestine.

Following the Second World War, the survivors of the holocaust in the Nazi death camps and their relations decided to settle in the area adjacent to Jerusalem. If the immigration had only been these hapless survivors, world opinion and possibly the Palestinians would have accepted and absorbed the relatively modest influx. Unfortunately America, by that time a very dominant power, was in a position to influence – and perhaps financially bully – its old wartime ally, Britain, regarding this part of the Middle East. The USA was pressurized to act in this way primarily because of the very powerful and vociferous Jewish-American vote that appeared to be presenting a biased picture.

On 14 May 1948, Britain was 'persuaded' to relinquish its long-standing international protectorate over Palestine, and the recently formed United Nations, under further strong American pressure, declared that a portion of that country would become the new Jewish state of Israel. It is difficult to see what basis in international law was used to justify this annexation of other people's land.

Unfortunately for everyone concerned, this small, newly created country adopted a strategy, used many times before in history, of swelling its population by encouraging massive immigration from all parts of the world. Jews, many from very affluent backgrounds, began arriving from America, Europe, Russia and even Africa. Eventually there was deemed to be insufficient land to support such artificially large numbers, so expansion into territory that they did not in fact possess became necessary. Parcels of land, some of them deep in Palestinian territory, were occupied in what came to be called the 'settlements'. The settlers pretty soon needed defending against hostile neighbours who, in some cases, had lost land and property that their families had owned for centuries and to which they possessed legal deeds and certification.

The people forcibly moved out of the areas of the settlements swelled the numbers being housed in the notorious refugee camps. It is hardly surprising that under the circumstances these camps became hotbeds of discontent. They were construed by the Palestinians and many others around the world as illegal, immoral and unjust.

Anyone who spoke out against these apparent inequities was branded a terrorist or a terrorist sympathiser. The people trumpeting these names for anyone who disagreed with Israel's actions conveniently forgot the actions of the Stern Gang, the Irgun Svie Liumi, the Haganah and other Jewish groups at Israel's beginnings. Many of the members or leaders of these groups, whatever title one chooses to give them, subsequently became presidents, prime ministers and senior politicians of the new country. Had they been terrorists?

Not all the members of the new Israeli population agreed with their erstwhile government's approach to its possible security problem, as witnessed in the many elections that have taken place in Israel since 1948. The hardliners have the greatest difficulty in presenting a majority front for their virtually racist policies. In fact, single political parties in the Israeli Knesset are usually forced to form coalitions with other unlikely parties to amass enough votes to form viable governments. There is clearly, therefore, a large proportion of the Israeli population that is not in accord with the repressive measures arbitrarily employed against the indigenous Palestinians by the Israeli Government.

The situation described above forms the background to the events now to be related.

On 14 June 1974, I was requested to take a Falcon to the VIP lounge at Tripoli Airport, where members of the Revolutionary Command Council (RCC) wished to travel to Gamel Abdul Nasser Airport (Tobruk), in eastern Libya. Once at the VIP lounge at 3 o'clock in the afternoon, nobody could be contacted to clarify the time

Self and the Palestinian Leader.
Round my neck is his Mother of Pearl gift for Lesley.

of arrival of our mystery passengers, so we played cards, read books, walked around the dispersal, drank coffee and relaxed in the lounge's comfortable chairs.

At about midnight we were told that our passengers were leaving the city and would be with us shortly. They arrived at 1 o'clock, accompanied by the Libyan Chief of Protocol, Mr Abu Shagour, who introduced me to my senior passenger, Yasser Arafat, dressed in his usual khaki fatigues, with designer stubble on the lower part of his face and his hallmark black and white kaffiyeh held in place with twin thick black silk cords around the upper part of his forehead.

We greeted each other politely with a formal handshake and I confirmed with him that he wished to fly to Tobruk. Yes, he verified, but we would only be stopping there to take on one more passenger and then we would be going to Cairo, where we would stay the night. The close proximity of this vilified enigma of a leader caused me slight nervousness. My only knowledge of him was from the many negative reports that I had previously read in the British broadsheet press and some critical remarks that had been broadcast on the BBC Overseas Service news broadcasts.

Deciding that my wife should be aware of exactly whom I was flying, just in case, I excused myself and telephoned her from the VIP lounge. The news probably ruined her night's sleep: just what I expected her to do about this revelation was never clear to either of us, but at the time it did seem to me to be a necessary precaution. Roused out of a deep sleep, Lesley staggered to the telephone in the pitch dark, unable to find the light switch on the way. After considering the possible gravity of my unexpected news she decided that she must write down the details, so she picked up a pencil and started to write on the pad that was always kept next to the telephone. She later showed me her notes scribbled in total darkness and, remarkably, they were easily readable.

In the event this much-maligned leader arrived at the Falcon very tired and was fast asleep shortly after take-off. The seven other passengers were younger and their roles in the delegation were obvious to me when I walked back up the cabin after levelling off at altitude to meet them individually. Three of them were studious secretary types, but the other four were quite clearly bodyguards. They did not say they were bodyguards, but their alert body language proclaimed their duties with no need for words of confirmation. No armament of any kind was visible, which confirmed that they were not amateurs at the protection business.

Over the Gulf of Sirte, the engineer served hot meals to the seven, but left their leader sleeping. Mr Arafat awoke, however, as we passed Benghazi, probably because of the aroma of fresh coffee wafting on the cabin air. He strolled nonchalantly up to the cockpit where I presented him with a copy of the map of our route. It was obvious that he was spatially aware and followed our position with great accuracy, knowing the name of every small cluster of lights on the ground. His conversation was light-hearted, family orientated and at times even jovial. As we passed abeam the Greco-Roman cities of Cyrene and Apollonia on the coast, he returned to his seat to enjoy one of our excellent hot evening meals.

He had just drained the last of his coffee as we greased the wheels onto the smooth tarmac of Tobruk's main runway. The taxi track was apparently blocked by blown sand, so we backtracked up the runway to the control tower where our extra passenger was waiting. The eight passengers joined the new one on the ground to stretch their legs and, I suspect, confirm the identity of the new man. The fuel bowser quickly arrived and soon the precious liquid was flooding into our empty tanks.

Whilst this was happening the controller ran down the steps from the tower to say that he had been the controller on duty on that fateful day about a year before, when we were scurrying westwards out of Egypt to escape both the SAM II missiles and the Egyptian Air Force. He asked whether I was afraid to return to Cairo after such an encounter, but I assured him that I had been there many times since that terrifying day and that I tried to adopt a philosophical attitude, but that I could never completely forget what had happened. He said that maybe I did not know at the time, but they had been well aware of our predicament. To prepare for the possibility of the Egyptian Air Force crossing the Libyan border in hot pursuit of our Falcon, they had activated all their missile defence systems and were quite prepared to take the entire Egyptian Air Force out of the sky if they had crossed the Egypt/Libya border, or even if they fired missiles or other weaponry at my aircraft from their side of the border.

It might have been helpful if I had known that at the time, I said; but then I thought a little deeper. Perhaps if I had known that I was flying over fully activated anti-aircraft missiles, I might have worried even more – that they would hit me by mistake instead of the Egyptians.

Twenty-five minutes after landing, our wheels left the ground and we were en route to Cairo. This time the Palestinian leader sat with us in the cockpit on the jump-seat. He followed our progress on my chart until, as we turned to port over the Qattara Depression to line up with Cairo's main runway, there was a loud explosion and all our eardrums hurt. 'What's that?' shouted our guest; I explained that we had apparently suffered a pressurization failure. As if to confirm my diagnosis a forest of white oxygen masks descended from the cabin roof. The co-pilot and I donned our own oxygen masks and our engineer, wearing his mask, helped Mr Arafat to fit one over his head correctly.

I explained to everyone that I was making an emergency descent in order to take the aircraft below 10,000 feet, where we could all dispense with the masks. Pointing the Falcon's nose vertically at the ground below and extending the airbrakes – called lift-spoilers in civil aircraft – we lost 30,000 feet quite spectacularly. Cairo control acknowledged our emergency manoeuvre and invited us to continue down to complete our landing if we wished. We accepted their invitation and, as a result, were rolling down Cairo's main runway less than an hour after taking off from Tobruk, a record time for us over the distance.

Colonel Shukri, the ubiquitous Cairo Airport intelligence chief, and two Palestinian chauffeurs met us outside the VIP lounge. The heat and humidity radiating from the sticky tarmac was stifling. Our passengers enquired whether the crew would be able find suitable accommodation in Cairo at 5 o'clock in the morning and we assured them that we were likely to find three suitable rooms at the Shepheards Hotel, so they arranged transport for us for after we had put the Falcon to bed.

The decompression at altitude was found by the engineer to have been caused by a ruptured main door seal. Whilst we did not carry a spare rubber seal, we did have a repair kit so we two pilots supervised the refuelling, thereby allowing the engineer to carry out a very professional repair, good enough for a pressurized return home the following day.

Arriving at the Shepheards we were relieved to find that our passengers had called half an hour previously and that three rooms were ready for our tired bodies.

The 'Do Not Disturb' notices hung outside the doors remarkably did as they were intended, allowing us to sleep until after normal lunchtime, when the heat forced us to seek the comfort of our cool showers. A walk over to the Hilton Hotel coffee bar satisfied the need for breakfast, and after a lively discussion on the afternoon's activity we browsed around the hotel shops, where I bought a few artificial gemstones – man-made alexandrite from Russia. As they were a fixed purple colour (whereas genuine alexandrite is a greeny brown, changing to almost red in natural daylight) there was not much point in the shopkeeper attempting to claim that they were genuine, so their price of 30 piastres (about 15 pence) each was probably correct.

With the three hours left before closing we decided to have another self-guided tour of the Cairo museum. There were always items to be discovered in this treasure-house of ancient Egyptian antiquities that we had never seen before. The place was cool, vast and interesting. I stated my preference of starting once again at the supine naked body of the unwrapped mummy of Pharaoh Rameses II, perhaps the greatest Egyptian Pharaoh of them all.

Leaving the museum as darkness and a cooling breeze heralded the evening's approach, we decided to remain in the Shepheards for the evening and forgo another session of Miss Nagwa Faoud's fascinating belly dancing in the cocktail bar of the Sheraton. We all agreed on an early night –a fortunate decision, as a messenger awaiting our return from sightseeing asked if we could be ready to take off at 7.00 the following morning.

Our principal passenger arrived at the airport on time, but only his four bodyguards returned with him to Tobruk. Shortly after levelling at altitude Yasser Arafat came up to the cockpit to give each one of the crew a thank you gift. This was a routine that he instituted on this flight and continued for every one of the many times that we subsequently flew him. These gifts, though not in themselves especially valuable, were very much appreciated. They were usually craft items made by Palestinian people in the different countries we visited and were always given to us 'as something for your wife'.

The short journey to Tobruk did not afford any opportunity for general discussion so the Palestinian leader removed his kaffiyeh and relaxed into his seat bareheaded to watch the North African coast drift lazily past the window. The sky was clear blue with just a few wisps of cloud over the higher ground to the south; with the rising orange ball of the sun slightly behind us, the visibility was magnificent.

It was impossible to prevent one's mind from drifting once again to the momentous battles fought out by Montgomery's and Rommel's forces thirty years earlier across these sand dunes passing below our port wing. The very names of the villages and towns sounded like a roll-call of recent history. Sidi Barrani, Mersa Matruh, El Alamein, the Qattara Depression and even our destination, Tobruk, all featured in BBC wartime reports as milestones along the road to an eventual allied victory. The German, French, Italian and English cemeteries at Tobruk testify to the ferocity of the fighting and many brave young men rest permanently under these desert sands. The fortunate ones have a headstone complete with revered name, but many headstones have no name while others do not even aspire to a headstone at all. They lie, at varying depths, in the cradle of sand, exactly where they fell. The only people who once knew their many resting places, themselves often died shortly afterwards, taking their knowledge with them. War is hell.

The Tobruk air traffic controller triumphantly announced that he could see us twinkling in the sky to the east of his field and that as we were his only traffic we were at liberty to land at our own discretion. The sand had been removed from his tarmac, he cheerfully informed us, and we could taxi back to the control tower after landing along the normal taxi-track.

A Range Rover awaited our passengers, who disappeared into the desert shortly after arriving. A fluky breeze was left wafting sand around the lonely control tower as we refuelled and prepared to return home. As if to remind us of events of long ago, a slinky desert fox carefully picked its way across the airfield, disappearing into the bright sun shining from the south-east. Perhaps it was the ghost of Field Marshal Erwin Rommel, always known as the Desert Fox – or was my imagination running riot?

To bring me back to more imperative action, one of our two electrical generators failed on take-off and whilst the Falcon was able to produce a reasonable supply of electricity from the remaining generator, a prudent shedding of all but the most important electrical loads would help the remaining generator to keep performing normally. A double generator failure in most aircraft is a serious emergency, to be avoided at all costs, so off went everything that was not necessary to actually fly the aircraft in acceptable comfort. We even dispensed with the coffee machine and the oven, so we must have been pretty desperate! To help us decide what services we should drop in these circumstances, Marcel Dassault had provided us with a list of the amperage of every service supplied by each generator. The vital services –flying controls, emergency hydraulic pumps, signals to raise and lower the main undercarriage, the various radios in both their transmit and receive modes – only drew modest electrical current values. If push came to shove and the second generator was lost for any reason, most of these services were reputed to be capable of being run from the aircraft battery, but no aviator would choose to put that claim to the test unnecessarily. Prudent cosseting of single electrical generators is a golden rule of survival for all pilots.

In the event, we arrived home with the second generator still performing perfectly and changing the failed component took our engineer about an hour in the midday sun, with some lifting from both pilots and its inevitable smothering of them in thick black grease. 5A-DAF was refuelled, serviceable and ready for anything that might be asked of it before we towed it into its hangar and left the airfield to join our families on the shores of the Mediterranean for the afternoon.

We subsequently flew Yasser Arafat on many dozens of occasions to most African and Middle Eastern countries, and sometimes to European and Far Eastern ones as well. We were always directed to fly him and his delegations by Libyan presidential and RCC senior officials, but whilst away from Tripoli we were authorized to change routes and destinations as requested by the Palestinian leader. All the rules governing the carriage of personal weapons for our senior Libyan passengers were also applied to the Palestinian passengers, with their complete co-operation. Whilst their baggage was never routinely searched, we had their word that no explosives or heavier armaments would be brought on board our Falcons or later, the Gulfstream IIs. I am confident that everyone abided by these stipulations – indeed, their bags were usually so small and light that no such possibility existed.

It is worth relating just a few of the more interesting incidents that occurred during our trips together.

The close proximity into which we were inevitably thrown over very long periods allowed me to observe his character. By the time we first met he had become an accomplished politician and a fervent leader of his dispirited people. He conducted himself in a calm, collected and well-organized manner, only stating his opinions after mature consideration of the subject under discussion. He was generally courteous and thoughtful of others, but he could be quite forceful when it became necessary.

Our early flights together were generally into and around the leading countries of the Middle East. Yasser Arafat frequently buttonholed me privately, in the quieter moments of our flights or whilst waiting for permissions to fly to his chosen destinations, wanting to know my views and world opinion about his people. During these discussions he revealed a remarkable capacity for remembering the actual words that world-famous politicians of many countries had used over the previous sixty or more years, regarding promises and undertakings they had made about his homeland. For instance, he could quote word for word the Balfour Declaration, whereas I only had a hazy knowledge of its existence.

Lord Arthur James Balfour was the Conservative British Foreign Minister in Lloyd George's Cabinet from 1916 to 1919. In the House of Lords on 2 November 1917 he made a speech which later became known as 'the Balfour Declaration', in which he undertook on behalf of both Houses of Parliament to consider supporting the case for an independent Jewish State in part of Palestine, on condition that all the rights of the Palestinian people would be completely safeguarded. He expanded his views with regard to limiting the numbers of such immigrants in order to avoid the danger of destabilizing the country and later outlined the methods by which the land involved should be purchased from its current owners at mutually agreeable prices.

Balfour's plan later became official British policy, but very few of its undertakings were subsequently acted upon and the chaos that we read about in our newspapers today as 'the Middle East problem' must be recognized as the direct result of these failures.

My answers to his questions as to my assessment of world opinion and views about the then current Israeli/Palestinian situation quite surprised him, although he did not say so directly. He was too much of a politician.

Being a native Yorkshireman, I spoke plainly and told him that the policies currently being followed regarding airliner hijackings, guerrilla attacks and terrorist outrages by Palestinians, that filled our daily newspapers, were totally counter-productive to his and the Palestinian people's aspirations. The world outside the Middle East consequently regarded all Palestinians as dangerous people, and probable legitimate aims were being submerged in storms of irrelevant violence. 'You are shooting yourselves in the foot. If you do not change your policies on violence, in my considered opinion your future is doomed,' I told him.

He questioned me closely for some time about specific aspects of their activities and I did my best to give him my honest view of how these appeared to the rest of the world, and their apparent effects on British public opinion in particular.

He was careful not to accept my outspoken assessment, but did not offer any counter arguments and the expression on his face showed tacit agreement. On later flights, when he raised the same subject again, he explored my determination to adhere to the views I had expressed, so I explained that I was first and foremost a pilot and no pilot would ever harbour sympathy with people who specialized in hijacking airliners: it would not be a reasonable stance for any professional aviator. He said that he saw my point.

At no time did he respond to my determined opinions regarding indiscriminate violence by attempting to justify past incidents, and at no time did he ever say anything derogatory to me, or in my hearing to others, about the Israeli people themselves. Neither did he reveal his own personal views regarding

Palestinian violence. He was obviously firmly of the opinion that the current British political standpoint regarding his people had become largely irrelevant and that Palestinian salvation lay mostly with the power of the United States of America. My observations since that time confirm that he was probably correct in this assessment.

When we landed in any country it was usual that Yasser Arafat, and maybe his secretary and a couple of bodyguards, would be treated to some kind of ceremonial welcome, with guards of traditionally dressed soldiers and often a military band to play everyone's National Anthem. His small delegation would then be driven away and we would only see them again when we left or were preparing to leave the host country.

Occasionally he would join us for colourful local meals outside the capital city, often in restaurants in distinctly rural settings, in vineyards and farmland. It always struck me that the venues chosen were selected primarily for their ease of defence against surprise attack as much as their culinary excellence, and the amount of armament on display reinforced that opinion. Perhaps I am being churlish about the food because the standard of meals that we all enjoyed on these occasions was often excellent and usually Arab in origin. The owners and staff were sometimes resident Palestinians.

Yasser Arafat adopted the habit at many of these occasions of announcing, mainly from across the table and loud enough for everyone to hear, that I – referred to as 'the Captain' – disagreed with the current Palestinian action regarding hijacking of aircraft and terrorist violence. Usually during these meals there would be one or two young men who rapidly betrayed their positions as fanatical hotheads dedicated to violence, in furtherance of their political ends.

I was apparently being encouraged to restate my views, which I invariably did with some conviction, whereupon I would be verbally attacked by the more extreme members of the party, sometimes interrupting each other to justify their extremist views. The arguments that invariably ensued were, to say the least, forceful and distinctly hostile. Yasser Arafat only intervened himself when overtly aggressive gestures were made against me personally. The gesture that caused the Palestinian leader to push his chair back and take verbal – and on one occasion physical – action was when one or more of my antagonists actually drew their hidden weapons, cocked the firing mechanism and laid them on the table with the barrel pointing menacingly towards me. Thankfully, his word was law in these circumstances and the culprits, shamefacedly, apologized to me profusely.

Unfortunately for my crew, who remained silent during these heated exchanges, Yasser Arafat – referred to as 'Abu Amer' by the Palestinians – was sometimes forced to leave the meal by pressure of work. In these circumstances the next senior diner was given the responsibility for our welfare. If he happened to be one of the people I had verbally crossed swords with during the evening, then the prospects for the standard of our subsequent hospitality were much reduced.

On one such occasion in Damascus, the capital of Syria, our senior passenger was called away from the evening meal for personal discussions with the Syrian President, Hafez Al-Assad. Unfortunately for us, the meal had been organized for everyone before we had had the opportunity to find any overnight accommodation. Normally at that time we would stay in the luxury of the newly completed Sheraton Hotel, but our reluctant host and erstwhile angry verbal opponent, who had earlier been introduced to me as the PLO's Chancellor of the Exchequer, announced that all the usual hotels in Damascus were full to overflowing because of the fighting in Beirut, the capital of the Lebanon, 60 miles to the west. As a result of this the Damascus hotels had filled up with escaping Lebanese.

Fortunately, after a protracted session on the unreliable Syrian telephone system, he announced that he had found accommodation in a 'nice hotel' on the other side of Damascus. Not suspecting this man's evil intent, we collected our suitcases and were driven late at night down some of the dirtiest back streets at the seedier end of the city, to what   only after he had driven away – we discovered to be a brothel. The resident pimp, who was carrying out the duties of receptionist, realized from our aircrew uniforms that for some inexplicable reason a serious error had been made, and set about looking after us as best he could.

The girls on duty were told that we were not potential customers and to do them justice, they looked after us thoughtfully and discreetly, as friends. There was no question of any approaches from them and they adopted a rather motherly attitude towards us. The room chosen for us, on the first floor, had three beds in it and whilst we were organizing our sleeping arrangements, two of the girls stripped the beds and refitted them with beautifully pressed pure white sheets. Bottled drinking water and glasses were placed on small tables by each bed and the girls showed us their bathroom, which had been specially cleaned for our use.

They explained that it was the only bathroom that they could use and that there was no lock on the door, so they undertook that one of them would stand outside the door when we wished to use the toilet, to prevent us being disturbed. They apologized for the line of skimpy underwear dangling from a line in the corner to dry, but explained that they had nowhere else to launder their clothes. Sure enough, whenever any of the three of us used the bathroom, one of the girls mysteriously appeared and smiled sweetly at us as we vacated this important room.

Whilst the building was definitely a brothel, at first glance it could have been mistaken for a low-grade tourist hotel. It was very clean, without opulence of any kind. There were no lavish reception areas, but the girls were quite smartly dressed and there was a much pleasanter atmosphere than one would perhaps anticipate in such an establishment.

It was probably reassuring to our wives that we all slept in the same room, although it broke one of our Special Flight stipulations that we would always demand separate rooms to help us achieve our necessary sleep. In the early morning, when our aviation services were needed, two of the girls 'on duty' turned out to be pretty young twins from Liverpool who immediately offered to walk down the street to buy us a takeaway breakfast before we left. We felt guilty refusing their kind offer because they were very genuine and I wondered whether they were in Damascus of their own free will or had fallen foul of the white slave traffic that had recently been publicized in the British press.

I talked to them very discreetly and offered to take them out of the country if they were in Damascus under some duress, which brought a small tear to each of their eyes. 'No,' they assured me, 'we really are here of our own free will.' Initially, they said, they had come out under the impression that they were to feature in some type of exotic cabaret, but it soon became apparent to them that the real money was to be made entertaining foreign businessmen who regularly passed through Damascus – mostly from Germany, France and Italy. 'We can return home anytime we choose, but we are making so much money that we will soon be able to return to Liverpool in some style,' they assured us.

Still sceptical, I asked one of them to prove to me that they were able to leave when they wished, so she went off and returned moments later with both of their passports in her hand and a wad of high-denomination US dollar bills that truly amazed me by its magnitude. I was therefore convinced that they were secure and relatively happy, and as our taxi drew up outside in the early dawn light, they both ran out after us, enthusiastically waving and shouting, 'Bon voyidge!' in broad Liverpudlian accents. We travelled to the airport without speaking to each other, deep in our own private thoughts and hoping that we would enjoy a *Bon voyage* as they wished.

Damascus Airport with the Palestinians was always somewhat of a lottery to us. When carrying the Palestinian leader we were usually met by young bodyguards openly displaying weapons of every size and calibre, although occasionally the same people were there, apparently unarmed. This meant that since our previous visit the Syrians had purged their capital city of the irritant of these overzealous Palestinian militias. Perhaps there had been an unfortunate incident that had caused Hafez Al-Assad to tighten up the rules, but we never heard of any specific extra problems.

The certain and immediate indicator to us as to the political climate prevailing in the city was if we were met at the aircraft by the smiling figure of big fat Mohamed. We never knew his family name, but he made himself an institution at Damascus Airport and to some extent, in the main part of the city as well. If he was there, then the Palestinian fortunes were riding high, but if he did not appear to welcome his leader he was assuredly in jail again.

Either way, nobody ever commented on his presence or on his absence, and questions from us failed to shed any light on his fortunes. We never even discovered his position in the hierarchy, or what his main functions were during our absence. He was a bubbly, 'can-do' kind of person, usually dressed in a crumpled grey suit, complete with waistcoat in colder weather – and the nights could be very cold in Syria on occasions.

We sorely missed his presence on the night of the brothel incident. His knowledge of religious history was astounding and whilst driving through Damascus he would lurch to a complete stop to show us sites that were important to Christians as well as Muslims, including roads, streets and buildings mentioned in the Bible or the Koran; places where Jesus visited during his lifetime were given due reverence and he would relate to us the parts of the Bible where these features were mentioned. Once on a tour of the Omyad Mosque in the centre of Damascus, on the fringes of the main souk he guided us out of an immense, white marble, paved, open-air square into a building containing many religious features important to his Muslim religion, and was pleased to show us a small, ornate pulpit at the far right of the covered building where, he claimed, Jesus had taught and preached. [See also footnote on p.15.] He confirmed that Jesus was very important in the Muslim religion as one of its early prophets, and he confirmed that during Jesus's lifetime this important mosque had been a Jewish synagogue and later a Christian church. As a mark of respect, the pulpit reputed to have been used by Jesus himself was never used by anyone else. There were three other pulpits of various sizes in the same building.

During most of our visits with his leader, he assumed the role of our guide, guard, friend, adviser and communications expert. Nothing was too much trouble for him and there seemed to be nothing that could not be obtained at the lowest possible prices from some friend or relation. The fruit from the Bakr valley was second to none in the world and from the Damascus fruit market we frequently bought large boxes of enormous black cherries, succulent sweet strawberries, raspberries, peaches and apricots, in season, to take back to our families in Tripoli. We were rarely in the city for very long, so the fruit always arrived home in pristine condition. Sometimes, it was being eaten in Libya within four hours of being picked off the tree in the Bakr valley.

If Mohamed disliked the price that we were being asked for some of the produce, he would take the correct amount out of our hands, throw it at the shopkeeper, pick up the boxes of fruit and put them in the boot of his car. The shopkeepers would stand open mouthed as he drove away without a backwards glance.

He usually drove us from the airport to our hotel in the main city in his beat-up off-white Renault. It was in such poor condition that the Sheraton doorkeepers would wave us away in disgust, or turn their backs as Mohamed approached, but he did not seem to notice their derision. He refused to acknowledge the jurisdiction of the Syrian Immigration and Customs officials and invariably drove us away from the airport via a back exit, where he cheerfully waved to the armed Syrian guards without reducing his speed. When an unwary young armed Syrian policeman stepped in front of him on one occasion, he drove straight at him. The poor man narrowly escaped disaster by hurling himself and his weapon horizontally into the bushes at the side of the road. 'Silly fool,' Mohamed exclaimed to us as we sailed majestically through the gates.

His nonchalant disregard of Syrian bureaucracy sometimes created severe difficulties for us on our return to the airport. If we were required to fly when Mohamed was temporarily unavailable, we sometimes used a public taxi and the driver would take us to the normal passenger entrance, where the Immigration officials sought to append their official stamp to our documents showing that we were leaving Syria – soon discovering that we had never officially entered their country in the first place.

Scenes of wild, French-style pandemonium consumed the Gendarmerie at these times and I am not quite sure just how we managed to talk ourselves out of these offences, which could have resulted in our incarceration behind bars. These threats were always taken fairly lightly, because we knew that if push came to shove and it appeared that we were about to be arrested, we had several usable lines of defence, or attack, if we were really threatened – but the necessity never actually arose. (If it had, the Palestinian leader, always reasonably close to President Assad himself, would have come to our rescue, and if that line failed we could have called upon the Libyan Ambassador to intercede on our behalf – and Libya's name carried a great deal of weight in Syria at that time.) So we smiled, were ultra polite and reason eventually prevailed.

One memorable time in Damascus started, as usual, with a ceremonial welcome for Yasser Arafat at the airport, and Mohamed once more taking us under his wing. The Palestinians were in some kind of ascendancy and everyone seemed to be brandishing lethal weaponry in worryingly irresponsible ways. The relief at settling into the five-star bedrooms at the Sheraton was short-lived and we had to cancel our dinner bookings when a Range Rover arrived with a senior Palestinian figure to take us for the evidently pre-arranged evening meal up in the hills west of Damascus.

The driver obviously fancied himself as a racing driver, explaining that the bullet-proof, armoured Range Rover was fitted with a seven-litre supercharged engine and could achieve more than 150 miles per hour. No amount of our pleading in Arabic for him to drive more slowly had any effect whatsoever. He wove his very heavy vehicle in and out of the traffic like a man possessed, breaking every traffic rule in existence. On the open road, he was even more lethal, reaching speeds that Range Rovers were never designed to achieve. Remarkably, we arrived at the chosen restaurant without killing anybody en route, but it was no surprise to anyone to find that none of the other guests had yet arrived. They filtered up to the long table in ones and twos over the next half hour and when everyone had arrived we were treated to a superb lamb couscous, followed by exotic sweets, dripping in fresh honey and cream.

Sure enough, I was expected once again by Yasser Arafat to expound my theories on the inadvisability of pursuing violent policies to achieve Palestinian political aims, with particular emphasis on the negative results achieved by aircraft hijacking. This time I encountered only mild verbal opposition and, out of my eye corner I was aware that the Palestinian leader wore a fixed smile that was perhaps more pronounced than usual. To my great relief, at the end of the meal Mohamed arrived with a message and when he had delivered his news, I grabbed him and pleaded with him to wait for us three crew so that he could drive us back to the hotel. Fortunately for us he agreed, and our return to the Sheraton was at a much more modest pace.

The next morning Mohamed showed us Saladin's white marble tomb on the outskirts of the city. This man Saladin (whose full name was Saleh ad-Din Yusuf ibn-Aiyub) conquered Egypt and Syria , took Jerusalem in 1187 and successfully defended his empire against the third Christian Crusade. Saladin was renowned throughout Islam and Christendom for his chivalry and generosity to the poor of all faiths. It now appears that he was far from the evil tyrant that Popes Gregory VIII and Clement III claimed in their justification for the third Crusade, led by the Holy Roman Emperor, Frederick I (known to the medieval world as Barbarossa) and his second-in-command, King Richard the Lionheart of England.

I clearly remember a second tomb, also in white marble, next to Saladin's; I believe that this was his wife's but cannot be certain. Close to the tombs there was an exhibition of ancient Muslim and Christian weapons, some of which appeared to be remarkably modern in that the designs had changed little in over ten centuries. There were many weapons that had not been used since the times of the Crusades. The swords and variously shaped curved cutting weapons were particularly vicious and many of them were trimmed with pure gold. Damascus steel, that formed many of the blades and barrels of a lot of the early guns was highly prized throughout history for use in weaponry – because of its resistance to corrosion, its ability to resist high levels of explosive force without fracturing and to retain a keen edge.

After the cultural tour we were taken into a nearby glass-blowing factory where the head blower fashioned personal, rich, sapphire-blue, ornate glass jugs for each of us as presents.

During the afternoon we relaxed by the swimming pool and dined early in the main restaurant, in preparation for a dawn start the following morning. As we left the hotel, and were in the process of organising a taxi, the throaty roar of a massive engine, a flurry of dust and a screeching of brakes announced the arrival of the dreaded armoured Range Rover. Our hearts sank. The previous night's budding Michael Schumacher at the wheel leaped out and literally threw our suitcases behind the back seat before we could see clearly just what he was throwing them onto. The tailgate slammed and we were off; we struggled to find our seatbelts, only to discover that none were fitted to the vehicle.

Our passage through the city was a nightmare. Mercifully there was little traffic on the roads as dawn was breaking, but any wheeled transport that had the temerity to appear in front of us had to be passed at nothing less than 100 miles an hour. Donkeys on their own or pulling produce to the market were particular targets for his animosity.

One particular donkey, which must have been deaf, did not hear our approach. As we passed the poor unfortunate animal, the wind that we created knocked it completely off its feet and a glance through the rear window revealed it, apparently suspended half a metre above the road with its legs stuck out at right angles and its huge rigid ears vertically upwards. It was like something out of a Thelwell cartoon. Traffic lights, road markings and Stop signs failed to impress this maniac. He managed to keep our tyres screeching almost continuously and I wondered how long they would withstand this punishment on what was a seriously overweight vehicle.

If driving inside the city had been a nightmare, the dual carriageway of the airport road was undiluted hell. I have flown jet aircraft at slower speeds than he reached on that road. Fortunately there were only about three cars to be passed, but each one needed two tight turns, executed at the very last minute, to overtake. This manoeuvre lifted the side of the car on the inside of the necessarily small turn and we proceeded for at least a hundred yards on two wheels. I was absolutely terrified each time and apart from shouting at him to slow down was unable to utter any other sound.

Relief came with an enormous bang underneath the car as one of the rear tyres exploded. Owing to the high speed it took some distance to bring the Range Rover to a stop and in the process we temporarily left the road onto the central reservation before lurching back to end up off the road to the extreme right of the slow lane. We were very thankful that crash barriers had not yet been fitted or some sort of serious disaster would surely have been unavoidable.

The nearside rear wheel was smoking heavily as we disembarked and flames were starting to appear quite close to the main petrol tank. Surprisingly, the driver produced a fire extinguisher, which eventually extinguished the flames but not the dense clouds of acrid black smoke. It looked very dramatic as it formed a vertical column about 30 metres high and when the tailgate was lowered to permit access to the spare wheel and the necessary repair tools, we took the precaution of removing our precious luggage and setting it down by the roadside in the fresh morning air.

We were aghast at what lay hitherto unseen beneath our suitcases. There were three shallow wooden boxes containing approximately twenty Czechoslovakian hand-grenades in separate small square wooden compartments in each box. Underneath the boxes were an indeterminate number of sub-machine guns, automatic rifles and loose ammunition of various types. I noted several Kalshnikov AK-47s and some small machine-pistols similar to the Israeli Uzi, but failed to recognize the rest.

Seeing the boxes of hand grenades reminded me of my time as a leading telegraphist in HMS *Plucky*, a minesweeper with the Mediterranean Second Minesweeping Squadron, in 1951. The corrupt King Farouk, with some British government support, was still in power in Egypt, but nationalism under the tacit control of Egyptian Army General, Mohammed Neguib, was creating havoc with the civil operation of the Suez Canal and sabotage of the canal's installations was a daily event.

The Royal Navy's response was to send all four Algerine Class ships of the 2nd Minesweeping Squadron to Suez to register a military presence. Remarkably, the ploy actually worked and the sabotage ceased for over three months.

HMS *Chameleon*, the squadron's lead minesweeper, was based in the Suez Canal at Port Said, its northerly end. HMS *Rifleman* and HMS *Sursay* were together in the Great Bitter Lakes, south of Ismailia, about halfway down while HMS *Plucky* took up station in the middle of the waterway off Suez at the

HMS Plucky *strutting her stuff off Port Tewfik at the southern end of the Suez Canal.*

southern end. Our exact position was just on the horizon, off the small town of Port Tewfik, with orders to make our presence felt amongst the local population.

This was a wide remit and one that our captain, Commander Wyatt, set about with some enthusiasm. We sailed around at our best speed, which was about 20 knots with a good following wind. Our main gun on the fo'c'sle was fired, away from the town, at floating targets in the water and depth charges sent up huge spouts of white water, but whilst we were at anchor we felt somewhat vulnerable to attack from underwater saboteurs who were known to be capable of attaching limpet mines to unwary British naval ships.

To counter this threat a constant stream of ship's divers scoured the underside of the ship at about fifteen-minute intervals. It must be remembered that Port Tewfik lay at the top end of the Red Sea, which was known to be full of almost every type of shark, some of them very nasty indeed. Whilst at anchor we lowered a small boat into the water alongside the ship as the divers swam underneath *Plucky* under the watchful eye of Lieutenant James, our TAS (Torpedo Anti-Submarine) Officer. A volunteer selected a hand grenade out of a stock of about sixty we carried in the boat; each time a diver climbed the ladder up into the boat, the volunteer pulled the pin of the hand grenade and dropped it in the water, where it sank and exploded some seconds later.

The mistaken idea of this exercise with the hand grenades was that we would frighten any marauding sharks away from our divers and if any saboteurs tried to approach the ship at the time, we would give them a severe headache. Several years later, following experiments by Jacques Cousteau, the French underwater scientist, it transpired that such small explosions act like a dinner gong for sharks and actually attract them to the site to gobble up any stunned fish; but in good faith, we thought that we were doing the right thing.

The volunteer who tossed *Plucky's* hand grenades into the sea from this small boat was me; hour after hour in the blazing sun, pulling pins and plopping them into the sea. It was a boring task which I decided to liven up in a most foolish way. Having accumulated a fair pile of grenade pins, I picked one up in my left hand and with a grenade in my right hand, with its intact pin obscured, I said to Lieutenant James, 'The pin has fallen out of this grenade. What shall I do with it?'

For someone who had been half-asleep, I was surprised at the remarkable speed with which he leapt out of his seat, lunged towards me and made to grab the grenade. I dodged out of his way just as he swung a serious punch at my head. Missing my chin by half an inch, he then surprised me by leaping over the side of the boat in his white tropical uniform, disappearing beneath the surface of the water. When he surfaced, I showed him that the pin was still in the hand grenade and that I had been joking.

Without comment he pulled himself back in the boat, grabbed my shirt and punched me with such force that I had a black eye for days. I certainly learnt the lesson and never even contemplated jokes with live ammunition ever again. Nor did I think about complaining about the TAS Officer's punch, because I knew that if I did Commander Wyatt would have dispensed even more painful punishment.

The small boats that came out from Port Tewfik to sell souvenirs to *Plucky's* sailors were manned by very friendly Egyptians who appeared to welcome our presence, so Commander Wyatt decided on a 'hearts and minds' exercise. We rigged the quarterdeck with a sparkling white canvas awning for a cocktail party and the First Lieutenant was dispatched ashore to invite the mayor, local worthies and their wives to attend the next day.

The ship was brought closer to the harbour and at the appointed time *Plucky's* two motorboats were waiting at the jetty to ferry the Egyptians on board. The mayor and about twenty others were thrilled to come aboard and everyone enjoyed the ship's hospitality for a couple of hours. As the mayor left, he asked Commander Wyatt whether the ship's company played football, to which he received an emphatic affirmative. 'Good,' he shouted up the gangway. 'The town football team would like to challenge you to a game tomorrow afternoon.'

As the population of the town could not have been more than 300, we reckoned that our team, which had recently won the Mediterranean Fleet Championships in Malta against teams from 2,000-man battleships, aircraft carriers and the like, stood a very good chance of winning against what was effectively a village team.

At the appointed hour *Plucky*'s intrepid eleven men landed on the jetty, supported by every member of the ship's company not on duty. I should add at this point that I was just a spectator – although I liked playing football, I was nowhere near good enough to make the ship's first team. However the scene that met us as we walked through the town to what amounted to a stadium was quite worrying. Banners across the street announced that this football match was between Egypt and Great Britain. There were thousands of people everywhere who had evidently arrived from as far away as Luxor, the noise was deafening in the stadium, but everyone was very friendly and appeared to be somewhat embarrassed.

No wonder they were embarrassed, for this casual game had grown from a 73-man ship's company team playing an Egyptian village team, into a full 'international'. The Egyptian referee who met our lads on the pitch was a well-known international referee, and when their players appeared, there were several famous names amongst them. It later transpired that none of the players lived in Port Tewfik at all. The Egyptians scored first and their supporters went wild, then they scored a second goal, although that was not a fair commentary on the run of play. *Plucky* gave as good as they received and the refereeing was very fair indeed. Just before half-time, we scored a magnificent goal from a long way out and the Egyptian worries became evident.

The second half was much more evenly balanced and we scored a sneaky second goal, and then, wonder of wonders, we banged a third one into the net, just before full time. Surprisingly, the Egyptians cheered our goals as enthusiastically as they had cheered their own. They just loved good football, whoever was playing, and on our return to the jetty after our 3-2 victory, we were escorted by a wildly cheering crowd of good-natured young people. Whilst we all wondered how they had produced such a high-powered team of players at such short notice, we never did find the answer.

Back to Damascus!

It was the hand grenades that worried us most because they all appeared to be primed and ready to explode by merely withdrawing the pin. What's more, being Czechoslovakian they were quite likely to be filled with deadly Semtex explosive, which was known to be unstable and could detonate from any sharp knock. The driver called me round to the damaged wheel to show me that the rubber of the tyre had mostly disappeared, but the metal of the wheel itself was almost glowing, nearly red-hot. We needed to reduce the temperature in order to replace it with the spare wheel, but there was no more left in the fire extinguisher and we did not carry any water. The solution, he suggested, would be for us all to urinate onto the hot metal and as if we did not fully understand him, he demonstrated exactly how to carry out this potentially dangerous procedure. Fortunately, we had all consumed good quantities of liquid with our breakfast, so we were able to oblige his demand for liquid and the steam spiralled upwards in the process.

As he loosened the wheel nuts it was obvious that, despite our noble efforts to cool the metal, the steaming rim of the wheel was still hot and as it finally fell to the ground I prevailed upon him to leave it there for a few minutes to avoid burning his fingers. Whilst we paused to allow the wheel and brake drum to cool, the driver bent down to retrieve his wheel spanner from the sand and, from somewhere within his clothing, an automatic machine-pistol fell onto the ground.

My ill-considered enquiry as to whether the weapon was loaded or not caused him to examine the safety catch, turn away from the Range Rover and fire a magazine full of ammunition towards a fence post about 20 metres away from the road. If he was aiming at the six-inch fence post, he missed. When the magazine was empty, he replaced it with a fresh magazine and handed the gun to me, saying, 'You try.' My firm dictum is never to argue with a man, whatever his demeanour, with a loaded gun in his hand, so I carefully took the weapon from him and took deliberate aim at the same post. He showed me how to select single shot and my first round took splinters off the side of it. Subsequent aimed shots either hit the post or produced more splinters. It was a very handy weapon indeed and I was pleased to find that my naval training had not all been forgotten.

Eventually the brake drum had cooled sufficiently to allow the new wheel to be fitted, but the original one was still steaming quietly on the ground. He picked up the hot wheel, protecting his hands with a cloth, and, to my amazement, placed it on the live hand grenades. I pushed past him, grabbed the wheel, took it off the explosives and threw it behind us. It was hot enough to scorch my hand. The only things I could use to insulate it from the grenades were my own and the co-pilot's suitcases, so I placed the two cases on top of them and carefully replaced the damaged wheel on top of the suitcases.

Turning to the driver, I enquired whether the grenades were, in fact, live. His answer was to pick one out of the box, withdraw the pin and hurl it 30 or so metres into the bushes, whereupon there was a very loud bang and a column of sand shot up into the air. We were spread-eagled on the ground long before the explosion, but the thrower remained standing upright, in the direct line of any stray shrapnel. I could see that he was about to pass a grenade to me to try, so I quickly closed the tailgate and sat down inside the vehicle. The time from withdrawing the pin of the grenade to its explosion was less than five seconds, a very short interval compared with grenades that I had used in the past, which had a ten-second delay. In my judgement, this made the Czechoslovakian grenades dangerous to use.

The final five miles to our Falcon were driven at more normal speeds and we were all very relieved to thank our driver for the eventful taxi ride before watching him disappear back towards the city, never to be seen again by any of us.

In October 1974 we were asked to fly from Tripoli to Marrakech with Yasser Arafat, for a meeting with King Hassan II of Morocco. He arrived with his two secretary/bodyguards early in the morning. I elected to refuel in Algeria en route and arrived outside the Algiers VIP lounge at about 10 o'clock. A group of Palestinians met us inside the lounge and informed us that we could not proceed to Marrakech because the United States Secretary of State, Henry Kissinger, had made a surprise visit and was currently in the presence of King Hassan II.

After an intense discussion, in which President Boumedienne became personally involved, it was decided that the Palestinian leader would need to wait in Algiers until Henry Kissinger had left Morocco. Exactly why the two should not meet, as they both wished to see King Hassan II, was never explained to me so I just accepted the decision as a *fait accompli*. The Algerian President kindly loaned us a handy palace to rest in, whilst we followed the fortunes of the American Secretary of State. I am not exactly clear just where the palace was situated in the hills behind Algiers because the police motorcycle outriders escorting us had an unfortunate crash on the way and I paid more attention to the care of the injured bodies than to the direction of the road.

The palace was surrounded by beautiful gardens full of raised beds of colourful, semi-tropical flowers surrounded by metre-high, beautifully clipped, green box hedges and scarlet gravel paths. Inside the almost oriental building, besides the staff we had the whole building to ourselves. There were about a dozen Palestinians and we three aircrew; we had a small snack meal served at a long, polished mahogany table in an ornate dining room with a heavily figured plaster ceiling.

In the heat of the afternoon following our meal, as we did not know how long we would have to wait, we all took an afternoon's siesta. The beds were large, very old-fashioned, polished carved wood and comfortable; my bedroom was huge. At one corner of the room an arched door intrigued me, through which I found a bathroom surfaced – floor, walls and ceiling – with a very pretty natural orange-coloured marble. The original French design was apparent throughout the building and I was inclined to walk into the furniture whilst gazing at the carvings on the walls and the complex designs in the plaster on the ceilings. The opulence of the bathroom persuaded me to indulge in a luxurious soak before dinner.

Relaxing in the wide, white, cast-iron bath, I realized that there was a second door in the wall opposite the door through which I had entered. Whilst drying myself after a most enjoyable soak, I tried the brass door knob to the second door and was somewhat surprised to see that it swung open revealing another room, slightly smaller than mine, with a single bed almost behind the door, beneath a window. Resting on the bed, working on some official papers, lay Yasser Arafat, with the soles of his stockinged feet pointing towards my dripping, towel-draped body. What made this encounter somewhat strange was that a Kalashnikov AK-47 lay along his body, with the muzzle pointing at me. As I stepped into his room without knocking, he raised the gun to his chin and removed the safety catch. As soon as he recognized me, he put the gun down and apologized. I, too, apologized to him for bursting into his room unannounced and hastily withdrew, slightly embarrassed.

At dinner, at the same long polished mahogany table, I reiterated my apologies and everyone had a good laugh at my embarrassment. The Palestinian leader sat directly opposite me, somewhere about the middle of the table. Half way through the main course, which I seem to remember was a spicy chicken dish, he threw me to the lions once again, by announcing to the room in general that 'the Captain' was of the opinion that the Palestinians were alienating themselves with the rest of the world by their violent tactics.

My heart sank and I found myself murmuring, under my breath, 'Oh no! Here we go again.' This time I had been pushed into crossing swords with two articulate young English speakers and one, seemingly more extreme, Palestinian with very little command of the English language, who spoke Arabic. For some unknown reason, aircraft hijacking became the main topic under discussion. Maybe these three were aspiring experts on the subject, or were involved with planning a specific hijack. Whatever the reason, when I decried such policies, they became decidedly militant and aggressive towards me personally and were unreasonably abusive.

I glanced over towards Yasser Arafat, who gave me a half smile and a surreptitious nod, which I took to mean that I should defend myself verbally, as best I could. It probably meant, 'For god's sake, shut up,' but if it did I was too deep into my demolition of their potential violence and its probable repercussions with the rest of the world to care a damn.

Perhaps I used too extreme language, which I interpreted into Arabic for the benefit of the non-English speaker, or perhaps I was dealing with uncontrollable fanatics who could see nobody else's point of view. Whatever the reason, the result was fairly dramatic. Again they both placed a handgun on the table, each one pointing towards my chest, which thankfully once more produced a cry of horror from the Palestinian leader. He jumped out of his chair, walked around the entire table, talking non-stop Arabic. As he reached each weapon on the table, he picked it up and threw it onto the lap of its respective owner. Returning to his seat, he asked me what the weather was like in Marrakech, and with some relief I launched into a detailed forecast that would have done Michael Fish justice.

As we sipped our coffee, the Algerian Chief of Protocol came into the room and announced that Henry Kissinger had just taken off from Morocco and that we were therefore free to go as soon as we liked. We took off at 11 o'clock in the dark, except for a sky full of brilliant stars, and at 1 o'clock in the morning landed at Marrakech. The airfield was in complete darkness, though the three-quarter moon was climbing high into the heavens giving us enough light to walk over to the control tower without the aid of any torches. The Palestinian leader was mystified. 'Where is the king?' he kept saying, but the only people around were some very young, bewildered-looking armed soldiers.

An army officer appeared and when I saw Yasser Arafat in deep conversation with him, I returned to the safety of our Falcon to await developments.

Fifteen minutes later, he returned to the aircraft, laughing uncontrollably, the tears rolling down his hairy cheeks. Through bouts of laughter, he explained that Marrakech was the Arabic name for Morocco – until that moment he had been unaware that there was an actual city called Marrakech, so his instruction to fly there clearly meant to him the capital of Morocco. But Rabat was the capital of the country, and that was where King Hassan II was waiting for us, complete with armed guard, military band and, by this time, a prodigious temper.

The co-pilot, Yasser Arafat and myself stood on the tarmac, at the foot of the aircraft steps, and laughed until we cried. At one stage we had to hold each other up to avoid one of us falling over. The two Moroccan soldiers standing some way away from us were obviously convinced that we had all gone stark raving mad. When the hilarity subsided I decided that we must make an effort to rectify our ridiculous position, so we flashed up the motors and flew with all speed to the capital Rabat, 150 miles to the north. Needless to say, by this time the king had taken more than a little umbrage and had taken his guard and military band back to his massive stone palace in the heart of the city.

We admitted defeat, ordered a taxi and booked into the Hilton Hotel, some way outside the palace gates. As we walked to our individual rooms, we still could not resist laughing about our ridiculous predicament. The following morning, we all relaxed over breakfast until the Royal Messenger called Yasser Arafat to the palace for his meeting with King Hassan II. A group of three local expatriate

Palestinians took us on a tour of the souk whilst the royal meeting was in progress, ending up at an open-fronted shop where craftsmen were constructing furniture for sale. At the time they were making various designs of small tables, inlaid with different types of colourful wood. We were asked by the shopkeeper which type of table we liked most, so we all three stated our preferences before being taken away for a mid-morning coffee. On our return an hour later, we were presented with the three tables we had admired, which had been made specially for us in our absence. They were parcelled up with brown paper and string, and we carried them back to our hotel, mystified as to who had paid for them. We presumed that they were presents from the Palestinians, but we later discovered that the shopkeeper was also Palestinian, so everyone received our sincere thanks.

Gifts from expatriate Palestinians were a common experience when it was discovered that we were flying their beloved leader. Some of them were completely overcome with gratitude and when we walked away from their shops or stalls, the whole family would spontaneously offer their thanks. It could sometimes be quite embarrassing, so we tended to keep the details of our passengers a secret and behaved more like ordinary tourists.

Returning to the Hilton, we were met by the Moroccan Chief of Protocol who, over lunch, told us a fascinating story. He said that King Hassan was a most resourceful leader of the country, and to illustrate his point he described an assassination attempt on his life by the then C-in-C of the Moroccan armed forces, General Mohammad Oufkir.

The king was evidently flying back to Rabat from a meeting with some of his ministers in Casablanca on 16 August 1972, when his Fan-Jet Falcon was attacked by three Moroccan Air Force Northrop F-5s, which attempted to shoot the civil aircraft down. The attack caused some damage to it, but the king survived the attempt without injury and the robust royal aircraft was able to land back safely in Rabat. Thinking about the incident, the king remembered that General Oufkir had proposed to him some months earlier that he was in favour of shooting down a Falcon carrying President Gadaffi of Libya using three of the Air Force's Northrop F-5s. The king had vetoed the proposal as being in flagrant contravention of international law, or that is what he apparently told his chief of protocol. Recalling that conversation, and having just been attacked in the exact way proposed by General Oufkir, convinced the king that the general was responsible for the attack on him.

He called Rabat Control personally, claiming to be the pilot, and asked General Oufkir to meet his aircraft on landing as the king had been seriously injured following an attack by unidentified fighter aircraft. When General Oufkir walked up the stairs of the Falcon he was met by a fully fit King Hassan at the top, wielding a loaded sub-machine gun. Eighteen bullets later, the general lay dead on the tarmac in a growing pool of his own blood.

Gen Mohamed Oufkir prior to his reputed demise at the hands of King Hassan II of Morocco.

To be honest, it is difficult to confirm all the details of this account of the general's demise. Some accounts of the incident have the aircraft as a Boeing 727, some have the flight taking place over the Mediterranean, while others allege that the killing of the general was inside the king's palace a couple of hours later. The main fact, however, is undeniable – King Hassan II of Morocco shot General Mohammad Oufkir, his C-in-C, on 16 August 1972 and killed him. It is highly probable the general had attempted to assassinate King Hassan an hour earlier.

On 14 November 1975 we were called out to the Tripoli VIP lounge for a short flight to Sirte, President Gadaffi's birthplace in the desert, midway between Libya's two main cities, where we landed on the main Benghazi to Tripoli road; this sounds more dangerous than in fact it was.

Waiting for us as arranged was a leading light of the Libyan administration, the ex-Minister of Communications, Sharif Ben Amer, a multilingual academic of great all-round ability who was always a pleasure to fly. His thoughtful demeanour and humorous approach to any problems occurring during any flight, and his lively conversational ability made him very popular with anyone who came into contact with him. He had undoubted natural charisma, which was always appreciated, especially by the better-looking lady diplomats we encountered around the Middle East and Africa.

His current position was non-specific. In the British Parliament he would probably have been described as Minister without Portfolio, but his real job was to act as the Libyan President's general adviser. He was a godsend to the Chief Pilot of Special Flight, being someone who readily understood complex problems, accepted responsibility and made quick, sensible decisions. Where Special Flight was concerned he would instruct the senior members of Libyan Arab Airlines in exactly what he wanted and heaven help anyone who was obstructive.

On this occasion, he was accompanied by Yasser Arafat and his own secretary. The routine of landing on the main road at Sirte was well established by this time, but Sharif Ben Amer could not resist sitting in the jump-seat in the cockpit to witness the whole procedure. We flew at relatively low level to a spot on the wide tarmac road indicated by our Omega navigation system, then at very low level over two buildings with windsocks on their roofs, at each end of a long stretch – perhaps two miles – of straight road. As if by magic, Libyan policemen would emerge from the buildings and stop any traffic before it reached the buildings. When the pilot was happy that the road was empty of motor vehicles, he would carry out one more run to examine the surface for obstacles, then turn and land into wind. There were no vertical obstructions of any kind to bother a pilot; in fact the highest features were the metre-high, wind-blown balls of prairie grass rolling across the desert sand, reminiscent of many of the old western movies.

A Range Rover usually met our passengers and, whilst they were away, we waited for them in a prominent 'lay-by' that had been thoughtfully created for that purpose. If our wait was planned to be longer than an hour or so, we would arrange for the police to stand guard on our Falcon whilst we walked half a mile north to the southerly shore of the Mediterranean for a refreshing swim in the clear blue water of the Gulf of Sirte. This time we were warned that we would be waiting about three hours whilst our two main passengers had a meeting with the Libyan President in his colourfully ornate Bedouin tent, about ten miles to the south of the road.

So off we went with our sun umbrellas, straw mats and a few bottles of orange juice for a couple of hours' relaxation on the beach. It was a very long, flat beach stretching over four hundred miles to both east and west, with not a single living soul to be seen. There are not many places in the world where it is possible to enjoy about a thousand nautical miles of beach just to yourself, but this was one of them. On a clear day, as this was, the curvature of the earth could be seen.

As we relaxed on the beach with a ball, I suddenly became aware of something bobbing up and down on the surface of the water about half a mile off the coast. It looked a little like a moored mine of wartime vintage, but we decided that that was most unlikely, so we all swam out to investigate. It turned out to be an old-fashioned, three-legged, butcher's block that must have been washed overboard from some passing ship. I decided that this substantial piece of wood would look nice on my patio back in Tripoli with a pretty flowering plant sitting on it, so we took a leg each and swam it ashore.

Back on the beach we found that it was quite heavy, so we left it on the sand above the high-water mark whilst we walked south, back to the policemen on the road, for some assistance. Luckily, a platoon of soldiers had arrived since our departure from the shiny white Falcon, and they were equipped with a short-wheelbase Land Rover, which they were only too pleased to lend us for a while. Equipped with a four-wheel drive vehicle and a couple of willing helpers we had the butcher's block stowed away in our baggage compartment in no time at all.

For some unaccountable reason the police and the army thought that we were quite mad and our salvaged flotsam caused them a great deal of hilarity.

The passengers, when they arrived, wished to fly further east rather than return home as originally planned, so we landed at Benghazi for fuel where the President's personal adviser had business with the Governor of Cyrenaica overnight. On landing at Damascus with the remainder of the passengers, where there was no ceremonial reception, we were relieved to see the smiling face of big fat Mohamed greeting us. Thankfully there was no sign of the supercharged Range Rover.

As Yasser Arafat was on his own, he joined us in Mohamed's decrepit Renault to be taken to his Damascus office in the centre of the city, before we settled ourselves down for the night in the luxury of the Sheraton. No food was needed until breakfast time the next day as we had all eaten well on board the Falcon after the stop in Benghazi. We shopped in the hotel's boutiques before retiring to bed and met around the bar to compare our purchases. I had bought some large strangely shaped pearls to be made into a pendant for a necklace for Lesley.

For the next hour the most onerous task that any of us did was to grapple with the tough little pistachio nuts on the bar as we each enjoyed a couple of small glasses of their best draught lager. The swimming off Sirte had made us tired, so we admitted defeat and wandered off to our rooms relatively early. During breakfast round the swimming pool the next morning a Palestinian messenger arrived to say that Yasser Arafat would like to fly to Jeddah, in Saudi Arabia, shortly after lunch.

In Jeddah we were met by an efficient group of smartly dressed young men, most of whom had lost their family houses and possessions in the Jerusalem area, on land that had effectively been annexed by Israel, so they were temporarily resident in Saudi Arabia's second city. Their leader departed for a meeting with Saudi officials and the Palestinians organized some pleasant airport hotel accommodation for us.

Unfortunately the meeting was over almost before it started and we had to drag ourselves away from our comfortable hotel to take the Palestinian leader to Cairo. The intention was to return to Tripoli, but when we requested take off clearance from Cairo Air Traffic Control, they informed us that there would be a two- to three-hour delay owing to repair work being carried out on their main runway. The weather was sunny, but being November it was quite pleasant outside, so Yasser Arafat and I took some comfortable cushions out of the Falcon and with our backs resting on the main landing wheels in the shade of one wing, we talked quietly together for a long time. The engineer kindly kept a steady supply of cool soft drinks lubricating our vocal chords as he and the co-pilot played cards, propped against the other pair of wheels.

The conversation started just as two particularly attractive Egyptair stewardesses strolled across the dispersal in front of us, heading for their Boeing 727 on the other side of the tarmac dispersal. Even seated, Yasser Arafat was unmistakable in his black and white kaffiyeh and as he was well known in Egypt the two girls' reaction at seeing the Palestinian leader sitting with the captain under the wing of an aircraft was respectful, but embarrassed. They giggled in a girlish kind of way and called 'Good afternoon' as they passed.

As we returned the greeting Yasser Arafat whispered quietly into my ear, 'Mine's the one on the left, which one are you having, Captain?' He grinned as I replied that if that was his choice I would take the one on the right. We laughed as the girls walked up the steps at the front of their Boeing.

Sensing a relaxed mood, I took the opportunity to comment on his proclivity to involve me and my anti-violence opinions whenever the more hot-headed members of his people were present in our company. He gave my statement some consideration, then replied that although he was the leader of the Palestinian people, he was only in such a position because he was 'at the top of the pile' when a leader was needed for purposes of international diplomacy.

His position, he judged, was a tenuous one and would only continue as long as he was seen to be promoting the obvious needs of his people. Some of those people were the younger members of families that had been wiped out in what they saw as random terrorist attacks against the Palestinians, and blatant illegal confiscation of their property. They wanted revenge for what were, in their frustrated opinion, unacceptable atrocities.

Although he was their leader, there was only so much that could be done with these groups by anyone in these regrettable circumstances, despite any awareness of the negative impact on world opinion of some of their actions.

'If public denunciation of the more extreme groups, or even some of the smaller violent pockets happened, how long do you think any leader's life would last, Captain?' he asked me. 'Without a leader, the Palestinian cause would be lost, as the Israeli strongmen are only too well aware. Consider my position. I am not a conquering dictator; I have no established army, no effective police force, no civil service, no administration machinery, no tax system to provide a useable income. I clearly lead only by consensus of the majority.

'When I hear someone like you expounding theories that I know inside me must happen if we are to progress at all, do you blame me for involving you in our politics? It allows me to discuss your views with others later and perhaps make them see the wisdom of what you say, without me having to claim them as my own personal views.'

It was then that he apologized for his ploy that resulted in landing my crew in the brothel in Damascus. I forgave him and he laughed a deep belly laugh. Up to that time I was never aware that he knew of our predicament that unfortunate night.

When I said as much, he said that the one thing he had established that was probably one of the best in the world was his foolproof communications system. He was able to contact and receive confidential replies from most of the countries of the world quicker than their own embassies could usually manage, he claimed. 'Put me to the test,' he invited, and on a few occasions, when urgent decisions were needed regarding our aircraft, I did utilize his advanced communications ability, testing the response time by sending duplicate requests through official embassy channels. His communications were always much quicker and to this day I have no idea how he achieved this.

Years later, when I asked him how his secure communications were so efficient, he said that he had studied the methods of Lord Louis Mountbatten, but would not elaborate any further.

On 9 June 1977 I flew Yasser Arafat to Cairo for a formal meeting with President Sadat of Egypt and this was one of the few times that the Shepheards Hotel let us down. In fact, there were no respectable hotel bedrooms available in the whole of Cairo, because five international conferences that were taking place in the city had claimed all the available acceptable accommodation before our arrival. About 2 o'clock in the morning of 10 June we pitched up at the Venus Hotel, complete with outside flashing lights, somewhere in the back streets behind the main railway station.

Yes, they had three bedrooms and by then we were not being too fussy, so we staggered upstairs with our suitcases to be met by a fat, middle-aged, droopy boobed, Egyptian 'lady', wearing a nylon headscarf and shuffling around in a pair of gaudy rubber flip-flops. The three of us went into the first bedroom, which was clean enough to convince the co-pilot to take it for his night's sleep. Next we found a room for the engineer, then I was led away by 'madame' to another room. I was just pulling back the bedclothes to assess the cleanliness of the sheets, when the door slammed and I realized that madame of the droopy boobs had closed the door but had neglected to leave the room. Her object was glaringly obvious as she sidled up to me and rubbed her left shoulder against my chest.

Realizing the full enormity of her action, I rushed past her, fought open the door and dashed back into the engineer's room. When the two of us returned to my room to confront the attack, the threat had disappeared, so I bade him goodnight and fished a portable 'door bolt' out of my luggage to bar the door from any possibility of a forced entry. Fortunately, our passengers wished to leave early the next morning and we all left the Hotel Venus with great relief.

The Palestinian leader wanted to fly to Riyadh, the capital of Saudi Arabia, but because of delays from Cairo Air Traffic Control, we were not able to leave until late afternoon. En route to Riyadh he told me that he had a meeting booked with Prince Zoltan who was staying with King Khalid Bin Abdulaziz in the palace. This news boded well for our accommodation and sure enough, royal limousines bore us all away to the peak of luxury in rooms decorated with miles of coloured silk fabrics, enriched with threads of pure gold. We enjoyed the opulence being lavished upon us and slept soundly until midday the following day.

Breakfast with Yasser Arafat and Prince Zoltan was followed by a shopping expedition into the old souk where we found ourselves trying out ancient long-barrelled flintlock weapons and some of the first bolt-action rifles that were used by colonizing Europeans in the Arabian Peninsula, before the establishment of the current Kingdom. When we returned to our transport, the weapons that we had been handling were all neatly packaged on the back seat for us. It was never clearly established exactly who had paid for them, so to be on the safe side we thanked everyone in sight.

When I tactfully enquired of Yasser Arafat whether any of his men had been involved in the gifts, he denied all knowledge, so I must presume that they were presents from someone within the palace. They have pride of place on my lounge wall to this day.

I only once saw Yasser Arafat really lose his temper. It happened while he was meeting President Sadat of Egypt on 22 July 1977, outside the VIP lounge at Cairo Airport.

A short while earlier, during our take-off from Tobruk, a squadron of Egyptian Sukhoi 21 fighter-bombers, perhaps sixteen in all, had swept in at very low level from the sea and without warning dropped a hail of bombs around Tobruk's main runway. The nearest bomb was about 200 metres behind us just as our wheels were leaving the ground, and the explosions severely rocked our Falcon, at a vulnerable stage in its flight. Yasser Arafat was occupying the jump-seat in the cockpit at the time and saw the whole incident very clearly.

Everyone was severely startled and somewhat annoyed, because we were unaware of any animosity between Egypt and Libya and wondered whether, in the circumstances, it was wise for us to continue the flight to the Egyptian capital.

In the event we received satisfactory assurances that International Air Traffic Control was still operating from Cairo, so I decided that it would be safe for us to land at Cairo Airport. Meeting the Egyptian leader on the tarmac outside the aircraft, Yasser stated quite forcibly, 'You bloody well nearly killed us all at Tobruk,' to which Anwar Sadat replied, smiling, 'No, no, no. We knew exactly where you were all the time and were just waiting for you to get airborne before we dropped our bombs.' Then the Egyptian President looked over the Palestinian leader's shoulder at me and said, 'Once again – sorry, Captain,' to which I gave a resigned 'tut' and a non-committal nod.

It was interesting for me to note the different forms of address used to the Palestinian leader when greeting him in different countries. He was addressed almost universally as 'President Arafat' throughout the Middle East and Africa; elsewhere he was usually referred to as either 'Chairman Arafat' or 'Mr Arafat'.

He was, of course, the undisputed leader of his people and therefore their *de facto* President. The different forms of address were merely a commentary on each particular country's current stance with regard to Palestinian politics. He did not at any time, by word or facial expression, register any acknowledgement of the differences in the various countries' forms of address. Leaders of other countries were invariably faced with Yasser Arafat's characteristic fixed outward half smile that betrayed little of his inner thoughts.

His country's economy could not be run in the way that most other economies were sustained. Palestine had, as I commented earlier, no tax system because there was no conventional income that could be taxed. Agriculture was at subsistence level and almost nothing was sold to anyone else, largely because the fertile sections of the country had been annexed by Israel. Bartering systems were common; there was no manufacturing industry of any kind. He once said to me that he did not even have anywhere to bury his dead.

It is not surprising, therefore, that much of his travelling was connected with raising funds on behalf of his people, for no country can survive without any money at all. The normal function of any government is to ensure a consistent supply of reliable funds for all its requirements. Because of the administration of the funds raised by him for the continuance of the Palestinian state, some wagging tongues put it about that their leader was living the high life in opulence and splendour.

In my experience this was never the case throughout the many years of my acquaintance with him. He frequently arrived back at our aircraft for the next leg of his flight, clearly exhausted from his meetings and the constant activity, having been unable to find anywhere to rest his head. On these occasions he would divest himself of his headdress and fatigue jacket, throw them on the floor in the recess between the two rows of seats as a pillow, shout 'Goodnight, Captain!' lie down and instantly fall asleep before the engines had even been started. The engineer would find him a conventional white pillow and a few blankets to make his erstwhile bed a little more comfortable and he would sleep soundly in this position for several hours before his next engagement.

These and many other clear examples were not the acts of someone who was living in the lap of luxury. This was the lifestyle of a man living in deprived conditions, in sympathy with his struggling people.

In most of the countries that we visited with the Palestinian leader we were met by larger or smaller groups of Palestinian people living in exile, sometimes away from their families. They existed as more or less autonomous entities that provided the necessities of life for themselves without outside support. Throughout these visits they assumed responsibility for their leader and his delegation's well-being and security. Their method of maintaining a standard of living that was sometimes better than average was by finding highly paid work in their host country, not through any criminal activity.

There were doctors, civil engineers, teachers, accountants and all manner of professions living in various forms of exile. Sometimes, if these groups were living in areas with ineffective police protection, their security arrangements became overtly high profile. In other words, they could be armed to the teeth and quite prepared to blaze away in protection of their leadership, although we never actually witnessed any such behaviour.

At other times the resident group merely provided access to the communications network while the government of the host country made themselves responsible for the delegation's accommodation and sustenance. From our point of view this was usually a much more secure and preferable arrangement and on occasions produced for us, the crew, some of life's little luxuries. One such example was when we arrived in the ex-French West African state of Senegal on 6 June 1977. Yasser Arafat was met by the local Palestinian group and was ushered away to prepare for a meeting with Senegal's President, Leopold Sedar Senghor.

As they left the airfield the group's leader told us that our passengers would be in Dakar, the capital of Senegal, for at least two days and recommended a nearby hotel for us to stay. Fortunately for us, the Senegalese Chief of Protocol made himself known shortly afterwards and dismissed our previous adviser's choice of accommodation as absolute rubbish. He had already arranged our hotel, he informed us. We were to stay in the five-star Oberoi down on the beach and would be quite comfortable there for a couple of days. He was quite correct.

That evening we explored the jungle city of Dakar. Its architecture is typically French-African, with a selection of impressive Catholic churches and several interesting markets. Each market had semi-permanent stalls grouped into self-contained sections selling their own particular products, rather like a typical French town market. There was an area that sold nothing but the myriads of spices used in local cooking and perfumes. Rare spices like frankincense and myrrh, both aromatic gums from East Africa, were on sale but were very expensive. The aroma of this section assailed the senses and was almost intoxicating. Another large area of stalls stocked every conceivable kind of fabric, in every known combination of colour; the effect was a kaleidoscope of vibrant colour covering over an acre. Other sections specialized in local crafts and intricate wood-carvings of a very high standard.

Bargaining, though expected, was not of the extreme variety used by traders in some of the blacker African countries to the east, like Chad. The stated prices were usually only a few percentage points above the seller's 'bottom line', so halving the price, as was necessary in many parts of Africa, only produced storms of derision from the stallholder.

The men, with a few notable exceptions, seemed to us to be generally poorly dressed, but the females, young and old, were colourfully draped in very fashionable robes with headdresses rather like flamboyant turbans. The older ladies obviously wielded great power within their family groups. Each family was seemingly dominated by a matriarchal figure and it was sometimes apparent that a single older lady controlled several stalls through her younger family members.

I should have followed my co-pilot's example and bought a couple of the large, beautifully carved, ebony or mahogany figures and heads that were on offer, but there were so many on each stall that I became bewildered. After a while I decided to buy a black ebony dugout boat, about 70 centimetres long, complete with seven jet-black native figures, each clutching a broad spear and a paddle. I was assured that it was an authentic carving of a Senegalese crocodile-hunting boat – by the numerous crocodile-skin products on sale, there must have been plenty of the gigantic creatures in the city's rivers.

Nevertheless, I took it for granted that this attractive black carving was a caricature of the real thing, as it would be inherently unstable with so many men standing up in such a relatively small boat. The fallacy of my deductions was glaringly illustrated when we stopped to look down from a bridge over a substantial river whilst walking back to the Oberoi. There on the surface of the water, less than 15 feet away, floated a full-size copy of the model I had just purchased. It was crewed by seven tall natives, shining black in the evening light, clutching spears and paddles whilst they gazed with intense concentration into the water. How the boat stayed upright when occasionally they all seemed to lean over the same side, was a mystery to me and none of my experience as a naval officer helped to explain the boat's remarkable stability.

The following morning, the Senegal Chief of Protocol joined us for breakfast on the balcony of our suite of rooms, overlooking the calm palm-fringed Atlantic Ocean with its gentle swells breaking lazily on the sandy beach, to discuss our

The co-pilot, left and engineer, right enjoying big game fishing in the
Atlantic off Dakar, Senegal. June 1977.

preferred choice for the day's activities. 'If you like,' he said, 'we have booked a boat for you to sample some big game fishing off the coast and it is planned to arrive at the hotel's jetty at 9 o'clock with all your meals and drinks on board.' The co-pilot and I were rather partial to hunting for marlin and the engineer agreed to join us, promising not to be seasick cruising over the gentle sea. We thoroughly enjoyed ourselves, trolling lures along the Atlantic swells, until about 6 o'clock in the evening when the sun hovered an inch or two above the westerly horizon, which meant that we would be docking in the obscurity of relative darkness. The self-proclaimed big game fishing experts had managed to catch nothing, whereas the total novice amongst us had landed a quite respectable Atlantic Blue tuna. There's no justice.

Back in the Oberoi bar, our host had ordered us three cool glasses of draught lager, so we presented him with our solitary catch, which seemed to impress him beyond belief. We were quite ashamed of our lack of prowess, in the circumstances, but the engineer had a beaming fixed smile all over his face. Then came something of a bombshell. The Chief of Protocol laid a substantial pile of 1,000 CFA (Central Franc Africain) notes on the counter and announced that everyone needed to sample the local girls when they travelled abroad, so we should follow his careful directions, take the money, which was sufficient for three of the best girls in town, and he would see us in the morning. We were left with no choice – he just stood up, placed the considerable amount of cash in my lap and left.

The dilemma of just what to do with our newfound wealth was soon solved as we walked down the drive from the hotel, and past a group of French nuns collecting funds for a local children's orphanage. Following a quick conference we agreed that this was the ideal place for the money we had recently acquired for shadier purposes. The multilingual nuns thanked us in French and the local Wolof language, and were so enthusiastic about our substantial donation that we were showered with enthusiastic kisses in true French fashion. One of our number, who shall be nameless, was so overcome with the enthusiasm of a particularly attractive young blonde nun that he even started chatting her up. Some people have no shame.

We left for Guinea-Bissau early the next morning and the Chief of Protocol came to the airport to see us off. There was a great deal of nudge-nudge, wink-wink, but nobody referred directly to our previous night's activities and we adopted a circumspect and businesslike attitude.

The tiny African country of Guinea-Bissau is one of the poorest in Africa, with a general life expectancy of its population, in 1977, of just thirty-five years. The President, Luis de Alemeida Cabral, whom Yasser Arafat had come to meet, must bear a great deal of the responsibility for the political and administrative chaos that was then prevalent in the country. His abortive policies of trying to merge with the Cape Verde islands out in the Atlantic were nothing short of disastrous. The Palestinian group resident in the country kept a low profile because of repressive measures used by the government from time to time.

Yasser Arafat was taken away by four local Palestinians while two others remained to take us to a rather seedy hotel where the food was barely edible. Thankfully, our chief passenger did not wish to stay the night and asked for an onward flight to Conakry that afternoon to meet Guinea's President, Ahmed Sekou Toure and his Prime Minister, Luis Lamsana Beavogui. Guinea was a renowned basket-case West African country, riddled with corruption and inefficiency. President Toure's oppression of all opposition within Guinea, whether political, military or just in local newspaper articles, was absolute. Even mild comments justified summary death penalties.

One of the most worrying aspects to me of landing in Conakry was a recent report that I had read in *Flight International*'s weekly accident summary. Apparently a medium-sized civil transport aircraft had landed there about a week earlier, refuelled and, during take-off, all its engines had failed, causing it to plummet into the jungle, killing everyone on board. An investigation team arrived from France in another aircraft and decided to stay in the country until they could find the reason for the crash. Unfortunately, like its predecessor, their plane, returning with no passengers on board, also speared into the jungle on take-off, killing the crew.

The reason for the two crashes, the air accident investigation team eventually discovered was that a consignment of sulphuric acid, used in the manufacture of car batteries, had arrived by sea and needed transporting to the town of Kankan, 200 miles up-country. Without a great deal of thought or care, they borrowed a fuel bowser from the airport, emptied out the fuel which, no doubt, was utilized as cooking oil, and filled the bowser with sulphuric acid.

Returning some days later to the airport fuel compound, it appears that only ineffectual attempts were made to purge the tanks of the bowser of their highly corrosive contents, before it was refilled with Jet A1 aviation fuel. As a result the two stricken aircraft tanks were filled with a mixture of fuel and sulphuric acid, in unknown proportions. They both taxied to the take-off point using the pure fuel with which they had arrived in Conakry in their internal tanks. Shortly after full power was selected, in both instances, the contaminated fuel surged into the jet engines, which are severely averse to even small quantities of sulphuric acid, causing them to fail.

I decided that we could not therefore rely on any fuel whatsoever from the airfield at Conakry, and decided that as Guinea-Bissau was only 180 miles from Conakry, our full tanks would be sufficient to return us to a reliable fuel source, which meant refuelling in Conakry would be unnecessary. We felt a lot happier with this decision and wondered whether this unreliable country would throw up any other surprises during our stay.

We were not to be disappointed.

There was only a very small group of five or so Palestinians resident in the country to welcome their leader, and the hotel that they showed us into appeared to be the only one in the whole city. Because of our schedule and short stays between stages, nobody had been able to eat since breakfast and everyone was hungry. Not needing to refuel we accompanied the delegation into the hotel restaurant as soon as we arrived in the city.

None of the crew was pleased with the food on offer, which appeared to be boiled rice of an indeterminate colour, with centimetre-long black pieces mixed into it. Without tasting the food, the co-pilot and I walked through into the kitchen to investigate what it was, which probably saved some or all of us from contracting any of several deadly diseases. The country was known to be host to the deadly Ebola virus, Lassa fever, blackwater fever and bilharzia, to name four, but many other parasitic and viral killers lurked in wait for the unwary visitor.

We found that the kitchen probably contained enough infective material to kill off an army. Cockroaches of various sizes were everywhere; there were rats, mice and other creatures, and after examining the rat droppings on the serving tables, we decided that the black pieces mixed into the rice that we had just been served were in fact rat droppings. It was pointless saying anything to anyone. Fortunately, we returned to the restaurant just in time to prevent any of our passengers eating the food.

It was then that we remembered the twelve meals that we had brought with us in the Falcon from Senegal and we thanked our lucky stars for the French chefs in Dakar. Returning to our Falcon with Yasser Arafat and his delegation, who were only too pleased to forgo a dose of Ebola virus, we started our auxiliary engine, activated the air conditioning and heated our hot meals in the aircraft's oven.

There was silence whilst we all ate our rather fine food and the ice in the cold box ensured that everyone could enjoy a refreshing cool drink. Afterwards, the delegation was invited to kip down for the night in the homes of the resident Palestinians. We announced that we would prefer to sleep on the aircraft where we had all the facilities that we would need. I am pleased to say that none of the crew, or as far as I am aware the delegation, set foot in that hotel ever again. It was a living nightmare – and I do mean 'living'.

The meeting with President Toure and his Prime Minister took place early the following morning and we left Conakry very pleased that we and our passengers had avoided any of its food, drink or fuel.

We flew north over Senegal, Mauritania, Western Sahara, Las Palmas in the Canary Islands to Agadir in western Morocco to top up our fuel tanks. The weather was perfect, as it usually is over this part of the Sahara Desert in June. Occasionally though, in the past, I have noticed thick fog being produced over Las Palmas by the cold Canaries current that wells up from the seabed after its long journey from the Antarctic, but there was no such problem on this flight.

Yasser Arafat flew with us in the cockpit on the relatively uncomfortable jump-seat and seemed in good spirits as we chatted about the landmarks passing below us in the different countries. His grasp of geography was clearly better than average and he was able to discuss potential routes for future flights from his memory, without reference to any charts – all, that is, except Marrakech.

As the sun set behind us, we overflew the Moroccan city of Fez on a direct track for Algiers and a short meeting with Algeria's President, Houari Boumedienne. On his return to the Falcon, I commented to Yasser Arafat that the Algerian President looked very unwell and he confirmed that his own worries about the long-standing Boumedienne's health had persuaded him to cut the meeting short, to ease the strain. Within a year President Houari Boumedienne was dead, to be replaced by Chandli Benjedid.

One of the airfields that I flew the Palestinian leader to on several occasions was at Kufra Oasis, deep in the Sahara Desert, close to the points where Chad, Sudan, Egypt and Libya meet. It is a wilderness part of Africa that must be approached by aviators with extreme caution. Unless one's aircraft possesses sufficient range to return to the nearest airfield, at Benghazi, should any unforeseen problem occur at Kufra, a small problem can easily escalate into a disaster.

This part of the desert is prone to sandstorms that are difficult to predict and can reduce visibility to less than a metre in minutes, so a thorough grasp of the meteorological causes of such phenomena is essential for all pilots hoping to land on this tricky desert airfield. On three occasions I was forced to refuse to fly to the oasis with Yasser Arafat when the visibility on the ground at Kufra was satisfactory at the time. I was of the opinion that the conditions were perfect for an instant sandstorm at any minute and on each occasion, at our predicted landing time, the visibility was zero and we would probably have crashed attempting to land.

When the depression causing the wind had passed and the sandstorm subsided, I was then able to fly him to Kufra safely, but the delays could be many hours – sometimes even days – and he always considered that I was being too cautious.

In May 1992, after I had left Libya, Yasser Arafat needed to fly to Kufra and persuaded the Russian pilot of a twin-engined Russian aircraft to fly him there despite the forecast approach of unpredictable meteorological conditions. The inevitable happened and after three attempts to land in a severe sandstorm, with insufficient fuel to reach any other airfield, the aircraft crashed in the desert, killing most people on board. The Palestinian leader survived but sustained severe damage to his head and was taken to the King Hussein Medical Centre in Amman, Jordan.

On 1 June 1992 I wrote to him in hospital, maybe unkindly, reminding him of the times that I had refused to fly him to Kufra when sandstorms threatened. I wished him a speedy recovery but it subsequently seemed that he never totally recovered from the accident and the resultant operation. He kindly sent me a reply from his Tunis office in July, though from the words he used some of his old sparkle was missing. I was sad to see a gradual deterioration in his health until his death in early November 2004.

How much better to remember him on the dark dispersal of Marrakech airfield, laughing so much that both of us could hardly stand upright.

It would be unreasonable for me to leave this chapter without giving my views on Yasser Arafat's peace-keeping efforts, although my close contact with him effectively ceased in 1983. Whatever his background before we first met in 1973, he was a man whom I came to regard as a tireless worker for his people. He strived in every way that he thought possible to persuade his people to cease the violence that many of them felt was fully justified.

History may show that he did not always make exactly the right decisions when dealing with Israel, but it will also show that most of their so-called 'offers' made to him during later 'peace' negotiations would have been impossible for him to accept; his own people would certainly have rejected them in any case. The terms appeared to the rest of the world to be carefully crafted statements which it was known from the outset could never be accepted, but aimed to show the Palestinians in a bad light.

Albert Einstein, in one of his more notable pronouncements, stated that anyone who achieved greater than 47 per cent correctness in their considered decisions throughout life had reached or exceeded 'genius level'. Yasser Arafat never aspired to being considered a genius.

Any offers to the Palestinian people or their leaders in the future should, in my opinion, address all their just grievances including the return of land illegally occupied for whatever supposed reason, reinstatement of the Palestinian rights to their own holy places, agreed sharing of Jerusalem, the dismantling of the iniquitous wall – most of which appears to have been built on Palestinian land –and the cessation of illegal water extraction, for whatever purpose, that renders Palestinian and Jordanian land infertile.

The expectation that the Palestinian leader – be it Yasser Arafat, Mahmoud Abbas or anyone else – could direct a cessation of armed incidents by such groups as the Popular Front for the Liberation of Palestine or Hamas is totally unrealistic. It is common knowledge that these and other groups have declared themselves independent of the Palestinian leadership and therefore outside its control. It is hoped that an atmosphere will eventually exist where such co-operation is possible, but that will only occur when the activists of these groups feel confident enough to join the majority of their people in peaceful coexistence.

Part of the way through my time as either Deputy or Chief Pilot of Special Flight – about 1975 to 1983 – there was a marked decrease in aircraft hijackings and other violence emanating from Palestinian sources. Although it could probably never be proved, I am happy to claim some of the credit for this decrease in the steady, unnecessary loss of life that occurred both before and after this period.

CHAPTER SEVEN

'The things that I did to Madame le Président'

By Christmas 1977, I was facing a family revolt. For various unconnected reasons I had either been the duty pilot or personally needed to fly for a large part of the previous four Christmas school holidays. This was unfair on the children because I was the one who organized several of their activities, like waterskiing, which they enjoyed. They felt cheated by my absence during their short holidays and enough was enough – 'We want our Dad!'

Accordingly, the flying programme was rewritten so that two of the pilots without grown-up children would take the duty over that period. Unusually, two weeks' advance warning of a flight was given that year, allowing the captain to organize all the domestics in time for the scheduled take-off on the evening of 23 December. The captain involved was a rarity in Special Flight who came to us from being Second Officer with a scheduled airline, whereas most of our captains were of ex-military background. The difference was one of personal perception of the nature of the job.

Unless there was an overriding reason – like illness, aircraft breakdown or utter exhaustion – we were expected to fly when required and to take our unique passengers to where they were needed, especially if prior warning of the flight had been given. Ex-military pilots found no difficulty in operating on this basis – after all their entire aviation careers had been conducted this way. Some ex-airline pilots, however, were so imbued with regular duty hours, followed by mandatory rest hours, that they became too inflexible to operate in Special Flight. To carry out such a duty/rest routine would have required three times the number of pilots that *we* needed to operate and that would have made an economical service impossible.

Don't get me wrong, our passengers were not unreasonable people and whenever it was tactfully explained to them that there was a need for a night's sleep, they invariably agreed and made their plans accordingly. Our method of operating never caused a problem in this direction – in fact, our major operating problem was not managing to secure enough flying to satisfy everyone.

This particular day before Christmas Eve, the duty captain was called out in the forenoon to fly the Libyan Foreign Minister to Benghazi – a fifty-minute flight. They had about two-hours' relaxation in the comfortable Benghazi VIP lounge whilst the Minister had his meeting, followed by a fifty-minute return to base. On his return to Tripoli, the captain declared that he was unable to fly the long-arranged flight scheduled for early evening because of his morning flight to Benghazi.

This was nonsense, of course, but if he declared himself unfit to carry out his duties, for whatever reason, a replacement must be found. The only captain available to take his place was me. Try explaining that to two children newly arrived from boarding schools for their vacation. Both the co-pilot and engineer, fortunately, pleaded to remain on the flight and stated that they had achieved sufficient rest throughout the day.

Our passenger was Madame le Président of Rwanda, Madame Juvenal Habyarimana, complete with six of her ladies-in-waiting, or whatever titles her servants adopted on these diplomatic visits. Surprisingly, Madame le Président was only about twenty-six years old, and much prettier and younger than I had expected. She wore long brightly coloured dresses that had obviously been created by top fashion houses and was fluent in English, French and Swahili. Her conversation was mature with a smiling, impish, bubbly overtone.

Whilst the Libyan Chief of Protocol, Mr Abu Shagour, had been settling the First Lady of Rwanda into the cabin of the Falcon, there had been little opportunity to ascertain her intentions. When we settled at our 40,000 feet cruising altitude and she was drinking her first coffee, I walked back to discuss her wishes. Our first planned refuelling stop was Damascus and our aim was to fly straight on to Kigali, the capital of Rwanda.

Unfortunately her husband was not expecting her until the next day, so we decided to contact the Libyan Ambassador and arrange to stay overnight in Damascus. She agreed, but the best-laid plans are no good until the wheels are on the ground. This leg of the flight was notable in that, as we crossed Crete heading east, we were belted from underneath by what seemed to be some kind of major explosion, followed at one-minute intervals by three more. The cause, even at 40,000 feet, was clear air turbulence caused by orographic lifting of air off the mountains to the east of Crete, but it was the most violent of any such turbulence I have ever encountered. The passengers did not appear perturbed so I thought that it was best to make no comment in the interest of not causing unnecessary alarm.

As we crossed the coast of Lebanon Air Traffic Control informed us that there was swirling fog and a sandstorm blowing at Damascus Airport and we would be unable to land, so I had to choose a substitute airfield. Beirut, in the Lebanon, would be the nearest, but they could be very pedantic and unhelpful with the paperwork for an unscheduled landing and we would be requiring suitable accommodation for a First Lady.

Larnaca, in Cyprus, was almost as near and as they were always co-operative with Special Flight, very flexible and had high-quality hotels close to the airport,

I decided to divert there. A bonus in my consideration was the fact that Archbishop Makarios, the President of Cyprus, was a very good friend of mine and if we encountered any diplomatic problems, I could always call on the top man to help. In the event, the airline station manager met us on landing and our passengers were whisked away in suitable luxury transport to a splendid five-star hotel within ten minutes of landing. After refuelling, we settled down in a hotel much nearer the airport to enable us to make an early start in the morning.

By 9.30 the following morning we were ready outside the VIP lounge, as arranged, but there was no sign of our passengers. At 10 o'clock the Libyan Arab Airline station manager arrived to tell us that the Cypriot Foreign Ministry had been informed of Madame Habyarimana's arrival and insisted on treating her visit with the pomp and ceremony due to Rwanda's First Lady. She therefore arrived at the VIP lounge, flags flying, with the mandatory police motorcycle outriders. We were very impressed, but could envisage problems later in the day with her arrival at Kigali, because the pomp and ceremony had taken an extra two hours and this made us behind schedule before we started.

However, everyone was very relaxed and in high spirits so we resolved to do our best to speed up the flight. The route took us south across the eastern Mediterranean, 40,000 feet above the Suez Canal and down the Red Sea for a refuelling stop at the Saudi Arabian port of Jeddah. My planning had allowed forty minutes from landing to take-off at Jeddah as I was familiar with the airfield, having landed there at least twenty times in the recent past.

Unfortunately protocol had again not entered my calculations and the Saudis, it seemed, were determined to carry out their diplomatic obligations to the full. There was an Arab guard for her to inspect and a sword-waving son of the King to impress the First Lady. To slow our departure even more, her royal host walked her over to the VIP lounge where a table full of delicious small eats and, being Saudi, non-alcoholic cool drinks had been prepared. It was impossible for her to refuse to sample these, and by the time I arrived to inform her that the Falcon was ready, she was standing in conversation with the Prince, a plateful of small squares of bread covered with lobster, prawn and caviar, and a fruit juice balanced between her fingers.

It was over an hour and three-quarters from landing at Jeddah before our wheels left the ground on the journey south. The weather was perfect and we could clearly see both coasts of the Red Sea as we made for our next refuelling stop at Djibouti, in a generally south-easterly direction. To our right lay Port Sudan, the country's only access to the sea and ahead we soon saw the Farasan Islands with the North Yemeni port of Hodeida, slightly to the left. The mountains of Ethiopia started to appear to the right, with its port of Asmara on the western coast of this long inland sea, busy with the bulk of Ethiopia's commerce.

Eventually, after a pleasant two and a half-hour flight, the bottleneck of the southern end of the Red Sea was visible and Djibouti control invited us to commence a slow descent into their airspace. It was with great surprise that on landing in the early evening we were met by a smart French army officer whom I instantly recognized as the same one who had welcomed Idi Amin three years previously. There was no honour guard for Madame Habyarimana to inspect, but all the usual courtesies were observed and she was whisked away with her entourage to relax and be pampered whilst we attended to the Falcon's needs.

When I entered the entertainment room to inform the First Lady that we were ready, the French host grabbed hold of my arm and whispered that our current passenger was a damn sight prettier than the previous person we had brought him. We laughed together as he explained that his days in Africa were numbered as the Afars and Issas were pressing for independence, and as the country represented only expense and problems to the French Government, they were likely to go their own way very soon.

It was quite dark as we climbed out over the mountains of Ethiopia on our last leg of the flight and although we had a fleeting glimpse of the disappearing ball of a bright orange sun at the top of the climb, it was not long before the whole continent of Africa was covered in its blanket of the densest black.

My major concern as we flew over the middle of Ethiopia was that we would not arrive at the international airport of Kigali until well after 10 o'clock at night and the Jeppesen air navigation instructions clearly stated that Kigali closed at sunset, which was two hours ago. A command decision was needed so I handed over to the co-pilot and chatted to the First Lady about the practical problems ahead of us.

I asked if she was sure that her husband, President Habyarimana, was really expecting her at what could be 11 o'clock at night and would he have arranged for his airfield to be kept open for her. She vehemently assured me that the airfield would be open and that he would definitely be there to welcome her. I explained that Rwanda was at the extreme of our range and that if I went there and the airfield was closed we would be very short of fuel to enable us to fly anywhere else. Very few airfields in Central Africa stayed open twenty-four hours a day and the nearest one, Entebbe, closed two hours after sunset, so would not be available.

She explained that Entebbe would be an unfortunate choice of diversion airfield because of strained diplomatic relations between the Ugandan and Rwandan Governments. I showed her the navigation chart and asked her to tell me which airfields within our range she would be comfortable visiting overnight. The one she preferred was Nairobi, the capital of Kenya. I explained that if we flew to Kigali and then diverted to Nairobi, we would be very short of fuel, but she was confident that Kigali would be open for her and that there would be no problem. I assured her we would do our best for her, but the safest plan would be to divert to Nairobi from our present position and stay the night. I even tried a line of flattery – I said that she would be arriving on Christmas morning after a night in Nairobi and what better Christmas present could her husband wish than his lovely –and I meant lovely – wife returned to him, safe and sound. She laughed, but was not persuaded.

Back in the cockpit I studied the alternatives, bearing in mind that everyone's safety depended on my decisions over the next few minutes. If I flew directly over Kigali, but retained my 42,000 feet altitude, I would be in a position to see with my own eyes whether the airport was open; if it was not, I could then close the throttle and glide using almost no fuel to Nairobi, with enough fuel remaining for a safe landing.

This course of action would satisfy everyone's wishes, but to be doubly sure I called Nairobi on the long-range radio and checked that they were available in an hour's time, should the need arise. They were very co-operative, saying that we would be very welcome any time at all and signed off by wishing us all a very merry Christmas.

As I feared, there was no response on Kigali's radio frequencies and when I should have been visual with the airport's lights, had they been illuminated, there was nothing but deep blackness. I called Madame up to the cockpit to show her Rwanda in total darkness and inform her that I was turning for Nairobi. She agreed, but as she returned to her seat said something most uncomplimentary about the President.

A little while later she returned to the cockpit to enquire why the engines had gone very quiet. I explained my tactics and showed her the lights of the fishing boats on Lake Victoria as we glided over. Satisfied, she asked if I could ask Nairobi Air Traffic Control to arrange for the Rwandan Ambassador to meet the Falcon on landing. When I made the request they were somewhat affronted, assured me that they had already made that arrangement and that the Kenyan Chief of Protocol would be joining us at the VIP lounge.

Things were going too well: something just had to go wrong, but I could never have anticipated exactly what was about to foul up the system. Kenya invited me to make a straight-in approach, which saved us even more fuel, so I landed at Nairobi with fuel to spare. The taxiway to the VIP lounge was specially illuminated so there was no possibility of losing the way round the airfield. As we turned off the main taxiway the tower informed me that I should look out for a female lion that had been seen in my area, and with that she appeared in the glow of the landing lights, strolling off into the darkness, unconcerned about our presence.

The tower explained that the elephants had poked a hole in the game park's perimeter fence and she had just come out to explore. She was heading back home, so there should not be any problem. It amazed me how relaxed they were about a lion in the middle of their international airport, but this was Kenya: she was behaving herself, so why should anybody create a fuss?

Outside the VIP lounge the Kenyan Chief of Protocol met us as planned, and we listened to profuse apologies about his being unable to find the key to open the lounge. He was acutely embarrassed, but two minutes later the situation became even more embarrassing when the Rwandan First Lady noticed that, about five feet up, one of the upper windows in the VIP lounge was open a few inches.

Madame Habyarimana said, 'Come on, Captain, give me a shove and I can squeeze in through that window.' Who was I to argue? She stood on the wide window sill and I managed to put my shoulder under her bottom, then – trying to be as discreet as possible – I pushed with the flat of my hand until she managed to prize the window fully open. She inserted her head through the gap and shouted for me to push a bit more. Reluctantly I did as instructed. Maybe I pushed too hard, because she shot head first through the window and in a flurry of long silk dresses, white petticoats and goodness knows what else she landed hands first on the floor beneath. An upholstered chair may have broken her descent, but the room was too dark to be certain.

She stood up, rearranged her smart clothes, dusted herself off and walked over to the door where she slipped the latch and let the rest of us into the lounge. After a session in the ladies' room, where she fully regained her composure, Madame le Président swept back into the room and in a most authoritative voice demanded, 'Bring some beer. The Captain wants a beer!' With that, as if by magic, a crate of twenty-four litre bottles of Tusker Beer appeared and was placed in front of the First Lady –on the floor between her legs as she sat in the middle of a lavishly upholstered, five-seat gold-trimmed settee. Some of her ladies-in-waiting were seated beside her, but she moved one of them and invited me to sit next to her.

The next problem was that the tops of the bottles were covered with the standard crown tops, requiring a bottle-opener, but Madame was not to be messed about. Without pausing, she plunged her hand into the crate, withdrew a bottle, placed it between her lips, removed the crimped top with her teeth and triumphantly handed the open bottle to me saying, 'There, Captain.' The First Lady similarly opened another bottle for herself and pushed the crate into the

President of Rwanda's wife. Madame Juvenal Habyarimana in traditional dress leaving Nairobi Airport.

centre of the room with her foot. What else could I do but thank her and drink? It tasted marvellous in these unusual circumstances. The co-pilot produced a conventional bottle-opener for the rest of the bottles and as the makings of a good party were taking shape when the Rwandan Ambassador arrived a few minutes later, he joined in.

Eventually the Ambassador remembered that his carefully arranged superior accommodation provisions would be thrown into jeopardy if he did not shepherd his unexpected responsibilities away from the airport. As they left I asked the Kenyan Chief of Protocol where he recommended the crew to stay the night. He kindly vouchsafed that the Kenyan Government kept ten rooms available at the Mount Kenya Safari Club in Nairobi for unexpected official requirements, and that we would be welcome to use three of them. We gracefully accepted his kind offer and he drove us there personally in his official black limousine.

The Chief of Protocol apologized on the journey into town for being unable to collect us in the morning because he would be leaving the country with his President, Jomo Kenyatta, on an official visit to Tanzania. I assured him that he had done quite enough for us and we could easily organize a taxi for the return to the airport. I was instructed to take note of his contact numbers and telex address and be sure to contact him personally if we were planning to pass through Nairobi again or were scheduled to bring somebody on an official visit to Kenya.

He would, he promised, make all the arrangements for us and if there were enough time he would organize a safari to one of the game parks whilst we were waiting for our VIPs. 'I shall never forget, as long as I live, the sight of you pushing the Rwandan First Lady through the top window of the VIP lounge and the flurry of silks and satins as Madame le Président hurtled head first on to the floor,' he said and lapsed into a hearty laugh once more. 'How she remained so dignified throughout the episode amazed me and I regretted my inability to stop laughing.'

As for various reasons we regularly landed in Nairobi, I promised to contact him in the future, but unfortunately we were never there long enough to take advantage of his kind safari offer.

The Rwandan Ambassador joined us for breakfast at the Mount Kenya Safari Club to discuss the schedule for the First Lady's return to Kigali. President Habyarimana had organized an arrival of full ceremonial, which was planned to commence at 11 o'clock. Working back from that gave us a take-off time of 9.30 from Nairobi, so the passengers needed to be seated on the Falcon by 9.15.

Armed with this programme, the Ambassador scurried off to gather his charges, which gave us time to settle our accounts with the club and take a relaxed taxi ride to the airport. Remarkably, our wheels left the ground at 9.30, the first time any of our flights with Madame le Président had taken off on schedule. The hour and a half flight to Rwanda took place in beautiful weather with the air so smooth, it felt as if we were floating on a cushion of the smoothest down. Our passengers were concentrating on preparing the First Lady for her part in the planned ceremonial and the smell of various expensive cosmetics became overpowering, even up in the cockpit.

None of the passengers had time to appreciate our low-level view of the magnificence of Lake Victoria in the morning sun as we crossed the borders, first into Tanzania and then into the highlands of Rwanda. We flew low and smoothed the Falcon onto Kigali's main runway so that we could appear at the end of the red carpet without the great and the good even being aware that an aircraft had arrived. The President later told us that the effect was almost magical. With the Rwandan Army band playing Christmas carols on this Christmas morning, nobody heard us land and taxi until we suddenly appeared alongside them, exactly on time, and the statuesque First Lady, resplendent in flashing golden silks and crimson accoutrements, floated down the gleaming Falcon's steps alongside the Guard of Honour.

It was one of those planned events that for once worked out perfectly, but our part in the proceedings was not yet finished. The Rwandan Chief of Protocol came up the steps as the inspection of the guard of honour was finishing and the

National Anthem was dying away, to ask us to join the proceedings. Fortunately, that morning we had all dressed in crisp white short-sleeved uniform shirts and smart navy-blue trousers, with shiny black shoes, so we looked the part as we were led to the seats immediately in front of the rostrum where the President and his Lady were the centre of attention.

They talked to each other for a short while as a troupe of native dancers arrived from each side of the rostrum to perform a warlike tribal dance, which they called a dance of welcome. With sharp flashing spears and vicious-looking knives being flourished about an inch in front of my nose, it was difficult to interpret the meaning of the dance as one of welcome. At times it looked as if the lead dancers, with their tight rippling shiny muscles, were about to impale me on their assegais. Not *all* the sweat standing out on my face at the end of the dance was due to the equatorial heat.

When the beating of the native drums and the dancing finished, the President stood and pulled a microphone towards him. He welcomed his wife back home on this beautiful Christmas morning and praised her notable achievements whilst away from his side. The majority of his speech was given in French and I managed to understand most of his points, but if anything related specifically to us, he kindly translated his words into English.

Halfway through his dissertation I translated one of his points, made directly to me, and shuddered. I thought that my interpretation must have been erroneous, but no, he repeated it in English and I had not made a mistake. The words boomed out of the loudspeakers all over the aircraft dispersal area: 'I especially wish to thank you, Captain, for the things that you did to my wife.'

The eyes of everyone in the audience turned to stare at me and I particularly remember the disapproving gaze of the British Ambassador. The First Lady's face broke into a beaming smile. The rest of my crew sniggered and whispered scurrilously. It was all most embarrassing and I blushed profusely.

I was convinced that the President must have made a grammatical error, but half wondered whether his wife had told him about the fiasco at Nairobi's VIP lounge as I remembered that, whilst propelling the First Lady through the upper window she was sitting virtually on my shoulder with my hands on her bottom. Whether that would constitute 'things that you did to my wife' or not, I was uncertain, but I definitely felt pangs of mild guilt. Had the spears and knives of the welcoming dance been some sort of a threat. Who could know?

He continued his speech by smiling and saying that he was grateful to me and wished to issue an invitation to my family and I to return to Rwanda for a vacation in the future to give them the opportunity of entertaining us properly. On first thoughts this was very kind and I should bear it in mind, but the chances of being able to bring my family back to this small country, almost in the centre of Africa, were remote indeed. The President finished, left the rostrum, came over to shake my hand and reiterated his invitation.

When the great and the good had left the scene and the detritus of ceremonial had been wheeled away, we started an engine and taxied to our overnight parking position. Whilst we were preparing the Falcon for our return flight the Libyan Ambassador to Rwanda came on board and said that he would like us to take the diplomatic bag back with us. 'What's her name?' shouted the co-pilot down the cabin, but fortunately the Ambassador did not understand his wit. He told us that it would take two days to prepare everything and he would also like us to take a Libyan member of his staff back to Tripoli, if I would be so kind. In the air I was in charge and made the decisions in consultation with the senior passenger, but on the ground the senior Libyan official was in control and I must co-operate with him – so if he demanded that I wait two days and take his official mail and a passenger back to Tripoli, there was no decision to be made by me.

The Rwandan Chief of Protocol was the next official to come aboard and he wanted to organize our social programme for us. Accommodation had been booked at the Hôtel Mille Collines ('Thousand Hills'), but as we looked like being forced to stay a couple of days, would we like to see a little of the country whilst in Rwanda? I asked whether any of the game parks were within range and he promised to enquire and meet us in the hotel in about an hour's time to let us know.

He gave us a government car and chauffeur for transport and left us to complete the Falcon's security arrangements. The hotel was comfortable and boasted a very big swimming pool, but we had just completed a full exploration when the Chief of Protocol arrived to say that he had arranged for us to spend two days in one of Rwanda's biggest game parks in the south of the country. Unfortunately, in order to drive there in time for the evening meal, we would need to leave almost immediately. We were all at the door with overnight bags and dressed in the best safari gear within thirty minutes. The opportunity of two days on safari in a little-known game park in the middle of Africa, instead of in a city hotel, was much too good to miss.

The chauffeur explained to us whilst travelling south on bumpy dirt roads that he had a problem, or rather, two problems. Firstly, he did not actually know the way – never having been south of Kigali before – and secondly, there had been a bloody massacre of a part of the Rwandan population two months earlier. To dispose of the bodies, huge trenches had been excavated along several valleys to accommodate the gruesome remains and now, with the heat of the equatorial jungle, the stench made these valleys no-go areas, so driving to our destination at the far side of the burial grounds concerned meant sticking to minor roads with very few signposts.

Knowing we would be travelling for some time, our curiosity demanded that we quiz the driver on the details of these horrific events, which I now relate as they were told to us. It must be borne in mind that the driver was a Tutsi and that his account of the massacre could have been biased in favour of his people.

The population of Rwanda in 1977 was about 6.5 million; the majority Hutu and the minority Tutsi. The Hutu were generally smaller people and the Tutsi of a much taller, almost statuesque, bearing. This difference in stature and a noticeable difference in intellect led to the Tutsi political and economic dominance over the majority Hutu. Violent eruptions by the Hutu against the Tutsi were all too common and efforts were made to ease the simmering situation by including ministers from both tribes in the country's government.

A few months before this Christmas the state radio station and the country's newspapers publicized that on a certain day the ex-king of the Tutsi – our driver thought that it was Kigeri V – would drive along a given route and as many Tutsis as possible should line the route to wave to their king. No explanation was offered as to why this particular king should re-enter the country years after his abdication and drive along Rwandan roads expecting this kind of homage, but the Tutsis turned out in their hundreds of thousands to line the route.

There was no car and there was no king. What actually happened was that a squadron of Harvards, a Second World War American training plane, equipped with machine-guns, flew low down each of the roads machine-gunning the mostly Tutsi spectators, until, according to our driver, there were 350,000 dead or seriously injured lying by the roads. We questioned the numbers but although the driver was adamant, I believe they must have been rather fewer than this. However many, these bodies were now the cause of the current stench.

It makes one sick to contemplate such brutality, but it has to be said that compared with the later massacres of the Tutsis and sympathetic Hutu by those same Hutu extremists, again organized and publicised on Rwandan state radio, brutality has now reached even greater heights and the most recent death toll exceeds one million, and could be nearly two.

These atrocities were known to the rest of the world, but nothing was done to abate the horrific massacres. The world's press reported the facts, but the United Nations sat on their hands and did nothing. It seemed that just because it was a small country in the middle of Africa, of little global economic interest, there was no need to take any action. President Clinton of America commented in his memoirs that his inactivity in the face of such known brutality has since caused him eternal shame. I am astounded that none of the African leaders considered this holocaust important enough to become involved. How could such brutality be tolerated in the twenty-first century?

We drove serenely on along those same roads with constant stops to ascertain the way from convenient passers-by, some dressed in ceremonial costume in honour of Christmas Day. After about twenty miles without guidance we stopped in the growing darkness alongside a family, walking to friends for a Christmas meal. Whilst our driver was conversing with what looked like the grandfather of the group, I noticed that he carried a very large stick or fence post, nearly six feet long and about two and a half inches in diameter. It was a substantial weapon, but I could not work out how he could use such an ungainly piece of wood. I was very soon to have an hilarious demonstration of exactly how he proposed wielding it.

We had stopped in the darkness on an upward facing slope with our headlights on full beam and about half a mile up the slope a man on a bicycle was hurtling towards us, his speed increasing with the aid of gravity from his downhill path. As he closed towards us, I realized that the poor unfortunate soul on the bicycle was totally blinded by our car's headlights. He aimed his cycle so that he was clear of the headlights but of course was unable to see the group of people standing talking to us.

I shouted, 'Look out!' as he careered straight at these unfortunate Christmas revellers at breakneck speed. At the very last minute Grandad appreciated the impending disaster and in an attempt to avoid any of his family being seriously injured, raised the huge stick until it pointed at the cyclist's chest like a jousting pole of medieval knightly battles. Grandad braced himself for the inevitable impact, which lifted the cyclist clear off the saddle, and like a veteran of such encounters he neatly dodged the riderless bike as it hurtled past downhill, to end up in an unfortunate heap in the nearest roadside bush.

Looking down at the rider lying motionless on his back, dressed in a long white shirt, I expected that the force of impact had killed the man, but as I shone a light on his face his eyes opened, he looked at the family and the car, and burst out laughing. The collision should have caused a couple of broken ribs at the very least, but if it had he would have been unable to laugh. What a lucky bunny he had been. Without many words, he retrieved the bike and resumed his journey, still laughing.

Our driver decided to leave in some haste before anyone tried to blame him for the accident and an hour later we passed through stout wooden gates, guarded by wildlife wardens and rangers. A great deal of documentation was issued to our driver without any money changing hands. He explained that for once the telephones had worked and everyone was expecting us. The half-mile from the gate to the accommodation revealed a young elephant quietly dozing, a speeding hippopotamus disappearing into the thorn trees and a glimpse of a cheetah with part of another animal in its mouth. This was a most promising start.

The bedrooms were comfortable – I was pleased to note that the beds were covered with mosquito nets and that the toilet arrangements were of a conventional nature. A small dining room served the clientele, perhaps about twelve in total, who other than ourselves were mainly of German and Belgian origin.

We were the subject of much speculation, having arrived in a presidential car with our own security guard and personal ranger who had joined us at the main gate. The food at this nature reserve was very good indeed and it was beautifully served, with obvious enthusiasm. Our Christmas dinner arrived in all its glory, complete with a bird that could have been a turkey, and was finished off with plum pudding and rum sauce. We all commented that we had been served much worse food in ostentatious five-star European hotels than these Rwandans achieved in the middle of the African bush.

At some ungodly hour, way before dawn, we were awakened for our first game drive of the day. Under the directions of the heavily armed ranger in the front passenger seat, we headed for the hills, but having climbed the first high ground the track took us down onto a flat plain with an area of water, about two hundred acres in extent, at its centre. On the edge of some low scrub, for all the world like a hedge, we left the car and proceeded on foot just as the sun was appearing over the lofty acacia trees.

A hundred metres out from the bank in what seemed to be shallow water, a sizeable group of hippopotamus splashed around chasing each other and really moving at some speed. The ranger whispered to us that the group had two much bigger male hippos with it, but he was worried that he could not see either of them. Our engineer asked if they were at all dangerous and his monosyllabic response, 'Yes', gave us very little comfort.

They are reputed to be capable of great speed out of the water, are known to stalk people when there are baby hippos in their group – and many small ones could be seen out in the water. If they came towards us, he said, we should return to our vehicle as fast as our legs could carry us, making as little noise as possible because they are blessed with very good directional hearing.

He had just managed to put the fear of Hades up us when I thought, 'If they are that dangerous he would not have brought us here on foot – his is just a story for the tourists'. But I was wrong. Adjusting the focus of our binoculars, I commented that some of the high reeds between us and the water were moving unnaturally. Our guard trained his glasses in the same direction, uttered a very rude expletive, and before anyone could gather their thoughts he set off at a speed that would have done an Olympic athlete credit towards our parked car, his Kalashnikov gripped firmly under his arm, leaving the rest of us standing.

This was obviously not an act for the tourists, so we followed suit although there was no hope of us catching him up. He reached the car and slammed the door shut before the rest of us had opened ours. 'What was it?' we asked, and in reply he pointed to the place where we had been standing. The tall reeds to the right flattened and out popped two enormous shiny black creatures that must have weighed three tons apiece, their heads moving from side to side in anticipation.

'They have poor eyesight,' our protector explained, 'but they will pick up any movement and they can move very rapidly.'

'Are we not safe, staying in the car?' I asked.

'No,' he replied, 'if they are spooked by a car, two hippos like that can easily tip it onto its roof and then proceed to pull it apart.'

'Let's go,' I said.

Sure enough, as we manoeuvred to leave they ambled towards us, which encouraged the driver to accelerate back along the track into the trees, until they disappeared from view. As he settled to a more sedate pace, allowing our hearts to slow down, we asked the ranger why there was so much armament in the car, because it did not seem to be the type needed to bring down heavy animals.

'You are quite right,' he replied. 'These are for killing people.'

'What people?' we asked.

'Poachers, criminals or any bad people, but we probably won't see any because we have killed most of them.'

Very encouraging, we thought.

As we picked our way carefully along the track through the trees, the ranger pointed out some of the shyer animals – monkeys, lizards and later on a medium-sized python. Tropical birds were everywhere and we eventually stopped the car beside a small stream where the ranger opened his door to show us the profusion of feathered creatures. There was everything from eagles to kingfishers, parrots to humming birds, in all possible colours and sizes. It was fascinating and as we sat beside that stream for some time, the bigger creatures came out for their early morning drink. A young female elephant appeared downstream and that seemed to remind our ranger of something, so he closed his door and gave the driver new instructions.

'Would you like to see the baby elephants?' he asked; but he had already decided, and there was really no choice. We turned off the track into what seemed like an open space, separated by thorn hedges into compartments. He jumped out of the car and made some peculiar animal noises with his mouth and fingers. Within five minutes half a dozen small elephants appeared slowly from the trees and we were invited to come close to them. 'These are our orphans. Do you like them?' he asked. They were pushing and playful – nobody could possibly have failed to like them. He produced a bunch of bananas from the car boot and we all fed the floppy young animals.

Although I have described them as small, they were about the height of a 15- or 16-hand horse and the one that I was feeding liked to lean on me and flap its ears around my head. That was fine until she stood on my foot. My cry of pain seemed to amuse her and she left her foot firmly on mine for about a minute, although not with her full weight on it. I'll swear that that baby elephant was laughing and eventually she lifted her huge foot off mine quite slowly and deliberately, and ran off bellowing. Who says that they do not have a sense of humour?

On the way back for breakfast we passed a small group of buffalo on the edge of some more water and a baboon walking slowly across the road to make us slow down, or so it seemed. At breakfast the other guests, who had also been out on their Boxing Day dawn safari, were bubbling with excitement at their experiences. Nobody else had been down to the hippos, so we warned them to be careful.

The two days in the game park kept us going from early morning until after dark both days and we saw most of Africa's wild game represented in that relatively small park. The journey back to Kigali was much simpler than our journey down on Christmas Day. There was no jousting to liven things up and having done his homework, our driver was much more familiar with the roads and did not stop every few miles to check the way.

Back at the Mille Collines the Libyan Ambassador joined us for dinner and informed us that there would be a further delay before our departure whilst his final documentation was prepared. It was late afternoon before everything was gathered together and our passenger, a Mr Mohamed al Hadi, was ready to leave, but as we called for take-off we were instructed to wait for a government delegation.

We could not guess what this involved, but we need not have worried. It was Madame le Président who came to the airport to thank us once more and bring us a present. Our gift consisted of about 100 kg of Rwandan coffee and another 100 kg of Rwandan tea divided into parcels with each of the crew's names clearly showing. It was a very pleasant surprise and we were most grateful. We were not treated as well as this on most of our flights and never before had the wife of the country's President come to the airport to wish us *bon voyage*.

Our route back to Tripoli took us firstly to Addis Ababa, the capital of Ethiopia, where for Air Traffic Control reasons we were required to stay overnight. I had not stayed in Addis since the days of its benevolent king and leader of the Rastafarian sect, the revered Haile Selassie, who fought the Italian dictator Benito Mussolini in 1936.

Mussolini eventually triumphed by using poison gas against the primitive Abyssinians, but after the British removed the Italian Fascist dictator during the Second World War, Haile Selassie was returned to power. This small, wizened-looking old man with a mind like a rapier brought peace to the region until 1974, when the head of the Dergue co-ordinating committee (who controlled the Army) threw the 82-year-old king into jail, where he died about a year later.

I was privileged to meet and talk with the King in 1974 when I was carrying General Jafar Nimeiri (sometimes spelt Zaffar Numeiri), the Sudanese President of his neighbouring country, back to the capital Khartoum. It was another example of a casual refuelling stop being used for unplanned important diplomatic discussions. The next day in Khartoum President Nimeiri came to the airport and presented me with a carved ivory elephant – in recognition, he said, of the important part I had played in creating peace between Sudan and its neighbours. Politics in this part of Africa were very secretive at the time, so no further explanation was given, but the present came with three kisses and two hugs from the smiling leader of the biggest country in Africa, so I must accept that his meeting with the King was very useful to them both.

For some years the oppressive Dictator of Ethiopia, Colonel Haile Mariam Mengistu, had been brutalizing the country, first as leader of the Dergue and later as self-styled President, using military aid from the Soviet Union. We could clearly see the terror he imposed on these peace-loving people. We arrived in Addis Ababa that night half an hour before Mengistu's draconian curfew and people were running in panic to clear the streets as we drove from the airport to the Sheraton Hotel. It was a total paradox. Inside the Sheraton all was sophistication and diplomatic calm. Outside, gunfire – some automatic – could be heard. I have seen curfews being enforced before in Africa, but shooting people who disobeyed, even by accident, was something else. It was a new depth of depravity. Two heavily armed soldiers were positioned on the doors of the hotel to ensure nobody inadvertently wandered off for a fatal evening's stroll after dinner. We had no intention of even opening a window in our rooms.

Mengistu, this most brutal oppressor, finally received his comeuppance in 1991, but not before he had ordered hundreds of thousands of killings of his own people. He had stayed in power by the simple expedient of exterminating anyone who was, might be, or was even rumoured to be in opposition to him.

On a previous visit to Addis Ababa, shortly after the old king had been deposed, I had pushed my luck whilst talking to the Ethiopian Chief of Protocol by asking him where King Haile Selassie was being held. At first he said that he was under house arrest but he amended that later, saying that he was in jail. As I had met and talked with him previously and as we had at least a day and a half waiting for our passengers, I asked whether it would be possible for me to visit the King in jail. 'Of course,' the government official replied, but each time I reminded him unlikely excuses were produced and eventually we left without my visit taking place.

Later statements put out by the government that Haile Selassie had died in prison were very vague on time and date. It is my belief that at the time I was asking the Chief of Protocol for permission to visit him, he was probably already dead and, for all I know, perhaps long dead. Truth is a scarce commodity in tribal Africa and convenient untruths are what often passes for diplomacy.

We had a pleasant evening with live music and Yarina, a stunning, light coffee-coloured girl singer, entertaining us throughout the pre-dinner drinks and later the meal. The food was of distinctly Italian flavour, reflecting their colonial past. Our comfortable en-suite double bedrooms were up to the usual Sheraton standard, but sporadic rifle fire could still be heard throughout the night. The heavy curtains and the drone of an old-fashioned air-conditioning system fortunately dulled the outside noise considerably, although gunfire in close proximity is always unsettling.

Our scheduled early morning take-off meant that we would be travelling to the airport half an hour after the end of the curfew. It was unbelievable that there were soldiers actually shooting at supposed curfew breakers as we drove through the city. We saw at least two, loincloth-clad figures fall to the ground as we passed, forty minutes after the end of the curfew. These were workers with early morning jobs who would probably have been sacked if they had arrived late at work. Talk about being between a rock and a hard place.

'Why are these people being killed?' we asked our driver.

'Many reasons,' he replied, 'but mainly because the soldiers on the streets either do not have a watch or, if they have they cannot tell the time.'

'Doesn't anyone complain?' we asked.

'Yes,' he replied, 'but only with graffiti on walls; it would be too dangerous to complain in person and the news media is all government controlled so it is impervious to human rights abuses.'

Let us get airborne as soon as possible, I thought. This country is like a macabre fantasyland.

The next leg of our return home took us out over the Red Sea again, to Jeddah for refuelling. It was a relief to be able to land in this heartland of the Muslim religion without the pomp and ceremony of carrying important people. An incognito landing, short taxi, quick refuelling, file the required flight plan, take-off and away were just perfect. We did not need any more tension or death and destruction for this flight. It was a beautiful day, the visibility was unlimited, everyone was friendly and helpful and we wished to keep things positive.

Larnaca, our next call, went one better – they had even organized twelve super VIP meals for us which we appreciated on the next section of the journey. By early evening, the sun overtook us in the heavens as we approached Tripoli International in the last of the evening light. We stopped outside the VIP lounge for the Foreign Office transport to unload their diplomatic bag and take care of the Rwandan Embassy passenger.

Lulled into a false sense of security back at base, we three crew were all occupied with the domestics of preparing the Falcon for its next flight and failed to notice that the Foreign Office messengers unloading the diplomatic bag had run off with the crew's presents from Rwanda. We had anticipated having enough fine tea and coffee for all the members of Special Flight for the next year, as had been the intention of the First Lady, but it was not to be. As we unpacked our own suitcases back at Special Flight's hangar, the engineer found a small packet of Rwandan tea that had been overlooked, so we left it in the Falcon's galley for future passengers. The Foreign Office failed to find any of our parcels of tea or coffee when enquiries were made the next day.

Trudi and Nigel, my children, eventually forgave me for delaying the start of their Christmas activities with the irksome necessity of duty. Whilst mandatory servicing was carried out on the Falcons later that week, we as a family took the opportunity of spending some days amongst the amazing Roman ruins of Leptis Magna, an hour's drive east of Tripoli. That exploration impressed my son so much that he was encouraged to write a thesis on the important links between foreign Roman cities and existing remains present in Rome itself. It was very well received and partially the reason for his university acceptance.

In 1988, after leaving Special Flight, my family and I were staying with friends in Nairobi when we passed a smart building with a shiny brass plaque outside proclaiming RWANDAN EMBASSY. As we had some time to spare in Kenya I went inside and spoke to the Rwandan Ambassador to tell him about the President's invitation to me of many years earlier. He kindly contacted Kigali and was told that the invitation was definitely still active. We would be most welcome, the reply continued, and I was to inform the President's office of our time of arrival.

The Silverback.
Dominant male mountain gorilla, who allowed us to spend a few hours with his family at nearly 14,000 feet up the Virgunga Volcanoes of Rwanda.

The next week had been organized by our Kenyan friends Biddy and Robin Davis and their son Charlie, to go on safari to Governor's Camp in the Masai Mara game reserve and onwards to the super-luxurious Mount Kenya Safari Club at Nanyuki. The earliest, therefore, that we could fly to Rwanda would be about ten days hence, so the Embassy contacted their President with our programme and was told that we had been booked in to Kigali, for a Mountain Gorilla Safari in the 14,000 foot Virunga Volcanoes National Park, for which we should allow at least two weeks. I enthusiastically accepted President Habyarimana's kind offer and dashed off to the Kenya Airways Office to book a flight.

Fortunately there were sufficient seats available on a scheduled Boeing 707 mid-morning on the day specified, so we informed the Embassy of our time of arrival in Kigali and anticipated meeting the famous mountain gorillas of the Virunga Volcanoes with great enthusiasm. Our times at Governor's Camp and the Nanyuki, Mount Kenya Safari Club were fantastic experiences which will never be forgotten by any of us, but they are outside the scope of this book, although I should add just a few words about the Davis family, our Kenyan hosts.

Their family had farmed in Kenya for generations, but their efforts were concentrated of late on providing animals, period furniture and people for big budget films being shot in Kenya and surrounding countries. For example, in such films as *Out of Africa, Gorillas in the Mist,* and *White Mischief,* the horses that Robert Redford (Derrick Finch-Hatton) and Meryl Streep rode, the deerhound that Meryl Streep (Baroness von Blixen) frequently cuddled and the furniture in most of the houses were provided by the Davises. They even inveigled Lesley, Trudi and me onto the set of *White Mischief* where we found ourselves driving two huge Brahmin bulls and 500 head of their females onto a railway track in the African bush ostensibly to stop an 1890 vintage steam train, along the outside of which Charles Dance (Lord Errol) was climbing in an attempt to get to Greta Scaatchi's (Lady Delamare's) bedroom compartment. Life was never dull in the Davis household and staying in their Nairobi home was an unforgettable experience – sleeping past dawn was an impossibility, with as many as possible of Biddy's nineteen pristine golden labradors as could cram onto a double bed squashing the life out of her guests.

We arrived in Kigali on schedule and were met by a presidential black Mercedes (which was for our use during our stay in Rwanda) and the President's secretary, who informed us that President Habyarimana was out of the country, but he sent us his best wishes and a programme that had been organized for us in detail.

Our base in Kigali was the Hôtel Diplomates, close to the presidential offices and the seat of government. Several days were spent sightseeing within twenty or thirty miles of the city and sampling the local food. We seemed to be in somewhat of a limbo, but there was a very well thought-out plan being instituted with our well-being at its core. Meanwhile, a couple of snags had cropped up.

The first was that our driver spoke no language that we could either understand or speak. French, German, Swahili or English sufficed for everyone else, but he spoke a language that as far as we could deduce was not spoken by anyone else. He even relied on us to arrange fuel for the car at the local fuel stations. One of the major Rwandan languages was Kinyarwanda, but the hotel director was unable to communicate with him in Kinyarwandese. The Foreign Minister, who was organizing our welfare, managed to supervise the driver but even he obviously had some difficulty. We did not wish to cause the man any trouble, so we communicated with him through mime and a series of hand signals.

The second problem with the driver was that he was over-keen on alcohol and in our own interests we used various subterfuges to keep him sober until we had finished with his services for the day. The standard of driving on the country tracks and roads was bad enough in its own right, but combining that with a dipsomaniac for a driver could have been a lethal combination. One of the common vehicles on the country roads was an agricultural machine that seemed to be a cross between a rotavator and a ride-on lawn mower. These vehicles were used for shopping and in the morning and evening for conveying the children to and from school in their smart uniforms. They must have been part of an agricultural aid programme, although it is unlikely the donor nation appreciated the many uses that were found for its gifts.

Just as we were becoming familiar with Kigali, our base was moved to the Meridian Hotel in Goma at the northern shore of Lake Kivu on the border with Zaire. The director of the hotel explained to us that Goma was at 8,500 feet and the President sent all his guests who were going to see the mountain gorillas at perhaps 14,000 feet, to stay at the Meridian Hotel in order to acclimatize. This precaution helped avoid the serious problem of altitude sickness, which in its worst manifestation could be fatal. He also explained that our stay in Kigali at 5,500 feet had been part of that acclimatisation.

We realized the next day how important these precautions were when Lesley sank quietly to her knees whilst running up the stairs to our room. I decided at that point that whilst staying at the Meridian it would probably be a better idea to take advantage of the lifts. It was also a good excuse to relax round the hotel's upmarket swimming pool as we acclimatised.

During our stay the Foreign Minister came over to discuss the short-term programme. He said that we would be moving over to Giscnyi in the foothills of the mountains on the following Tuesday morning for a day with the gorillas, which would entail a great deal of climbing and meant that we would be still at the Meridian on the Sunday. We had already noticed that most of Rwanda was very religious and everything came to a standstill on the Sabbath, so we asked the Minister what we could do in Goma on a Sunday. He called over the director, chatted for a short while and eventually announced that we should take our car over to Ruhengeri to see 'Mrs Clark'. Apparently we would be very welcome after lunch if we took a freshly baked cake, which the director would provide for us. We were left most intrigued.

Having failed to come up with a better idea we dragged ourselves away from the swimming pool and, complete with a splendid-looking, freshly baked cake, set off for Ruhengeri and Mrs Clark's typical English country cottage, set in a jungle clearing surrounded by acres of beautiful tropical flowers. The garden surrounding the house had low box hedges around the flower beds and the gravel paths had archways over them blossoming with old-fashioned roses that gave off the loveliest perfume. The periphery of the garden was surrounded by higher box hedges for privacy, with lower viewing points to allow the cottage windows to overlook the typical Rwandan countryside downhill. Inside her home everything was beautiful antique furniture with lace cloths and embroidered curtains, as would be seen in fine estates of Victorian England. We were amazed. There followed an afternoon that none of us will ever forget.

Joan Clark, a very attractive mature lady, overflowing with a zest for life, met us before we were out of the car. 'Oh, you lovely people,' she exclaimed, 'you could not possibly have come at a better time.' A bit over the top, we thought, after all it's not a particularly special cake. 'No, not the cake, it's you arriving in the President's car at this moment. This afternoon we are having tribal dancing in the field and we did not have anyone important to dance to, but your arrival in the President's car is perfect. Even better, this afternoon's dances are "fertility dances" and they will dance to Trudi. At eighteen she is ideal, so you will sit in the places of honour.'

After coffee and cake we trooped out to the field in casual procession, with cheers and hoots from hundreds, if not thousands, of local Hutu and Tutsi families who packed the open area, leaving rows of seats at the end nearest the house, where we were seated with our host directly behind us. The scene from our privileged position was truly awe-inspiring and caused a shiver of excitement. The backdrop was the high wooded peaks of the Virunga Volcanoes a few miles away, with their decoration of thin white stratus cloud worn almost like an old lady's shawl, sloping down past the canopy of the verdant primary jungle, with more cultivated fruit trees in the foreground leading into fields with small mud huts, not in organized villages, but dotted around individually. Each had its own cooking fire with smoke spiralling lazily into the sky in myriads of almost straight vertical columns. Around us was a sea of jet-black bodies in various degrees of nakedness, which in this context seemed perfectly natural. Indeed, at less than 1 degree south of the Equator at midday with the huge ball of the sun burning down from the heavens, any but the most minimal of clothing would have been superfluous.

The dancing started with the synchronized throbbing of dozens of native drums of all sizes and the shrill piping of wind instruments rather like large wooden flutes. Immediately, two lines of ebony-skinned, powerfully athletic young men about sixteen or seventeen years old, filed into the open space, dressed only in loose loin cloths, with six-foot long spears grasped firmly in their hands and various gleaming knives hanging from belts at their waists.

Each phase of the dance ended with the dancers rushing at us, but mainly Trudi, and stopping not much more than a foot away where they stamped their bare feet on the ground until the earth shook. Around the lower part of their ankles small cymbals crashed together during the stamping, which with the increased intensity of the drums produced an almost hypnotic effect, the finale coming when all weapons were drawn and pointed closely at Trudi. The raw smell of heavily perspiring powerful bodies, the flashing weapons, the shaking of the ground under their feet and the crescendo of the drumming made an unforgettable performance even more spectacular.

If we had not felt obliged to act the part of VIPs with a degree of seriousness at this juncture, we could have become very frightened indeed. The weapons the boys were brandishing were not replicas – they were genuine killing instruments and the arrows in the bamboo quivers strung across their backs were tipped with locally produced deadly alkaloid poisons, with no known antidote. The whole thing was absolutely exhilarating and made us feel like royalty.

During pauses between the dances, we learnt a little of Joan's life in Rwanda. She was an American married to a British coffee planter, but when the bottom fell out of the coffee market and they could not sell their crop on the world market for the price it had cost them to grow the beans, her husband decided to go back home. Joan refused to leave and set up her home at Ruhengeri in this delightful single-storey home, which she called a cottage.

It was a most attractive home and certainly bigger than any cottage that we had ever seen. It sat on top of a gentle rise with the mysterious Virunga Volcanoes a few miles to the west; to the east, down a 2,000-foot slope, were fascinating views of the villages that had housed the estate workers in the past. In each village there were avocado, pawpaw and banana plantations surrounding the low mud huts, where mothers prepared food and children played noisily together.

But this rural tranquillity belied the simmering tensions that existed under the political surface and which were destined to erupt within the next ten years. Here on this beautiful Sunday afternoon, nothing seemed further from possibility than a genocidal massacre, with 30 per cent of the population being cruelly slaughtered.

Joan's 'cottage' was surrounded by a couple of hundred acres, on which she grew the most beautiful tropical flowers. These were her means of livelihood and she had established a thriving market both in the country and on a global scale. She fully admitted that the Ambassador and members of the British Embassy in Kigali had helped her considerably with transportation of the flowers, and many airlines had been persuaded to carry her produce at advantageous rates.

She made a worthwhile profit from her venture, which apart from her living requirements she ploughed back into the local economy. These weekend native dances were her effort to sustain the ancient tribal rituals, which she had seen were rapidly dying out and without her kind of support would inevitably be lost forever.

Dian Fossey had lived in the Virunga forests supporting the mountain gorillas for several years and had been murdered eighteen months previously whilst working with these endangered, misunderstood primates. Joan and Dian had become very close friends and the mention of Dian's name brought tears to her eyes. There was a mystery behind the death which has never been solved; several aspects of the killing were very confusing.

Shortly before her death Dian had met an American backpacker who had wandered into her domain. He apparently turned out to be a less than wholly desirable character with a drug habit and a commensurate shortage of money. Dian was being paid reasonably well and according to Joan, he became 'a bit of a nuisance'.

Dian had actively campaigned for the welfare of the mountain gorillas with ministers of the Rwandan government, and Joan thought that she might have become a major irritant along the corridors of power in Kigali. On the surface the ministers publicly spoke highly of her work, but rumblings of discontent about Dian and her famous boss, the anthropologist Dr Richard Leakey, had reached Joan's ears in the months before her death.

The killing of Dian Fossey in December 1986 was unusual in many respects. Her body was discovered lying in the main room of the house she had built, high in the forest of the Virunga Volcanoes. She had clearly been shot at close range, but the room was full of articles of great value: hunting rifles, expensive cameras, cash (in the form of $100 US notes) and a great deal besides. Nothing had been taken, which ruled out an attack by any of the local people who could not have resisted such valuable items if they had been responsible.

The world's media speculated on all aspects of the killing and seemed to point an accusing finger at the Minister of Wildlife Affairs who was on record as being very critical of Dian's work, but no charges were ever brought and the case was dropped for lack of evidence. Everyone that we spoke to about her death was still quite shocked and there was a noticeable reluctance to offer any opinion.

Shortly after our visit to Rwanda, Biddy and Robin Davis came to the country escorting an American film crew making the film *Gorillas in the Mist*, with Sigourney Weaver playing the part of Dian Fossey. They also had an actress playing the redoubtable Joan Clark, who failed to catch her character. Our family were firmly of the opinion that the result would have been much better if Joan had been allowed to play herself in the film, but evidently that would have broken some immutable actors' union rules. The film company commented on Dian's death, and indeed depicted it, but not wanting to tread on any government toes they avoided any overt controversy.

Before leaving Joan's 'cottage' we had to meet the parrot. To look at, he was an ordinary African grey with a vibrant crimson tail. 'Be warned,' said Joan. 'He loves men and passionately hates women. If either of the girls come within range of his beak, there will be blood on the carpet; but you, Neville, can do anything with him.' It was surprisingly quite true. He was consumed with passion when I took him on my hand, but if Lesley so much as came within a yard, he adopted an aggressive stance and prepared to attack. In the wild there were clouds of African grey parrots in the tops of the tall avocado trees throughout tropical Africa, and we conveyed many of them back to Tripoli in the two Falcons as pets for some of our passengers, but I had never before encountered a parrot like this one. When he saw that we were preparing to leave, he wriggled inside my clothes and would have come with me if I had not returned him to his cage. We laughed at his antics all the way back to the Meridian in Goma that night.

The director informed us over dinner that we would be climbing the volcanoes the next day in search of the mountain gorillas and that we should retire early because we would have to leave at 5.30 in the morning. Lesley said that she knew that she would die of altitude sickness up the mountain and that I should take her body back home for burial. We all, quite rightly, laughed that little speech off and assured her that she would be fine, but we decided on the lift up to our room to be on the safe side.

Leaving the hotel in the morning before dawn, we noticed that just before the sun rose a heavy mist enveloped the whole countryside about fifty feet above the ground. It looked most eerie and the morning cooking fires outside the tidy mud huts on the hillsides added to the mysterious atmosphere. The ever-present peaks of the volcanoes and the abundant multicoloured birdlife were nothing short of spellbinding. It was truly magical.

In the general direction of Ruhengeri, at the start of the tropical forest, we left the car at a small wooden building where we were introduced to our three game wardens/trackers/guides. They were small enough to be pygmies, but they spoke good English and conducted themselves in a most authoritative manner. They had prepared stout sticks for each of us and announced that they would carry all our equipment, including the packed lunch that they had prepared. We protested that we only had two cameras and some film, but they insisted and took everything superfluous to the task of actual climbing off us and carried it themselves. Finally they asked whether any of us had a cold, 'flu or sore throat, or felt unwell. If the answer from anyone had been in the affirmative, we would not have been allowed to proceed further. Being closely related to human beings the gorillas were susceptible to human diseases and any infection could wipe out a large proportion of the world's remaining mountain gorillas.

Within a few minutes of entering the forest we were all eternally grateful for their consideration in carrying our spare equipment. Not only were we climbing quite steeply, but clear water ran down every branch and leaf which made the ground underfoot slippery and muddy. The trackers frequently grasped the girls' hands and physically lifted them over obstacles along the path, but being a capable young man I spurned such help, with the result that many times I found myself flat on my back with every creepy-crawly in creation on me and my clothes coated in thick, greasy mud.

As we entered the jungle at 10,000 feet, under a solid canopy of trees and with little sunlight filtering down to our level, we could see that we were walking up a slope along a packed-earth path. Within about a mile the path disappeared and our trackers cut the creepers and saplings with their machetes so that we were obliged to walk on a carpet of various-sized vegetation. This was very difficult and unexpected and our legs were frequently trapped between the fallen branches. We had all anticipated a steady path, rather like one sees in a Johnny Weissmuller Tarzan film, but real life, it seemed, was somewhat different and not as clinical.

After about an hour's slipping and sliding on the sap that spurted from every frond and getting our legs stuck between the cut branches, we suddenly burst out of the jungle into a five-acre clearing with tall pampas-type grass everywhere. The sunlight blinded us and it took a little while for the eyes to adjust. When we were finally able to take in our new terrain the trackers urged us to keep completely quiet and still. The reason soon became obvious when a large herd of about eighty wild buffalo wandered across our path. These were dangerous creatures in the open, responsible – according to the game wardens – for more people's deaths than any other animal in Africa; because we were upwind of them, they were becoming agitated and their sensitive noses told them that we were too close for their comfort. Eventually they lumbered off on their original track, sniffing the air suspiciously. As they passed they flattened a huge swathe of tall grass which would have been a useful path were it not leading in the wrong direction.

At close quarters the enormous, aggressive-looking buffalo had unsettled us; so, nervously continuing, we listened carefully to any instructions or gems of wisdom our trackers might impart. Suddenly, when we were halfway across the clearing, a crashing and banging announced the arrival of a family of wild boar, which we were told to poke with our sticks if they became too inquisitive. The look of the tusks on the lead animal convinced me that poking it with a stick would be a useless gesture so I stood perfectly still whilst they ran past. Shortly before we re-entered the jungle on the far side of the clearing we had a long-range view of a black rhino and prayed that it would remain long-range until we were all back deep in the jungle again.

Progress along the freshly cut uphill trail must have been very slow, but we moved as fast as we could and the trackers seemed satisfied with our rate of progress. Breathing became a laboured task, requiring more effort the higher we climbed, due to the shortage of oxygen at altitude. The guides grinned encouragement as we puffed and wheezed our way along. Eventually, our guides became excited as they pointed to a group of huge nests made from substantial creepers and other branches about two inches thick and looking like huge crows' nests, between five and seven feet off the ground. Each of the dozen or more nests was almost full of fresh gorilla droppings, perhaps 20 lbs of the stuff in each nest.

The lead tracker gathered us round and explained that these were the gorillas' last sleeping quarters, which they construct afresh every night. In the morning before they leave, they defecate into each nest to ensure that no other gorilla is tempted to use their accommodation and thereby become a threat to their territory. There is some logic in their actions because if they save their energy and return to the same nests each night, there would be a danger of finding the homes occupied by another gorilla group. As, to protect their territory, this would result in a fight to the death peace is ensured by moving on every night. The other advantage of constantly moving is the cleanliness aspect – with a new home every day, parasites are left behind and much endemic disease is thereby avoided.

Before we left the nests, our guides said that we would shortly be near a family group of gorillas and removed our sticks, as these are considered aggressive implements by the silverback male leader. If the silverback were to look directly into our eyes, we were instructed to lower our heads so that our eyes were not visible to him. Looking directly at him could be interpreted as a challenge and only a fool would choose to challenge, at close quarters, an angry wild animal weighing a third of a ton. If for any reason the silverback became curious and approached closely, which would be unusual, we should make subdued guttural, grunting-type noises, copying the sound that the female gorillas made all the time. The trackers made these noises from their first sight of the group until we eventually left, so when required we followed their example intermittently, as a reasonable precaution.

Progress along the track without our sticks was hilarious. We frequently fell over and must have made much more noise than the game wardens wished, but they did their fair share of acrobatics themselves so nobody was too worried. To make progress somewhat more uncomfortable the ground beneath the cut branches was covered with a thick carpet of a kind of nettle. Unlike the ones found in the British countryside, these African nettles were about four feet tall, fleshy and somewhat similar to cow parsley or small hogweed, with leaves about six inches across. Although grasping them with bare hands resulted in a mild sting, as soon as we let go the sting ceased and no further discomfort was felt. Because they grew everywhere it was impossible to avoid these mild irritants, and eventually we pushed past them with impunity. One of my spectacular dives resulted in my grabbing something slimy and alive. Remembering the trackers' warnings of the many poisonous snakes native to this jungle, I instinctively withdrew my hand.

Closer examination of the creature revealed a giant earthworm, nearly eighteen inches long and almost as thick as my wrist.

A short while later we emerged from the trees into an area that was a carpet of nettles. As the trackers stopped cutting, we realized that we were surrounded by fifteen or sixteen adult gorillas with about twenty baby ones scampering around them. They all stopped eating and looked curiously at us as if they were assessing whether we posed any threat. We looked back at them in wonderment and clicked away with our cameras, fearing that they would disappear as quickly as they had materialized.

All of us – gorillas and humans – stood still while we copied the trackers with our own imitations of the grunting noises clearly to be heard. We were relieved when a few minutes later these powerful creatures, looking uncomfortably similar to ourselves, stopped staring and resumed their eating. To our surprise we could see that they were eating the nettles. They swept their arms forward and deftly grasped the nettles with their hands, delicately pushing each bunch into their mouths, whilst they chewed away incessantly.

The digestion of so much vegetable matter had the predictable effect of causing uncontrollable wind. They farted noisily in a constant fanfare, but when they came closer we were surprised to notice that there was no smell emanating from them whatsoever, not even any distinctive body odour. After about half an hour it became obvious that we had become accepted by the group, except for the boss man. When the silverback arrived on the scene a crashing and banging of the undergrowth announced his arrival and he burst from the trees with an explosive leap into the nettles. He fixed us with a steady gaze, as if not very pleased at what he saw, then deliberately turned his back to indicate that we were of no consequence.

He swiped an armful of nettles into his mouth in a further disdainful gesture then walked slowly over to a large rock shaped in a curve at the back, with a raised flat horizontal stone about two feet off the jungle floor. The rock gave the impression of an outsize armchair and he proceeded to use it to sit in, leaning his powerful back on the vertical curve. When he was quite comfortable he slowly lifted his arms and placed his huge hands behind the back of his head, then to add to his general air of disdain he crossed his legs and pointed his size 25 feet straight at us. From 15 yards we could appreciate his expression, which clearly proclaimed, 'Now, you're all here with my permission. One wrong move from any of you and you're dead.' Everyone understood his terms and we all grunted our acceptance, or so it seemed. The ladies of the group ignored him completely and their expression seemed to say, 'He's just a great big show-off.'

Our first real physical contact with any of them came when one mother's two babies, about the size of large spaniels, pushed between my legs and sat down on the other side of Lesley and me. Without so much as a grunt, the mother grasped me by the legs with her hands and without tipping me over lifted me to the opposite side of the path to her two offspring, actually moving me about half a yard without leaving a single bruise. Seeing where she wanted to go, Lesley stepped backwards to avoid being bodily removed as well.

A further demonstration of their gentleness came when Trudi fainted, flat out on the ground, or to be more accurate on the nettles. The faint was probably caused by a combination of the extreme effort needed to reach the gorillas, the heat from the burning sun that had burst through the tree canopy whilst we stood in the small clearing, and the lack of oxygen at nearly 14,000 feet. We were concerned for her, but perhaps not as concerned as two of the female gorillas which came over to help. They were seriously worried and gently lifted her feet and legs about a foot into the air before slowly lowering them back to the ground; then they walked towards her side and each of them carefully lifted her hands and arms. All the while the two mothers chattered to each other like nurses in a hospital. Finally they placed their hands under her head and seemed to be about to lift her when Trudi returned to consciousness and sat up of her own accord.

We were pleased – but the two female gorillas were ecstatic. They chattered in a high-pitched tone, ran a few feet away, then returned to assure themselves that Trudi was still functioning normally. Meanwhile the silverback watched the proceedings with a detached interest, shifted his position and recrossed his legs. His expression seemed to say, 'Leave it to those two, they're a wow with poorly children.' Throughout the drama half a dozen baby gorillas sat close by in silence with their eyes growing wider and wider as they saw their mothers doing what they do best, looking after children.

Needless to say, we were amazed, not only at the gentleness of these powerful animals, but at the concern which they clearly demonstrated to an unconscious human being, and also the fact that their instinctive first action was to raise Trudi's feet and legs, which doctors advise us is the correct procedure for treating a faint. Was it coincidence, or were their survival instincts more highly developed than our own? It gives me a creepy feeling to contemplate too deeply along such lines.

Afterwards the young gorillas played a game of unfastening our shoelaces and trying to remove them from our shoes. Eventually the mothers took them all away for their afternoon feed and we were forced to retrace our steps down the mountain in good time before the blanket of darkness trapped us all in the jungle and we found ourselves building nests for the night.

When we returned to the game wardens' building, bottles of expensive foreign beer were produced and savoured as if they had been the finest champagne. We were thanked for our behaviour in the company of the gorillas and on our journey up the volcanoes. 'Group Nine', as this family of gorillas was known, was seemingly reserved solely for the President's personal guests and visited less than once a week. Some famous guests had in the past disregarded the trackers' instructions, and some had become hysterical when seeing the gorillas at close quarters for the first time. Unfortunately our guides refused to divulge the names of the high and the mighty who had lacked the common sense to behave as the trackers instructed.

The exhilaration we all felt as we returned to apparent civilization at a lower level was not entirely due to the increased density of oxygen. The whole experience of spending time with the gorillas left us euphoric and we repeatedly recalled the minor incidents along the way to each other with something approaching disbelief. The experience had been beyond our wildest expectation and something that we would not have missed for anything. We will remember the smallest detail for the rest of our lives.

President Habyarimana had certainly fulfilled his invitation to me, made from the rostrum, when he thanked me for 'the things that you did to my wife', and I cogitated on the justice of my family enjoying such hospitality when it was solely due to an ex-airline, Special Flight captain refusing to carry out a planned flight with Madame le Président. We had as a result enjoyed unbelievably memorable and unique experiences, such as money could not buy. Returning from the long evening drive to Kigali to our old rooms in the Hôtel Diplomate, we lay exhausted on our beds, periodically chattering like the gorillas to each other, reliving the events, hardly able to believe that it had all happened.

A few years later, when President Habyarimana of Rwanda and President Buyoya of Burundi were returning together from Bujumbura to Kigali in a Fan-Jet Falcon 20, they were shot down whilst attempting to land at Kigali International Airport. Everyone was killed. The weapon used to destroy their aircraft was a sophisticated Soviet shoulder-launched missile that must have been specially obtained for the purpose, for they were not even available to the Rwandan national army. This atrocity had been carefully orchestrated by agents of the Hutu militia who continued to carry out one of the most despicable campaigns of sustained genocide and massacre the world has ever seen. The methods used by these murderers were nothing short of disgusting and the trials of some of the people responsible are still being conducted to the present day. Both Rwanda and Burundi are still suffering instability from the aftermath of the killings and a return to a normal life is still a long way off.

When last contacted, Joan Clark was running an orphanage for many of the children left on their own. Many of the Rwandans we met are now either dead or numbered amongst the killers. It makes us all very sad.

CHAPTER EIGHT

A Surreptitious Dose of Death

In early December 1977 it was announced on Libyan Radio that Major Abdussalem Jalloud had stepped down from his position as the country's Prime Minister. He had held the post since 1 September 1969 and was a very hard working and loyal supporter of his President's wishes and instructions. Over the years there had been many wild rumours about a supposed profligate lifestyle, especially whilst travelling overseas. These rumours usually originated from some unnamed foreign oil company worker who had apparently claimed to have seen him making merry in this or that country. When questioned these so-called witnesses claimed that the alleged incidents had taken place in countries thousands of miles from where he actually was at the time.

I know this to be true as on several occasions I was personally flying him to conferences, meetings, gatherings and sometimes funerals in far-distant lands at the same time that he was rumoured to be whooping it up in Rome, Paris, New York or London. He did travel a great deal, usually in our Falcons, and was sometimes away with us for weeks at a time, but between meetings he often stayed in the same hotels that the crew used, invariably chatting to us on his return each day to update us on possible future plans.

He and other members of his delegation would sit at our table in the restaurant and have a coffee with us to relax. If we were in the bar he would sometimes buy us a bottle of beer whilst he enjoyed a fruit juice. On many occasions I needed to see him in his room to discuss changes of routes or unavailability of airfields. On these occasions I normally found him writing at his desk in preparation for his next official appointment, or deeply involved in telephone conversations with host government ministers. It was pure work, not riotous fun.

We did have some fun, however, whilst flying Major Jalloud, but definitely not in any planned way. On 27 December 1976 we flew him and the Libyan Ambassador plus their families to Madrid for a conference with the Spanish Prime Minister, Señor Carlos Arias Navarro, in the aftermath of the political chaos following the death of General Francisco Franco. Having been the infamous dictator of Spain for thirty-six years, he had directed that on his death the country should once again become a monarchy, naming Prince Juan Carlos his successor. The mechanics of this seismic decision created turmoil for many months and various groups both inside Spain and in many of the surrounding countries jockeyed for political influence.

En route to Madrid, we landed in Lisbon, the capital of Portugal, to touch base with political opinion in that country, before launching into detailed discussions with Prime Minister Navarro.

In Madrid, Major Jalloud and his family were guests of his Ambassador, whilst we stayed in the Hotel Cuzco, fairly close to the famous Prado Museum. In response to my enquires regarding the proposed programme the Ambassador assured us that we would be returning home to Tripoli in good time for the New Year, so we resolved to keep in touch, whilst indulging in some modest sightseeing. The Ambassador kindly provided us with transport and suggested a fairly ambitious itinerary. Unusually, on the first night the engineer went off on his own to a restaurant he had visited previously, which proved to be a disaster for him.

Apparently he ate a reasonably large fish, cooked whole, and by the time we met up with him the following morning, he was writhing in agony. He was so ill that the hotel doctor admitted him to hospital for detailed tests and treatment. The co-pilot and I relaxed in the Cuzco and ate in their restaurant that evening. We shared a lovely paella, a Spanish dish for which their chef was justifiably renowned, and when we saw the state of the engineer, whilst truly sympathetic we were doubly pleased with our choice. We felt almost guilty, behaving like tourists and enjoying ourselves, with the engineer by this time back in his hotel bed, existing on bottled water and pills and looking decidedly green. It seemed somewhat unfair, but such misfortune can happen to anyone travelling and despite our concern we managed to enjoy ourselves.

To make matters worse, or better, depending on how you look at it, the Ambassador came to see us on the evening of 30 December to say that the meetings had become somewhat protracted and we were unlikely to be able to return to Tripoli for an estimate of about a week. He was trying to make some arrangements for us, but would not be certain of success until later that evening, and he conveyed the Prime Minister's regret that we would not be able to spend New Year's Eve with our families.

This delay would, however, allow our engineer time to recuperate, but we were intrigued as to what arrangements the Ambassador was cooking up for us. Full of enthusiasm, he met the two of us later that evening and produced three very ostentatious invitations, with gold borders and many Spanish coats of arms, for a New Year's Eve celebration in a prestigious venue in the centre of Madrid. Details of just what the 'celebration' was were a little short on substance, but when we later showed the invitations to the hotel manager to pick his brains on the expected protocol, he was highly impressed and explained that only royalty or rich industrialists normally received such invitations. Money could not buy a place at these tables, he assured us, which had us worried over what the dress would be. By this time he too was becoming concerned, so he accompanied us up to our room to vet our wardrobe.

We both had dark lounge suits, but the normal luggage space restriction in the Falcon prevented us carrying more formal dress. 'The suits will be perfect,' he assured us, 'though some guests will be either in uniform, or even tails; but whatever you do, you must not take a camera. None of the guests will appreciate being photographed, especially later in the evening, and some of the men might even be accompanied by their mistresses. There will be a meal the like of which one rarely experiences, so be careful to be very hungry when you arrive, and do not have an alcoholic drink before going.'

It was a most intriguing prospect. The engineer was still recuperating and, as the very thought of food did funny things to his stomach, he chose to stay at the Cuzco. In the event, his decision was probably a wise one, but it left us with a surplus prestigious invitation and, knowing nobody in Madrid at that time, we were forced to waste this ostentatious gift.

Stone cold sober, ravenously hungry and attired in our very best, the co-pilot and I rendezvoused at the bottom of the six entrance steps, as invited, and were surprised to see a red carpet leading into what appeared to be an official government building. Spanish military guards dressed in steely suits of armour, complete with swords at their belts and long pikes in their right hands, lined the entrance. A fair-sized crowd of sightseeing Spaniards was held at bay by metal barriers manned by a platoon of smart policemen and our attempt to ascend the entrance steps was momentarily delayed by the arrival of an open coach drawn by four jet-black horses. The two lady occupants in sparkling tiaras were accompanied by gentlemen in the full-dress uniforms of senior Spanish army officers. They must have been well known because a murmur of appreciative recognition ran round the sightseers as they arrived.

Ascending the top step, invitation in hand, we were met by a smiling host who scrutinized our sparkling invitations and snapped his fingers towards a serious young man about fifteen metres away, who came smartly over and was introduced as our personal butler for the evening. His name was Felipe and he would attend to us until we left.

'When is that likely to be?' I enquired.

'Sometime after six in the morning, I expect,' came the reply.

We had been warned. This was shaping up to be a long and very pleasant night.

The actual details of what followed became somewhat hazy as the evening progressed, but as I recall we were led to a table beside what appeared to be a stage or dance floor. The table, about five feet wide, was covered in a pristine white lace cloth with a beautiful vase of tastefully arranged colourful orchids in the centre. A single setting of silver cutlery and a single glass was placed in front of us and as there was no programme or menu to be seen we presumed, mistakenly, that this indicated that just one course would therefore be served, and perhaps the glass would be filled with a drink of some kind.

Our butler stood slightly back, out of earshot, and signalled to the appropriate waiters when he judged that some kind of action was needed. The room was dimly illuminated mostly by the candles that twinkled everywhere. There were even some quite high up the walls on little ledges and as we gazed around we could see that the room was a high, stone-built, central hall of distinctly Gothic proportions. We were never enlightened as to the name of the building and as we had arrived in the Ambassador's chauffeur-driven car, we were not very sure where in Madrid it stood.

A very convincing clown – dressed in white baggy spotted pantaloons held up by fluorescent orange braces, with enormous red floppy shoes and a huge straw boater resting as far as we could see on a bright red spherical nose – arrived at our table clutching a basket full of hats, masks and general merrymaking equipment. A selection of these colourful items was chosen for us, but the clown was not happy until everything had been tried on personally for a perfect fit and exact colour coordination. As he juggled his basket to find the hats and masks that fitted each of us exactly, he chatted quietly away in perfect English with a pronounced cockney accent. When our butler sauntered over to assist our choice, the clown switched instantly into fluent classical Spanish.

The butler explained that whilst the meal was in progress we did not need to wear the hats, masks and neckerchiefs, but that if and when we danced we must wear our mask and preferably the hat and neckerchief also. The co-pilot and I commented that there was little chance of us dancing with each other, under any foreseeable circumstances; our butler agreed but proceeded to point out that many of the other tables were over-provided with eligible ladies and that one of his duties was to make discreet arrangements, at our request, at the beginning of the New Year. Things were most definitely looking up.

He snapped his fingers and two bowls of beluga caviar, nestling on beds of crushed ice, instantly slid onto the table by the silverware, and a basket of delicate crackers appeared between us. Another waiter ceremoniously uncorked a bottle of vintage Bollinger champagne and poured two glasses, returning the bottle to its ice bucket alongside the table. From its elevated mezzanine position the orchestra decreased a few decibels to a pleasant level for dining, and the meal had begun.

Everything was delicious and between each course a programme of dance and/or song, each lasting between ten and fifteen minutes, entertained the guests; judging by the tumultuous applause for each act, they were greatly appreciated by everyone. The first act, between the champagne/caviar and the dry sherry/soup, was an explosion of flamenco with the whirling red silks of a stunning young Spanish girl and a statuesque matadorial male in black, clicking heels, castanets and just about everything else. It was a veritable whirlwind of fierce confrontational activity and mesmerizing sound.

Each course was accompanied by a full bottle of the appropriate beverage, which the two of us were expected to demolish before proceeding to the next course. It was a truly daunting task, but we felt, quite wrongly, that we were the sole representatives of Great Britain at this function and that we should not under any circumstance let our country down.

We therefore consumed the full bottle of Harveys' best dry sherry from Jerez, after the bottle of champagne from Epernay, and along with the brace of roast quail each we shared a bottle of the finest Chablis. Mercifully, a two-litre bottle of pure cool spring water from a spring on the Spanish side of the Pyrenees arrived at the table along with the mouth-refreshing lemon sorbet – and we were not even halfway through the meal. Whilst tenors thrilled us with music by Verdi, Puccini and Bizet, guitarists caressed us with classical and popular rhythms from the latest London stage musicals.

We both lost count of the subsequent courses at this stage, but we were certainly not beaten. There was a spaghetti dish along with a bottle of Chianti Ruffino, a duck dish complete with a bottle of Rioja, a beef dish with a powerful red Burgundy, and eventually a sweet almond and apricot dish with a sweet white wine.

We looked at each other and heaved a couple of sighs of relief that we had lasted the course without actually falling flat on the floor in the process, but apparently we were not finished. More cutlery arrived followed by a savoury dish served on large croutons, with thick ham, four liquefied cheeses and what appeared to be a dash of Angostura bitters. No alcohol, we both remarked thankfully, but we were wrong. Felipe asked me my date of birth and forthwith half a bottle of vintage port appeared on the table with 1933, the year of my birth, on its label. We were later convinced that the vintage port was our final undoing.

When I stood up in search of the toilet, my left leg developed a distinct tendency to buckle underneath and I only managed to maintain a vertical posture with superhuman concentration.

The bells and hearty music of the actual New Year came and went, but soon became a distant memory. We were all wearing our masks and other accoutrements, as instructed; the stage/dance floor was quite full of guests in motion, which we were content to observe from a sitting position. Unfortunately, Felipe would have none of it and insisted that we should dance. 'We have no partners,' was treated as a weak excuse and he made us glance around the room and select the most attractive female prospects. A large group directly across the floor from us included two young ladies who we noticed had not danced up to that time. They were in their early twenties, dressed in rather opulent ball gowns and could have been twins – or maybe there was only one and we were seeing double. Anything was possible at that stage. Even in our befuddled state, one thing was quite clear – they were extremely attractive young ladies and it was obvious that the only reason they had been left sitting in their seats was that their group contained only two older men, who were unable to dance with all their female guests.

Felipe pinpointed the young ladies and strode authoritatively across the floor during a pause in the music to open negotiations with the butler of their group – all very civilized. When their butler had done his stuff, the two young things both stood up, gave us an encouraging wave and our butler confirmed that they would welcome the opportunity to dance.

Finally out of excuses, we had no alternative. When the music restarted we strode across the floor, introduced ourselves and before many minutes we were whirling round the floor like experts. Well, that's what it felt like, but the girls were clearly much more talented dancers than either of us and all we really achieved was not actually standing on their feet in the process; but they flattered us with kind comments about our dancing prowess and when the music stopped, we were asked to join them at their table to be introduced to their party.

We were pleasantly surprised to be told that the older couple in the group were the owners of the Harvey Sherry empire, from Jerez, and the others were members of their family. They were very lively and quickly produced a couple of extra chairs, instantly accepting us into their group, so Felipe dutifully crossed the floor to look after our interests for the rest of the festivities.

The conversation was animated and light-hearted, we were made to feel part of the Harvey family and were included in all the subsequent hilarity. My dancing partner giggled in my ear that I must be very drunk because I had asked her the same question three times already. This came as a complete surprise to me, so I had to presume that she was correct in her assessment. Thank heavens there was no immediate prospect of my being needed to fly.

Hot steaming mugs of consommé were served about 3 o'clock. Afterwards, three more shows of flamenco, operatic arias and songs from the popular musicals were interspersed by music for more dancing by the guests. A full Spanish breakfast arrived at about 6 o'clock, including poached eggs and some delicious thick-cut ham.

A spontaneous mock bullfight was staged by masked guests in military dress uniform. The most memorable feature of the performance, above the general humorous shambles, was that the gentleman taking the part of the bull evaded all attempts to bring him down, eventually returning unopposed to his seat, whilst the banderilleros, picadors, toreadors and matadors all ended up in a writhing heap in the middle of the floor shouting, 'Where's the bull?'

At about 8 o'clock we took our leave of the Harvey family, found Felipe to reward him for his unstinting services and ventured out into a cold, clear-blue, sunlit Madrid morning. If anything there were more spectators there to see everyone leave than there had been the night before to witness the arrival. Out on the street, the co-pilot and I decided that a cup of coffee was urgently needed. If we had been in full possession of all our faculties we would have asked someone to direct us to the nearest coffee bar, but instead we decided to find one on our own. We walked for many miles around the Old City of Madrid and just as we were about to admit defeat, discovered the perfect venue; even more important, by that time it was lovely and warm. Lingering in the cosy atmosphere we speculated on our position relative to the venue of the night before. To our chagrin when we emerged from the coffee bar, we found that the scene of our entertainment was only two buildings away. If we had turned right instead of left when leaving the Ball we would have had only about twenty metres to walk.

Finally admitting our parlous state, we hailed a passing taxi and sped off to the Hotel Cuzco, where we slept all that day and the following night as well. No sustenance beyond a constant supply of cold bottled water was needed until the following morning's breakfast.

Discovering that our aviation services would not be needed for at least another two days, we dived into the nearby Prado Museum and Portrait Galleries to absorb a day's culture. El Greco, Goya, Botticelli, Michelangelo, Leonardo da Vinci, Titian and Bellini all became our friends before the end of the day, but some of the most memorable images were those of the cruelty of the Spanish Civil War of 1936-39, when Generalissimo Francisco Franco defeated the Republican army of the Communist Spanish Government with overwhelming military help from Hitler and Mussolini.

Three days after our unexpected New Year's festivities, we had all recovered our normal fighting efficiency, including the flight engineer. The Prime Minister decided to fly to Lisbon for further discussions with the Portuguese Prime Minister. His delegation was still bolstered by his family and included Ambassador Gariani, the Libyan Ambassador to Spain, and his family. To complete the family atmosphere, the Portuguese Prime Minister welcomed them all to Lisbon, accompanied by *his* family. They all departed the airfield in a convoy of black Rolls-Royces, preceded by the usual motorcycle outriders and the wailing of police sirens.

The following morning we flew back to Madrid. This time, the Portuguese Prime Minister and his family swelled the delegation to a total of ten, which presented me with some difficulties in a Fan-Jet Falcon only equipped for nine passengers. Some adaptability with the seating of the children eventually helped us to maintain a semblance of legality during the flight. At Barajas, Madrid's international airport, our two prime ministers were met by Señor Navarro accompanied by his wife. After the usual displays of affection, the twelve of them filed into three waiting black Mercedes and, flanked by the obligatory police posse, they departed for the official residence and further rounds of political discussions.

We, on the other hand, sought our usual sanctuary in the Cuzco Hotel which became our base for a further round of opportunistic Spanish sightseeing, whilst more serious business was conducted within the Spanish portals of power. To our surprise, Major Jalloud and fellow Revolutionary Command Council member Muktar el Qirwi, each accompanied by a personal secretary, arrived at the Falcon three days later to fly back to Tripoli – but the families, having probably stayed in Madrid for some New Year shopping and returned home on the scheduled Libyan Arab Airlines flight, had vanished.

Prior to this Madrid/Lisbon flight, in the early part of 1974 I was booked to fly, possibly with Major Jalloud, to Benghazi. We arrived at the Tripoli VIP lounge with Falcon 5A-DAG in good time but finding no potential passengers we settled down with our books inside the lounge to await developments. After about an hour some activity at the other side of the lounge attracted my attention and I noticed that the British Ambassador, Peter Tripp, had arrived with his family. He settled them in a couple of easy chairs and wandered over to me, ostensibly to pass the time of day. Sitting on my chair arm he casually enquired who we were expecting to fly.

'We're not too sure,' I replied, 'but there is a possibility that our chief passenger will be the Prime Minister.'

'Could you do me a great favour?' he enquired and led me over to the other side of the room where we were away from anyone else. 'If you do fly the Prime Minister,' he continued, 'would you raise the question with him of the compensation that should be due from the Libyan Government to British Petroleum for his government's recent nationalization of all BP's Libyan oilfields and equipment?'

'Just wait a minute,' I responded. 'I am the captain of an aircraft whose primary duty is to fly designated passengers safely from wherever we pick them up to nominated international airfields. No part of my job entails carrying out political negotiations between governments.' Negotiating this compensation was quite clearly the task of the British Ambassador, in discussion with ministers of the host country. 'This is your job, not mine.'

'I will let you into a secret,' he replied. 'I have been Ambassador to Libya for three years and this is my last day. I leave Libya tonight for good. In the three years that I have been here, I have never spoken to a single member of the Libyan Government.'

Without giving it any thought I blurted out that I was appalled that what must be one of the prime tasks of any 'head of mission' had been neglected for this period of time, especially considering the high cost of maintaining a presence as high profile as that of the British Embassy. I was aware, at the time, that Peter Tripp's predecessor, Ambassador Maitland, who later became Britain's man at the United Nations, was very highly thought of amongst Libyan ministers, because they had told me so on many occasions. He had even been invited to give talks on Libyan television on one of his favourite subjects, desert ornithology.

Perhaps my outburst was a little unfair, because any country's ambassador is constrained by the instructions that he receives from his own Foreign Ministry and I was not aware what these instructions had been over the preceding three years. He accepted my criticism with some discomfort, but reiterated his request that I raise the subject. Feeling somewhat embarrassed at my tactlessness, I agreed that in the unlikely event of a private opportunity arising, I would bear it in mind. Standing up to end the discussion I enquired what magnitude of compensation would be considered adequate to BP. 'They value their assets at £60 million, but they would be content with £50 million,' he replied.

In the event, it turned out to be an unusual flight. The Prime Minister arrived after about three hours, in quite good humour, and we embarked him, along with his secretary and two others. As we taxied past the control tower, we were asked to hold our position, the air traffic controller informing us that there was some problem with the runway at Benghazi and likely to be one or two hours' delay. After a short discussion Major Jalloud decided to stay in the aircraft in our present position, to enable us to get airborne as soon as possible; so we started our auxiliary engine to maintain the air-conditioning, lighting and the coffee machine, and shut down the main engines to conserve fuel. I left the radio on loudspeaker and walked back into the cabin to join the passengers. The Prime Minister sat in one of the larger seats at the front of the cabin, whilst the other three were in earnest conversation with each other at the rear of the aircraft.

As I drew level with Major Jalloud he smiled and invited me to sit down at his table for a game of cards. I accepted and the engineer brought two coffees and a couple of fresh packs of cards. We chatted on light-hearted subjects until eventually he seemed to be tiring of playing cards, so we just talked over our second coffee.

When I slid the subject of compensation for BP into the conversation, his face lit up and he countered with the fact that as the installations were on Libyan territory, they must all belong to the Libyans, so no compensation was due. I pointed out that the wells had quite clearly been developed in good faith with money from the company and that if no compensation were forthcoming, the world and future potential investing countries could regard the Libyan government as a severe risk and refuse to put their assets into the country. This, I claimed, would not be in Libya's best interests. The subject was batted to and fro for a further ten minutes or so before Air Traffic Control interrupted with our clearance to take off for Benghazi.

He must have felt reasonably relaxed, as he chose to fly to Benghazi seated with us on the relatively uncomfortable jump-seat in the cockpit between the pilots, where he sustained a constant casual conversation. He enquired about our families and any problems that we might have living in Tripoli, and discussed some of his own family problems through being Libya's Prime Minister. After landing, he gathered his three colleagues and walked smartly over to Benghazi's VIP lounge, instructing me to join him later when his future movements would become more clear.

Perhaps twenty minutes later, with the Falcon fully refuelled and ready for its next flight, I walked over to the VIP lounge in the gathering gloom of the evening twilight. Inside, Major Jalloud's companions had disappeared and he was in earnest conversation with the President, Colonel Gadaffi. I stood inside the very large and lavishly furnished VIP reception room where they could both see me; but instead of waving me over, as I had expected, they both stood and walked towards me.

One of them held my right shoulder, without addressing me directly, and we all walked outside into the cool evening air. As we promenaded slowly up and down, the Prime Minister mentioned that he and the President had been discussing my assertions that it would be in Libya's best interests to compensate BP for the nationalization of their oilfields and equipment. The two of them reiterated the philosophy of the nationalization of foreign assets and I repeated my belief that the lack of compensation would leave Libya vulnerable to charges of malpractice, which, if supported by the international community, could well spoil Libya's financial standing in Europe and, indeed, amongst her allies in Africa.

The conversation was good-natured, with smiles on everyone's faces and even the odd joke. One of them asked what figure would keep all parties happy and I stated that such negotiations would be none of my business, but expressed the opinion that £60 million should satisfy everyone. For good measure, I suggested that this figure would seem far less than the value of the output from the BP wells for a single year.

The conversation ended abruptly and they repaired to the VIP lounge, instructing me to return to Tripoli without any passengers as soon as we were ready. The Falcon was airborne within ten minutes and as we flew home we consumed three of the VIP meals we had brought from the Air France chefs in Tripoli on our outbound leg.

On the 13th November 1973 we waited in Falcon 5A –DAF outside Malta Airport's VIP lounge ostensibly for Prime Minister Dom Mintoff's return to Tripoli.

Late afternoon, amid the wailing of police motor cycle sirens, suprisingly to us, Archbishop Makarios of Cyprus escorted by Dom Mintoff, emerged from the lounge and asked to be flown to Cyprus.

During the Archbishops party's embarkation, the Maltese Prime Minister called me from the cockpit to request that I ask 'His Beatitude' to remove his trademark tall black hat to confirm his state of baldness. Evidently he could not be persuaded to remove his hat during his week long stay in Malta and substantial bets were at stake on the Patriach's baldness.

Archbishop Makarios of Cyprus in his normal greek orthodox robes leaving Benghazi VIP lounge for his return to Nicosia.

Fortunately the opportunity soon arose to clarify the position because with his hat in place he was unable to secure his seat belt due to the sloping ceiling in the cabin. Dom Mintoff howled with mirth at the news of his guest's total baldness and declared that I had helped his short-term financial position considerably.

The Cypriot leader proved to be a jovial passenger, most appreciative of his smooth flight to Nicosia via Benghazi. On his midnight arrival in the country's capital the air traffic instructions were, however somewhat vague. The controller asked me to execute an instrument landing system (ILS) approach, but urged me to descend as steeply as possible.

An ILS approach is, by definition, at an angle of 3° to the ground and to make it steeper conflicts with the ILS instruction. Some negotiation ensued which only served to confuse the position further, so I announced that I was abandoning the ILS instruction as I was clearly visual with the airfield. I intended spiralling down from overhead onto the threshold of the runway.

This announcement pleased him enormously, so I continued on that basis.

After landing the controller ran over from the tower and explained that General Grivas, despite his previous friendship with Archbishop Makarios, had recently become a sworn enemy and had declared his intention of killing the Patriarch. With that plan the General had taken up position five miles out underneath the ILS guide path, armed with heavy artillery and was listening to the ATC radio, preparing to kill Makarios as he came into land.

I am pleased to confirm that my unorthodox approach defeated Grivas's intentions.

About ten days later I was waiting outside the Tripoli VIP lounge for the Foreign Minister, Major el Houni, with the auxiliary engine purring away, when Major Jalloud appeared and waved towards me – which suggested that our senior passenger had been changed. Arriving alongside him, I could see that he had a wide grin on his face and as we entered the cool of the lounge he said, to me, 'I just wanted to tell you that we have decided to pay £60 million compensation to BP.' I replied that they would be happy with that and expressed the opinion that the rest of the world would take note of this statesmanlike act.[1]

---

[1] When I mention this story to my friends, they all automatically express the opinion that I must have been handsomely compensated by BP for the success of my diplomatic efforts. To set the record straight, let me say that sometime later when my family was financially devastated by involvement with Lloyds of London, where Lesley and I were both names, I contacted a senior board member of BP, to give him my opinion that morally I should be eligible for some compensation from them for my efforts on their behalf. The meeting took place in their head office in London, but the senior executive was unsympathetic to my claim, challenging me to provide proof. I gave him the dates of my conversations, which preceded BP's actual receipt of

He then informed me that the Foreign Minister had been detained, and asked me to fly to Malta to collect Dom Mintoff, the Maltese Prime Minister, and bring him to Tripoli. It turned out to be a most peculiar day because we brought 'The Dom' to Tripoli dressed in khaki shorts, a T-shirt and sandals, and returned him to Malta's Luqa Airport two hours later, where we waited for him for about an hour. We then flew him, still dressed in shorts, back to Tripoli along with his secretary and returned them both to Malta in the evening.

In the early days of my time in Special Flight, statistics recording left a little to be desired and flights with members of the Libyan government were only noted as RCC (Revolutionary Command Council). Consequently, when any query arose regarding the names of the actual passengers years later, unless any member of the relevant crew had a memory like an elephant, it became a matter for conjecture. I tried to be more specific in my personal flying logbook, but eventually a system was instituted where the actual names of our passengers were recorded on the operational flight returns.

The important details of the next flight were initially difficult to identify. However, records do exist as to the actual date and time of the incident, because it involved the total loss of a perfectly good Japan Airlines Boeing 747 jumbo jet through terrorist action.

Any doubt has now been clarified by a friend working in the archives of the authoritative aviation weekly magazine *Flight International*, who has supplied me with the date and time of this incident. His information coincides exactly with an entry in my personal flying logbook.

At 4.30 on a very still, hot, dark, Tripoli morning on 23 July 1973, the insistent ringing of the telephone dragged me out of bed. As it was the Prime Minister on the other end of the line I somehow managed to conceal my surprise

---

compensation by about three or four weeks, and he confirmed to Lesley and me that their own negotiations through industrial and diplomatic channels had been completely stalled prior to the surprise announcement by the Libyan Oil Minister that their company was to be compensated. Nevertheless, he refused to even consider payment of any kind and we left his office confirmed in our view that the majority of high-powered business executives are morally bereft.

Regarding the aforementioned 'proof' that was apparently so crucial to BP: during a later flight with the Prime Minister, it became clear to me that even he assumed that I would have been compensated by the company; so, anticipating some future dire need, I stated that no such compensation had been sought at that time, or offered by the company. I could foresee that there would be difficulty in such a case, as I had no cast-iron proof of my assertions. He replied emphatically that he would provide me with a letter from his office, signed by him, stating my part in the compensation negotiations. No such letter ever reached me, however, and no opportunity to raise the subject again presented itself. He was, it must be said, a very busy man and I expect that the matter just slipped his mind.

at being awoken at this ungodly hour. He told me that a potentially dangerous situation was developing at Benghazi Airport and that I should meet him at the Tripoli VIP lounge with one of the Falcons as soon as possible.

Selecting a co-pilot and engineer on the way, we made it to the airport in record time, expecting to be involved with the usual lengthy wait, but this time it was different. Major Jalloud was actually at the aircraft before we had divested the gleaming white machine of all its red engine covers and was seated inside the cabin before the engines had been started. A suitable flight plan was accepted over the radio and we were headed for take-off in minutes.

Just after the wheels left the ground, the Prime Minister came up to the cockpit, strapped himself into the jump-seat and proceeded to update us on the drama that was unfolding 500 miles to the east.

It appeared that a routine scheduled Boeing 747 of Japan Airlines, en route from Amsterdam to Tokyo via Anchorage over the North Pole, with a full load of passengers, had been hijacked during the night of 20 July. Five hijackers were involved in the piracy, but the make-up of the disparate group had not been established at this early stage. It appeared that there were two members of the Japanese Red Army Faction, perhaps one from the German Bader Meinhof group and two Middle Eastern Arabs that no known group acknowledged, although they apparently claimed to belong to a previously unknown organization calling themselves 'The Sons of Occupied Territories'.

Later statements from Al Fatah and the Popular Front for the Liberation of Palestine disclaimed any connection with any of these pirates. The only female member of the group, rumoured to be Japanese, had been fiddling nervously with the pin of a hand grenade in her pocket. Unfortunately for her, she fiddled too much and withdrew the firing pin completely, thereby blowing herself up and wounding a male Japanese cabin attendant in the process.

As the stricken airliner meandered through the skies of Europe, seeking a haven, the various governments below disabled their airfields with heavy equipment towed onto the runways to deny landing. It flew down the length of Italy, across Greece, Cyprus, Lebanon, Syria, Iraq and Saudi Arabia, before the exhausted captain declared an emergency and was allowed to land in Dubai. It remained on the ground in this Gulf state for three days, whilst various demands flew around like confetti. At one stage it was reported that they demanded the release of the Japanese, Kozo Okamoto, who was serving a life sentence in Israel for his part in the Lydda Airport massacre, but that was mentioned only once, then forgotten.

When the jumbo left Dubai, Saudi Arabia closed its airspace to the aircraft and Bahrein, Abu Dhabi and Kuwait refused any services. The captain declared an engine emergency over Syria, where he was allowed to land in Damascus, and stayed for only three hours. By 6 o'clock in the morning, they had just been turned away from Beirut and Cyprus and were heading for Athens, who similarly refused landing permission and informed the hijackers that the Greek Air Force were scrambling fighters to force the 747 out of Greek airspace.

By this time fuel on board the jumbo was starting to fall to a level where range and endurance were becoming serious concerns. The Greeks firmly shepherded the heavily loaded Boeing into Libyan airspace south of Crete, and it was at this point that the crew established radio contact with Benghazi Air Traffic Control and ourselves, in our position at 40,000 feet 100 miles west of Benghazi, over the Gulf of Sirte, heading east at best speed. We listened as the control tower informed the hijackers that landing permission was refused and that a detachment of army Centurion tanks was being positioned along their main runway to prevent the 747's landing.

At this point, the Prime Minister asked for the cockpit microphone and authoritatively took charge of the situation. He threatened the hijackers with severe consequences if they did not leave Libyan airspace immediately, and they responded by saying that they were all fully prepared to die, as their kamikaze ancestors had been thirty years earlier. He asked them what their passengers thought of such action and received an insulting reply. The Japan Airlines captain came on the air and assured the Prime Minister that these people were fanatics and were determined to make a world-shattering gesture regardless of loss of life. He also reported the death of the female hijacker.

Silence reigned for about five minutes, when a seemingly demented Japanese hijacker came on the air screaming with rage. He said that if landing permission was not received within ten minutes he intended to crash the 747 and all its passengers and crew onto the most populous part of Benghazi city. Major Jalloud talked in Arabic to the Benghazi control tower and, as if by magic, every light in the whole city was extinguished so that it became impossible to say with any certainty exactly where on the ground the city lay.

The chief hijacker, beside himself with rage by this stage, screamed that they would find the centre of the city with the jumbo's huge landing lights. With just two minutes remaining, after further Arabic from the Prime Minister the control tower announced that the tanks were being withdrawn from the runway and that the Boeing 747 could land in fifteen minutes. As the tanks moved to the side of the tarmac, we landed our Falcon and adopted a position to survey the scene from near the VIP lounge.

Standing outside our aircraft we saw the jumbo make its lumbering approach, touching down early, right at the beginning of the runway. It stopped about halfway along the wide tarmac strip, facing north towards the sea and about a mile away from us. Instantly, the emergency disembarkation chutes were deployed and the passengers hurtled down the rubber slides onto the ground. Several of them suffered minor injuries, but none appeared to be seriously hurt. As the last person cleared the port wingtip, running towards us across the airfield, an ear-splitting explosion blasted the aircraft apart and flame enveloped the white fuselage and wings.

Those who were able redoubled their efforts to escape, but others – those nursing arm and leg injuries, children and the elderly – were moving more slowly, assisted by the cabin crew. The whole bizarre spectacle reminded one of a stampede as the phalanx of running people spread across the sand and grass towards us. The huge aircraft burned fiercely behind them with, from our helpless perspective, the pulsating red ball of the rising early morning sun nervously peeping over the horizon in the eastern sky, the pronounced heat haze shimmering from the despicable conflagration raging along the full length of the stricken jumbo and its fleeing passengers.

The saddest sight of all was the vertical tailfin of the Boeing, with its bright red Japan Airlines phoenix emblem slowly being consumed by the flames. I found myself emotionally drained by the experience. Maybe the stress of the build-up to the tragedy (in which I could only offer advisory input to the Prime Minister, the key player in this macabre drama) had taken its toll. There was huge relief that there was apparently no loss of life, but this dying aeroplane was such a sad sight that I found tears coursing down my face and when I turned towards the Prime Minister, I could see that he also was weeping. We stood and held each other, as we quietly sobbed on each other's shoulder.

What a waste – a perfectly good aircraft destroyed on a whim. The whole disgraceful act produced nothing whatsoever, either then or in the future. In fact it was never clear why these terrorists had hijacked the jumbo in the first place. They never gave a plausible reason – or if they did nobody heard about it; there were no changes in anybody's policies, no ransom, nothing.

The hijackers were bundled roughly into jail on the Prime Minister's orders, from where they were eventually put on trial and later returned to their own countries to face the consequences for the useless gesture that had inflicted agonies of torment on the jumbo's innocent passengers and crew. When I glimpsed the Japan Airlines captain he too had tears rolling down his face: all he could say was, 'What have they achieved, what have they achieved?' His tears were obviously tinged with great gouts of raw nervous tension from his 88-hour ordeal.

Our part in the tragedy was then over. The Prime Minister, Major Jalloud, had performed admirably to achieve a successful conclusion to this atrocity, without any loss of innocent life whatsoever. After half an hour, whilst the wreckage was removed from the runway, we left for Tripoli and a late breakfast –

but not before examining the enormous smoking hole that had been burnt into the tarmac of Benghazi's main runway by the blazing 747. The normality of the rest of the day seemed somewhat of an anticlimax, so we decided to head for the beach with our families for a session of water-skiing and contemplation of the day's bizarre events.

On 15 August 1974 we left Tripoli, bound for Rome, with the Prime Minister, Major Jalloud, and a member of the Libyan Embassy in Italy.

Our parent company in Britain, Court Line Aviation of Luton, a predominantly package holiday tour operator equipped with BAC 1-11 aircraft painted in a variety of unlikely pastel colours, had recently been encountering financial difficulties. The previous day the world's press had reported that a group of British banks had put together a rescue package so everyone in the company relaxed in the knowledge that their jobs had been saved.

We landed at Rome's military airfield, Ciampino, at lunchtime and all of us, passengers and crew, took up residence in the new Cavaleri Hilton in a very pretty leafy suburb of Rome. Libya's Prime Minister had come to Rome for meetings with Italy's new Prime Minister, Signor Aldo Moro. The weather was very hot and as we were instructed to hold ourselves in readiness to fly, because political events were changing very rapidly, it seemed appropriate to gravitate around the crystal-clear swimming pool in suitable states of undress.

It was our third visit to this flagship hotel, so the resident – or semi-resident – aspiring Sophia Loren and Gina Lollabrigida look-alikes regarded us, not as potential customers for their various services, but more as old friends. They knew that we were aircrew for politically important people and therefore refrained from enquiring too closely into the names of our passengers, while we, realizing the nature of their business, did our best to avoid cramping their style. Occasionally, we even pointed out prospective customers for them and in turn they alerted us to the waiters who were prone to double-charge for refreshments. We all chatted amiably around the pool over the fresh lime juices which the girls occasionally bought for us, and enjoyed the relaxing ambiance.

A year later I took my family to stay in the hotel and introduced Lesley and the children to the film star-like girls. My young sixteen-year-old son was most impressed and after listening to one of these beauties haggling with an American visitor (a potential customer) for some time, we all became aware that her bottom line price was 74,000 lire. As the four of us climbed the baronial staircase up to our room, to change for an afternoon's sightseeing, my young son who perhaps was not quite so innocent, sidled up to me and asked, 'Dad, could I borrow seventy-four thousand lire?' I had obviously failed in some aspects of his education.

On this occasion the crew were required to stay within the confines of the Cavaleri Hotel, so we instituted a chess tournament at the side of the swimming pool. By lunchtime the next day, when the score was fairly even in numbers of games won, the co-pilot – who was not playing at that time – wandered off to buy a British newspaper. He returned in a state of unusual agitation, clutching that morning's *Daily Telegraph*; 'We're all out of a job,' he announced and sure enough the headlines of the *Telegraph* proclaimed: "Court Line Aviation Bankrupt". 'All the company aircraft around the world are grounded.'

The chess tournament was forgotten as we pondered on the effects for us personally. Technically, we were not able to fly, as the company held all our aviation qualifications and insurances in its Luton offices, which had been sequestrated and sealed. Our two Fan-Jet Falcon 20 aircraft were the property of the Libyan government, so they were not affected by the ensuing turmoil. After batting the subject around for a couple of hours it became obvious to me that I had no option but to brief the Prime Minister of the change in our status.

After a snack lunch, I walked up to Major Jalloud's room on the first floor and knocked on his door, which opened almost immediately with our PM laughing and saying that he was expecting room service; but he invited me in. There were four other people in the room: our two passengers, the Italian Prime Minister, Signor Aldo Moro, a smartly dressed man seemingly in his mid-fifties, and his secretary. Judging by all the paperwork scattered everywhere they were obviously involved in an intense meeting, so I made to excuse myself and leave, but they would have none of it and asked me to sit down. They said that they were having a mini-break and a light snack and that it was quite convenient to talk for a few minutes.

I quickly outlined the Court Line bankruptcy problem as it affected us and whilst the gravity of our new position was sinking in, Signor Moro asked how our families enjoyed living in Tripoli. He asked where we were staying and told me that he had been attached to the Italian Embassy in Tripoli in his younger days and that his family remembered the 'Golf Club' –in fact a beach club with access to golf, although the main activity was water sports – with some affection. When I told him that my family were members of the adjacent 'Underwater Club', he commented that the UWC was always a closed membership in his day and he was only allowed there by invitation. I gave him my card and invited him to return in the future.

Unfortunately, a couple of years later, when he was again ousted from power as Italy's Prime Minister by Signor Giulio Andreotti, Signor Aldo Moro was kidnapped by Italy's home-grown terrorists, the Red Brigades, and summarily executed – so my invitation necessarily lapsed.

Having given the Court Line problem some consideration Major Jalloud outlined a plan, which I welcomed with enthusiasm, whereby the two leading pilots formed a new company, assumed the Court Line contract in its entirety, while the Libyan government would continue to pay to the new company the same amount that they were paying to Court Line for their contract. To cut the resultant complicated financial arrangement down to its basics, this would have allowed us to double everyone in Special Flight's salary overnight and still maintain a financially viable company as a separate entity. What could possibly cause any objection? I reasoned. On the strength of that prime ministerial preference I telephoned a lawyer in London and ordered an off-the-shelf company, as suggested.

Major Jalloud sketched out what he had outlined in writing, handing it to me with the statement, 'You now work directly for the President's Office. We'll sort out the small details when we return to Tripoli.' Thanking him, I left his room so that they could get on with their governmental meeting.

Secure in our new-found employment arrangements, I retired back to the pool to continue with the chess tournament.

Over the next four days, the frenetic activity involved in Major Jalloud's meetings intensified and various high-powered individuals came and went. I once glimpsed Italy's President, Giovanni Leone, meeting him in the Cavaleri Hilton foyer, and various noisy convoys of black Mercedes limousines conveyed him to government offices around Rome.

It came as some surprise, therefore, when the Libyan Foreign Minister, Major Abdul mun'im el Houni, came into my room on 19 August and asked me to take him and his family to Cairo that afternoon. I told him that the distance would not allow us to fly directly to Cairo, so we would need to stop for fuel en route, adding that we would normally refuel in Benghazi, about halfway, but that we could easily refuel in Athens if that suited him better.

He elected to use Benghazi, as I expected, so I was able to file a flight plan on the telephone. Before he left, I reminded him that the aircraft was sitting at the Italian Air Force base of Ciampino – not, as was more usual, at Rome's international civil airport of Fiumicino.

He arrived at the Falcon at 2.15 that afternoon in good spirits, accompanied by his Egyptian wife, her father and their son. The Alitalia VIP catering had done us proud once again and we had incredibly fine gourmet meals on board, which made the three-hour flight down to the North African coast most enjoyable.

At Benghazi, we taxied up to the VIP lounge as usual, just as the huge bright red evening sun was descending into the desert sands behind the main building.

We were completing our post-landing checks in a relaxed state of mind, when Colonel Gadaffi, submachine-gun under his arm, and a detachment of his very smart hand-picked bodyguards in their immaculately ironed light khaki uniforms marched alongside the aircraft steps, to be met by the Foreign Minister in plain clothes at the top of the steps. The President glanced up at me in the cockpit and smiled, but I was not entirely convinced that I was not about to witness something very unpleasant indeed. Alarm bells were quite definitely ringing round my brain. The smiles were there, but the body language told me something quite different.

Major el Houni sauntered down the steps, greeted his leader and they talked intensely for a couple of minutes, before strolling over to the VIP lounge, with the posse of élite presidential guards a short distance behind. They could not be described as 'marching', but they were formed into a tidy phalanx that moved as one. The whole atmosphere was full of foreboding, so I switched my mind up three gears and felt like a coiled spring, about to snap into action.

My mind was turning cartwheels trying to make some sense of this unexpected injection of tension. The Foreign Minister's family members who had been left on the Falcon gave no clue as to the reason for the deteriorating situation, but none of them spoke a word. They did not need to – their fixed agitated expressions confirmed my worst fears. A Yorkshire expression that I remembered from my schooldays came to mind: 'There's trouble at t'mill, mark my words' – and there certainly was some kind of trouble; great heaps of it.

I decided to play my part in the unfolding drama as straight as possible until somebody asked me for a decision, which they surely would very shortly. The crew serviced the Falcon for its next leg, which then seemed most unlikely to proceed as planned. When we were totally ready for take-off I filed a flight plan for the next leg to Cairo and walked boldly into the VIP lounge to inform the major players.

Passing the potential firing squad in the vestibule, I saw to my surprise that the great hall of the VIP lounge was empty except for two prone bodies, stretched on the deep-pile Chinese carpets, facing east. At first, I wondered whether there had been some kind of nasty accident but as my eyes adjusted, I could see that the President and the Foreign Minister were praying together. I tactfully withdrew from sight and waited. Presently the two supplicants rose without audible sound and I made my presence known. On seeing me, the Foreign Minister broke away from the President and walked over to me. As he approached, I quickly assured him of our complete readiness and awaited his instructions.

He said that we would not now be going to Cairo that evening, but I was to take his wife, father-in-law and child to the Omar Khayyam Hotel in Benghazi for the night, organize accommodation for them and rendezvous back at the aircraft at

9 o'clock the following morning. I acknowledged his instructions, turned and left the two leaders together. Passing the President's guards outside, I walked through them with a positive *Ma as salaama* (goodbye), which left them with incredulous expressions as I departed.

Establishing that all three of Major el Houni's family were in possession of valid passports, we left the airport by the normal passenger arrivals exit to avoid any diplomatic involvement, and travelled the 12 miles to the Omar Khayyam in two Benghazi taxis, passing the British Second World War army cemetery on the way.

At the hotel, we suffered the usual 'No rooms, all full, you must all sleep in the one room,' so I decided to use what little power I possessed and produced my shiny Arabic and English presidential pass to the hotel manager. The results were electric. Five of their best rooms were found instantly and willing hands carried our luggage up to the first floor without being asked. Our average tips were accepted as if they had been solid gold and the level of the service moved up several gears.

In the morning a breakfast spread was placed before us, superior to anything we had experienced before at the Omar Khayyam and two hotel courtesy cars were provided to transport us back to the airport in good time for our designated rendezvous. By 9 o'clock we were stationary outside the VIP lounge with the auxiliary engine purring away and the smell of fresh coffee wafting along the cabin. The Foreign Minister bounded up the steps shortly after nine, relieved to find his family already aboard and in good health.

Our wheels left the ground at fifteen minutes past nine and two hours later we touched down at Cairo International Airport. No explanation was forthcoming at that time regarding the military reception at Benghazi the night before and we were left completely in the dark until our return to Rome the following day. Our old Egyptian friend Colonel Shukri met the Libyan Foreign Minister and his family as we drew into the dispersal and a car whisked them away without any arrival formalities. Their departure was so quick and so sincere that I completely forgot that I had paid out of my own pocket for all the rooms at the Omar Khayyam the night before, and that the total had been quite hefty. Ah well – 'Win some, lose some'. I was just relieved to conclude this particular flight without any severe nastiness and was airborne returning to Rome within the hour.

We stopped off at Malta this time for fuel, to be on the safe side, and arrived back at Ciampino whilst darkness was falling. The Cavaleri Hilton had kindly kept our rooms for us in our absence and the girls round the pool hardly realized that we had been away. A senior member of the Libyan Embassy in Rome, who met us at Ciampino, told us that the reason for the tension in Benghazi the night before was that the Foreign Minister, Major el Houni, had left Libya permanently, following some disagreement, and had decided to take up residence in Cairo along with his family. The broad truth of this statement later became clear when a campaign was mounted in the Tripoli press denigrating the former Foreign Minister to the Libyan population. My feelings of foreboding, it seems, had been justified.

There was no time for any more chess as the Libyan Prime Minister needed to go to Paris early the following morning for a meeting with the French Prime Minister, Jacques Chirac. Paris is renowned for its grand hotels, and at the French government's insistence we were all booked into the Georges Cinq, perhaps one of the finest. I can state unequivocally that the beds in that hotel were the most comfortable that I have ever slept in – it was like sinking into a warm sea of pure white goose down; the pillows were just as luxurious and the overall service perfect.

At the conclusion of the high-level meetings with M. Chirac at midday on 23 August, we left Paris for Cairo with instructions to refuel in Malta. Our eight passengers included Major Jalloud, with a secretary, Muktar el Qirwi (a fellow Revolutionary Command Council member) along with his wife and child, and three members of the Libyan Embassy in Cairo. This time our Falcon was met by President Anwar Sadat, who after a short discussion at the airport whisked everyone away in the obligatory convoy of black limousines, flanked by the usual noisy police motorcycle outriders in their smart gleaming white uniforms.

Taking up our familiar residence in the Shepheards Hotel, by the side of the Nile, we later walked to the Sheraton in the sultry heat of a typical Cairo August day for our evening meal in their coffee bar. By mutual agreement we followed our food with a relaxed session of Nagwa Faoud's accomplished belly dancing, under the bright twinkling stars above the outside cocktail lounge. As usual, she sat at our table between her bouts of energetic gyration, but this time there was a group of particularly angry Arab gentlemen seated at a table opposite – when Nagwa threw a chiffonous veil onto our table during her dancing the tension level escalated to the point where an early withdrawal to the basement casino became clearly advisable.

Arriving in the casino much earlier than planned left me somewhat harassed and I should have spent the rest of the evening as a spectator rather than risk my hard-earned US dollars on the green baize. It felt wrong and it was wrong, so to teach me a firm lesson fate rapidly deprived me of a modest stake in its entirety. Our engineer settled himself down at the blackjack table and acquitted himself quite well over the following two hours, but the co-pilot fared little better than I had done. Nevertheless, we were all in good spirits for our moonlit early morning walk across the deserted Zamalek Bridge, back to the Shepheards.

At lunchtime the following day we left for home, but not before selecting perfumes and goodies from the duty-free shop at Cairo Airport, for our wives. The Egyptian Libyan Embassy passengers who had been on the Falcon from Paris remained in Cairo, but the others returned with us to Tripoli. Fortunately a strong easterly jet stream was blowing at 41,000 feet, enabling us to fly home without the necessity of refuelling in Benghazi on the way.

Unfortunately, at the time of the Court Line collapse, I was Deputy Chief Pilot of Special Flight and not yet the Chief Pilot. This meant that my plans for the future administration of our work, drawn up with the Prime Minister in Rome, had to be agreed with the then Chief Pilot. Regardless of presidential preference, the latter felt that the responsibility for setting up a new company was too great for him to contemplate and therefore decided – despite my protestations to the contrary – that he would place the responsibility for the Flight's future with the national carrier, Libyan Arab Airlines.

It proved very difficult indeed to balance the onerous demands of Libya's Presidential Flight, which insisted on our aircraft being available to fly government ministers and visiting heads of state – twenty-four hours a day, 365 days a year, anywhere in the world – against the subsequent interference and petty bureaucracy inflicted on us by the constantly and rapidly changing hierarchy of Libyan Arab Airlines. Impossible situations developed, which some members of the government interpreted as less than full co-operation from members of the Flight themselves, but in truth the unnecessary conditions forced on us by some members of the airline restricted the normal operating methods which had evolved with our customers over several years.

It would be wrong to presume that we resented co-operation with Libyan Arab Airlines in general, just that various members of the airline presumed that they were responsible for decisions which closely affected the movements of the President and his government. They were *not* in charge, and eventually a government minister would inform them of their misappreciation, but by that time an unnecessary shambles had been created and some senior minister severely inconvenienced.

Special Flight's unwise involvement with Libyan Arab Airlines eventually resulted in such constant interference that our prime task of flying the President and government ministers efficiently was made almost unworkable – to the point where the previous Chief Pilot resigned and left the country, leaving me doing my best to pick up the pieces as the new Chief Pilot. Forging an efficient unit was work that I very much enjoyed, but the Flight would have been many times more effective for being its own separate company, as Major Jalloud had wished when Court Line went bankrupt.

The following will serve as an example of the bizarre situations that I subsequently became involved in. It took place whilst requesting diplomatic clearance for a flight with President Gadaffi and Sharif Ben Amer deep into Central Africa.

The captains of Special Flight were all quite capable of arranging these necessary diplomatic clearances by direct contact with the Chief of the Libyan Civil Aviation Department, Mr Abuzakuk or more often his talented deputy, Mr Ahmed Adnan el Gabsi. It was found over the years that if such requests were sent via telex they were rarely answered, but that success only followed personal contact with the local official in the different countries who actually granted these permissions. It was also necessary to make allowance for the actual time in that particular country. Knowing who these vital people were and how to contact them, complete with their names and those of key members of their families, was the secret of Mr Adnan's almost infallible success.

As their involvement with Special Flight increased, the airline decided that these crucial clearances – that could ensure the success or otherwise of very long and involved journeys – should be handled by the Chairman's office, in the centre of Tripoli. One such demand for diplomatic and flight clearances had disappeared completely somewhere within the airline offices, and because of the impending urgency of the matter I drove into the crowded city to take up the problem with the Chairman himself, Mr Mohamed Badri Hassan.

I was eventually shown into his presence and explained the urgent need for these important documents within the next forty-five minutes. He was seated behind his large, brown, leather-topped desk, rotating nonchalantly round on his swivel-chair, simply not comprehending the seriousness of potentially inconveniencing the country's President, whilst at the same time exuding confidence and superiority. Suddenly his door burst open and a group of the most unlikely airline employees barged into his palatial office, walked behind the Chairman's desk, pinned him in his swivel-chair, lifted the chair containing their erstwhile leader and removed both into the large vestibule outside.

It became apparent that this group of twenty or so airline employees, holding various positions all the way from airline captain down to car park attendant, constituted the recently appointed 'Airline Committee'. They immediately set up a quasi court, with defenders, prosecutors and much semi-legal verbiage and, to cut short an hour's subsequent proceedings, the final outcome was that the Chairman was sentenced to death there and then for fraud and embezzlement on a moderate scale.

Now, a little unpleasantness is one thing, but a death sentence is something else, so I decided that 'exit stage right' had become appropriate. The important clearances were still, however, outstanding and time was rapidly running out, so Mr Adnan's help was obviously needed. Without any exaggeration, within ten minutes of sitting down at his desk I was able to walk away with all the written diplomatic and flight permissions needed.

The eventual fate of Mr Badri Hassan was much better than it might have been. The committees such as the one I witnessed had been instituted by the government to root out corruption in the country's institutions, and though they were sometimes quite effective they were perhaps occasionally a little overzealous. Mr Hassan went to jail as a result of this kangaroo court, and I later saw him on Libyan Television apparently confessing to accepting commissions on aircraft ground equipment purchases made for the airline. I have no knowledge of exactly how long he remained in prison, but I was told by a representative of the Libyan Foreign Ministry that some years later he had been rehabilitated and promoted to the post of Libyan Ambassador to Jugoslavia. He was not, therefore, executed.

It should not be assumed from this little story that all Libyan Arab Airlines chairmen were of questionable experience. Even before our unfortunate closer relationship with the national airline, there had always been certain parts of our operation that needed to be carried out through Libyan Arab Airlines. The routine maintenance of all our aircraft was always processed by Special Flight through the administrative offices of the airline in co-operation with the President's office. Previous chairmen had expedited our aircrafts' routine downtime most professionally and as a result we were always pleased to co-operate with them by taking spare parts or replacement crews to grounded Libyan Arab Airlines aircraft, using the flying time as useful 'Crew Training Flights'.

One such very experienced chairman whom we sorely missed when he gave up his chairmanship of the airline to become one of the country's senior judges, was Mr Ahmed A. Zawi. During my time in Libya he had progressed from Financial Director of the airline to become one of its most successful chairmen. He was a pleasure to work with, always had a grasp of the situation, and his experience invariably showed him the best way to solve any problem. His negotiating tactics were simple: he would listen carefully to your outline of the latest problem and its consequences, whereupon he would bounce the ball back into your court by saying, 'Right, I now know what the problem is: tell me the possible solutions.' He trusted senior managers to do their job to the best of their ability and as a result they performed beyond the normal call of duty, round the clock if necessary. Additionally, he knew all the members of the Revolutionary Command Council personally. I am still proud to number Mr Zawi and his family among my very good friends.

Following the departure of Major Abdusalem Jalloud as Prime Minister, the next holder of the post was a small, good-natured gentleman who was not an ex-military officer. His name was Abdu Ati Obeidi and one of his first long-distance flights, on 10 December 1977, was to carry out a series of meetings deep in the heart of Africa, on behalf of the Organization of African Unity (OAU). He filled the Falcon with eight other passengers for the flight, some of whom were embassy representatives of the countries we were destined to visit.

We first touched down in Algiers, where the Algerian President, Mr Houari Boumedienne, who the new Libyan Prime Minister was due to meet, had recently been taken ill. Instead of waiting for his recovery we left for our next destination, Nouakchott (capital of Mauritania), without meeting him. It was too far for a single leg, so we refuelled in Agadir, Morocco, en route.

At Nouakchott we were met by Mokhtar Ould Daddah, Mauritania's long-term President, who had been in power for sixteen years as both President and Prime Minister. I had flown him many thousands of miles around Africa some years before, and, quite embarrassingly, he gave the new Libyan Prime Minister a peremptory handshake on first meeting, before pushing past everyone else to throw his arms around me with many warm embraces, as if no one else existed. He then lectured the assembled company of visiting dignitaries on my qualities as a pilot, and how fortunate the Libyan government was to have such a dedicated aviator flying them around.

The speech was all the more impressive because it was delivered by this tall, slim, old man dressed in the swirling, formal, sky-blue robes of the desert Tuareg people, and spoken in good English with an attractive French accent. The light desert breeze kept his robes constantly moving, revealing a ceremonial sword around his waist swinging from a white leather belt, which for some reason seemed to give his carefully chosen words added emphasis. My rather weak 'Thank you' at the end of his address seemed quite inadequate, but under the circumstances anything more on this bleak sun-baked desert airstrip would have been superfluous.

The visiting delegation and their hosts retired to the VIP lounge, no doubt to discuss each other's tactics at the upcoming gathering of the OAU, scheduled for Libreville in Gabon. The annoying attacks on Mauritania by rebels from the Polisario Front of Mauritania's northerly neighbour, Spanish Sahara, were scheduled for debate and a common front would obviously be helpful.

Despite Mokhtar Ould Daddah's sincere invitations to stay the night as his guest, Abdu Ati Obeidi insisted on pressing on to Upper Volta, on the fringes of the equatorial rain forests, for his next meeting. Two hours after landing in Nouakchott we were therefore airborne again heading east towards Timbuktu in

Mali. Overhead this fabled city of ancient, legendary riches, we swung south to pick up the Volta River, one of West Africa's major rivers.

Our aim was to land at Ouagadougou International Airport, in Upper Volta's capital city, which lay equidistant between the White and Red arms of the Volta River. (The Red Volta is called 'Black Volta' in some books, but the locals and most atlases call it the Red Volta because of its colouration by the bright-red earth surrounding its banks.) These facts were somewhat academic to our arrival, because night had fallen over Africa shortly after take-off from Nouakchott and the land was now in darkness except for the myriads of cooking fires far below and the countless stars twinkling overhead. There was no visual horizon because the intensity of the stars and the brightness of the cooking fires were so similar that no visible line existed between them. The whole firmament blended as if we were flying in a goldfish bowl.

A night landing at Ouagadougou pleased me because it removed the danger of flying into any of the enormous hawks, eagles and vultures that cruise effortlessly overhead during the day. The nice little birdies were all tucked up in bed, until dawn. All the aircrew within the Flight usually enjoyed a visit to Upper Volta because the local people were friendly towards us and bargained good naturedly for the well-made African artefacts in the local markets. They distrusted and generally disliked politicians of any origin, both their own and other people's, because corruption had been rife amongst the ruling elite since France had relinquished responsibility for the country in 1960. In 1983 the then President, Thomas Sankara, changed the country's name from Upper Volta, which perfectly described the place, to the rather bizarre Burkina Faso, which he said meant 'the land of the incorruptible men'. Considering that this country was and still is renowned as one the most corrupt in the whole of Africa, his new name was regarded by its peasant population as a bit of a joke.

It is a relatively poor, landlocked country that in ancient times covered a huge area, but France, in its eagerness to divide and rule, had given much of Upper Volta's land away to its neighbours Mali, Ivory Coast, the Gold Coast, Togo, Benin and Niger. This left a poor, agricultural, landlocked area capable only of subsistence farming, but the French found these other countries more profitable and left Upper Volta in abject poverty, with a per capita income in the 1970s and 1980s of only £75 per year. That amounts to a daily sum of only 20 pence to provide food, clothing and all the other essentials for life, which is an impossibility for anyone, anywhere.

We were met at the airport in the searingly hot and humid, mosquito-laden conditions, by Upper Volta's President, Monsieur Sangoule Lamizano who rapidly removed our nine passengers from Ouagadougou's airport in a fleet of black Citroën limousines, this time without the usual police outriders and their annoying sirens. Everyone ignored the need for fuel for the Falcon and any thought of accommodation for the crew. They just left and the place grew quiet, except for the incessant cicadas chirping away in the bushes and the occasional small monkey dashing past the circle of light around the aircraft.

I walked over to the fuel compound with my clutch of fuel carnets issued by the world's major oil companies, but the refuellers were singularly unimpressed with any of them. 'You'll only get fuel for cash,' they assured me.

'What type of cash?' I enquired.

'US dollars,' they replied.

'How about CFA [the local currency]?' I enquired and they laughed uproariously. I assured them that I had US dollars, but only in large denomination notes.

Without hesitation, they replied, 'Five-dollar bills only.'

'Could you fill up the aircraft now and allow me to pay for the fuel in the morning when the banks are open?'

'No!' came the deafening response, so reluctantly we were forced to leave the fuel tanks empty overnight, which carried with it the danger of condensation gathering in them and being drawn into the jet engine on take-off. No amount of persuasion, bribery or anything else would soften their hearts and I was eventually forced to admit defeat.

Our next hurdle was locking up the Falcon safely and finding transport into the city. The air traffic controller kindly telephoned for a taxi to come for us and also contacted the Ouagadougou Hotel, our usual bolthole in this savage country. He offered to watch over the well-being of our Falcon and keep the light illuminated around it throughout the night, but his offer to shoot dead anyone coming near the aircraft did worry me slightly. He backed up his offer by pulling a huge elephant gun from under his desk and smiling.

'How much do you charge for these extra services?' I asked.

Quick as a flash he replied, 'A hundred US dollars.'

'I will give you the money in the morning,' I assured him and he seemed happy, but I worried just what kind of a hole he would blow in my beloved Falcon if his aim was not true or the sights on his ancient weapon were not properly adjusted.

The receptionist at the Ouagadougou Hotel welcomed the three of us and found us three perfectly adequate en suite rooms. What's more, he produced some scrambled eggs on toast for our bedtime snack. At 10.30 at night, after a tiring day, a pilot cannot ask for more than a clean, comfortable bed, a clean bathroom and well-cooked scrambled eggs on toast, along with a bottle of local beer. It may not have been gourmet fare, but it tasted marvellous to us.

We slept the sleep of the just and did not peep outside our bedrooms until past 10 o'clock the next day. The big oblong swimming pool outside our bedrooms was surprisingly clean and full of chlorinated water, so while we enjoyed bacon and eggs beneath a two-metre umbrella by the deep end, we planned the day. Firstly, after breakfast it was off to the local bank to change my US$500 travellers cheques for fresh new US$5 notes, and then to the airfield to refuel our aircraft, not forgetting the $100 note for the erstwhile overnight guard.

The taxi eventually dropped us at the arrivals building and the officials gave us a hard time because we had eluded the immigration procedures the night before and therefore were not officially 'in' the country. Lots of smiles and gouts of schoolboy French and our misdemeanour was forgiven. I cannot remember whether actual bribery featured in our release, but it probably did at some stage. The air traffic controller was sitting outside his elevated glass room, on the balcony, overlooking our white Falcon, with his ancient weapon on his lap, as he read a James Bond novel. Ouagadougou International Airport was not exactly a hive of activity and more than three aircraft a day would constitute work at fever pitch for the staff.

The fuel arrived at the behest of the controller and my fistful of US$5 bills brought a smile to a shiny and very black face. Our engineer tested the quality of the fuel with every known test and then he tested it all over again. The sight of the fuel bowser driver, in his worn khaki clothing, standing there in the blistering heat – with many hundreds of green US$5 bills stuffed into his two shirt pockets, some even spilling out until eventually he was forced to fill every other pocket that he possessed – was almost comical.

The engineer emptied all the wheel bay and under-wing water traps until pure fuel streamed onto the concrete. All the other aviation domestics were completed and a member of the Upper Volta Foreign Ministry arrived to organize a platoon of soldiers to mount a 24-hour guard on the fully fuelled Falcon. No more hundred-dollar bills needed. The air traffic controller who had successfully stood guard for me throughout the previous night was ecstatic when I honoured our agreement and gave him his $100, even volunteering to supervise the platoon of soldiers throughout our stay for no further payment. I felt that he was sincere when a small tear rolled down his cheek as he spoke. What $100 represented to him, I can only guess, but considering it was a year's average salary in Upper Volta it was obviously an important contribution to his family's future well-being.

Back at the hotel, we cruised up and down the pool trying to work up an appetite for lunch, but just as we had finished swimming the Libyan Prime Minister, Mr Abdu Ati Obeidi, joined us for a chat. Their meetings with the Upper Volta President would not start until the next day and there was due to be a dinner, hosted by Monsieur Sangoule Lamizana that evening in our hotel. The host government were due to arrive with a big delegation and he would like us to join the nine-strong of the Libyan delegation, probably to make his delegation seem somewhat larger. We all agreed with his request and arranged to meet in the reception area at 8 o'clock that evening.

To cope with the oppressive jungle heat 150 miles north of the Equator, I wore a very light cotton safari suit which allowed whatever breeze there was to circulate round the body. Mr Sangoule Lamizano and his party arrived at the hotel with gifts for all the members of the OAU delegation, including ourselves. My gift was a bronze statuette, 15 inches high, of an armoured prancing horse, with a seated armed rider, dressed in the costume of a thousand years earlier. Apparently he was the figure of a legendary hero who had reputedly galloped into Ouagadougou leading a small army, at a time when the country was under attack from the Sudanese. He and his men had killed the attackers and restored the country to its rightful rulers. The statuette sits nicely on my mantelpiece to remind me of that fateful night, when I looked death in the face.

We were seated in a banqueting hall that comfortably held the thirty or so diners. We were each given our own menu from which we selected our preferred main dishes. President Sangoule Lamizana was placed at the central curve of a horseshoe-style dining table, with Mr Abdu Ati Obeidi on his left side. I sat on Mr Obeidi's left. My co-pilot was two places removed from me, further down the table on the left, but close enough for me to hear his food order. The meal started with a French-style hors d'oeuvre during which the waiters took our main course order. I cannot say with any certainty which of us ordered first, but I was aware that both the Prime Minister and I ordered the same main course, 'Well-done steak'. Simultaneously, my co-pilot ordered steak tartare, which seemed to me to be highly dangerous. Raw beef with a raw egg on top in Central Africa seemed to me to be very risky indeed, but who was I to advise on his food? He was a big lad and could make his own decisions.

The meal progressed as anticipated and the conversation around the table was interesting. Although we were not experts, we were all required occasionally to offer opinions on the complex world of modern African politics, so we tried to be as tactful as possible with our replies. When the main courses started arriving on the table, the first person to be served was the guest of honour, the Libyan Prime Minister. He looked down at his meal and for some inexplicable reason picked it up, and placed it in front of me, saying, 'We both ordered the same main course, so you have this one, Captain.' I wanted to refuse, but I could not think of a tactful way of doing so, so the plate stayed in front of me as the second 'well-done steak' arrived quite quickly and was placed in front of the Prime

The Emir of Kuwait, Jaber al Ahmed al Jaber. Greeting the Libyan Prime Minister outside the Kuwait VIP lounge. (Major Abdusalem Jaloud) on an official visit.

Minister. To make a fuss at this stage and try to change the meals back would have been ill mannered, so I accepted the Prime Minister's preference, whatever the reason.

I was horrified to see the raw minced steak arriving in front of my co-pilot, but the conversation was louder at that time and I was unable to make any comment to him. Nothing further of note happened throughout the meal and the evening ended with two short speeches – one from the President of Upper Volta and the reply from the Libyan Prime Minister. As the main guests left the hotel to return to their accommodation, we sat for a while discussing the evening, then decided to retire to our rooms for the night.

I awoke some hours later feeling absolutely dreadful. Although it was quite dark I became aware that I was having serious difficulty with my vision. I shivered and poured with sweat in alternate bouts and eventually decided that I was about to be sick. On the way to the toilet I passed out completely and sometime later awoke, lying in a pool of warm liquid which I assumed was sweat, stretched out on the floor, but still wishing to find the toilet. This presented a major problem as I was unable to stand up without lapsing into total unconsciousness and even when I was conscious, I could not see. Crawling in the direction that my memory told me the bathroom should be, I fared little better, as the effort was too much and I drifted between complete numbness and some kind of bodily awareness. I obviously could not reach the toilet, no matter how much effort I devoted to the task, so I gave up the struggle and proceeded to be violently sick where I lay. A knowledgeable doctor later told me that this act of evacuation of the stomach probably saved my life.

That was later, but for the present, I was certain that I was in the process of dying. My simple mind nagged at me to make some effort to stay alive. It was very important, something somewhere seemed to be saying, but I could not fathom out just what I had to do to keep living. The whole thing seemed to be slipping away as I drifted back into unconsciousness.

How long I lay there, I have no idea, but when I resumed the conscious fight with whatever was happening, I grabbed a towel, or maybe it was my shirt, and tried to clean myself up. It was then that I realized that I could actually see again, not clearly, but some of the objects in the room started to make sense out of the all enveloping, surrounding haze. Trying to stand up, I slid remorselessly to my knees, but I somehow eventually reached the bed – not along it as normal, but clear across it, with my head and arms on the far side, a few inches off the ground and my feet on the nearside floor, draped over the mattress like a wet towel.

In that position, which seemed to me at the time to be something of an achievement, I considered my situation. Firstly, I felt terrible, but just what kind of terrible, I find hard to describe. My stomach felt as if there was a knife through it, and with all the warm liquid around, there could well have been a knife. Breath was agonizingly difficult to force into my lungs. My heart was pounding like a steam-hammer and the brain could not function on any particular subject for longer than a few seconds. Lying face down over the bed, with the head just clear of the ground, and a not very pretty backside facing the ceiling, draped half off the bed, eventually seemed to improve the operation of the brain. After some time in that ridiculous position, I realized that thoughts could be retained for maybe a minute, instead of a few seconds. Coming back from 'somewhere' felt very reassuring.

Some time later, my co-pilot came into the room to find out why I had not shown up for breakfast. The very idea of food nearly sent me off again, but after he had turned me the right way round and covered me with a sheet, I was able to ask him to find a doctor urgently. The doctor arrived quite quickly, it seemed to me, but time was a dimension that was causing my brain a serious problem, so he may have been longer than I calculated.

He was a Frenchman of about thirty-five years of age who introduced himself as the Chief World Health doctor for Upper Volta. We talked in short bursts as conversation taxed my whole body, which he appeared to understand. He took a multitude of readings – blood pressure, temperature, pulse, lung capacity – and examined my eyes, tongue, teeth, ears, fingers and the multitude of bruises that I had sustained hitting the concrete floor repeatedly during the night. His bedside manner was very professional and I found his slight French accent very comforting. He produced a fresh bottle of Evian water and urged me to sip as much as I could as often as possible. When he had finished he sat down in a chair by my bed and chatted with me for a very long time, probably an hour or two, before excusing himself to bring more equipment from his car.

He returned about five minutes later with what appeared to be a typewriter, but it turned out to be a very compact, portable electro-cardiograph machine. After sticking his little suction pads all over my chest and legs, he took several traces of various heart functions and sat at the opposite side of the room, under a window devouring the electronic information.

His first words were, 'You know that you nearly died in the night, don't you?'

'It felt something like that,' I replied.

'I can carry out laboratory tests to confirm my diagnosis, but they will be superfluous,' he went on. 'You have been artificially infected with botulism, almost certainly in a meal that you consumed yesterday evening. We will establish the actual strain, but it is almost sure to be Botulus 'B'. We have a particularly virulent strain in Ouagadougou and it is routinely harvested from infected people, by some groups, to kill their enemies. It is usually administered in freshly cooked meat, where it is either injected into the meat after cooking, or the meat is coated with the infective material.

'You must be grateful that you are alive,' he continued, 'the last four people I was called to see, who had been infected in this way, all died. You must have a very strong heart to survive this attack, but I have to tell you that your heart has been damaged and there will be a danger of future associated heart problems. You must have an anti-toxin injection now and stay in bed. I will come back to see you every day about this time. If you eat, it must be just light meals, but I don't expect that you will feel much like eating for a few days after your recent experience.'

He thought that it would be about five days before I would be functioning on all four cylinders again and he warned me not to even contemplate going anywhere near an aircraft until then.

He also warned me against being bitten by mosquitoes. The anti-toxins he administered could, he said, nullify most malarial protection, so I should stay there and use my mosquito net at night. With that, he left.

I had much to consider. The only meal that I had eaten the evening before was the one, given to him, that the Prime Minister insisted should be mine. Who would want to harm the Prime Minister and why did he pass the meal to me? These are questions that I have never been able to answer satisfactorily.

My health recovered enough to enable me to fly the Falcon back to Tripoli, without passengers, about a week later. No mention was ever made about the change of meals in Ouagadougou, with its disastrous consequences. Perhaps nobody realized – but I wonder . . .

My heart did show signs of deterioration a few years after this infection, exactly as the World Health doctor in Ouagadougou predicted. The deterioration was first detected by Dr Dirhan at the oil company clinic in Tripoli, during my routine six-monthly aircrew medical inspection. At first the blood pressure increased steadily as shown in my subsequent medical checks, then certain heart, sinus rhythm irregularities manifested themselves, until atrial fibrillation was confirmed and medication became essential. My pilot's licences were withdrawn because of my heart irregularities, shortly after leaving Special Flight in 1983, forcing me to abandon the aviation career which I loved so very dearly, and through which I enjoyed real success in my chosen field.

The resultant loss of my aviation income was disastrous to the family causing us to sell most of our assets that had been built up over the whole of a long aviation career, in order to keep ourselves financially viable. Five houses and a farm that we owned were sold to cover our commitments. Even our home was at one time owned by someone else, but we fought to regain possession and recently succeeded in recovering ownership. Life became very tough indeed for us over the following few years but we must be thankful for living through this dreaded poisoning and Lesley and I make the best of what we are now able to afford and are physically capable of doing.

Just how my co-pilot managed to eat raw minced steak and raw egg without acquiring any dreaded infection on that fateful night, whilst I was struck down in this terrible way whilst eating a perfectly conventional cooked meal, remains a mystery to me. The World Health doctor attending me in Ouagadougou was also baffled as to how anyone would even consider ordering such a potentially dangerous mixture as steak tartare in the insanitary conditions prevailing in Upper Volta.

Major Jalloud, although technically out of office, never really faded from the political scene during the remainder of our time in Libya. He regularly reappeared to assume key negotiating and diplomatic missions, when serious events in international affairs needed the cool head of an experienced statesman to solve apparently intractable situations.

CHAPTER NINE

Rendezvous with Evil

To the righteous soul will be said: O thou soul, in complete rest and satisfaction. Come back to thy lord, well content thyself and well pleasing unto him. Enter thou, then, among thy devotees. Yea, enter thou my heaven. *(This verse from the Koran was apparently recited by 45-year-old Sheik Yamani when he was expecting to be killed within minutes by Carlos the Jackal.)*

In telling the story that follows I will, so far as I can recall, include the words used by various heads of state. These were the statements on which, acting in good faith, I based my decisions at the time. Although this may seem irrelevant it is of the utmost importance to me personally. Had I known all the truth at the time, I would possibly have acted differently.

Early in January 1976, I was telephoned by a senior minister from President Gadaffi's office. Though I cannot be a hundred per cent certain, I believe it was a close confidant of the President called Abdul Majeed Gaoud. It had been decided, he said, that there was a diplomatically sensitive flight required to Algiers and that instructions from on high were that it *was* to be piloted by 'the Chief Pilot'. I was also fortunately the duty pilot, so the request caused no problem.

Naturally I tried to ascertain the nature of the flight and why it was so diplomatically sensitive, but was told that details of onward routing would be discussed with me by the Algerian President, Colonel Houari Boumedienne, and that this fact was not to be divulged to any other member of my crew. He also assured me that if for any reason, after I had spoken to President Boumedienne, I was unhappy with the proposed flight, I would be fully supported in refusing the task.

Intrigued though I certainly was, I had flown President Boumedienne on previous occasions, found him to be friendly and co-operative, and was therefore not too worried at the prospect of flying him again. Would that life were that simple!

We arrived at Algiers International Airport in the early evening and were parked away from the airport buildings and the VIP lounge on a stretch of steel

Somerfield tracking[1] about two hundred yards from anyone else. As we were refuelling, a black Mercedes came alongside and the uniformed driver asked for me by name. Collecting my flight bag, I jumped aboard and in the gathering darkness was taken to the VIP lounge where I was ushered into a room off the main lounge into the presence of President Boumedienne, who was relaxing in an armchair, sipping coffee and talking with his Foreign Minister, Abdel Aziz Bouteflika. We all shook hands, embraced and I seem to remember being kissed on both cheeks. He recalled how I had flown him to the southern Algerian airport of Tamanrasset about a year previously. The Foreign Minister reminded him that he had also been a passenger on the same flight and that when a sandstorm had arisen whilst we were on the ground everyone had wondered whether they would be stuck for the night. 'Not with me as the pilot,' I had foolishly remarked. In the event, the weather improved and the sandstorm subsided.

A cup of coffee arrived and Foreign Minister Bouteflika made some excuse and left, so I sat in his vacant armchair on the instructions of the President. On our own I could see that he was agitated, but he still insisted on ten minutes of small talk about our families and life in Libya, finally asking how President Gadaffi was keeping. I replied that I had not seen him for about a month, but that he was fit and very active when I last saw him. He asked me to give him his kind regards when we next met, but in the event the opportunity did not materialize for over three months and I confess that I forgot the greeting when the next opportunity presented itself.

I interrupted his speculation about the weather by cutting the protocol and telling him about my instructions from Libya. He winced and looked at the floor. After a pause in reflective contemplation he seemed to look past me at the distant wall with severe concentration, so much so that he caused me to turn around to see if some threat was lurking in the corner of the room. Whereupon he stood up, gripped the back of his armchair, fixed his gaze about foot above my head and almost blurted out a request for me to fly a passenger and three of his companions to Mogadishu, the capital of Somalia. Something did not add up, so I said, 'This is a normal task for me, just like flying you to Tamanrasset or Timbuctou, as I did last year. There must be something else – is there a problem of some kind?'

His voice faltered as he announced, still not meeting my eyes, 'The passenger

---

[1] Somerfield tracking is a series of thick steel panels, interlocked with each other to form a hardened surface for aircraft on what would otherwise be unsafe soft ground. It was invented by British engineers for the Royal Air Force supporting the Eighth Army operating aircraft in the North African desert during the Second World War. In some African countries this temporary covering for taxiways and hardstandings has been in use now for more than sixty years and shows little sign of being replaced with anything more permanent.

is Carlos, who has been living in Algiers since he hijacked the OPEC oil ministers in Vienna, just before Christmas.'

I stood up, protesting that there was no way that I would agree to fly Carlos the Jackal. Being in the same country as him gave me enough cause for concern, let alone having him in my aircraft. This man appeared to me to be a nutcase who killed for pleasure. He and his supporters had just killed half a dozen people in Vienna, at the December OPEC summit meeting a short while previous to which he had shot three members of the DST (The French Secret Service), two of whom died instantly; at the same time he shot and killed Michael Mourkharbal, his Lebanese ex-colleague – all in Paris, where it might be expected that the French would be well prepared.

'These Secret Service Agents were not naïve idiots,' I went on, 'yet he completely outwitted them. This man must be very dangerous indeed. He is ruthless and very well trained by the Spetznaz and the KGB, for starters, according to the world's press. I may be able to handle dangerous fools for a short while, but psychopathic killers with university degrees in the art of assassination [from Patrice Lumumba University in Moscow] are not something that I would like to test my wits against. I like living too much. We are going back to Tripoli,' and I walked towards the door.

'Stop,' he said, 'stop! I have not told you everything.' I was convinced that he was about to offer me serious money, but I was wrong. 'If you do not agree to fly Carlos to Mogadishu within the next few minutes, he and his men are going to kill Sheikh Yamani, the Saudi Arabian Oil Minister, and Jamshid Amouzegar, the Iranian Oil Minister, within one hour. They will be dead before you land in Tripoli. The other oil ministers will then die, one every hour, including the Libyan Oil Minister.' To add emphasis to his words he led me over to the window where he pointed to a DC9 with lights glowing along its line of windows, which, he said, belonged to Austrian Airlines and contained the OPEC hostages from Vienna under the control of the hijackers.

'If you can find me another cup of coffee,' I responded, 'I will just sit here for a few minutes and give my decision some more consideration, sir!' The coffee arrived immediately.

The murderous threat sounded to me to be in line with Carlos's normal operating procedure and I definitely did not wish to be responsible for the deaths of Sheikh Yamani and the other oil ministers, so I reasoned to myself that if I flew him exactly where he wished to go, he would have no reason to hijack us to anywhere else. If he shot us in the air with high-velocity bullets, they would be likely to penetrate the Falcon's fuselage, cause an explosive decompression and kill everyone on board.

Ilich Ramírez Sánchez, better known as Carlos the Jackal.

The main danger to us, it appeared to me, was Carlos losing his temper and blazing away uncontrollably. Likewise, if he took an irrational dislike to any of the crew on ethnic, political or personal grounds, we would be at risk whilst on the ground. But if he killed us, or destroyed the aircraft, he would have made a very powerful and influential enemy – the Libyan President. Carlos already had enough enemies in the intelligence services of most of the Western world. Forcing Colonel Gadaffi, a Muslim leader, to actively seek his downfall would probably be the last straw and would surely destroy him.

Equivocation was no longer an option because Algeria's President had gone very red in the face, the deep lines of tension stood out on his forehead and his hands had started to shake. I judged that he was not far away from a heart attack. Draining the dregs of coffee from my cup I announced that in the circumstances I was prepared to take the flight. Tears appeared in the President's eyes as he shook my hand and said, 'We will all be permanently in your debt.'

Whilst the diplomatic ramifications were arranged I was asked to collect the rest of my crew and return to the VIP lounge. When we stepped out of the car the Algerian Chief of Protocol announced that there would be a short delay, and to save us waiting at the Dar el Beida airport for longer than necessary we had been booked into a well-known Algerian restaurant for a meal. As the driver was given instructions we thanked him, and off we sped into the city of Algiers.

Halfway through a very fine meal a youngish, thickset man of similar build to myself, but heavier with a boyish round face, excused himself and sat down at the table. He conversed with us in fluent English, the waiter in fluent French and the *maître d'* in fluent Arabic. Suddenly I realized that this Spanish-looking twenty-six-year-old was the renowned linguist, Carlos the Jackal, but I had been forewarned. My co-pilot had no prior knowledge but deduced the truth within about five minutes. In a hushed voice, because he was no fool, he said, 'You must be Carlos.'

'No,' he responded, 'my name is James Richardson and I am third secretary in the British Embassy here in Algiers.'

By way of proof he dropped a red British diplomatic passport onto the table, which I picked up and examined. Sure enough, it was a genuine British diplomatic passport proclaiming that the bearer was James Richardson and that he must be accorded diplomatic immunity. The photograph stamped with the approved indented letters was certainly the man at our table, but all three of us knew that this man was, in fact, Carlos.

We were immediately immersed in the murky world of espionage, assassination and intrigue, where nothing is quite what it seems and where people make statements containing no basis of truth whatsoever. They are actors on a criminal stage and some of them are consummate actors who can weave stories out of thin air that defy even the most penetrative mind. We were in the company of a master of such arts and I must confess that I was fascinated with his prowess. I was also somewhat scared. How could I possibly cope with such an incisive mind over the period of days that fate had ordained we would be together. Could I be the foil to his deadly act without offending him in the process and pushing him into drilling me fuller of holes than a colander? I thought perhaps I could. Anyway, I'd give it my best try.

The nerve of the man! He had actually come to our table in that restaurant to check us out and decide whether he would deign to fly with us to Mogadishu, or whether he would dial the telephone number he had memorized and detonate the explosives he had placed under the seats of Sheikh Yamani and Jamshid Amouzegar and just disappear into the desert to lie low in the tents of his Tuareg friends. This was the depth of the man with whom I would be crossing verbal swords for longer than I cared to contemplate.

Leaving the restaurant, Carlos disappeared without any of us realizing that he had gone, probably into the maze of backstreets behind Algiers Old Town, whilst we returned to Dar el Beida with our chauffeur and the black car. The official wheels of departure had certainly been oiled in our absence because we were not even required to render a normal flight plan. The Algerian Chief of Protocol had already done this, and asked us to call in at Tripoli to collect a Libyan Foreign Ministry official who would be coming with us to Mogadishu.

A red Ford Hertz rental car drew alongside the Falcon as we completed the pre-flight checks and out stepped a girl and three men, one of whom seemed to be in some pain as he tried to walk towards the aircraft, with the aid of two walking sticks. The car was left exactly where they stepped out of it and I often wondered whether Hertz ever saw it again, or if it even was a Hertz car in the first place, because none of the four passengers seemed to give it any regard whatsoever as they walked away and left it sitting on the dispersal.

The four came up the aircraft steps with the girl and one of the men helping the injured young man as best they could. They settled themselves in the Falcon cabin with the injured man being installed in a double seat, one of his legs resting on the seat in front of him. Carlos came up to the cockpit to announce that they were all ready to go and I told him that the Chief of Protocol had asked us to fly in the first instance to Tripoli to collect a Libyan Foreign Ministry official.

This was agreeable so without further ado we requested clearance to taxi. Not only were we given immediate permission to taxi, but a British Airways 747 and an Air France 747 airliner, both full of passengers, were moved out of the way to allow us to do a rolling take-off without delay. Service like this from Algiers Air Traffic Control was unheard of, especially for a small business jet like our Falcon 20. They really did wish to get rid of us. As we taxied to the runway I looked out for the Austrian Airlines DC9 that was reputed to contain the hijacked OPEC oil ministers, but surprisingly it was nowhere to be seen.

Levelling off at 41,000 feet, as we headed east the coast was clearly visible and the lights of Tunis appeared in front of us on the horizon. Carlos was very tense and kept appearing in the cockpit on trivial pretexts, so I showed him the lights of Tunis as they became brighter. He became even more agitated and said that they were 'a bunch of awkward bastards'. I said that we usually had very good service from Tunis whereupon he replied that they had closed the airfield a few days previously to prevent him landing, even though he had not requested permission to land. He was, in fact, flying from Vienna to Algiers and apart from overflying had no interest in Tunis. They were obviously very nervous, I suggested, knowing his reputation and that the DC9 contained the captured oil ministers. He seemed to like the reference to his 'reputation' and I filed the fact away to assist me to cool his ruffled feathers, if necessary, later in the flight.

At Tripoli International we were met by Mr Abu Shagour, the Libyan Chief of Protocol, who told us that the Foreign Office official who would accompany us to Mogadishu was driving back the 1,000 miles from Benghazi so it would be better if we took a night's rest and arranged to leave in the morning. We agreed wholeheartedly with this sensible suggestion and put the Falcon to bed in record time, albeit with a full load of fuel, ready for take-off the next day. Our unusual passengers were last seen disappearing into the VIP lounge, under the expert guidance of Abu Shagour.

At the appointed time of 8 o'clock, we re-embarked our unlikely group of passengers, plus the newly arrived Libyan official. I will call him Abdul, but as I have derogatory remarks to make about this unfortunate young man and do not wish to cause him any embarrassment, that is not his real name. As we climbed up to our cruising altitude of 21,000 feet, on a course of almost due south, the huge ball of the sun was quite high in the heavens to our left.

The Sahara Desert spread out before us and the short shadows emphasized

Leaving Benghazi VIP Lounge.
Mr Abu Shagour, Libyan Chief of Protocol with sunglasses.
Major Abdusalem Jaloud, Libyan Prime Minister, in battledress, without hat.
President Siad Bari of Somalia on left.

the irregularities of the sandy terrain. Undulating sand dunes neatly arranged in south-east/north-west lines could easily have originated on an artist's palette. After leaving the neat cultivated groves of olives, citrus fruit, cherries, apples and bananas, indicating the limit of Libya's cultivated terrain, our southerly track enabled us to see a camel caravan travelling with the sun at its back, westwards towards Algeria. We could even make out from the four- or five-mile distance, the light blue of their Tuareg robes.

Half an hour later, Sebha, with its massive runway and unique fort, came into view and we were invited to commence our descent for a straight-in approach at our first refuelling stop. As I positioned the Falcon with the threshold of the wide north-south runway just below the nose, a voice burst into the cockpit loudspeaker, saying, 'I'm just behind you flying the morning Boeing 727 and I think that we should make this one a race, Neville.' It was Captain Krema, the Chief Pilot of Libyan Arab Airlines, and a very capable aviator, so I accepted the challenge and accelerated. We touched down in line astern with a three-minute interval, which enabled me to be hooked up to a refuelling bowser before his 727 drove alongside near the airport buildings. My passengers could hear the radio on the loudspeakers and were calling derisory comments from the cabin. The hilarity helped to cool fevered brows and lower the obvious tension behind us. Carlos and his compatriots remained on board during our Sebha stop to avoid any publicity, and I prayed that Captain Krema did not leap energetically into the cabin to accuse me of cheating in the race to touchdown.

Our next leg took us from Sebha to Ndjamena (formerly Fort Lamy), the capital of Chad. Travelling into a less reliable area of Africa, in aviation terms, we always attempted to arrive with plenty of fuel so we could go somewhere else should the need arise. With this in mind, we climbed to 44,000 feet where our engines burned less fuel for any given distance flown. As I was levelling off, gently throttling back the engines and adjusting the trim of the control surfaces – in short flailing my arms and hands around the cockpit like a one-armed paperhanger – I felt something cold and hard stuck into my right ear.

Not able to give the intrusion my full attention because of the delicate care needed to set all the controls at the optimum for maximum range, flying in the rarefied air at this altitude, I grabbed the offending article and was surprised to discover that it was the barrel of a Colt .38 Special revolver. This particular one was silver, not just in colour, but real silver and very pretty indeed. The right hand holding the lethal weapon was Carlos's, so I gently but firmly pushed his hand away and told him to stop buggering about if he did not wish to end up a smoking heap in the jungle below.

'Don't you want to be hijacked?' he asked.

'What's the point?' I replied casually, 'We are taking you where you have said you want to go.'

He said, 'You're right. There wouldn't really be much point, would there?' and with that he placed his gun in my right hand.

His bravado gave me two problems. Firstly, I needed my right hand to activate the Falcon's autopilot and allow it to operate from the aircraft's Omega satellite navigation system, and secondly, I needed to check on the status of the weapon that Carlos had just thrust into my hand. Was the safety catch on? Was it loaded? Was it on a hair trigger that could fire with imperceptible pressure? What exactly did he expect me to do with this rather heavy, showy firearm?

I solved the problem by lifting my right hand and slowly placing the Colt .38 Special into my left hand, so that he could clearly see the whole operation. With my now free right hand, I made the switches needed to complete the cruising configuration, set the latitude and longitude of the next waypoint on the Omega with the co-pilot's confirmation of the numbers, and coupled the navigation system to the autopilot.

Satisfied that everything was then in order for the next 2,000 miles and with the co-pilot in temporary control of the aircraft, I unstrapped my seat belt and invited Carlos to come with me back into the cabin. The other passengers, and indeed the aircraft engineer, must have had somewhat of a surprise seeing me, for the first time, with Carlos's prize silver revolver in my right hand and Carlos backing into the cabin away from me. We settled into two vacant armchairs opposite each other and folded out the table between us so that we both had something substantial to lean on. Slowly and deliberately I placed the Colt .38 on the table near Carlos, with the barrel pointing in my direction, but not directly at my chest because by now I had established to my own satisfaction that the gun was certainly loaded and that the safety catch was underneath the ammunition chamber on the palm of my hand, so I did not know its actual position. Following my naval training I therefore had to assume that the gun was live and treat it with the utmost respect.

There followed a succinct lecture by me to Carlos outlining the terms on which I was prepared to continue the flight. In the interest of all our safety, no weapons of any kind were to be produced during the rest of the flight and I would prefer that all weapons now being worn by the passengers should be removed, set to safe with the ammunition removed and placed carefully inside their luggage, where they should remain. To clarify my request – for realistically that is what my statement amounted to – I assured him that none of the crew would attempt to frisk them or check whether they had any weapons concealed in their clothing, but that it would be safer for everyone if the firepower was stowed safely away. He looked me directly in the eyes, but passed no comment.

'We have hot VIP food and drinks on board,' I said, 'which will be renewed at our refuelling stops and we can assure you all of our care to attend to any requirements. You only have to ask any of the crew for anything, but while you are on board, you must remember that we have an onerous job to do that sometimes can be technically demanding. Please assist us and help keep everyone as safe as possible.

'We have prepared several charts for you, showing our route and refuelling airfields. Let me know if any of these countries give you any cause for concern, and if it is possible (which it probably will be) I will organize refuelling somewhere more agreeable. If anyone wishes to fly in the cockpit to check that we are travelling in the right direction and listen to the radio, there is a jump-seat between the two pilots with its own seat belt. You may come up front and strap yourself in, one at a time, but please keep quiet if the local Air Traffic Control is talking to us on the radio and allow us to attend to aviation matters during the take-off and landing phases. It is fairly certain that if one of us dies during this flight, everyone will die and it will not be a pretty scene.

'Now, I would like to know why you gave me that Colt .38 in the cockpit after we had gone through the hijack routine. Was it just a game?'

'Well no,' he replied, 'I was checking how dangerous you were.'

329

'What would you have done,' I asked, 'if for some insane reason I had been tempted to point the gun at you?'

'That's simple,' he said, 'I would have pulled this small machine gun out from my shoulder holster and put at least nine bullets into you before you had brought the Colt up to point at me.'

With that he produced, in about half a millisecond, what looked to me like a very small black Israeli Uzi Machine-pistol and cocked it ready to fire. Point taken, I thought.

When I had seen the four hijackers coming on board the Falcon in Algiers, I heard someone call one of them Khaled. That must be the girl, I said to myself. She must be Leila Khaled, the young girl who had hijacked a TWA Boeing 707 to Damascus in August 1969. Later, following extensive plastic surgery in the intervening months to change her appearance, on or about 6 September 1970 she tried to hijack an El Al Boeing 707. The Israeli sky marshal on board shot and killed her Nicaraguan accomplice, Patrick Arguello, who pulled the pin on his hand grenade and rolled it up the aisle, where happily it failed to explode. Leila Khaled then pulled several hand grenades out of her bra, whereupon she was jumped by a number of male passengers who wrestled her to the floor, preventing her from detonating the grenades.

She was arrested at Heathrow in London when the El Al aircraft landed, but was exchanged for 150 BOAC passengers who were later hijacked to Dawson's Field in the Kingdom of Jordan.

The radio crackled into life, requesting confirmation that we were level at Flight Level 440 (44,000 feet), so I returned to the cockpit. Ndjamena control continued that we had a UTA 747 5,000 feet below us on a reciprocal course, but in view of the altitude separation we were safe to continue on our present course. The French pilot of the 747 joined in saying that he could see us, because we were leaving what appeared to be an almost permanent white contrail straight down the middle of Africa. 'We are passing underneath you in one minute,' he added and asked for the air temperature at our altitude.

'Minus 64ºC,' we told him.

He responded, 'That's bloody cold.'

Then we saw the 747, and because it was less than a mile away, the Boeing jumbo looked enormous. I turned to point the huge aircraft out to our passengers and saw that they were stripping themselves of their weaponry and dutifully stowing the various armaments in their luggage. It was quite comforting to see that my little lecture had been heeded and that they were prepared to cooperate. Maybe we would live long enough to land in Mogadishu after all. When they subsided back into their seats the engineer/steward served them a meal, which looked very good indeed.

Carlos shouted up to the cockpit, 'This meal needs a good Burgundy. Don't we have any on board?'

'No,' I replied, 'remember that we come from Libya, which is a dry country.'

'Now you tell me,' and he clicked his tongue in a resigned gesture.

It was very reassuring to see that all the passengers, including Carlos, seemed to be relaxing and the tension that pervaded the atmosphere earlier was rapidly dissipating – except, that was, for Abdul, the young Libyan Foreign Ministry gentleman. His body language and facial expressions were clearly antagonistic towards the other passengers and I resolved to have a serious word with him at the earliest opportunity.

Our passengers, especially Carlos, were dedicated egotists. In fact they were a bunch of prima donnas – dangerous prima donnas – who needed thoughtful handling if disaster was to be avoided. The last thing any of us needed was a serious confrontation amongst the passengers. It was abundantly clear to me that unless the Libyan could be persuaded to cool things whilst he was on board, we would all end up in mortal danger.

On the ground in the Chadian airport of Ndjamena, where the passengers had originally elected to remain on board, the heat and 100 per cent humidity made the cabin unbearable after the air conditioning was closed down during refuelling. A little black gentleman in uniform pedalled over on his bicycle and announced that he was the immigration officer and could he see the passports of anyone who would be staying in Chad. When I replied that we were just refuelling and none of the passengers would be remaining in his country he was happy, so I gave him a cool fizzy orange juice to oil the wheels of diplomacy. When he had finished and was jumping back on his bike I asked whether it was all right for the passengers to walk round the aeroplane whilst refuelling was in progress. 'Sure,' he shouted as he disappeared back into his air-conditioned office.

All of them except the injured young man stretched their legs for a few minutes and the co-pilot took our flight plan up to the control tower. He returned as the refuelling was finishing so I chased everyone back on board, but not before noticing that Abdul upset Carlos verbally every time they were in close range. I somehow managed to separate Abdul from the OPEC hijackers and led him round to the tail of the aircraft where I explained how dangerous it would be to upset any of our other passengers and asked him to avoid any abrasive verbal contact with them until we reached Mogadishu. 'Carlos will kill you without even thinking about it, if you upset him, so for all our sakes you must cool it. Try to put a smile on your face, sit at the back of the aircraft where none of the others can see you and just read a book or something.' His reply was not very encouraging. As he climbed the Falcon steps, he tossed his head back and said petulantly that everyone had to die some time, and with a fixed expression on his face he walked to the back of the cabin.

The next leg of our flight was planned to take us to Entebbe in Uganda and would last about 3 hours 50 minutes with a favourable wind. Normally, with a flight of this length, I would be inclined to stop for fuel en route, but the only realistic airfield available was Bangui in the Central African Republic and remembering being slapped into jail on my last visit, I was not too keen to repeat the performance.

Levelling at 43,000 feet I managed to persuade Chadian Air Traffic Control to allow us to fly in a straight line, direct for Entebbe and leave the established civil airway, which had several dog-legs and would have been 250 nautical miles longer. That permission saved us just over thirty minutes of flying time and if we struck unpredicted adverse meteorological conditions would be a great help – in fact, it could be a lifesaver.

Not having eaten so far, we two pilots took it in turns to enjoy a rather good meal courtesy of Tripoli International's catering section, washed down with the engineer's hot coffee. As we passed over Fort Archambault, near the Chadian border with the Central African Republic, the ground appeared to have standing water between the jungle trees wherever one looked. There had been a major flood in the area and the rivers could not clear the water away. It looked like hundreds of miles of marshland. I wondered what had happened to the people living in this south-east area of Chad, but when I looked on the Michelin map it showed very few towns or villages. This part of Africa was obviously barely habitable most of the time.

With no one to talk to on the radio in this part of Africa without resorting to high frequency transmissions, I handed over to the co-pilot and walked back to update the passengers on our progress. Sitting opposite Carlos across the table, I gave him an update on our progress and showed him how far we had travelled along the planned track. There was little to point out on the ground except unbroken jungle with areas of standing water. 'The mosquitoes must be terrible down there,' I commented. 'The wet and humid conditions are exactly what they need to thrive.' He laughed and said that he would rather pass over this part of Africa in an aeroplane than risk it on the ground.

I agreed and commented that he had not yet introduced me to his compatriots, so he turned to the injured young man and announced that this was Hans-Joachim Klein who had taken a couple of bullets when Vienna's Special Command Unit had tried to storm the OPEC building. The rest of the hijackers had been in the main conference room with the doors closed and Klein, along with the Lebanese hijacker, Joseph, was left in the badly lit corridor outside. Commander Kurt Leopolder, leader of the unit, opened fire on them both before he had a clear view of the hijackers and one of his bullets bounced off the wall and hit Klein in the stomach where it shattered and caused serious internal injuries, piercing his duodenal artery, pancreas and colon. He took a second bullet in his leg, but this was a minor wound and a third bullet hit his hand knocking his machine gun to the floor. He shouted that all the oil ministers would be killed if the unit did not withdraw. Perhaps persuaded by a hand grenade thrown down the corridor by Klein with his left hand, and the fact that Kurt Leopolder was immediately seriously wounded by one of Klein's bullets, the unit withdrew and left the hijackers holding the entire first floor.

Hans – Joachim Klein, a member of the Baader-Meinhof terrorist group.

Carlos then turned to the 23-year-old girl sitting behind Klein. This was Gabriele Kröcher-Tiedemann, a seasoned campaigner, who distinguished herself in the OPEC operation. A sixty-year-old Austrian police inspector, Anton Tichler, and his colleague Inspector Joseph Janda were the only guards outside the OPEC conference chamber. Seeing the hijackers approaching, bristling with weapons, Tichler apparently lunged at Carlos and grabbed his Beretta sub-machine gun, but as Carlos was very fit and athletic he easily pulled his hand and gun free from the Inspector's grasp; Kröcher-Tiedemann, standing close by, shot Tichler in the back of the neck causing devastating wounds, and for no apparent reason except possibly as a warning to anyone else thinking of climbing up from the ground floor, she opened the lift, dragged his bleeding body inside and pressed the button to send him down to the ground floor.

His body, with its macabre injuries, stayed spreadeagled, half in and half out of the lift without anyone taking any remedial medical action until he finally died. A few moments later the hijackers in the conference chamber noticed an Iraqi security guard, a very big man called Hassan Saccd al Khafiri, backing towards one of the doors, but Kröcher-Tiedemann strode up to him and pressed her pistol into his chest, whereupon the Iraqi threw his arms around the hijacker and squeezed her tightly to him, trapping her gun between them. As she was being bodily removed

Gabriele Kröcher-Tiedmann probably the most ruthless of the hijackers at the OPEC conference.

from the room in the grip of his bear hug, she managed to draw an Uzi machine-pistol and shoot him dead. She did not appear to be a very attractive young lady, but was certainly endowed with a resourceful mind.

Turning to the seat behind me Carlos introduced a Palestinian with a very badly damaged left side to his face. He had obviously suffered severe burns to half his face that available plastic surgeons had been unable to fully rectify. 'This is our explosives expert, Khaled,' Carlos claimed. 'He positioned fifteen kilos of C4 plastic explosive around the conference chamber so that had we been attacked it would have removed most of the upper floors of the building.' Khaled was obviously not his real name and he spoke English slowly, but not very often. I had difficulty talking to him because one's eyes were constantly drawn to the awful mess of the left side of his face. My co-pilot cruelly named him 'Crumple Chops' and the name stuck – but not when addressing him directly. None of the crew would wish to offend anyone with such a disability, especially one who could blow us all in an instant to kingdom come.

Carlos clearly enjoyed boasting about his recent exploits and was proud of his successes as he saw them. The press had reported the death of a Libyan security guard during the OPEC siege and Carlos told me that this large, well-dressed bodyguard, Yousef Ismirli, who was listed as an economist, had jumped on him at an early stage, grabbed tight hold of his heavy Beretta sub-machine gun and wrenched it from his grasp. Ismirli had no idea of the workings of the big weapon and fumbled ineffectively with its levers and buttons. This allowed Carlos enough time to draw an automatic pistol from underneath his leather jacket and shoot Ismirli in the hand, causing him to drop the Beretta. Carlos then told me that the Libyan just would not die, or back off. 'I emptied my entire 9 mm magazine into him, slowly, expecting him to drop with each bullet, but he kept clawing at me. I eventually fired nine bullets into him before he fell.' That version differs considerably from the eventual semi-official report which states that the shot to Ismirli's hand was followed by one to his right leg, one to his stomach and the final one to the back of his neck – four bullets in all.

At this stage I remembered that my bedtime reading at that time was *The Day of the Jackal*, by Frederick Forsyth and it might be with me in my flight bag. As I fiddled about in the depths of the black leather holdall, the hijackers grew nervous as I had persuaded them to bury their beloved handguns deep inside their luggage. Fortunately my hand soon emerged clutching the blood red paperback book and as I was face to face with Carlos the Jackal, I prevailed upon him to sign the book as a memento of a very long and very tense flight. He signed it, 'CARLOS, Ilich Ramirez Sanchez', and added that the 'Jackal' title was sheer bullshit!

The Day of
the Jackal

*The name
is sheer "bullshit"*

Carlos

Ilich Ramírez Sánchez

Upon reflection I am not convinced that calling him 'the Jackal' in this context *was* bullshit – some of his methods of operating were very similar to Frederick Forsyth's fictional character. His group produced bogus passports and other documentation of perfect quality for him, enabling him to assume other identities at will. As required for his 'operations' he could become any one of at least ten other people, complete with full documentation, historical background and recent movements. He also employed specialist weapons' manufacturers to produce, for unusual tasks, specific weapons that could be concealed in innocent-looking tools. There certainly were similarities with 'the Jackal' in my opinion.

I asked him whether it was true that he had shot three senior members of the DST, the French Secret Service, in Paris as had been hinted at in the world's press, but never really confirmed. He said that he had been living comfortably in London at the time – and when he said 'comfortably' he really meant the word, complete with serious amounts of money, top hotels and a bevy of glamorous young girls swooning at his lifestyle. When the leadership of the Popular Front for the Liberation of Palestine summoned him to Paris in June 1975, he was angry at having to leave the London high life.

In Paris, he found that the previous local PFLP head, Mohamed Boudia, had been assassinated, probably by Mossad, the Israeli secret intelligence service. Knowing that Boudia carefully examined the underside of his car before opening the door and would have spotted an external explosive device, his assassins placed a pressure mine under the driver's seat.

Leaving one of his mistresses houses in the rue des Fosses St Bernard, Boudia examined his car carefully before unlocking the door. As his right buttock touched the upholstery of the seat, an almighty explosion ripped him and the car apart before his other foot had even left the pavement.

Instead of replacing Boudia with Carlos the Jackal as he had expected, Dr Wadi Hadad, the leader of the PFLP, along with his second in command, Dr George Habash, had decided that Carlos was too much of a loose cannon and instead sent Michel Moukharbl – a short, smartly dressed Lebanese from Beirut, with a supercilious stare – to take over in Paris. It appeared to be a very strange choice as this interior decorator was thrown in at the deep end, in the murky world of espionage and mayhem that swirled around the backstreets of the French capital. He was not even a member of the Popular Front.

Carlos and Moukharbel agreed on one thing, but not much more – Boudia's assassination must be avenged. So Carlos produced his list of privately investigated anti-Palestinians, from which the name Joseph Edward Sieff, the Jewish President of Marks & Spencer, the British department store, was produced. With revenge in mind the two renegades flew from Charles de Gaulle,

Paris, to Heathrow, London and took up residence with one of Carlos's old girlfriends, Nydia (Maria Nydia Tobon di Romera, a 37-year-old Colombian émigrée lawyer, who was obsessed with tales of Che Guevara.) She and Carlos had a flat in Comeragh Mews, with other flats in Chester Road and Coleherne Road – so tracking them would have been quite difficult, even for MI5 and the Special Branch.

It was from the mews flat that Carlos set off on his own to kill the President of Marks & Spencer in his palatial house in St John's Wood. He was armed with a flick knife and an old gun, which he had never fired before, containing only five bullets. Having carried out no reconnaissance he marched up to the front door and rang the bell, which was answered by the maid who told Carlos that Mr Sieff was upstairs changing for an evening function. Carlos asked which was Mr Sieff's bedroom, and as she pointed her hand to a door at the top of the stairs it immediately opened and out stepped Mr Sieff in crisp new shirt and black trousers, asking who was ringing the doorbell.

Carlos pushed the maid aside and murmuring some excuse strode up the stairs, pulling out his gun on the way. In the doorway of the room Carlos fired at Mr Sieff's face at very close range. The bullet knocked out several of his front teeth and lodged in the back of his throat, whereupon he collapsed to the floor. Carlos claims that he fired a further two bullets, but irrefutable evidence showed that only one bullet was fired and only one empty cartridge case was ever found. Carlos left the house after the shooting and walked off down the street to hail a taxi.

Mrs Sieff found her prostrate husband on the floor, with blood pouring out of his mouth and a gurgling sound emanating from his throat. She turned him face down to allow the blood to pour onto the floor, made sure that his airway was clear and summoned an ambulance. Her act of common sense saved her husband's life. His extra-strong teeth had slowed the bullet as they shattered into tiny fragments, and placing him face down drained the blood from his throat. Paramedics and the surgeons did the rest. The single bullet was removed from the back of his throat and two weeks later he was recuperating in Bermuda. Carlos admitted that he was ill prepared for this job and would never carry out any operation again with so little preparation and such unsuitable weapons.

Over the next few weeks the pair of conspirators flitted backwards and forwards freely, between London and Paris, building up caches of weapons and explosives in both capital cities. The arms were usually kept in holdalls or suitcases in the flats of Carlos's various girlfriends. These innocent participants often smuggled heavy suitcases through various frontiers without the slightest knowledge of their contents.

At Wadi Hadad's direction, Carlos and Moukharbel joined forces with members of the Japanese Red Army in Paris to attack various embassies and other designated targets. On one of his many visits to Lebanon Moukharbel was arrested and handed over to the DST in Paris, after a sinister list of names of important people in Paris and London and diagrams of buildings was discovered in his briefcase.

Marie-Teresa Lara, a young Venezuelan girl and her flatmate Nancy Sanchez Falcon, an anthropology student at the Sorbonne, had a convenient apartment at 9 rue Toullier, in the Latin Quarter, which was large enough and ideally placed to provide a secret refuge for Moukharbel and Carlos. After his erstwhile boss's arrest in Beirut Carlos realized that the rue Toullier address would soon become unsafe, because – as he quite rightly assessed – Moukharbel's ability to withstand the DST's professional interrogation was non-existent.

On 27 June 1975, in the early evening, Carlos was enjoying a noisy party with three young Venezuelan students, Leyma Palomares, Edgar Marino Muller and Luis Urdaneta Urbina, whilst the owners of the flat were away on holiday. Commissioner Herranz had learned from Moukharbel the details of 9 rue Toullier and that his colleague who carried out all the killing was a man called Nourredine who lived there with him. The Commissioner collected his two colleagues, Raymond Dous (who had distinguished himself in the Algerian war) and Jean Donatini, a good-looking young man from Epernay. Normally they would all have been carrying Manhurin semi-automatic weapons, but as it was Friday they had returned their guns before setting out, to avoid wasting time at the start of the weekend by having to return to the office to hand them in. This turned out to be a fatal decision.

Privacy being at a premium in the crowded flat, Carlos was sitting in the bathroom, on the toilet seat, talking to Leyma Palomares, when Herranz appeared in the flat. As Leyma emerged from the bathroom ahead of Carlos, the Commissioner spoke aggressively to her, causing her to lose her temper and rip his warrant card out of his hand. Carlos and the other partygoers calmed her down and Herranz examined all their identity papers. He asked Carlos questions about the Beirut stamp in his passport and received the response that anyone could go there as a tourist. Herranz searched Carlos, but found no weapon. Dous showed him photographs of himself and Moukharbel and asked where he had been on 13 June. As the questioning became more insistent, Carlos threatened to appeal to his ambassador, though which South American country he was claiming to originate from that day was not clear.

Trying to placate the policemen, Carlos offered Herranz and Dous a J&B whisky. The Commissioner accepted but Dous was dispatched to bring Donatini and the other passenger from the car. Leyma persuaded Marino to sit down next to her on the bed, picked up her cuatro (a four-stringed Peruvian instrument), and announced that she would sing to him. As she plucked at the strings, Carlos excused himself and went into the bathroom. He returned with a long-barrelled, Czech CZ Vzor 52, 7.62mm sub-machine gun down the back of his trousers. This was a fearsome weapon that could fire eight rounds a second.

As Leyma sang the Venezuelan song 'Barlovento' in full voice, Dous, Donatini and Moukharbel appeared at the top of the stairs. Carlos was surprised at Moukharbel's gaunt appearance after what must have been days of aggressive questioning. He looked haggard and frightened, but that did not stop him springing into the room, pointing to Carlos and pronouncing, 'This is him, this is Nourredine!'

Carlos's right hand came out from behind his back and with the words 'Bloody traitor', the long Czech barrel spurted a foot-long blast of flame and exploded in an ear-splitting noise as he blasted Moukharbel with enough firepower to sever his spine. As he fell backwards Carlos swung round and fired a second burst into Herranz, who fell face first onto the parquet floor and smashed his front teeth as he hit the ground. Donatini, the closest to Carlos, was hit in the face, which was blackened with gunpowder. Dous was spun around by the force of the next impact, but before landing on top of Donatini's body he was dead.

In the flat below, where Incarnacion Carrasco was hosting a dinner party, two bullets whistled through the ceiling, through the dining table and buried themselves in the floor. The party round the table looked at each other in amazement and two of the guests decided that this must be some unique entertainment organized by their host. It was only when their host fainted that they realized that something more momentous must be taking place. They opened the front door to see a well-built man coming down the stairs four at a time, with an enormous gun in his right hand. He crossed the footbridge into the next house's courtyard and descended into rue Toullier, where he forced himself to slow down, replaced the gun down the back of his trousers and calmly walked past an armed police patrol.

Of the four men hit by Carlos's barrage of bullets, only Herranz was still alive. The students left in the flat found a taxi to take him to the Cochin hospital where several bullets were removed and he later recovered. Examination of 9 rue Toullier revealed Savile Row suits, cashmere overcoats, Nina Ricci ties, Italian designer leather shoes, Christian Dior sunglasses and Marks & Spencer cotton vests. The police were baffled. Pierre Ottavioli of the Brigade Criminelle declared that he had seen many things in his time, but three bodies in a heap in one room....

Without condoning such brutality, I had to be realistic. Not many men, even in the murky world of espionage and international violence could confidently take on the resources, might and professionalism of the French secret police in their own backyard with complete impunity. He had absorbed his instruction from the Patrice Lumumba University of Moscow very well indeed.

This was a man to be reckoned with and whatever view one had on his methods, motives and politics he had to be treated with the utmost respect, especially in the very close quarters in which we now found ourselves. It was not just my life that was at risk from this assassin, but also the lives of the other two members of my crew and they had accepted my decision to convey this graduate of terror to Mogadishu without question. If to preserve our lives and limbs I had to swallow a dollop or two of humble pie, then so be it.

At this juncture the engineer brought very welcome coffee and cakes for everyone and created an opportunity for Carlos and me to discuss wider topics.

He had severely shocked me by revealing that one of his main boltholes had been London. From all that I had read about his nefarious activities in Europe and the Middle East, it always seemed to me that he lived in some of the more exotic parts of Europe. London was too close to home for my liking, so I asked him his views on the British Royal Family. It was a ridiculous question to a dedicated Marxist/Leninist assassin and left the stage open for him to be completely defamatory, but maybe the warmth of the coffee was having a soothing effect as he replied, 'I really don't know much about them. You see, I have never slept with any of them to the best of my knowledge.' Then slowly he added, 'Well, none of the men anyway.' What I really wanted to know was whether any of the Royal Family was actually on the list of people that he needed to assassinate; from his nonchalant reply and smile I became convinced that they were not.

Silently I said to myself, 'Well, that removes the necessity of me trying to kill you.'

I asked him next if any of the world's powers or intelligence services, such as the KGB, the CIA, Mossad, MI6, the DST, the Stasi or any of the Arab terror networks wished to kill him, which would be the one that he feared the most. Without pausing for thought, he replied, 'None of them, but there is a "Black Department" under the direction of a shadowy group in the British Establishment. A death sentence by this Black Department would frighten the shit out of me. They never fail.'

He did not elucidate, but his body language told me clearly that he knew that such a department did exist and that he really did not wish to discuss the matter any further. I took the hint and changed the subject.

Whether such a Black Department does exist or not, his information must have come from either Moscow University, the KGB or the Stasi (the then East

German secret service); he was certainly convinced of its existence and appeared genuinely frightened of its ability to terminate.

Hearing a radio call from Bangui Control I excused myself and returned to the cockpit. We were over the jungle airfield of Obo, close to Zaire's border with the Central African Republic, and Bangui wanted to hand us over to Kisangani Control as we entered their airspace. Wishing us a good flight the controller quipped that we were not refuelling in Bangui these days. Had we taken offence? he asked. Not wishing to prolong the exchange, I replied simply, 'Yes' and left the frequency. I did not fancy a second night in a Bangui jail.

Above the airfield and town of Isiro, the virtual capital of Africa's remaining pygmy population, we could see a large body of water lying across our track. I had just established that it was Lake Albert (recently renamed Lake Mobutu Sese Seko by the Zairian President of that name) when a familiar face emerged in the cockpit between us two pilots. 'Is that Lake Victoria?' Carlos cheerfully asked. I explained its two names and said that it was an unusually salt lake, owing to its shallow depth and high rate of evaporation because of the oppressive heat at only 2º North.

'Lake Victoria,' I continued, 'is fifteen times bigger in surface area than Lake Albert and much deeper. It is the second largest freshwater lake in the world and the largest in Africa. It is also the source of the Nile, which is the longest river in the world. We will see it in about half an hour.' On this occasion, to relax him I invited him to sit on the jump-seat between the two pilots, as the view ahead was magnificent and getting even better as the flight progressed. We switched on the cockpit loudspeaker so that he could hear that nobody was trying to land him into a trap. The fabled Mountains of the Moon could be seen on the west bank of Lake Albert; once we were over the lake, Kisingani Control handed us over to Entebbe Control.

Entebbe welcomed us to their airspace, adding that the controller was Jacob, one I knew well and who asked if we would be staying the night. I told him that we needed to press on to Mogadishu after refuelling.

'Neville! You will regret it. There's a new cabaret at the Leopard's Lair in the Kampala Hotel and it is very good indeed.' This reply surprised Carlos considerably.

'How the devil does he know your name, and why are you given this sort of service?'

So I explained that we often dropped in to Entebbe and he either recognized my voice or read it on our flight plan from Ndjemena. 'If we stay overnight, he usually comes over to the Leopard's Lair, buys us a bottle of beer and introduces us to his girls. He provides most of the bar girls for the nightclub and ensures that we are not ripped off with the prices. If we buy a girl a drink, it's a bottle of beer at the normal price, and the same for us – not a sticky green at some vast expense.'

'I've misjudged you pilots,' he said. 'I thought you were a dismal bunch, but it seems that there is another side.'

The co-pilot joined in and said, 'He has to watch it,' pointing at me, 'he knows that if he does anything naughty I shall tell his wife when we get back to Tripoli.'

'Are you sure that you have to go straight on to Mogadishu?' I asked. 'It will be nearly 9 o'clock when we arrive in Somalia at this rate.'

'Yes,' he said, 'lots of important people are waiting for us and they would not be amused if they heard that I was pissing it up in some nightclub with a couple of pilots and an engineer, whilst they waited on the tarmac at Mogadishu – though I am tempted.'

This prompted me to ask, 'Who is your current boss?'

'Wadi Hadad, the leader of the PFLP,' he replied.

'Does that mean that it was they who organized the Vienna OPEC operation then?'

'Yes. You don't think that I organized the vast amount of weapons and explosives on my own, do you? The six of us walked into that building with big canvas Adidas sports bags, each stuffed with weaponry. There must have been over 350 pounds of lethal hardware in those bags and we just sat in our Vienna rooms and waited for it to arrive with various PFLP, couriers, mostly female.'

'Is Hadad likely to be pleased with the OPEC result when you arrive?' I asked.

'He will be furious,' Carlos said. 'He ordered me to kill Sheikh Yamani and the Iranian Oil Minister Jamshid Amouzegar at the outset and to persuade *you* to fly us to Mogadishu, as a bargaining counter. I was forced to let them go alive. He will certainly not be pleased, but who cares. He's a miserable shit at times and he's never pleased. He rarely gets his hands dirty, just directs other people to risk their lives in his kind of politics.'

'There!' I pointed forward to what looked like the Indian Ocean because we could not see the far side of it. 'That's Lake Victoria in all its glory,' and in this light it did indeed look glorious with the sun behind us and a yellow glow shimmering on the water like a golden blanket. The tiny fishing boats danced around on its surface like so many jewels. The 26,815 square miles of water seemed to be fluorescent and endless. Up to the north of the lake, the start of the Nile snaked off to the west and tumbled over the Murchison Falls before briefly entering Lake Albert and out again along its northerly track to the Mediterranean, 4,150 miles away.

Landing in Entebbe was a routine procedure. The only dangerous aspect was the need to keep a beady eye out for the vultures and sea eagles that could destroy an aircraft by hitting an engine at high speed, or crashing straight through the fuselage. The truth is that they are relatively stationary at anything up to 10,000 feet as they wheel round and round in the thermal currents of air, so the aircraft's speed becomes the impact velocity – just a tiny dot in the sky that in the twinkle of an eye becomes an eight-foot wingspan and a 20 kg disaster. A keen lookout is the only real antidote to the dozens of feathery threats suspended innocently in wait.

My tactic in these conditions was to extend 15 degrees of wing flaps to enable me to fly as slowly and safely as possible, thereby giving the huge birds time to descend out of our way after their first sight of our aircraft, and giving us the ability to turn away from them with alacrity if we saw them first, before we actually collided.

The first potentially catastrophic encounter I had with our feathered friends was on 15 December 1958, as a student in 738 Squadron at the Naval Air Station at Lossiemouth and the memory stayed with me for the rest of my aviation career. On that clear, calm, wintry afternoon our Commanding Officer, Lieutenant-Commander Jock McCandless, breezed into the students' crew room and selected four of us to join him for an hour and a half's low-level battle drill in the Aberdeenshire low-flying area.

We were all flying Sea Hawk FB5s, a beautiful single-seat fighter and low-level battle drill was the kind of flying that all student pilots at our stage enjoyed. It was thrilling flying at not much above treetop height, and the 'arrowhead' formation at extended intervals allowed a constant lookout for aircraft or any other conflicting objects – five pairs of eyes straining to keep everyone safe was usually a foolproof insurance against airborne collision. To keep us on our toes, a further Sea Hawk FB5 was airborne, to attack us as we closed with a mock target; then we would all be involved in a no-holds-barred dogfight and our gunsight cameras would positively certify who shot down whom. This was ripping stuff and lookout was all-important.

Jock McCandless was renowned as a hard taskmaster who had been known to treat students who did not perform perfectly very harshly indeed, or so we all thought. Our nerves were at full stretch during the Commanding Officer's hour-long briefing as we scribbled his instructions onto our flying overall kneepads. Walking out to the line of shiny grey and white fighters outside the crew room, the students checked with each other that their understanding of what Jock demanded of us was accurate. We were a formation, so all our actions must be synchronized. When Jock's raised hand fell on completion of our pre-starting checks, all five sets of starter cartridges fired simultaneously as nervous fingers depressed the starter buttons at precisely the same time.

The formation take-off went like clockwork and the five of us stayed down very low over the sea matching our leader's height and speed. The flight proceeded professionally and the radio calls gave everyone confidence that we were all assisting each other as was required of us, reporting any important facts to Red Leader, Jock's call sign. I was tail-end Charlie at the back of the formation when, as we were flying down a valley near the town of Huntly, my keen eyes saw a huge flock of medium-sized birds rising from the tree tops, seemingly straight at the leader. Only a few seconds separated Red Leader from impact and possible disaster.

As calmly as I could I reported, 'Red Formation from Red Four – Birds, pull up.'

Like a well-trained circus troupe everyone, including me, instantly pulled up to about 400 feet and my mesmerized eyes saw that just one bird out of the thousands in the flock was continuing upwards. Higher and higher I climbed, but this pigeon seemed intent on hitting my aircraft – and sure enough, it succeeded.

Trying to avoid the inevitable, prior to the impact I clearly saw that it had folded its wings around it, trying its very best to descend. My speed as the pigeon and I collided was about 500 miles per hour and the impact sounded as if I had been shot down by an anti-aircraft shell. Where the left side of the front of my cockpit had been before the collision, there was now a gaping hole about nine inches across and the throttle lever was somewhat bent towards me, although it still functioned normally. My head and chest were covered in blood, the Sea Hawk had depressurized and the noise of the rushing air persuaded me to extend the airbrakes and slow down.

I announced that I had experienced a bird strike and was returning to base with fuselage damage, and climbed immediately to a thousand feet. Red Leader designated one of the other Sea Hawk students to escort me back to base and report on the external damage to my aeroplane. The guide came alongside and reported that there was a hole in the port side of the cockpit and that the canopy was covered in what looked like blood. It was difficult for me to hear exactly what he was saying because of the excessive wind noise. I tried to tell everybody that I was not injured as far as I knew. I could not explain the large quantity of blood and doubted whether they understood me, due to the now heavy background noise.

My guide led me into a formation landing and as we cleared the runway I was instructed to shut down the engine on the taxiway. No sooner had the engine started to wind down when the canopy was ripped open from the outside and several men in white overalls arrived at the side of the cockpit and proceeded to hoist me bodily upwards. Before I knew it I was in the back of an ambulance hurtling to the base hospital, shouting to everyone that I was not hurt. They wrongly presumed that I was just being brave and took no notice – as if in response they showed me my helmet, which was red with blood, so they insisted that I lie still. On arriving in the operating theatre, an astute surgeon had me washed down and sure enough, there were no injuries on my body whatsoever. Not a single scratch could be found. It was later established that all the blood belonged to the unfortunate pigeon, not me. Thanks to our naval engineers the Sea Hawk was cleaned, repaired and back on the line in pristine condition for flying the following morning.

Funny though the outcome was, the trauma of that incident never left me and over the years, when some of my less fortunate colleagues died through ingesting various birds into their engines, which almost invariably exploded, I became doubly careful in the company of our feathered friends and always viewed them as potential attackers whilst airborne.

On the ground at Entebbe, refuelling was most efficient and Carlos, Gabriele Kröcher-Teidemann and Crumple Chops were taken over to the airport duty-free shop by one of the ground crew, where they purchased the latest French perfume and the very best of drinks – not just any old champagne, but Dom Pérignon 68 vintage; not just brandy, but Courvoisier Napoleon Cœur de Lion in gold-plated bottles; and not just red wine, but Château Lafitte 1970. These bottles were all expensive, very expensive. They must have had money to burn. On return to the Falcon with their purchases they were met by Abdul, who was most disapproving of them buying alcohol.

Carlos went very red in the face at the confrontation and passed me saying that he was going to kill him, whereupon he tried unsuccessfully to pull his holdall full of weapons from the luggage rack. With some difficulty I prevailed upon him to calm down and he eventually subsided, made a few jokes, but avoided eye contact with Abdul. The last words that I heard Carlos say on the subject were that he would kill Abdul when we were airborne and throw him out of the plane. I neglected to inform him that no door or window in the Falcon could possibly be opened in flight once the aircraft's wheels were off the ground, a trump card that I kept up my sleeve. Without revealing my actual words to Abdul, I persuaded him to keep quiet until we arrived in Mogadishu, or stay in Entebbe. He obviously liked living dangerously; perhaps he was brave, but if so it was very ill-advised in our current circumstances.

The weather forecast for the flight from Entebbe to Mogadishu showed that we would cross a very active warm front and that severe turbulence had been reported by preceding aircraft. On the climb-out from Entebbe we crossed Lake Victoria, the surface of which had then changed to a deep red with the changing colour of the evening sun, still at our backs. Coasting in on Victoria's eastern shore we passed the Kenyan metropolis of Kisumu and could see the game reserves of

Nakuru dead ahead, and Samburu slightly left. We looked set to pass directly over Mount Kenya and beyond over the Meru game reserve where Elsa, Joy Adamson's lion, was released and unfortunately subsequently killed by poachers. Sadly, both the Adamsons were also killed some years later, possibly by the same group of poachers.

Ahead, near the Somalian border, the build-up of angry looking cloud confirmed that we were shortly in for an exciting ride. Nairobi Control informed us that if we deviated 30 degrees right and resumed our course for Mogadishu as we coasted out above the Indian Ocean, we would avoid the most violent weather ahead of us. As night descended and the sky blackened ominously, we were grateful to comply with Nairobi's advice.

The track between us and Mogadishu in a straight line was like an Olympic fireworks display, with the most brilliant lightning tracking in all directions. The clouds responsible for this electrical activity were huge. In Europe it is usually possible for us to fly over the tops of the cumulonimbus clouds that are responsible for the violent air currents that produce extreme turbulence. In Africa there is a meteorological line lying east – west that moves north and south with the seasons. It is called the Intertropical Convergence Zone (ITCZ), where the extra cold air from the Antarctic collides with the searing hot air of the tropics. It produces some of the most violent cloud precipitation and resultant electrical activity that can be experienced anywhere in the world and aviators treat this zone with the greatest respect. To avoid it they are prepared to deviate from the track to their destination – sometimes by hundreds of miles.

The Falcon 20's maximum safe altitude was in the order of 45,000 feet. We were flying at that altitude and the dark cumulonimbus cloud straight ahead of us towered up to about twice as high. These bubbling beauties – they looked like gigantic moving cauliflowers growing their florets bigger before one's very eyes – were levelling off in excess of 90,000 feet, well into the stratosphere. It was worth our trouble to circle round the worst of the inevitable violence as we had plenty of fuel and an extra half hour or so on the flight would not inconvenience us too much.

Preparing for action I illuminated the 'Fasten Seat Belts' signs in the cabin and we pilots took an extra pull on our own belts for good measure. The engineer removed all the coffee cups and plates from the passengers' tables and warned them that we would shortly be flying through turbulence. He then came up to the cockpit and strapped himself into the jump-seat – seeing the fireworks intensifying around us, we probably all prayed a little to our respective gods. There were obviously mighty forces at work, too close for our comfort.

On entering the cloud itself the Falcon's airframe was pounded by big hailstones and despite our full de-icing precautions ice could be seen building up on the wings. The hot air being diverted from the engine onto the wing leading edges by the anti-icing system was causing the ice build-up to crack and fly off over the top surface of the wing. Hopefully none of the larger pieces would be sucked into either of our engines as it would severely damage the turbine blades and in the worst case could cause the engine's compressor or turbine discs to distort – at the speed they were rotating there would be a danger of them exploding the engine.

Grappling with such considerations I was taken totally by surprise when a huge bolt of lightning struck the starboard wingtip with a blinding flash and an enormous bang. It was just like being in an active war zone and a backwards glance told me that our intrepid bunch of assassins in the cabin were very chastened indeed. The next strike hit the Falcon somewhere on the tail producing less noise but a great deal of illumination. This really was a bravura performance that the weather was staging for us, but remarkably all the aircraft's systems continued to function normally. *Inshallah* ('God willing' in Arabic), they would remain functioning.

Nairobi Control handed us over to Mogadishu Control and I confirmed with them both that we were experiencing extreme turbulence at 45,000 feet. They wished us the best of luck and Mogadishu gave us permission to approach their airfield from any direction we preferred in order to allow us to manoeuvre and avoid the worst of the weather. We were the only aircraft in their airspace that night. Somali radar assisted us by telling us where the most intense cells of electrical activity were in relation to our position, allowing us to take early avoiding action.

Conditions were certainly very uncomfortable, but as we coasted out over the Somali coast with the Indian Ocean beneath us, we could again see lights on the ground and the air seemed to be transformed into a silky smoothness. I dispensed with the 'Fasten Seat Belts' signs, the engineer unstrapped and went back into the cabin to make us all a welcome cup of coffee. Some of our intrepid assassins were a funny whitish-green colour, but none of them had been forced to use their sick bags. After the coffee a more normal pink colour returned to their cheeks and the odd smile could be seen – perhaps of nervous relief.

A rhyme came into my mind, frequently recited by petty officers in the Navy when their junior ratings were being severely seasick in a violently rolling warship: 'You're bloody good kids in harbour, but Oh! my Christ, at sea.' Maybe it was the abashed look on some of the passengers' faces that brought this particular rhyme to mind.

We flew north-east along the Somali coast for about 400 nautical miles, letting down to 5,000 feet over the sea, and when we were visual with the Mogadishu airfield beacon just south of the city, were invited to land. As we taxied up to the

VIP lounge, clear of the normal airport buildings, a substantial welcoming party could be dimly seen in the darkness, so we stopped about twenty feet away from them and shut down both engines.

The welcoming party was very subdued, almost surreptitious at first, and I was quite surprised that Gabriele, Carlos and Crumple Chops insisted on retrieving their holdalls, which (as I was very aware) contained a veritable armoury of lethal weapons, before they would leave the Falcon. I didn't recognize anybody in the twelve-strong welcoming committee until, from round the outside, a tall figure with very little wispy grey hair on an almost bald head and dressed in a smart lightweight pinstripe suit, came towards me with his hands outstretched. 'Captain Neville!' he almost shouted, as I was pulled towards him to endure his hugs and kisses on both cheeks. It was Mohammad Siad Barre, the longstanding President of Somalia whom I had had the privilege of flying for many thousands of miles in the recent past.

'How is Dick? Is he with you?' he asked, referring to one of our other engineers who had looked after him on a previous flight.

'No,' I replied, 'he is presently on leave at home in Harpenden.'

'Harpenden,' he repeated as if he was recalling something in the past. 'You know, I believe that I was in Harpenden once, with a delegation concerned with equipment for purifying drinking water, but I do not remember much about it except that the weather was beautiful.'

He held on to my hand and led me away from the other people who all seemed to be talking Arabic at once, some of their tones less than friendly. When we were standing by his official presidential car he asked conspiratorially how my passengers had been en route. I replied that they had behaved reasonably on the aircraft and had given us very little cause for concern during the flight, though I would far rather not have been pressurized into flying them. He understood and seemed somehow relieved. 'I would much rather have nothing to do with them either,' he replied.

Getting into his car to leave, he wound his window down and asked me to remember him to Dick when I returned to Tripoli. 'Of course,' I agreed, wondering what hold these people had over the President of this huge country with its small population. I never discovered the answer.

Siad Barre, as he is usually known in the West, was one of Africa's survivors. He came to power in October 1969 in a bloodless military coup, which deposed his ineffectual predecessor, Abdelrashid Ali Shermarke. At first, he courted the Soviet bloc, but found them too dour and unproductive, so he shifted his allegiances to the West, which contained Somalia's former colonial rulers with whom he felt more comfortable, and who helped him to modernize his impoverished country with generous aid packages.

He survived a very serious car crash in May 1986 when his driver collided with a bus on a country dirt road outside Mogadishu. He suffered major fractures to his head and chest and was flown to a hospital in Jeddah, Saudi Arabia, for treatment under the king's surgeons. The next year saw him surviving an army coup attempt which he is reputed to have quashed with brutal ferocity. In 1991 Somalia erupted into clan warfare when the warlords of the different clans slaughtered members of opposing clans in their thousands, in vain attempts to gain power.

The warlord Mohamed Farrah Aidid eventually prevailed after untold amounts of vicious killing of the Somali people. Intent on publicizing the symbolism of personally ejecting Siad Barre from the country, he took a group of photographers to the border with Kenya and had himself pictured kicking the very capable 72-year-old President out of the country. Unfortunately for him, when he returned to Mogadishu to display his triumphal pictures, a rival warlord and his clan had seized power in Aidid's absence and civil war erupted once more with renewed ferocity.

Three months later, Aidid regained power at the cost of an estimated 250,000 further Somali deaths. Today the country still festers in a self-inflicted trough of misery, with no law and order, and the almost universal poverty that cripples the economy. Its farms remain unproductive for the lack of means to sow crops and even with the deaths of over 25 per cent of its five million population it cannot feed the remainder. The only plentiful item available in Somalia seems to be Kalashnikov automatic rifles and mounds of suitable ammunition. It appears that everyone from about ten years old upwards, male or female, owns one of these weapons and most are prepared to blaze away with impunity.

How stability can ever be returned to this now chaotic country is impossible to even imagine. The Americans appreciated the seriousness of the problem in 1993 and tried to help restore some order out of the chaos, but they received a bloody nose for their concern, as was documented in the book and film *Blackhawk Down*. The ordinary Somali yearns for the days of peace and stability under Mohamed Siad Barre, when the country was economically successful and they could export their agricultural products over the whole of the Middle East.

That night in early 1976 we arrived at the Mogadishu Hotel after the normal dinners were finished so the Director invited us all to a meal, prepared especially for us, in the great banqueting hall. The Somalis, then, were proud of their prowess with breeding cattle and we were to dine on a huge side of local beef of the highest quality. The Somali Chief of Protocol presided over the meal, but for some reason Carlos was asked to choose the wine. He selected a Grand Cru

Vintage Burgundy, Chambole Musigny, which should have been a very fine dry red wine that I had previously enjoyed in perfect conditions in France.

The waiter poured a small amount into Carlos's glass and he dutifully took a sip. He felt the bottle with his hand and instructed the waiter to fill everyone's glass. As the wine was being poured, he leaned over to me from his seat on the opposite side of the table and said, 'You wouldn't believe it, Neville, but these fucking animals have had this fine wine in the refrigerator. It's almost frozen; it will be ruined. Would you believe it?' I replied that the temperature in the room was so high that he would be well advised to drink it before it became too warm.

After the meal – which, having anticipated that we would be too late to find any food at all, my ravenous stomach really enjoyed – the Somali Chief of Protocol announced that he must go to the docks to meet a foreign visitor arriving by ship. Tables had been reserved for us, however, in the hotel's nightclub and he hoped that the entertainment would be to our liking. This particular nightclub was housed in a spacious canvas marquee near the Indian Ocean side of the hotel and had been divided into numerous discreet sections, all with good views of the stage and dance floor.

The arrangement worked out quite well as the gentle breeze blowing through the various open entrances relieved Mogadishu's intense heat and high humidity. The only drinks available, as I remember, were bottles of Carlsberg or Heineken lager beer, served ice cold. All our passengers sat together in one of the sections – even Hans-Joachim Klein staggered down on his walking sticks to participate. We three crew members decided that having survived by the grace of God thus far, we would relax some distance away. We were all tired from the arduous flight and sneaking off to our individual rooms was uppermost in our minds.

The set-up in the nightclub was designed to discourage such behaviour and as we sat down in the gloom of the dimmed lights, in the middle of a particularly fine cabaret act by two girl singers and a male dancer, performing the latest hits from the London stage, we were virtually issued with a girl each. They just appeared, like magic, in the spare chairs at our table. The three young ladies introduced themselves and sat down gracefully at our table. They were slim, well-proportioned, almost statuesque, coffee-coloured girls who spoke perfect English and were probably the most attractive and accomplished hostesses that any of us had met anywhere in Africa. They did not quite merit the accolade of 'drop-dead gorgeous' but in our fatigued state they came pretty close.

How they retained their attractive figures with an occupation demanding the consumption of quantities of beer each night was baffling, but there was one drawback to their company. They had been schooled that their temporary partners *must* have at least one dance with them when the dance music was playing.

It may not appear to have been much of an imposition, depending on one's state of mind at the time, but after midnight, following a day like ours and a heavy meal with wine, even one dance needed superhuman effort.

The girls were at great pains to make clear that they were not prostitutes and any advances in that direction would have been futile, unlikely though this may seem. To support them in their claim of chastity, local policemen were much in evidence outside the club, armed with guns and baseball bats. Even the professed Don Juan, Carlos, and his group were seen to leave the marquee without Somali female accompaniment. At one stage the badly injured Hans Joachim-Klein was noticed attempting to dance with one of the girls using his walking sticks for support – and he was stone cold sober at the time, which speaks volumes for the girls' powers of persuasion.

Eventually, sleep became essential, so we sloped off to bed.

The following day we slept late and I was awoken by the Libyan Ambassador to Somalia, who invited me down for a coffee and asked if we could take three Palestinians back with us and drop them off in Baghdad, Iraq.

The northerly route back home, via Baghdad, Istanbul and Athens, was only a few miles more than the southerly route that we had chosen, inbound to Mogadishu. It therefore made very little difference from an aviation standpoint, so I took out the charts and we discussed the distances involved. I explained that we would need to refuel between Mogadishu and Baghdad and suggested that the most convenient suitable airfield appeared to be Jeddah, in Saudi Arabia. However, the severely unstable weather that had smashed into us between Entebbe and Mogadishu was now centred close to the Red Sea and I would be unwilling, I told him, to consider planning a landing in Jeddah in these meteorological conditions without having extra fuel on board for possible emergencies. The precaution, I suggested, was an extra landing in Aden to refuel – a decision, it subsequently transpired, that saved us from disaster.

He agreed with my suggestions and offered to arrange diplomatic clearances for the flight. Subsequent events showed that he should really have checked with the proposed passengers, because as well as the dice being heavily loaded against us due to the probable weather, his confirmation of Jeddah as a suitable refuelling stop very nearly conspired to have us all killed because of other serious problems as yet unknown to me – there were much safer alternative airfields that would have been available to us, given fuller information. This was yet another example of the folly of being forced to take decisions about a flight with the important details withheld, supposedly for security reasons. It does nobody any favours to be secretive and clandestine if you are also very dead.

In this murky world of intrigue and deception that we were presently plunged into, nobody volunteered any more than they were absolutely forced to reveal. Information was judged to be on a need-to-know basis. What people did not know could not be discussed.

'How are the passengers that we brought to Mogadishu?' I asked, only to be told that they had already left the country. The Ambassador did not comment on where they had gone, though I later deduced that they must have gone to Aden, the capital of South Yemen, 720 nautical miles north of Mogadishu. This country was heavily influenced by the Soviet Union and by then its two million population was severely regretting the departure of the British who had protected them from 1839 to 1969, when it became the only Arab Marxist state in the world. The per capita income and living conditions pre-Marxism were high, but that changed for the worse with communism.

Subsequently South Yemen descended from being a very prosperous trading nation into abject poverty. I lived and worked in and around Aden many times throughout my career in the Royal Navy and enjoyed a friendly relationship with many of its native Arabs. Returning several times whilst flying for the Libyan President, I almost invariably met someone who knew me well and was keen to recall old times.

We were asked by the Libyan Ambassador to wait until the following day to depart, so we made good use of the facilities for some welcome rest and recreation. The shallow sea near our hotel was like stepping into a warm bath, but I am never comfortable walking in shallow water in such conditions in bare feet – there are many nasty beasts prepared to bite, sting or grab the unwary foot. I much preferred swimming, even in water as shallow as a foot deep, in order to view the sea bed, coral and the activity of the many multi-coloured fish through a mask whilst breathing through a snorkel tube and using rubber flippers to propel me through the water – very quickly, if necessary.

The underwater world has always held a long-term fascination for me since my teens in the early 1950s, cruising the Mediterranean with the 2nd Minesweeping Squadron. This interest was later consolidated when my naval duties took me to the jungles of Ceylon, manning what was then a top-secret wireless station north of Colombo. The job gave me ready access to the crystal clear waters and abundant sea life of the nearby Indian Ocean.

Strangely enough the beach that we had chosen to swim from proved to be close to the Foreign Embassy district of Mogadishu and, because of the restricted visibility in the sandy water, I blundered into the rather portly Russian Ambassador who was stationary in water about a metre deep, bobbing up and down like a jumping bean and having an earnest conversation with the British and Italian

Ambassadors. I swam on after apologizing for interrupting their impromptu diplomatic meeting, which they were conducting in a language that I was unable to understand.

The following day we dutifully taxied our Falcon up to the VIP Lounge at the appointed time of 12 o'clock, but there were no passengers to be seen and no communication was possible with anyone to clarify the situation. It seemed that there was nothing for it but to find the playing cards and adopt our usual waiting mode. The first hour was taken up by a leisurely lunch provided by the Mogadishu Hotel, but it was teatime before any news was forthcoming when a Libyan Embassy messenger came to say that our passengers would be arriving in about an hour. They eventually arrived at the VIP lounge two and a half hours later carrying large heavy suitcases and canvas holdalls, which the engineer stowed in the luggage area at the front of the passenger cabin.

They did not appear to be armed, which came as a pleasant relief following the antics of our previous passengers. A small disgruntled-looking man in his mid-forties appeared to be the senior passenger, along with an older man in severely creased jacket and trousers. They were accompanied by Crumple Chops and another younger man who gave the impression of being quite frightened, though he did not seem to be under any duress from the other passengers. They all spoke English in varying degrees, but the young man's responses to my questions were noticeably monosyllabic.

My attempts to discover the passengers' names from the Ambassador were frustrated by one of his staff calling him urgently to the telephone, but names were less important with Palestinians, as already mentioned. They could legitimately have three different names and sometimes they had different passports in each name. For instance, Yasser Arafat was more often called Ben Amer, the name of his father, but if he'd had an elder son called Yousef, he could also have been called Ben Yousef. By that reasoning I could be either Neville C. Atkinson, or Ben Richard, my father, or perhaps Ben Nigel, my son. Some of the more clandestine Arabs deliberately used this triple identity anomaly to cause the utmost confusion.

The two-hour flight to Aden was conducted in perfect weather and we landed at Khormaksar International Airport, on the southern tip of the Arabian Peninsula as darkness was falling. Whilst the Falcon was being refuelled our four passengers stretched their legs walking around the plane and chatting amiably to each other. Sure enough, when I climbed the steps to the top of the control tower, where I had spent the better part of 100 or so hours during my naval aviation days, the local controller, Omar, came rushing over with a cry of 'Neville!' as my feet reached the top step. Hugs, kisses and the odd tear followed as we recalled old times.

'Do you have as much air traffic as when we were here?' I asked him.

'When you were here we handled between a hundred and a hundred and fifty aircraft a day. Now,' he said, 'we are lucky to see ten, even on a busy day.'

'What a shame, for an airfield with a two and a half-mile, high loading, wide runway with infrastructure to match. That's less than one an hour.' He agreed and said that the powers that be could change their minds five times in one day and cancel all their decisions the next. 'For anyone aiming for maximum efficiency and safety,' he said, 'it is completely frustrating.'

He commented that our flight to Jeddah could become very interesting indeed, with some atrocious weather being forecast. 'If you look north from here,' he said, 'you will see a lot of very lively lightning illuminating the night sky and the whole system slowly moving eastwards. At the moment Jeddah is in the clear, but the wind is at right angles to the runway and increasing. You should not hang around if you're aiming to spend the night there.'

Taking his advice, I did not hang about and we were soon climbing into the sky with alacrity. Fortunately we were immediately cleared to 45,000 feet and it looked as if we might be able to skirt around the worst of the weather to the east. With Hodeida, the port of North Yemen, visible below us it seemed that we were going to be lucky, but anything could happen in the next 1,500 nautical miles. Leaving the flying and the radio to the tender mercies of the Omega navigation system, the auto-pilot and the co-pilot I walked into the cabin to discuss the potential problems that might lie ahead with the senior passenger.

I gave him a chart and showed him the port of Hodeida, slightly out to the right below the Falcon, and discussed at length my proposed route to Baghdad. He seemed only partially interested. When I asked for his name and those of the rest of the passengers in case we were asked for them by Air Traffic Control, he seemed slightly upset and fished his hand into his pocket, pulling out about a dozen passports. He almost threw them onto the table towards me, saying, 'Take your pick.' I examined the first three red diplomatic passports that all had his photograph, clearly stating that he was embassy staff of different countries around the Middle East, with each name different. Whether all the other passports were his I failed to discover, because he scooped them all up into his right hand, rather tetchily, and replaced them in his jacket pocket.

I asked what my response should be if we were questioned about the identity of my four passengers and he replied that I should let him know when such information was requested. This was a most unusual situation, but it was obviously not going to be easy to discover my passengers' identities and this particular one was becoming upset with my questioning. Reluctantly, I bade him goodbye and returned to the cockpit.

The engineer/steward, who had been unconsciously eavesdropping on my conversation, stood between we two pilots and quietly commented on my failure to discover his identity. I suggested that the passengers may be hungry and it might be a good move to serve them their evening meal. He agreed and by the way they launched into the food, it looked as if it was their first meal of the day. No sooner had they drained the last of their coffee, when one by one they drifted off into fitful sleep with a great deal of snoring, allowing the engineer to join us in the cockpit as we made our way north along the Red Sea's easterly coast.

About an hour and a half later and without warning, we suddenly hit some moderate clear-air turbulence, no doubt associated with the forecast bad weather. The 'Fasten Seat Belts' signs had to be illuminated and the Engineer had to check that all the passengers' seat belts were secured, which meant waking up the crotchety quartet. Jeddah Control informed me that their weather was rapidly deteriorating and that a moderate sandstorm had hit them from the east, but that the visibility was assessed at 1,000 metres at the present time and the airfield would remain open for as long as possible. Twenty minutes later, they contacted us again to say that the sandstorm was now 90 degrees across the runway and that the wind strength had increased to 60 knots, with gusts of up to 70. Visibility had fallen to less than 20 metres and they were intending to close the airfield to all landings and take-offs until the storm abated.

Without further ado I elected to divert from my current position to Riyadh, Saudi Arabia's capital, which although it was 500 nautical miles further east, was still just within our safe range. At 45,000 feet we were flying at the most efficient altitude and our speed was the optimum for maximum range, so nothing needed changing. All our calculations, however, were checked and double-checked. A forced landing at night in the Saudi Arabian desert, possibly in a sandstorm and without the benefit of engines, did not appeal to any of us.

Provided that Dassault's published fuel-flow figures for the Falcon 20 were accurate, that Riyadh Air Traffic Control did not force us into any unnecessary scenic tours of the countryside and that we were allowed to approach their airfield in a gentle descent, we would have sufficient fuel on board to carry out a safe landing. We were, however, operating in a part of the aircraft's 'flight envelope'[2] that few pilots willingly choose to explore.

I did not declare a fuel emergency because as long as everything went 'as

---

[2] The 'flight envelope' is a graphical depiction of all the safe operating parameters discovered in the original flight testing of a new aircraft before it comes into service. It displays range and endurance figures at various altitudes, acceptable centre of gravity movements allowed and a great deal of other technical data.

published' we did not have an emergency, although such a declaration would be the next option if any further problems occurred. The senior passenger was asked to come up to the cockpit for me to explain why we were unable to land in Jeddah and what my intentions were under these circumstances. He was not overjoyed with the news, but I was unable to find any logical reason for his discontent. We had always planned to land in Jeddah, which was almost on a straight line to his requested destination, so a change to another airfield in the same country should not create a problem. After all, it was only a refuelling stop and would take at most half an hour. The Saudis were known to be very efficient with petroleum products – after all, they were sitting on a virtual underground lake of the crude product, so there was little about jet fuel that they did not understand.

About half an hour later the engineer came up to the cockpit and said that he thought that I should come back and see what was happening in the cabin. Engineers do not make such requests lightly, especially not when the pilots are grappling with a potential emergency, so I jumped out of my seat and walked back into the cabin. 'Alarm' is not an extreme enough word to describe accurately my reaction to the picture that met me as I strolled into the cabin.

The passengers had removed some of their baggage from the luggage holder at the front of the aircraft and were unpacking a veritable armoury of weapons, and readying them for use. There was all that might be needed to start a mini war, including hand grenades and explosive devices, rocket launchers and automatic weapons in a variety of sizes and calibres.

'What's this all about?' I asked somewhat foolishly in as forceful a voice as I could muster. 'What on earth do you intend to use all this weaponry for?'

I felt somewhat like a schoolmaster who had stumbled upon a group of schoolchildren lighting up cigarettes behind the bike shed and struggling to find the right words.

The senior passenger looked at me as if I was a piece of dirt that he had just discovered on his shoe. Wadi Hadad, the leader of the notorious Popular Front for the Liberation of Palestine (PFLP) –as I later discovered the senior passenger to be – was rather lost for words for a minute. He looked almost sheepish and a little guilty. He came up to me with some hand-gun or other firmly gripped in his right hand and conspiratorially placed his other hand gently on my right shoulder.

The whole scene had a strong resemblance to a Mafia thriller where the Don Corleone of the group had discovered that his partner had double-crossed him and was gently pulling the guilty man towards him, before he raised his other hand and blew the traitor's brains out. Fortunately for me this was not his actual intention. He explained in a quiet voice, so that only I could hear him, that when we landed in Riyadh the Saudis would certainly kill them – reason unspecified –

so the four of them were intending to go down the aircraft steps blazing away with every weapon they possessed and kill as many Saudis as possible.

It took a few seconds for this scenario to sink in, finally penetrating my brain that after succeeding to deliver this bunch safely onto the ground, my crew and I were destined to die in a withering hail of bullets – Saudi or PFLP, it made little difference. Wadi Hadad was seriously suggesting that all this was about to happen within the next ten or fifteen minutes.

'Just hold fire,' I said. 'Why on earth do you imagine that the Saudis will want to kill you?'

'They don't like us,' he replied.

'Well, I don't like lecherous creeps chatting up my attractive wife, but I don't automatically solve the problem by vaporizing them with maximum firepower.'

'It's no good trying to change our minds,' – meaning *his* mind– we will hold our fire long enough for you to get clear before we start firing.'

That assurance gave me no consolation whatsoever. If this proposed 'war' ever started, as he seemed sure that it would, our three lives would not be worth a candle. After all, he had made it clear that he did not like us in the first place, so why should we be spared? I did not like this little man and I certainly did not trust him to keep his promises, so an alternative must be found that avoided the seemingly inevitable bloodbath.

'Please wait while I explore what alternatives might still be open to us,' I said and hastily returned to the cockpit.

The co-pilot asked what the problem had been, so I told him that our senior passenger was giving every indication that he was stark raving mad. Unless we could come up with an alternative to landing in Riyadh, he was organizing himself to start the Third World War. Then, realizing that I was alarming my colleague I changed tack. Picking up the aeronautical charts, I asked if there was anywhere else that we could land other than Riyadh.

'Not with this fuel state,' he said, pointing to the fuel gauges, which were indicating perilously close to zero.

'Let's not give up hope yet,' I encouraged him. 'That bastard is not going to fill either of us full of lead if I can help it. How far is Bahrain away from Riyadh?'

'Along the civil airway, or direct?' he asked.

'Direct,' I replied.

His dividers flew along the line on the chart and he announced that it was pretty close to 250 nautical miles. Thinking back to my time fighting SAM II missiles over Cairo in this very same Falcon a few years before, I remembered that the fuel consumption with the engines set to idle power was very low indeed. Unfortunately the Falcon 20's operating manual gave no official figures for fuel flow in closed-throttle, glide conditions so I had to base my calculations on memory alone.

Two minutes later, after frantic scribbling on a navigation sheet, I announced that I believed that if we closed the throttle on both engines there and then, and if Bahrain permitted us to glide straight towards them, we could just about make it to the end of the runway. We would perhaps lose both engines taxiing into the dispersal, but even that prospect was better than us all ending up with ventilation holes from head to toe. We all agreed that the plan could work given a fair wind and moderate luck so Wadi Hadad was summoned to the cockpit.

'We are very short of fuel,' I informed him, 'but we have calculated that it might just be possible to make Bahrain. Would that be acceptable to you, and would that avoid your proposed holocaust?'

After a couple of minutes of silence, with a perplexed look on his face, he replied that if none of them needed to leave the aeroplane whilst it was refuelling in Bahrain, that would be acceptable. As he left the cockpit he turned and asked where Bahrain was on the chart. This shattered me. This organizer of death and destruction all over the Middle East, in numerous countries both Arab and otherwise, did not appear to know where one of those countries was geographically situated. I showed him on my navigational chart and he thanked me as he returned to his seat.

The engineer reported that they were packing their arsenal back in the bags and stowing them in the luggage compartment. One serious problem appeared to be improving, but it was left to me to arrange a landing in faraway Bahrain without going down into the Arabian Gulf on the way.

Informing Riyadh Control that the flight was being diverted to Bahrain, I requested an immediate handover to Bahrain Air Traffic Control.

'Don't you like our fuel?' he joked, but without waiting for my reply cleared us to contact Bahrain Control on their airfield frequency.

Mercifully a cockney voice replied to my opening radio call and I realized that the Royal Air Force still operated the control tower in this key Gulf international airport. He instructed me to squawk 2135 on the Falcon's radio transponder, which enhanced our radar return on his screen. 'Got you,' he almost intoned, 'you are twenty miles south of Riyadh at forty-five thousand feet, there is no conflicting traffic and I have no inbound aircraft other than yourselves at this time.'

'Thank you,' I replied. 'I would like to declare an emergency. We will be very short of fuel by the time we reach your field and I would like to commence an immediate gradual descent, and continue it right on to the end of your runway.'

'You are cleared as requested and we will do all we can to assist you. I have you in firm contact and you have 235 miles to run. Our weather is fine with fifteen knots of wind right down the runway and unlimited visibility. You will be clear for a straight-in approach from your present position.'

What comforting words they were. There was somebody left in the world who was actually doing his best to help us. We could not ask for more.

It was a great relief and I allowed myself to think that perhaps we would make it safely onto the ground after all, barring unforeseen problems. Our fuel gauges showed that we had less than 240 lb of fuel remaining and we were burning the precious liquid at our rate of descent at an indicated 6 lb per minute. Our gliding speed, with engines set to flight idle, gave us approximately forty minutes to engines stopped. Unfortunately the near end of the runway was forty-five minutes' flying time away. Both of us pilots repeated the calculations over and over again, but whichever way we checked the calculations we always ended up in the sea a few hundred yards short of the runway.

I felt cold sweat dripping down my back as I coaxed the Falcon onwards without using any harsh control movements that would increase the drag and hence increase the fuel consumption. Thinking back to the Dassault factory near Bordeaux, where I had explored the inside of the fuel tanks with the company test pilots, I remembered the Chief Pilot, Bernard, showing me half a dozen little nooks and crannies that had been formed inside the tanks when they were fitted inside the wing. He had said, 'Remember Neville, all those little pockets contain fuel and the gauges do not allow for them. There are probably about six or seven gallons of ungauged fuel there altogether and that's the best part of fifty pounds after the gauges read zero.' I fervently hoped that he was correct, as we fought to make the end of the runway at Bahrain that night.

The controller helped us as much as he could, but there was only so much he could do to influence events. We were now coming down to factors like the weight of the aircrew and passengers. I looked at the co-pilot and realized that he was a hefty young man – but at least we only had four passengers, which made us a little bit lighter than the typical Falcon for which the figures were worked out, thereby slightly increasing our potential range. 'Did you polish the wings at Mogadishu,' I asked the engineer, because a shiny clean aircraft uses less fuel for a given distance than a dirty aircraft. I really was searching for any crumbs of comfort but there were very few.

Suddenly a voice interrupted my calculations. 'You are just passing thirty miles at five thousand feet and I am increasing the intensity of my runway lights. Can you see the runway?' the controller asked.

'Yes, bright and clear,' I was pleased to reply.

'I will decrease the intensity of the lights as you approach to avoid blinding you. You are clear to land, the wind is a steady twelve knots straight down the runway and the surface is dry.' I kept the undercarriage and flaps housed until the last few yards to avoid increasing the drag unnecessarily early, but the kiss as we smoothed our dear old Falcon onto that black tarmac was almost sensual.

We had made it, thank God, but the fuel gauges had been reading zero for the last few miles. As we turned to clear the runway, the starboard engine gave a warning cough, but still kept rotating. It gave another two coughs as we turned towards the marshaller, who was energetically waving his marshalling bats, so I closed it down and brought the Falcon to the chocks using the port engine only. Completing the closing down checks I shouted, 'al Hamdulillah!' (something close to 'thank God'), which seemed good Arabic to use in the circumstances as I slumped back into the captain's seat very relieved indeed. We had just proved that the Falcon 20 could fly nearly 150 miles further than its operating manual claimed, but the 250-mile glide had been something of a fiddle factor on my part.

We were airborne again in 35 minutes, with full tanks of fuel and only a short distance to go, but remarkably and much to my relief the British air traffic controllers at Bahrain dispensed with the normal documentation required when an airborne emergency is called.

Bahrain to Baghdad was a two-hour flight, without incident, in smooth weather conditions. It was pleasing to see a Range Rover draw up alongside us as we stopped outside the main airport building. The driver and his passenger, who appeared to be Palestinian, unloaded our passengers' luggage and drove out of Baghdad's international airport with all our passengers. The driver's words and body language seemed to convey to me that having the leader of the PFLP suddenly dumped on them in the middle of the night was not a prospect that they found attractive. There was certainly no joy in their welcome of the man who must have been their leader – none of the usual smiles, kisses, hugs or even handshakes, just a rather melancholy slouch as they closed the car doors and disappeared.

Neither we nor any other member of Special Flight ever saw Carlos or Wadi Hadad again, which was just how we liked it. Two years later, in March 1978, Wadi Hadad – the 49-year-old leader of one of the world's most dangerous groups – died in an East German hospital, ostensibly of leukaemia, but rumours abounded at the time that he had been poisoned; those in the know claimed that the Iraqis were responsible. Perhaps they had not been too pleased at being forced to host such a renegade group when we delivered him to Baghdad two years earlier.

Carlos was eventually arrested by the French DST under most clandestine circumstances, in the Ibn Khaldoun hospital in Khartoum on Saturday 13 August 1993. He had been undergoing a painful operation on his right testicle at the time and before he had fully recovered from the general anaesthetic, he found himself being whisked away, with the Sudanese government's connivance, in a French government Fan-Jet Falcon 20 similar to the one in which we had flown him from Algiers to Mogadishu seventeen years earlier.

According to the official DST report he was apprehended at Villacoublay military airbase outside Paris, which just shows that intelligence services can say anything to justify their actions, with scant regard to the truth in any situation. The reason given for his arrest was that he did not have a passport or any identity documents. The fact that he was trussed up like a chicken at the time, inside a narrow sack, with two hoods over his head, does not appear to have been worthy of mention. Inevitably Carlos's past actions subsequently earned him a life sentence which he is currently serving in isolation in a French jail.

After dropping our unwelcome passengers in Baghdad, we debated whether to rest in the Iraqi capital or press on, unanimously deciding that it would be preferable to put some distance between ourselves and these epitomes of evil. We therefore elected to fly on to Istanbul before seeking a bed. The Hilton, off Taxim Square in the heart of Istanbul, provided us with the comfort and safety so badly needed and everyone slept the sleep of the exhausted until 2 o'clock in the afternoon.

Athens was chosen for refuelling en route to Tripoli, because our friend Aristotle, the chief refueller at Athens International Airport, could be relied upon to fill the tanks without too many awkward questions about the flight details, while the food provided by their VIP catering section was definitely of gourmet standard. The Greeks sent us on our way with the minimum of fuss, fully replenished, but we all felt a great sense of relief as the coast of Libya peeped its head above the horizon. The landfall in our home country was between Cyrene and the partially sunken Roman city of Apollonia. During their occupation in 630 BC the ancient Greeks named this part of Cyrenaica 'the Land of Milk and Honey', because of its fertile soils and the ideal climate that provided abundant harvests.

It was evening before I taxied Alpha Golf into Special Flight's secure hangar at Tripoli airport – the relief felt by everyone at being safely home was palpable. After relaxing and enjoying huge dollops of tender loving care from our respective families, we all woke up the next morning with a surprising and mysterious 'flu-like infection that took us about a week to shake off. The severe stress and nervous tension involved in carrying some of the world's most notorious terrorists had taken its inevitable toll.

Looking back at the flight, it had been a complete nightmare from its beginning to our eventual final release in Baghdad.

I just hoped that Sheikh Yamani of Saudi Arabia, Jamshid Amouzegar of Iran and most of the other oil ministers on board that Austrian DC9 appreciated the magnitude of what had been done for them. Even Carlos – if his word can be trusted – confirmed to me that he had ignored Wadi Hadad's order to execute these two oil ministers, purely because I had made their reprieve my premier demand in return for flying his team to Mogadishu.

I include in this statement the other oil ministers, as I later discovered that Carlos's explosives expert had placed plastic explosive under the seats of Sheikh Yamani and Jamshid Amouzegar in the DC9 and had wired their detonators to a remote control in Carlos's possession. It is difficult to see how such explosive charges could possibly have been detonated inside a medium-sized aircraft without blowing everyone on board to kingdom come – and all the other ministers, I was told, were still on board at that time. No acknowledgement of our sacrifice during those horrendous six days has ever been made.

It is possible that some might be tempted to criticize my actions in agreeing to fly these evil people, and my methods of establishing what might seem to have been an almost friendly relationship with the various passengers during the flights. To them, I would say that my sole intention at the outset was to save the lives of the oil ministers, in the situation described to me by the Algerian President and later by Carlos himself. As the flight progressed, it became necessary to take actions to preserve the lives of my crew. On each occasion I took what I considered to be the safest course, to the best of my ability.

CHAPTER TEN

Lost Political Opportunities

Our arrival in Libya in the early years of the Revolutionary Command Council's administration gave us the opportunity to observe the political posturing of the world's powers as they adapted to the new realities of post-monarchy Libya. My observations arose from privileged discussions with the country's new leaders, but Lesley's – amongst the shopkeepers, garage owners and ordinary Libyan people with whom she came into daily contact – were no less relevant and confirmed the overall picture that I could clearly see.

A major factor much in evidence during our early days in the country was an underlying pro-British sentiment that was deep-seated within the Libyan psyche. Consideration of the recent past partially explained this– after all, during the Second World War our Eighth Army had removed the belligerent Germans who treated them abominably, and the long-hated Mussolini and his Italians had also been efficiently ejected. They largely forgave us for installing a partially corrupt and inefficient monarchy, but now that what they regarded as an unfortunate mistake had been corrected by the Revolutionary Command Council's 1 September revolution, it was our commercial honesty that appeared to impress them.

Generally, if a British company signed a contract for work, the job was subsequently completed on time, on budget and commissions to intermediaries were kept down to an acceptable level. Furthermore, the British had a reputation for maintaining their installations long after completion, without rip-off charges being imposed, even if such maintenance had not been part of the original signed contract. Whereas contracts with our commercial competitors were frequently seen to overrun on cost, and rarely finished on time, if any work outside that already contracted was subsequently needed to keep the installation operating efficiently, massive and unfair charges were often imposed. The competitors' habit of winning contracts by paying large commissions to swing the decisions in their favour could not be kept secret for very long and caused untold resentment amongst Libyans.

However, the above facts only partially explained the pro-British ethos that we encountered and the remaining reasons may be difficult to accept, considering our colonial track record. The ordinary Libyan man in the street – or indeed, in the desert – liked working with our engineers, designers and oilfield roustabouts because we treated them as equals and if they lacked knowledge of a particular expertise, we started with the very basics and taught them, right there on the ground, without making a big deal about anyone's shortcomings.

Another desirable attribute that we offered, almost as an incidental by-product, was that we spoke English, which most people in Libyan commerce realized was essential in the modern world. Whilst working alongside our people they improved their grammar and pronunciation, considered by them to be very useful for future employment.

The French were the next in preference as working partners, but they were treated with much more suspicion because of their active and current colonial activities in neighbouring African countries. Another couple of apparent problems with working with the French was the excessive price that they often quoted for their work, and their reluctance to speak either English or Arabic. Studying the French language was regarded by Libyans to be somewhat of a useless exercise in the context of international commerce to which the North Africans generally aspired.

Nevertheless, it was recognized that the French produced some very fine civil and military aircraft and around this time there was a period when French aircraft were preferred against the products of most other countries. In my opinion, this was a sound aviation decision. At that time their aircraft were robust, easy to maintain and very reliable in desert conditions, while their cost was competitive compared to the United States, British, German and Italian aircraft of a similar category that were on offer. Little wonder that the Libyans chose manufacturers like Dassault and Aérospatiale for many of their civil and military needs. Our own original aircraft in Special Flight were, indeed, Avions Marcel Dassault Fan-Jet Falcon 20s which, at the time of their acquisition, were probably the finest business jets available anywhere in the world.

Air France had also gained the contract for running and providing the aircrew and some of the aircraft for the Libyan national carrier, Libyan Arab Airlines, but this had been a follow-through of their existing contract during King Idris's time.

Prior to the 1 September revolution, most of the country's income came from handouts negotiated with the various oil companies, which had concessions to extract crude oil from the Libyan desert. Only a small proportion of the value of such exports remained in Libya and by the time these meagre revenues had navigated the complexities of corruption and bureaucracy that were deep-seated within the so-called oil ministry, precious little remained to improve the lot of the ordinary Libyan citizen. Indeed, these anomalies, the squandering of the country's resources and a pervading air of general administrative corruption were at the seat of the perceived reasons for the 1 September revolution.

I am not making the case that King Idris was a bad ruler, or that any of the Royal Family was necessarily corrupt, but rather that the administration that this 85-year-old man presided over appeared to be inept and incapable of running such a huge country efficiently. Libya covered over 1.7 million square kilometres, many times the size of the British Isles, had a population of under three million largely rural people, and the King was not versed in anything approaching modern concepts of government. He came to power as the choice of the British Government in 1950. Since 1916 he had been the leader of the important desert tribe, the Sanussi, who had close links with the Mahdi of Khartoum – the man whose army defeated and killed Britain's General Gordon in Khartoum on 26 January 1885.

The mainstay of the King's government had been the Shalhi family who, by 1969, had manoeuvred themselves into widespread positions of power. The King's prime confidant had been Busairi al Shalhi, who until April 1964 had been the King's official adviser and Court Chamberlain, but was removed from the scene when he spectacularly smashed his Ferrari at high speed into a heavily loaded 'Calabrese' lorry on one of the tortuous mountain roads south of Tripoli.

Rumours of assassination abounded, largely because Busairi's father, Ibrahim al Shalhi, had been murdered in a Benghazi street in October 1954 by a nineteen-year-old Sanussi prince who resented his influence with their religious and tribal leader, King Idris – the forty-fourth descendant in a direct line from the Prophet Muhammad. This meant that King Idris was the de facto leader of the entire Muslim world, a very important religious figure.

The King was distressed at the loss of his friend and adviser (who had been married to Eve Pinnock, the English daughter of a British civil servant). Busairi's pronounced anti-British sentiment is reputed to have owed much to his time at Exeter University, where he claimed that he was very badly treated. After her husband's spectacular death, in line with Muslim tradition Eve married his brother, Lieutenant-Colonel Abd al Azziz al Shalhi; but it was the other brother, Umar al Shalhi who, exactly five years after the accident, in April 1969 forsook his life as a playboy businessman and stepped into Busairi's shoes as 'royal councillor', the King's closest adviser.

With the appointment of Lieutenant-Colonel Abd al Azziz al Shalhi to command the Cyrenaican Defence Force (CDF), essentially the Royal Praetorian Guard, a force that considerably outnumbered the Libyan Army, the Shalhis' power base was becoming impregnable. For the second time the eighty-year-old King Idris announced his intention to abdicate, which encouraged the Shalhis to consolidate their prime position for seizing power, by drawing the Libyan Police under their direct influence.

In the event, the whole apparently corrupt Shalhi organization came crashing to the ground when twelve junior army officers seized power in a bloodless coup at 2 a.m. on 1 September 1969. King Idris and Umar al Shalhi were relaxing in a hotel in Bursa, north-west Turkey, on the Sea of Marmara, when news of the successful revolution reached them. The King refused the new administration's offer for him to return home as an 'honoured citizen', and instead flew to Cairo via Athens, where he was welcomed and granted asylum by Egypt's leader, Gamel Abdul Nasser.

Umar al Shalhi immediately dashed to London to see Michael Stewart, the British Foreign Secretary, to request overt intervention to reinstate the King. His idea of Britain launching an aggressive attack on Libya from its leased bases in the country, with the aim of reinstating King Idris, was a wild suggestion that found no political sympathy whatsoever. He therefore flew to New York, intending to make his proposals to Spiro T. Agnew, Nixon's Vice-President. The State Department blocked his efforts to reach any influential politician, but – rightly or wrongly – he left the US convinced that a covert operation funded by himself would not be opposed by the United States.

From his base in Geneva he therefore financed and launched an abortive counter-coup attempt, which originated at Bridge of Allan in Scotland on 9 August 1970 and was finally stopped in April 1971 when Italian Intelligence arrested the conspirators at the Adriatic port of Trieste. The murky world of espionage, counter-espionage, double-cross and murder – which threads through the whole of Umar al Shalhi's plot – is covered by two ex-*Observer* journalists, Patrick Seale and Maureen McConville, in their excellent 1973 book, *The Hilton Assignment*. The title arose from the local Libyan name for Tripoli's main jail, 'the Tripoli Hilton'.

The plot was apparently known about by the American CIA, Britain's MI6, the Russian KGB and certainly by Libya's Revolutionary Command Council, as well as several of the smaller intelligence establishments around the rest of Europe, so who finally blew the whistle and brought the whole thing to an end is anybody's guess. I have no extra knowledge, neither have I discussed this period in Libyan politics with any of the main players, so my views are purely personal.

Shortly after this period, my family and I appeared on the scene in Tripoli, Libya's capital city. I had a serious job to become immersed in, but the work was interesting, enjoyable and well within my capability. Lesley relieved the load by taking full control of the inevitable domestic problems and most of the family's finances, involving me only when airline tickets were needed to convey the children to and from their respective schools. She relished the challenges that this role inevitably threw up and took great pride in dealing with the more complex problems.

Her efficient and courteous manner when dealing with our more senior passengers was obviously appreciated by them, and she was often taken into their confidence on the telephone, where complicated political problems were developing and decisions needed when I was unavailable. She eventually qualified as a supervising international air stewardess and was responsible for some of the high standards of cabin service that most of our passengers expected. Her services were always freely given and never financially rewarded.

As she became more experienced, the tasks that she was given increased to the point where on occasions she was working almost full time. When the Prime Minister decided that the inside of our Fan-Jet Falcon aircraft cabins urgently needed refurbishment, he turned to Lesley for suitable designs, giving her a free hand in the choice of materials to be used and the ergonomics of the seating. She was so successful with the Falcons that she received international acclaim for the result and was given further work in designing and commissioning the cabins of two Grumman Gulfstream IIs that the Libyan government purchased for Special Flight. This work entailed her having to fly Concorde many times to Savannah, Georgia for design and material decisions with the chosen firm, Cooper Airmotive (based at Redbird Airport, Dallas, Texas) and supervising the actual installation of the equipment chosen and the matching materials at Redbird itself.

In late 1972 Britain's diplomatic policy towards Libya was inconsistent and impossible to predict. Throughout the following five years many thousands of British and American oil company personnel worked in the country in comfortable conditions, in Benghazi, Tripoli and the many desert exploration and production oil wells. They were well liked by the Libyans with whom they worked, even if a few

Lesley supervising the finishing touches to the gulfstream cabin installations.

of them arrived off Heathrow flights in this 'dry' country as drunk as skunks. Immigration officials routinely gave the offenders a bed for the night and sent them on to the desert installations the next day, sober and embarrassed.

British businessmen arrived in the major cities seeking contracts to supply industrial machinery, portable buildings, oil exploration equipment and all the other essential requirements, including expertise, needed by a burgeoning economy. Naturally they checked in with the British Embassy for commercial advice and assistance with finding hotel beds for their stay in the country. Unfortunately when we later met these commercial executives as they tramped the streets of the city, lost and unable to meet Libya's decision makers, their overriding complaint was the lack of assistance or even interest from the Embassy. On many occasions we took these people home with us to feed them and provide beds for the night, as there was little hotel accommodation available in Tripoli itself at that time.

There did not appear to have been a commercial attaché in the British Embassy for long periods of time. Some of these captains of British industry were under the distinct impression that the previous holder of this post had left Libya without being replaced. This was an astonishing state of affairs, considering the services offered by Britain's competitors. Even little Malta had a go-getting commercial attaché in its embassy, who guided his country's business executives to all the user ministries.

A decision appeared to have been taken at very high level in the British Foreign Ministry to downgrade our country's commercial activity in Libya. And this was at a time of huge unemployment problems in the UK, where companies were regularly failing for lack of orders. Regardless of these considerations, when we discussed our experiences with members of the Embassy whom we met socially, there was an apparent attitude that commerce was not a nice subject to be discussing.

The magnitude of the work being effectively discouraged was well into the hundreds and thousands of millions of pounds in value and must have represented untold numbers of British jobs. Our country could then ill afford this cavalier attitude. To make matters worse, our broadsheet press periodically published insulting stories about the Libyan government and at times the Libyan people themselves. There was frequently little or no truth contained in the articles and several times, when I was on leave back in the UK I telephoned the editors of the papers involved and asked why they had published such patently untrue statements. Their response was always the same: 'We receive handouts from the Foreign Office periodically and if we do not publish them exactly as written, they punish the paper by withholding key future information from us. We do not have the ability to confirm the veracity or otherwise of the information that we are given.'

To be specific, the news editors I contacted on this subject were from *The*

Times, the *Daily Telegraph* and the *Observer*. The articles concerned were so inflammatory and provocative on occasions that my family sometimes seriously considered staying in Scotland on safety grounds and not returning to Libya.

When we did return as planned, not only was there no danger whatsoever, but nobody either in government or the expatriate community knew anything about the source of the story or the reasons for publishing it. This misinformation was regarded, with some justification, as entirely provocative.

There was clearly a dislike for Libya's new administration lurking somewhere in the prevailing British foreign policy. We noticed that some of the wealthier members of the King's old administration were treated remarkably well on their visits to London – on investigation they appeared to have closer ties to some of our diplomatic decision makers than was, perhaps, healthy in the circumstances. Some eventually took up residence in and around London on a more permanent basis. Many of the people to whom I refer had known members of our diplomatic corps since their schooldays at Stowe, Winchester, Eton, Harrow and other similar establishments.

The old school tie being used, through these discontented Libyans, to denigrate the new Libyan government and its leader had the effect of minimizing the innate pro-British Libyan sentiment which, handled sensibly, could have done so much for our country at a critical time in our industrial development. Damn it all, they liked us. What could possibly be gained by forcing them to *dis*like us? This backward thinking flew in the face of what diplomacy should, in my opinion, be about, the aim of which should surely be to encourage other people to like us and our nation, thereby exercising an influence that could be mutually beneficial. Commerce cannot thrive in an atmosphere of hatred and we desperately needed our expertise and products to be available on the world market. Without such demand we could not hope to survive, let alone prosper.

Regardless of the commercial suicide adopted in our diplomatic policies, it never failed to amaze me that we would apparently consciously seek to make enemies of a wealthy country capable of doing great harm to our global interests.

In about mid-1973 we seemed to take leave of our commercial and diplomatic senses completely. We were probably being leant on by America to be part of some grand plan of which I had no knowledge. Maybe some dirty backroom dealing on the international stage, of which all but a privileged few were unaware, was taking place, but about this time Britain stopped supplying military hardware to Libya and pushed her completely into the Russian camp. It was so sudden and unexpected that the move really did smack of a shady deal in which we said to Russia something like, 'We'll give you a free rein in Libya, if you wind your neck out of Cuba, Turkey and the western Balkans.'

I am not suggesting that this scenario was fact. I am almost certain, however, that there was some such arrangement at this time. My certainty was confirmed a couple of years later when I found myself in the company of the CIA Head of Station one day, and the head of the Libyan section of the Russian Secret Service, the KGB, the next day. At the same time, I flew and hosted for two days four members of the Russian Politburo, as they were introduced to me. They all indirectly referred to 'an agreement' or 'our agreement', the meaning of which was unmistakeable: some 'arrangement' would seem to have been made between the two major power blocs.

Nothing was announced, but the steady supply of Hercules transport aircraft and Chinook helicopters stopped, the re-equipping of air-to-air missiles for the predominantly French military fighters ceased, Britain's contract for Centurion tanks for the Libyan Army was terminated and countless smaller agreements for military or quasi military material were not fulfilled. The cut-off point was so sudden and unexpected that the last four C-130 Hercules which were being flight-tested for delivery to Libya were arbitrarily embargoed and left standing on the factory dispersal at Marietta, Georgia, where they remained for many years. It was impossible for the factory to reassign the aircraft to anyone else because they had already been purchased and paid for by the Libyan Air Force (which also subsequently paid for them to be kept fully serviced the whole time that they sat, like mascots, outside the Lockheed main offices, in resplendent Libyan Air Force colours).

Simultaneously, a massive amount of Russian military hardware arrived in the country. Huge numbers of MIG fighter aircraft of the latest marques were complemented by still more Sukhoi fighters and Tupolev long-range bombers, all equipped with state-of-the-art missiles. The latest Russian Army tanks arrived in such numbers that it appeared that Libya then possessed almost as many sophisticated battle tanks as the combined German, Italian and British armies deployed in the Libyan desert at the height of the Second World War.

The Russians were desperate for Libya's petrodollars and the favourable deals on offer from the Soviets may have been sufficient to cause the switch of their armed forces to Russian 'materiel', but it was done in such a way that it convinced me that some secret agreement between the major powers was involved. I only regret that I was not able to persuade anyone to allow me to strap one of the latest Russian fighters to my backside to put it through its supersonic paces. It would have been nice, but the opportunity never presented itself.

The Russian personnel who accompanied the military hardware were not very popular with the ordinary Libyan people, and lived mainly in closed camps within existing military establishments. The few Russians whom I met were pleasant enough, but they had no money of any kind and always seemed to want to sell something for cash. Most of them spoke some English, and grew exasperated with the Libyan Air Force personnel for not being careful enough with the batches of sophisticated missiles whose homing heads needed protection from the rays of the sun. One senior Russian engineer was incandescent with rage when he found that about a hundred air-to-air missiles had been ruined by storage in the full glare of the desert sun. When I talked to him at the Libyan Air Force base at Okba he told me that he was arranging for them to be shipped back to Moscow. He shouted at me that the cost of just one of these small missiles would buy him a house in Russia and keep him and his family in relative luxury for the rest of their lives. He was probably correct.

When President Gadaffi came with us he often flew in the cockpit, sitting on the less than comfortable jump-seat between the pilots. It was common practice on these occasions for us to conduct our radio communications over the cockpit loudspeakers so that he could clearly hear any instructions given to us, and our responses. The main reason for joining us in the cockpit was that he was invariably accompanied by armed bodyguards and sometimes other colleagues from the Revolutionary Command Council who talked so much, trying to impress him with their wisdom and perspicacity, that he was unable to gather his thoughts together, or complete any preparatory work.

Most of the times that I flew him he was contemplating having to make a speech to an assembled multitude as soon as he stepped from the aircraft, or very soon afterwards, and he liked to use the one or two hours available to him in the cockpit to jot down a few notes to remind him of the major points he needed to make. Very occasionally, if he was particularly pleased with a turn of phrase that he intended using in his dissertation, he would explain the context to me with a broad smile on his face, and after he had read the relevant passage would ask for my opinion.

I was always scrupulously, if tactfully, honest when asked by him for my opinion on any topic – it would have been foolhardy of me to have made critical remarks about his favourite nuggets of information, coated in humorous overlay. The need to criticize his style never, in fact, arose – which is surprising when you consider that he was writing his words in Arabic and reading them out to me in English, without losing any of the underlying meaning or style.

When he was satisfied with his notes, he usually relaxed and opened the conversation on any subject that interested him. Many of his chosen topics contained matters of a personal nature which were discussed in complete confidence; I have thus restricted my comments to subjects we discussed which I judge will not cause any embarrassment or offence.

The world's press and certainly the British press, at this time, carried out a consistent character assassination of President Gadaffi. Whenever he responded to past, current or future political and economic situations, he was mostly misquoted, sometimes misunderstood because of mistranslation of his words and almost always rudely criticized for his seemingly extreme views. If he made no such comments then the journalists involved would invariably invent some, without fear of being challenged.

In response to numerous enquiries as to my opinion about the balance of his mind during my time as Chief Pilot of Special Flight, I can truthfully say that I found him decisive, lucid, astute, incisive and a very pleasant person to be privileged to fly. If asked about his mental capacity I would certainly judge that his mind and IQ were very much above average. Those members of the press who publish denigrating articles questioning his sanity are in my view beneath contempt and the Libyans are quite correct in making no comment on these scandalous remarks.

Once he was satisfied that I would give him an honest answer to an honest question and not chicken out with a safe reply that I expected him to like – as most of his entourage were accustomed to doing – he would ask me a straight question that I could not avoid.

On one occasion, on a flight to Tobruk, he asked me what in my opinion the British people thought of him. There was absolutely no way to sugar the pill, so I turned, looked him in the face from a distance of about six inches and replied that the British people generally hated him intensely.

'Why?' came his surprised response.

My mind rapidly considered my future with no job. 'Because,' I replied, 'you are providing arms to the IRA that are used to kill their fathers, brothers and sons, not to mention the ordinary people of Northern Ireland, in large numbers.'

He said he understood that the IRA were freedom fighters, and there followed a moderately heated discussion over the next thirty minutes during which I did my best to outline the true situation of 'The Troubles' in the Province calmly, but as forcefully as I could manage. He countered my arguments with points that had obviously originated from some persuasive representatives of the IRA, with little regard for the truth and some very advanced blarney, where religious freedom was heavily confused with statements about the majority being downtrodden by the minority and with the brutal British Army squashing the ordinary people under their boots. I did my very best to set the record straight and portray the mess that was Northern Irish politics in a clear and truthful manner.

Eventually, one of us changed the subject to a more light-hearted one and we discussed the realities of our life in Tripoli. I remembered that one of the Tripoli expatriates had asked me if I ever had the chance to enquire of either the President or the Prime Minister if the issue of alcohol from the Tripoli duty-free store to eligible expatriates would take place before Christmas, as had happened the two previous years. He gave a rather non-committal response that he expected so and then frowned as he asked, 'Why do you want to know about alcohol? You have my full permission to have as much as you need.' I smiled and thanked him, saying that I had heard the rumour, but that his words now made it official. He grinned amiably.

The truth about our unique permission to have alcohol in Libya wasn't quite as simple as that because although we kept alcohol in our houses, the pilots and engineers of Special Flight were rarely able to consume anything beyond the odd can of beer since we could be called out to fly at any time of the day or night, 365 days a year. The slightest sniff of alcohol on our breath would certainly have been detected by our non-drinking passengers and as aircrew are banned from flying after consuming the dreaded liquid, the prospect would not have been very favourable.

We delivered the President and his entourage to Tobruk as requested and returned to Tripoli without any other passengers.

On the return, empty leg, my co-pilot offered his opinion that the conversation with President Gadaffi was a very tricky one, particularly when I had announced that he was sending arms to the IRA and followed that statement up with a full-scale protracted argument on the subject. The co-pilot said that he had looked around the cockpit for a little hole that he might be able to climb into.

'Perhaps it would be better not to unpack your case too quickly in Tripoli,' he advised. You might need to leave Libya in a hurry and not have time to repack it again.'

'That was not my assessment,' I said. 'The President was inviting me to give my opinion and I feel quite strongly about the subject, so as I was never likely to have such an opportunity again, I decided to give it my best shot. He can totally ignore me if he chooses, but at least he is now aware of what the ordinary British citizen thinks.'

'We'll soon find out,' was his reply; and sure enough we did not have long to wait.

Five days later I was called to the VIP lounge and found that my main passenger was again the President. As we waited outside the lounge the Libyan Chief of Protocol, Abu Shagour, came aboard and asked me to come with him as President Gadaffi wished to see me.

The VIP lounge was empty apart from the country's leader. He waved me towards his table and invited me to sit down. Two cool bitter sodas arrived and after the steward had retired, he looked me in the eye and said that he had been giving my arguments about the IRA a great deal of consideration. 'We have taken the decision, as a result,' he said, 'to terminate all supplies of military materials to Ireland and everyone concerned has been informed of that decision.'

He obviously expected a response from me, so I thanked him. I may have burbled some other inanity, but there did not seem to be anything else for me to say regarding this momentous announcement. 'Should I inform the British Embassy?' I asked. He said that I could tell them of the Libyan decision, but that he did not wish to be interviewed on the subject and thought it probably best to play the whole thing down.

Eventually, a car arrived outside the VIP lounge with two passengers and the President led the way on board the Falcon with Sharif Ben Amer and what I took to be an armed bodyguard. At the top of the steps, on embarking, President Gadaffi removed the magazine from his gun and pulled back the cocking handle, thereby ejecting a round from the firing chamber, which he picked up and dropped into his jacket pocket. The poor bodyguard attempted to do the same, but was not quite as slick. As he removed the weapon's magazine he managed to spray several rounds onto the crew's baggage in the luggage compartment. As he ejected the final round from the breech of his weapon it flew just past Sharif Ben Amer's right ear, where it landed at the back of the cabin.

The sight of this tall, athletic, young uniformed bodyguard on his hands and knees grovelling around the floor of the aircraft to retrieve his wayward bullets was hilarious and both the President and his senior adviser collapsed into peals of laughter at the incongruous sight. When, just after take-off, our engineer served the passengers three of the fine French meals that we had brought with us, one of them pointed to the bodyguard and shouted, 'Be careful if you give him a cup of hot coffee – he might throw it all over the floor!' By this time the bodyguard had recovered his composure and accepted the comment with nonchalant equanimity.

We were flying east en route to Benghazi and as we passed the oil refinery at Marsa Brega three quarters of the way across the Gulf of Sirte, I went back into the cabin to ascertain what our main passenger would like us to do after landing at Benghazi. He told me that they were having a meeting in the VIP lounge and should be ready to return to Tripoli around sunset. The mood in the cabin was very relaxed as if they were travelling to meet a group of old friends, which could well have been the case.

Taxiing towards the VIP lounge, I disturbed a magnificent group of about twenty lavishly dressed camels, some of them pure white, so I dispensed with the engines earlier than usual and freewheeled to a stop without causing the camels

Our Falcons on the Benghazi Road near the President of Libya's home at Sirte.

undue panic. The robed riders had dismounted and took up positions either side of the approach path into the building and as their President and Sharif Ben Amer walked into the lounge a restrained murmur of welcome greeted our passengers. Later, after the Falcon had been prepared for its return to Tripoli, half a dozen of these senior Bedouin sauntered out of the building and asked to look inside the aircraft. We provided a series of guided tours around the outside and into the cockpit. Maybe I misjudged the situation, but it seemed probable that this was the first time that most of them had been inside a flying monster. They were proud people and were not about to appear overly impressed with this modern machinery. After their tour we invited them into the cabin and the engineer provided everyone with cool soft drinks. Three of them even managed a few words of English, intermingled with their normal guttural Arabic. It did not take a genius to realize that these smartly robed Bedouin were inherent leaders of men, who probably wielded infinite power amongst their own desert people.

As they started to walk back to the meeting, one of the English speakers asked us if we would like to see their transport, pointing towards the camels. We three aircrew eagerly accepted and walked over to the beautifully obedient animals, sitting together on some clear sand near to the lounge. When we had reviewed the finely groomed camels and remarked at their sparkling leather harness and saddles, each of us was asked to choose one to climb aboard. We were not strangers to sitting on camels, but none of us could claim to be experts. As we rose into the air on three of the tall white animals, each of us spied the modern rifles stowed handily alongside the saddles. Our questions about the need for such lethal armament fell on stony ground and we failed to discover the necessity for such weaponry. A suitable photograph was taken to record the scene for posterity.

When the meeting was finished, they all came outside the ornate Benghazi VIP lounge and said their farewells to our passengers. They mounted their camels for the return home, wherever home happened to be in the thousands of miles of the Sahara Desert to the south. As we climbed away from Benghazi's main runway and turned our nose towards the west, we could clearly see the line of camels and their white-robed riders passing the British war cemetery on the Benghazi road, following a route to bypass the main city and heading towards the countless miles of undulating yellow sand.

Our return journey took us right towards the huge ball of a bright red setting sun that, at this time, was two of its diameters above the desert, before sliding quite quickly down towards the horizon. By the time that we passed the midway point across the Gulf of Sirte, the bottom of the red globe was just touching the line of the desert. Both our main passengers came up to the cockpit in turn to gaze over to their left to see the sand, which by this time was almost as red as the setting sun itself. It was, of course, the terrain where President Gadaffi had lived, played and worked as a small boy and where his family were still living.

As we coasted in over the small town of Misratah near the ancient Roman metropolis of Leptis Magna, I glanced down at the land to my left, not knowing that in a few years' time these olive groves would be the scene of a major setback to the Libyan government that would create serious long-term difficulties.

On 4 March 1978 the Prime Minister of the German Democratic Republic (East Germany) was visiting the country and it was decided at the last minute that he should have the opportunity of meeting Libya's President. It was early evening and someone in authority must have suggested that it would be safer for the journey to Sirte, where the President was staying, to be conducted by helicopter than for them to use Special Flight's fixed-wing aircraft. Perhaps they were worried about us landing on the unlit road at night, although we had instituted procedures by that time which would have ensured everyone's safety.

When the Libyan Air Force were contacted at their air base at Okba, on the western edge of Tripoli, the only serviceable helicopter available was one of their older French Aérospatiale Super Frelon SA 321s, which had given many years of reliable service, but (as I learned later) was not cleared at that time for night operations. Nevertheless the flight took place in perfect weather, on a moonlit night, with unlimited visibility and the helicopter arrived at Sirte on time, without incident.

Preparing to take off for its return flight, a peculiar shudder shook the aircraft when the third engine was started. It was severe enough for the pilot to make a note of the vibration on his knee-pad. Later, when cruising at 1,500 feet at a leisurely 105 knots, the vibrations recurred, so the pilot reported the problem to Air Traffic Control and announced his intention of making an unscheduled landing in his current position to investigate the problem. He executed a normal landing at the edge of an olive grove about 20 miles south of Misratah, but his ability to effectively investigate such a mechanical malfunction was strictly limited. Firstly, he was not carrying a qualified engineer, secondly, he had no lighting, and thirdly, the probable area of the malfunction was higher than he could possibly reach.

The four passengers – the East German Prime Minister and his secretary, the Senior Adviser to the Libyan government, Sharif Ben Amer, and Libya's experienced Chief of Protocol, Abu Shagour – disembarked and whilst the pilot was ineffectually removing panels and replacing them, they strolled around the olive grove, enjoying the brilliant, still, moonlit night. Eventually the pilot called Air Traffic Control at his base at Okba, on his single-sideband, high-frequency radio and reported his abortive investigation. He then announced his intention of embarking the passengers and returning to Okba.

The correct action, in the circumstances, should have been for him to secure his unserviceable aircraft, organize road transport for him and his passengers back to base and arrange for an engineering team to carry out a full investigation of the malfunction in daylight. Perhaps the seniority of his passengers, or frustration at the delay and a modicum of panic clouded his judgement. Whatever the reason, he started the engines and lifted off. Five minutes later, near his cruising altitude of 1,500 feet, an explosion was heard by witnesses on the ground and the Super Frelon crashed into a field killing everyone on board.

It was a terrible waste of human life and all of it totally unnecessary. The signs were clear, the procedures were in place, but the pilot took entirely the wrong decisions. Here was a case for a verdict that invariably upsets me in the extreme. From the facts that I was given, it was a clear case of pilot error.

The world's media, invariably looking for intrigue and conspiracy theories, published wild stories that the explosion was caused by a bomb that must have been placed on board, intending to kill the President. Other theories postulated involved portable ground-to-air missiles and an army revolt, all of which was pure rubbish. The board of inquiry, which involved a team of the maker's engineers, found that the engine gearbox had disintegrated due to a crack in one of its main gearwheels. If the pilot had followed standard operating procedures and had left his helicopter on the ground, as he should have done, the fault would have been discovered the next day and easily repaired.

The loss of Sharif Ben Amer and Abu Shagour was a bitter blow to the Libyan Government and their places were almost impossible to fill completely. Two months later, the lesser post of Chief of Protocol was given to an ex-Libyan Arab Airlines manager, Nuri Masmuri, who eventually grew into the job and was never afraid of asking for our advice on difficult or unusual diplomatic situations. He had a well-developed sense of humour and frequently recruited us to help him create mild panic with bumptious junior government functionaries who were giving him a hard time.

Sharif Ben Amer was a more difficult person to replace. He was a consummate linguist, experienced, diplomatically astute, usually smiling and very pleasant to work alongside. I suppose the nearest to a replacement was more than a year later when a former civil servant called Majid el Gaoud was established in an office in the Azzizia Barracks, not far from that of the President himself. He slowly accepted more and more of the responsibilities that had formerly been Sharif Ben Amer's, but he took some time to settle completely into the very onerous duties he had been given.

My contacts within the British Embassy confirmed to me that the Libyans had terminated their arms supplies to the IRA, as indicated to me, and that this undoubted improvement was maintained for over ten years. The flow of weaponry was apparently restarted following a scathing attack in the British Press on the sanity and integrity of Libya's President and the Revolutionary Command Council, but by this time I had left the country so am unable to comment on the detail. It seems likely that the similar type of terminology used in most of the broadsheet dailies indicated that another Foreign Office briefing was behind the insulting language. What on earth were we as a country trying to achieve?

Some time later, in perhaps 1980, I was introduced socially by the head of one of the American oil companies to two smartly dressed Irishmen, whose accents betrayed their origins as either Dublin or further south. They were very personable, smooth talking, smiling gentlemen whose reasons for being in Libya were, to say the least, highly suspicious. They claimed to be businessmen, but when asked the nature of their business they giggled playfully and answered that they were involved in import/export. My enquiry as to exactly which companies they represented received ludicrous answers and when I enquired which products they were trading in, I was immediately told, 'Pharmaceuticals'. When I announced that I was interested in pharmaceuticals, they were unable to clarify the types of chemicals involved and following my enquiry as to whether their main activity was importing or exporting they became nervously embarrassed and made an excuse to move away.

Lesley and I avoided them both for the rest of the evening and I never saw them again, but I could not erase some of the phraseology they had used from my mind and I later became convinced that I had probably just spoken to the source of the misinformation that the RCC had been given years before, regarding the situation in Northern Ireland. Everything that I later learnt about these two men confirmed my first impression. It should be noted that some people are prone to referring to materials as 'pharmaceuticals' when they really mean explosives.

In the early years of Libya's new administration, President Gadaffi and the RCC really did achieve many lasting improvements for their country, which were clear for all to see. The infrastructure around the capital was upgraded and new tarmac roads were driven to the previously ignored desert towns, even as far as Sebha in the deep south. There was employment for everyone who wished to work and the poverty-stricken people who had been living in what was generally referred to as 'the cages', on the edge of Tripoli, soon found themselves occupying new houses in their home districts. What's more, they were each given the deeds to their new homes, including the land on which they were built, without charge.

Each district had a modern, newly built school for their children and if there was a shortage of qualified teachers, they were brought in from abroad. The police were modernized and their efficiency improved. New hospitals were built, the old ones modernized and to provide qualified doctors and consultants, professors arrived from England, Italy, Malta and Egypt, to teach and examine the new medical students until they achieved the highest standards of medical practice.

Libya's oil industry needed the latest technology to operate at the optimum level, so, lacking sufficient Libyan engineers, American, British and Italian oil engineers were encouraged to work in the oilfields and some of them, I understand, are happily working there to this very day. We are not talking small numbers of people employed in this industry, but rather tens of thousands.

Throughout President Gadaffi's time in power, he has waged a constant war on corruption, but it is a never-ending battle. He is assisted in these endeavours by his own rather frugal requirements, probably acquired during his childhood, living an almost Bedouin existence. Large personal bank deposits beyond one's immediate needs are not part of his concept of life. He does not yearn personally for excessive luxury, as was demonstrated to me on a flight taking him to a meeting in Sebha and an overnight stay with the intention of flying on the next day to a desert airstrip near the Tibesti Mountains.

The then Chief of Protocol, Mr Abu Shagour, showed me to my bedroom, which was a very simple room in a stone-built house, with a camp bed, no mattress, a single sheet and a tiny pillow. There was no glass in the windows and as there were mosquitoes outside I felt very vulnerable to the nasty creatures' attack. Without thinking, I told my guide that this room would not be satisfactory. I would be cold, bitten to pieces, uncomfortable and because of a perceived lack of sleep, would be unfit to fly anyone the next day.

'Hang on,' said Abu Shagour, 'this is the best room available and was the one chosen by us for President Gadaffi; but as he is expecting to be working all night, he instructed me to give his room to you. I can hardly go back to him and announce that the room is unsatisfactory, can I?' I agreed with him. In the event, sleep did come, but only after I had slaughtered a dozen flying hypodermic needles.

It is hardly surprising that the President became very popular indeed with his own people, for ordinary Libyans could see their standards of living improving before their very eyes. The courts dispensed justice that seemed fair and not too extreme. If there was a death penalty, nobody was aware of it. Expatriates who broke the law of the country by manufacturing alcohol and selling it to Libyans were summarily expelled back to their own country – not incarcerated in jail or given hundreds of lashes with a whip, as is the case in many other Muslim countries.

Sometimes the arrival in an area of their President induced extreme panic amongst local officials. One such example was a flight I made with President Gadaffi on 30 June 1976 to a small airfield near the town of Labraq in the Jebel Akhdar (Green Mountains) about seventy miles east of Benghazi. En route from Tripoli, the President again flew with us in the cockpit – probably to escape his seven-strong delegation in the cabin, who were being unusually loquacious.

There was evidently to be some kind of open-air function at which the country's leader was to make an important speech, so he scribbled away on his notepad whilst we busied ourselves with the duties of aviation. Satisfied with his notes, he closed the pad and talked to me about the state of some of the beaches near to our home on the westerly outskirts of Tripoli. After about five minutes of domestic discussion, he pitched his voice up a couple of decibels and announced that he would like me to give a message from him to the British people.

I replied that whilst I would do so if he wished, I could only relay such a message through the British Embassy in Tripoli, and that perhaps it would be better if he gave it directly to the British Embassy himself or through his own Foreign Minister. 'Impossible,' he answered and explained that successive British ambassadors had shown themselves to be too pompous for him to have any meaningful discussion.

He continued that the Libyan people regarded the British as friends and would like to work with them to everyone's mutual benefit. I was to emphasize that Libyan commerce was not inextricably linked to the Soviet bloc and that there were plenty of prime opportunities that were available for co-operation with his country. 'Your press,' he continued, 'should remember that it is a mistake to constantly discuss Libya as if it were a First World Country like Britain, France and America. We are still Third World. We're improving, but nevertheless we have no cities like Manchester, Washington, or Paris and we have insufficient resources to create such places, even if we wanted to. There must be room for co-operation, even if it is only because you need our oil.'

Realizing the importance of what he was saying, I attempted to write his words verbatim on my navigation sheet, but there was only room for about twenty of them after which I had to rely on memory. These were probably not his actual words, only my recollection of them some time later. He made more points that I cannot now recall, though I did pass on all his comments shortly afterwards to a senior official within the Embassy. There was no response whatsoever, not even an acknowledgement of my message.

During a pause in the conversation I remarked to the President that most of the military leaders of African countries were generals, yet he had remained a colonel. 'Is there any chance of your promotion to General in the near future?' I enquired.

'No chance whatsoever,' he replied. 'Our army already has one general, Abu Bakr Unis, and that is quite sufficient. Besides,' he went on after pausing, 'heads of state in Africa who suddenly become generals tend not to live very long, so I am quite happy as a colonel.' We both laughed.

I invited President Gadaffi to stay in the cockpit for the landing at Labraq, because the runway was very short for a jet aircraft and landings were usually quite interesting. Overflying the unmanned field, I could see from the windsock that there was almost no wind to help us slow down, so I took the unusual precaution of warning the passengers to strap themselves into their seats as tightly as they could and after touchdown I deployed the tail braking parachute which proved remarkably effective in reducing our speed over the tarmac. This had the effect of almost halving the landing run and increasing our safety margins considerably, but to demonstrate the dangers lying in wait at the end of the runway, I jettisoned the parachute and taxied to the very end of the runway. There the President clearly saw the 100 foot sheer drop, ten feet beyond the end of the tarmac.

The danger must have been appreciated, because on my next visit the runway was 500 metres longer. The Libyan Air Force Commander later thanked me profusely as he had always been apprehensive that one of his aircraft would one day spear off the end of Labraq's short runway.

A fleet of black BMWs arrived at the Falcon to convey our passengers to their rally and as there was no refuelling facility, we quickly prepared to spend the afternoon as guest of the district's Chief of Police. He arrived in his blue and white limousine to convey us on a sightseeing tour of the Jebel Akhdar, stopping at a very good restaurant for lunch. During our relaxing time sipping coffee a message came through on the COP's radio announcing that the rally was coming to an end and asking for us to be transported back to Labraq.

I listened to that call and there was no note of urgency in the message whatsoever, but the senior policeman shot into the air as if he had been electrocuted. His mind must have registered: President, Aircraft, Panic. He drove like a maniac and on one of the numerous narrow mountain roads we inevitably came up behind a new white Peugeot pickup, driven slowly by a very old man in his Friday best robes. Perhaps he had just bought the car and was being very careful; perhaps he was partially blind and was concentrating very hard. Whatever the reason, the cacophony of the police horn supplemented by one of the loudest sirens possible and a multitude of flashing lights failed to impress him in the slightest.

Every time the irate policeman pulled out to pass the slower vehicle, which he must have attempted at least six times, the old man swerved across the road to block his path. This was very ill advised, as this policeman was armed and contemplating using his gun. Eventually, by dropping a couple of gears and nearly killing all of us, he passed the Peugeot, swerved in front of the pickup and slammed on the anchors –a foolish manoeuvre, causing the old man to hit us at about 10 mph right in the police car's boot.

The Chief of Police was blazing. He strummed his fingers menacingly on the Peugeot's roof and demanded driving licence, receipt for buying the car, insurance, taxation certificate, identity card and every other certification he could think of. When he had all the certificates in his hand, he tore them all up into tiny pieces one by one and scattered them willy-nilly on the evening breeze. As he walked back to his own vehicle, he shouted back something to the effect that if the old man did such a thing to a policeman ever again, he would personally shoot him dead. With that, we drove back to the Fan-Jet Falcon, even faster. Our passengers did not arrive for at least two hours, so the panic had been unnecessary.

How that old man ever managed to obtain all his documentation again worried me for weeks. Registering his car, with no supporting paperwork, would not have taken less than six months (perhaps appreciably longer), but if he had not deliberately swerved in front of the police car to prevent us overtaking, I reckon he would have escaped with a mild verbal chastisement.

The return flight to Benghazi for refuelling and straight on to Tripoli was routine from an aviation standpoint, but President Gadaffi flew most of the way after Benghazi in the cockpit and we had a lively general conversation on a variety of subjects including matrimony and family life in general. I was left with the firm conclusion that here was an educated man, with a well-developed sense of humour, a very lively mind and a huge job to do in dragging his country into the modern age, without losing what were historically the best attributes of his people. One major problem must have been how much education and what type was the right amount for this stage of development of what a few years previously had been predominantly desert families whose daily survival was of prime importance.

Britain should have been at the forefront of assisting him in his endeavours. Instead we denigrated him and his ideas at every opportunity. One of our newspapers coined the term 'mad dog' when referring to him. Here was a man who could sustain an erudite conversation in a language that was not his native Arabic – how many of the journalists insulting him could do likewise? Here too was a man who would argue point for point yet was courteous enough to agree when a more logical assessment of a problem was put to him. This was not the action of an unbalanced person, but of someone with an open, lively mind.

Our Embassy should have been capable of establishing avenues for constructive discussion, capable of progressing commercial interests for both countries' mutual benefit. Insulting Libya and its President, as we appeared to be doing, achieved nothing positive for our economy.

Work at the many desert oil wells employed whole fleets of cars, and four-wheel drive was somewhat of a rarity, though highly desirable, in soft sand. Flying the Oil Minister down south to Sebha for him to visit some of the remoter installations in 1975 resulted in his being repeatedly stranded in the sand. On his return to Sebha, covered in grime and driving a conventional car, which had been stuck fast for long periods, he explained to me that he had made several abortive attempts to contact British Leyland to purchase Range Rovers; he also wished to purchase Land Rovers.

As the British Embassy had been unable to provide any help he asked me if, on my next visit to the UK, I would make formal contact on his behalf with the board of British Leyland and order a thousand Range Rovers and a thousand Land Rovers. He also asked me to propose that the company should investigate setting up a servicing base in Tripoli to provide spare parts and maintain the vehicles as a joint venture. He further stated that this would be an introductory order with guaranteed repeat orders. The service base could be financed by the Libyan Oil Ministry following agreement with British Leyland, and the training of Libyan engineers could be negotiated as a part of the overall deal. They were prepared, the Oil Minister said, to pay ahead of delivery for 70 per cent of the purchase price, in cash, the final 30 per cent being held by an agreed British bank and made available to the company on completion of the order.

As agreed, two weeks later, I telephoned British Leyland from London and eventually spoke to a director who claimed to be responsible for overseas sales. His response to my firm order for 2,000 vehicles, which I anticipated would have him jumping for joy, was unbelievable. He asked me to telephone him back two days later, which of course I did, only to be told that this particular gentleman was away for ten days on holiday. I attempted to discover who else could expedite the order and was assured that the man to whom I had originally spoken was the only one with the authority to proceed in these circumstances.

Two weeks later, I spent nearly two hours on the telephone locating my British Leyland contact who, when I eventually reached him, claimed to have forgotten the original proposal. He then stated that he would need to discuss the Libyan Oil Minister's order with the rest of his board. When he actually telephoned me back two days later he said that, it had been decided that the company's allocation for the whole of Libya for the next two years was five Range Rovers and no Land Rovers.

I just could not believe what I was hearing. A major British company was turning down a firm order for 2,000 vehicles, which with the maintenance package at 1975 prices could not have been worth less than £20 million. Hardly surprisingly, British Leyland later went out of business due to an alleged lack of orders.

In 1976, Libya shifted their four-wheel drive vehicle requirement to Toyota and have been driving their Land Cruisers around the Sahara Desert ever since. It is estimated that to date they have bought around 10,000 Land Cruisers and Toyota has apparently established a maintenance facility for their support in Tripoli.

Apart from being a lost opportunity for the UK, such incompetence was eventually destined to cause the company's failure. No enterprise, however attractive their products, could possibly succeed by refusing orders of this magnitude. Whether there had been a political input behind the scenes of which I was unaware is a matter for conjecture, but the British Leyland director responsible denied any such interference when questioned by me at the time.

President Gadaffi's statement about British industry being welcome in his country inspired me to examine our own operation of Special Flight. The major maintenance of our aircraft was carried out by a Swiss firm based in Basel, called Jet Aviation. They maintained and carried out major overhauls on large and small business jet aircraft for many European, Middle Eastern and African countries. Most of these aircraft were used by the respective Heads of State.

'Jet' carried a massive stock of ready-use spares, and had a workforce of highly qualified, keen engineers headed by a human dynamo of an engineering director called Eli Zelouf. Eli was the finest 'can-do' man I have ever met. Nothing was too much trouble for him and he kept his specialist workshops as clean as surgical operating theatres. If he did not have the exact spare part needed for a particular repair within an acceptable timescale, he would remove the equivalent part from one of Jet's own fleet of aircraft, to replace it with the new part when the manufacturer eventually delivered. Nothing stood in the way of the speediest possible return to service, whatever the problem.

A radio call to Eli, twenty-four hours a day, 365 days a year, whilst flying over Europe was sufficient to galvanize the whole team into immediate activity and I have experience of being airborne from Basel within an hour of landing, following a complete main-wheel and undercarriage leg change. This incident happened to occur on a Sunday afternoon whilst Jet Aviation was closed, when I was carrying a cabin full of Libyan government ministers, en route to Cologne/Bonn. They were whisked away by Eli at Basel for suitable entertainment whilst the repair took place.

Nevertheless the substantial sums of money required for Special Flight's major maintenance, like new engines and routine component replacements, could have been earned by a British company if a suitable one could be found and I considered that it was my duty to investigate the available alternatives, to establish whether this money could instead be earned by a competent British organization, thereby supporting British jobs, and whether a similar maintenance package could be achieved at lesser cost. My first investigation was of a company that I had used for maintenance whilst I was Commanding Officer of a Naval Air Squadron. It was based in Cambridge and was many times the size of Jet Aviation's Basel operation. They had been reliable some years earlier, but their task at that time was mainly the supply of personnel for on-site maintenance. Special Flight had its own engineers who performed those tasks perfectly, so that type of help was not needed.

Enquiries revealed that if we used this company our aircraft would be required to arrive in Cambridge between 10 o'clock on Monday and 12 o'clock on Friday; aircraft could not be maintained during the company holidays, which covered about six weeks of the year. They carried a very small stock of parts for Fan-Jet Falcon 20s and most parts would need to be ordered direct from the manufacturer, to be fitted after arrival. A potential delay caused by the French customs authorities had to be expected. Their workshop facilities were manned on restrictive hours and contained only a small part of the test equipment available within Jet's Basel facility.

Examples of their charges for sample routine work revealed that almost all of the work was more expensive than the Swiss company and their hourly labour charges appeared to be higher. The extra thousand miles that would be necessary to fly to reach them from Libya would increase the costs even further.

The flexibility necessary to operate Special Flight demanded reliable, adaptable maintenance, at times without advance warning of an aircraft's arrival. Downtime for engineering work needed to be the absolute minimum. After investigating this and all the other possible British companies carrying out such work, it became quite obvious to me that none of them could match Jet Aviation's performance. The contract therefore stayed with Eli Zelouf and his team, who continued to support us in all aspects of Special Flight's successful aviation operations.

That attempt on my part to improve our maintenance performance and support British industry could be described as a failure, but it provided me with proof positive that our present arrangement with Jet Aviation at Basel could not be bettered, in both price and efficiency, for the efficient operation of our aircraft.

My next involvement with trying to assist a British company with work in Libya was during a flight with the Minister of the Interior and Minister of Municipalities. A British civil engineering company, Howard Humphreys, was near to signing a provisional second-stage contract for the installation of a new sewerage system for the city and surrounding district of Tripoli. This was a massive contract worth approximately £2 billion, and many other companies

Special Flight's new Gulfstream II being built at the Gulfstream factory in Savannah, Georgia, USA.

were jealous and evidently prepared to pay millions of pounds in gratuitous commissions – or to put it more crudely, bribes – to steal the nearly finalized contract for their own country's engineering companies. Germany and Italy featured strongly as competitors. As the ministers were discussing the contract and who would finally be given the work, I took the opportunity to extol the virtues of Howard Humphreys – which was difficult as up to that point I had never even heard of them. I worked on the principle that if they were bidding for this huge contract and were British, they must be worthy of consideration.

Nothing was likely to be decided that day, and as I was collecting the ministers from Benghazi two days later I made it my business to find out as much as possible about Howard Humphreys before I next saw them. It would not be ethical for me to make direct contact with the company, but I had friends who knew some of their engineers and I was able to discover many of the company's strengths in the civil engineering world without emerging from my self-imposed anonymity.

It was one of the ministers raising the subject of Tripoli's sewers when we next met which gave me the opportunity to calmly and almost disinterestedly launch into the international work that Howard Humphreys had recently successfully completed. He and his colleagues seemed impressed, but whether they were surprised at my increased knowledge about constructing sewers since we had last met, or my willingness to discuss a 'dirty' subject which most people shied away from, I was never quite sure.

Whatever the reason they must have been impressed with something, because Howard Humphreys was awarded the full contract a few days later. As a matter of record they did a splendid job, which was completed on time and on budget. Two years after completion a handful of their engineers returned to Tripoli and carried out work to ensure the system ran at the planned efficiency in the future. I was told by the Libyans that this follow-up work was carried out without further charge, not even for the engineers' accommodation or their travel expenses. The Libyan government was suitably impressed with this service.

When talk of building an international airport at Tripoli was first mooted by the Libyan government in the mid to late 1970s, the potential work attracted French, Italian, German, Spanish and even Greek civil engineering interest. Their representatives arrived in droves and apparently were prepared to make huge donations into the bank account of anyone who might be able to secure the work for their companies. The frenzy was almost obscene and much of it grossly unethical, so I did a little homework and found that a major British civil engineering company, Sir Alexander Gibb and Partners, had made a bid for the construction work.

Over the following few weeks I discussed the proposed prestige building with most of the remaining Revolutionary Command Council members, because of course Special Flight would be one of the users of the new facilities. During these conversations I dropped the odd snippet of information about Sir Alexander Gibb's company, where I thought it would do the most good, including lesser known facts about their first-class track record in the international civil engineering world, successfully completed projects, the size of the company, their willingness to employ and instruct local student and qualified people for the actual work and their use of local materials. Some of these details provoked useful debate with the country's decision makers. Perhaps my input was minimal, but it certainly did no harm and when the Prime Minister announced to me that Sir Alexander Gibb was to be awarded the contract, I smiled and said that I hoped that they would build an airport of which Libya and its people would be proud. They did. The contract value was £2.2 billion.

The contracts with Howard Humphreys and Sir Alexander Gibb should have created and sustained many British jobs over the years, which gives me a certain sense of achievement; but in order to dispel any supposition to the contrary, let me state unequivocally that I neither received nor requested any financial reward for promoting the British companies. I considered that, in the unique position in which I sometimes found myself, it was my duty to promote British business interests to the best of my ability.

This book is not, of course, the whole story – most of life's exciting experiences are interspersed with periods of enjoyable normality and even near boredom. I have therefore selected a small proportion of the more interesting events and described some of the people who featured in our lives at that time.

The one great regret I have concerning this period in my life is the consequences of that meal in Ouagadougou on 11 December 1977 which, as an airline captain with a damaged heart is unemployable, effectively destroyed my aviation career. Had I been given the option I would have remained in Libya for much longer, but my sudden unwelcome medical condition could not be ignored and eventually left me with little choice in the matter.

My personal reward came from enjoying an eventful and interesting job for nearly ten years, and being privileged to meet and spend time with some of the world's movers and shakers.

Epilogue

In writing this book I have relied heavily on copies of statistics, flight operations returns, and the memories of my family and some of the contemporary members of the Libyan Special Flight. My aircrew flying logbooks have provided some confirmation of times, dates, passengers and crew involved in the various incidents.

I should point out that not all the events portrayed in the book necessarily took place on the flights described. In the interest of continuity and narrative, where many flights were carried out with the same individual personalities, I have sometimes related the details of separate flights as if they occurred on the same one. This was done deliberately in an attempt to make the reading of the text more interesting and I hope that any such distortion of the facts can be regarded as acceptable author's licence.

Many of the names of people appearing in the text have been changed to avoid embarrassment to the individuals concerned. I regret being forced to take this action, but certain people within the publishing world have advised and in some cases insisted that such changes be made. I also regret if the resultant anonymity upsets any of those involved who would rather have seen their names in print – or indeed *vice versa.*

I have endeavoured to retain the feel of the actual incidents as they occurred and hope that by doing so I have portrayed some of the tension and fear that was felt on many occasions, without reducing any of the humour inherent in other parts of the dialogue. Perhaps I could have been more politically correct at times, but I believe that by so doing the impact of the opinions and views being expressed would have been lost.

Index